ELEANOR OF AQUITAINE,
AS IT WAS SAID

Eleanor of Aquitaine

AS IT WAS SAID

TRUTH AND TALES ABOUT
THE MEDIEVAL QUEEN

KAREN SULLIVAN

The University of Chicago Press CHICAGO AND LONDON

The University of Chicago Press, Chicago 60637
The University of Chicago Press, Ltd., London
© 2023 by The University of Chicago
All rights reserved.
No part of this book may be used or reproduced in any manner
whatsoever without written permission, except in the case of brief
quotations in critical articles and reviews. For more information, contact
the University of Chicago Press, 1427 East 60th Street, Chicago, IL 60637.
Published 2023
Printed in the United States of America

32 31 30 29 28 27 26 25 24 23   1 2 3 4 5

ISBN-13: 978-0-226-82583-0 (cloth)
ISBN-13: 978-0-226-82584-7 (e-book)
DOI: https://doi.org/10.7208/chicago/9780226825847.001.0001

The University of Chicago Press gratefully acknowledges the generous
support of Bard College toward the publication of this book.

Library of Congress Cataloging-in-Publication Data

Names: Sullivan, Karen, 1964– author.
Title: Eleanor of Aquitaine, as it was said : truth and tales about the medieval
    queen / Karen Sullivan.
Description: Chicago : The University of Chicago Press, 2023. | Includes
    bibliographical references and index.
Identifiers: LCCN 2022056910 | ISBN 9780226825830 (cloth) | ISBN
    9780226825847 (ebook)
Subjects: LCSH: Eleanor, of Aquitaine, Queen, consort of Henry II, King of
    England, 1122?–1204. | Queens—France—Biography. | Queens—England—
    Biography. | BISAC: HISTORY / Europe / Medieval | HISTORY / Europe /
    France
Classification: LCC DA209.E6 S85 2023 | DDC 942.03/1092 [B]—dc23/
    eng/20221130
LC record available at https://lccn.loc.gov/2022056910

For my sister, Aline Sullivan

CONTENTS

INTRODUCTION

The kingdom of England was in a state of disarray. Richard the Lionheart, its king, had been taken captive by a vassal of the Holy Roman Emperor as he was returning home from the Third Crusade and was being held prisoner in a castle in Germany. John, Richard's younger brother, was taking advantage of his absence by spreading rumors that the king was dead and that his vassals would have to swear loyalty to him as their new ruler. He had bound himself to Philip Augustus, the King of France, to whom he had given homage for Richard's continental lands, "and for England as well, as it was said."[1] In February of 1193, it was widely expected that the French were about to attack England with the assistance of their Flemish allies and attempt to raise John to the throne. But that invasion never occurred. The country's coastline had by that point been fortified, according to the chronicler Gervase, a monk of Christ Church, Canterbury, "by the command of Queen Eleanor, who was ruling England at that time."[2]

The fact that Eleanor of Aquitaine, the onetime Queen of France, current Queen of England, and mother to King Richard, was exercising power in England in the early 1190s is not in dispute, but this power was never perceived as hers. We are told that when Richard saw Eleanor in Sicily, as he was heading off on the crusade, "He sent back his mother to look after his land, which he had left, so that his holdings would not diminish."[3] It would be Eleanor who, together with Walter of Coutances, Archbishop of Rouen, would raise the enormous ransom that the emperor demanded for Richard's release; Eleanor who, again with Walter, would travel to Germany to deliver that ransom and reclaim her son; and Eleanor who, having brought Richard back home, would reconcile him with the penitent John.

Yet in all the accounts from these years, this is Richard's story, John's story, or Philip's story, not Eleanor's. Despite the magnitude of what Gervase of Canterbury is asserting—that the queen was in charge of England during this time—he makes the statement only as an aside, in a subordinate clause. In a similar manner, when the Augustinian canon William of Newburgh recounts how John patched up his differences with Richard, he mentions that this was done "with their mother mediating [*mediante matre*]."[4] It is Richard or John who functions as the subject of the action, while Eleanor serves as the means through which that action takes place, in an ablative absolute. Chroniclers like Gervase and William view Eleanor as functioning, not as a ruler in and of herself, but as a placeholder for the ruler to whom she had given birth while he is away or otherwise occupied. For this reason, if we are to tell Eleanor's story, we must read the historical sources that mention her as closely and attentively as we can, but we must also read them in a way they were never intended to be read, paying attention to a figure their authors never expected us to focus on, and we must consider other, more literary sources about this queen, which are ultimately no less illuminating.

It is not that Eleanor's contemporaries failed to respect her for her high birth, her great inheritance, and her ability to return, time and again, from defeat. According to a genealogical record from late thirteenth-century Limoges, "In the year 113[7], on the fifth ides of April, . . . William, the Count Palatine of Poitou, the last Duke of Aquitaine, died at Saint James in Galicia, leaving behind a single daughter of thirteen years of age by the name of Eleanor."[5] As the heiress to the county of Poitou and the duchy of Aquitaine, Eleanor wed the seventeen-year-old Louis "the Younger," the son of Louis VI "the Fat," King of France and her father's overlord. Within two weeks, her husband had become Louis VII and she his queen consort. In 1147, Eleanor accompanied Louis on the Second Crusade, traveling with the army through Germany, Hungary, Bulgaria, and Constantinople to Jerusalem. The crusade proved a disaster, and the marriage foundered in the years that followed. In 1152, an ecclesiastical council at Beaugency pronounced Eleanor and Louis related within the forbidden degrees of kinship and dissolved their union. Yet within eight weeks of the divorce, Eleanor had married Henry, the young Count of Anjou and Duke of Normandy, and within two and a half years, this new husband had become Henry II, King of England, and she a queen for the second time. Her years with Louis had produced only two daughters, yet her union with Henry resulted in at least five sons, one of whom died at an early age but three of whom became crowned kings, and three daughters, two of whom became crowned queens.[6] In 1173, Eleanor's three eldest sons rebelled against their father, and, because she was implicated in their schemes, she was arrested and imprisoned in various English castles for sixteen years. Yet after Richard became king in 1190, she effectively ran England while her son was occupied with warfare abroad. When John ascended to the throne in 1199, she became more involved in diplomacy than ever before and twice led armies into battle. Repudiated by the King of France and incarcerated by the King of England, Eleanor became even stronger in the aftermath of these adversities, for which she did not fail to earn the admiration of her peers.

Yet despite how formidable a character Eleanor proved to be over the course of her long life, medieval chroniclers say remarkably little about her. In the twelfth and the thirteenth centuries, clerics composed over 120 chronicles, histories, and annals which made reference to the queen, but all but one do so only in passing. About her marriage to Louis, they are almost entirely silent. Suger, Abbot of the Benedictine Abbey of Saint-Denis and regent during Louis's absence on the Second Crusade, alludes to Eleanor twice in his writings without dwelling on her either time. Odo of Deuil, another monk from Saint-Denis, accompanied the royal couple on this expedition and wrote a chronicle of what he witnessed, but he never mentions the queen by name, and he abandons his narrative just before the army arrives in Antioch, where her behavior would for the first time become an object of widespread discussion. In contrast to the events of the early years of Eleanor's life, the circumstances of her divorce from Louis, her quick remarriage to Henry, and her involvement in her sons' rebellion are addressed by a large number of authors, but never in more than a sentence or two. Medieval chroniclers composed lives of other female rulers, including Emma of Normandy, Margaret of Scotland, Matilda of Tuscany, and Elizabeth of Hungary, and they wrote, if not biographies per se, then lengthy accounts of the deeds of Eleanor's husbands and sons in their chronicles, often with elaborate portraits of these men and evaluations of their accomplishments.[7] Yet only one writer, John of Salisbury, a diplomat and sometime secretary to the Archbishop of Canterbury, addresses the queen with more than a glancing reference, and even he devotes a mere page and a half to her. After her death, few authors mention her, and when they do, it is mostly to say, "Eleanor, Queen of the English, died," with a brief notice of the year and, perhaps, the place of her burial.[8]

If medieval chroniclers were so silent about Eleanor's life, it may have been because so much of what they knew about her was based on hearsay. It was expected that chroniclers would base their accounts on their own firsthand observation of events or, if that was not possible, on consultation of well-informed and trustworthy sources. John of Salisbury declares in beginning his *Historia pontificalis* (1164) that he will write "nothing . . . except what I know to be true, by sight and by hearing, or what is supported in the writings or by the authority of reliable men."[9] The deeds of a king can be established with confidence because a ruler of this sort issues commands, receives ambassadors, and leads armies into battle. What he does of importance, he typically does publicly, in front of many people who can then testify to what they saw or even write down what happened. Yet a queen most often functions as an intercessor, appealing to the king to forgive someone he might be inclined to punish or assist someone he might be inclined to overlook.[10] What she does of significance, she typically does privately, in conversations with her husband or son to which others are not privy or, worse, in encounters with lovers which are purposefully hidden from view.[11] When the chroniclers discuss Eleanor's divorce from Louis and remarriage to Henry, they state, "It was said [*dicebatur*] that it was she brought about that contrived repudiation through her own skill,"[12] or "It is . . . said [*dicitur*] that, even during her marriage to the King of the French, she aspired to be wed to the Duke of Normandy."[13] When these authors turn to her sons' rebellion against their father, they report that these sons acted "on the counsel of their Queen Mother, that is, Eleanor, as it is said [*sicut dicitur*],"[14] or "under the influence, as it is reported [*ut fertur*], of their mother."[15] With their use of indirect discourse, these chroniclers acknowledge that they do not know, as a positive fact, that Eleanor brought about her divorce from Louis, her marriage to Henry, or her sons' rebellion against their father, but only that people around her alleged that she did these things. As the tag "it was said" signals, what the chroniclers convey about Eleanor was a tale transmitted from one person to another even before it was written down in their chronicles.

Already hesitant to speak about Eleanor because they would have to rely on hearsay, the chroniclers were even more hesitant to speak about her because this hearsay so often concerned love affairs. During the Second Crusade, while the royal couple was staying at the court of Eleanor's uncle, Raymond, Prince of Antioch, in what is now Turkey, something occurred that provoked great anger between the spouses. The chroniclers who allude to this incident do so vaguely and evasively. As we shall see, the primary sources for this episode—John of Salisbury; William, Archbishop of Tyre; and Gerhoh, an Augustinian canon at Reichersberg Abbey in Upper Austria—report that Eleanor was alleged to have engaged in some sort of marital infidelity, but two of these authors leave unclear whether she was guilty of this crime, and none of them does more than hint at the identity of her lover. Other chroniclers who speak of this incident do so mainly to establish that they are not going to speak of it. Gervase of Canterbury states, "After King Louis of France returned from pilgrimage in Jerusalem, there arose discord between him and his queen Eleanor over certain things that had happened during the pilgrimage about which it is perhaps better to be silent."[16] Richard of Devizes, a Benedictine monk at Saint Swinthin's in Winchester, likewise attests, "Many know what I would that none of us knew. This same queen, during the time of her first husband, was at Jerusalem. Let no one say any more about it. I too know it well. Keep silent!"[17] These two authors assert that they know why Eleanor and Louis clashed during the crusade, but they make clear that they will not disclose what they know and that others should not do so either. In the thirteenth century, the story developed that during the crusade, Eleanor had engaged in a dalliance with a "Turk" (that is, in contemporary parlance, a Muslim) who was ultimately identified as the great Saladin, Sultan of Egypt and Syria and a man as famed for his chivalry and courtesy as he was for his military prowess. But even in the twelfth century, during Eleanor's lifetime, rumors circulated that if she and Louis divorced, it was because she had broken her marriage vows with various men, and that if she was able to remarry so quickly, it was because she had already contrived an understanding with young Henry.

If medieval chroniclers were interested in Eleanor's alleged love affairs, it was because they were interested in kings' and queens' *mores*. Like *ethos* in Greek, *mores* in Latin indicates the type of person someone is as revealed by the decisions that person makes, which is why it can be translated as "moral character." Because moral character is often revealed by one's actions, especially when those actions are repeated, the term can also often be rendered as "manner of life" or "habits." Gervase of Canterbury writes, "It is the duty of the historian . . . to teach the deeds, manner of living [*mores*], and lives of those he portrays truthfully."[18] William of Tyre refers to his chronicle as containing "many things about the habits [*moribus*], lives, and corporeal appearance of kings."[19] Since Livy and Plutarch, historians had studied the moral characters of rulers in particular, in the belief that they would prove instructive to their civic-minded readers, teaching them what to imitate and what to avoid. The Benedictine monk William of Malmesbury, in his *Gesta regum Anglorum* (1125–40), refers to history as that which, "through the pleasant recounting of deeds, excites its readers to cultivate their manner of living [*mores*] with examples, so that they will pursue the good and avoid the bad."[20] Chroniclers sought to educate royal women as well as royal men through such history lessons. When the monks of Malmesbury sent Henry's mother, the Empress Matilda, a copy of William's volume, they informed her, "This kind of book used to be written in antiquity for kings and queens in order to instruct them in life with examples, so that they will follow the triumphs of some and avoid the misfortunes of others and imitate the wisdom of some and scorn the folly of others."[21] Because interest in moral character was so embedded in the historiographical tradition, it shaped the way in which chroniclers and, by extension, anyone educated in the liberal arts at this time made sense of human beings, including rulers. It is only someone who governs herself well, by cultivating her moral character, these authors assumed, who will be able to govern her realm effectively.

Given the general interest of medieval chroniclers in *mores*, the question was always what sort of moral character Eleanor possessed. This queen was never a flagrant adulteress. Whatever accusations were made against her during her lifetime, she never forsook her husband to live with another man. As a result, the issue was never what Eleanor was observed to have done by those who witnessed her behavior, but what she was *imagined* to have done by those who believed themselves to grasp her moral character. When William of Tyre considers the incident at Antioch, he writes, "She was, . . . as was seen through manifest indications both before and after this time, an imprudent woman."[22] He believes that Eleanor was unfaithful to her husband on the Second Crusade because, from what he had heard about her behavior both before and after this eastern sojourn, she was the type of woman who would be unfaithful to her husband. Similarly, John of Bellesmains, Bishop of Poitiers, wrote to Thomas Becket, Archbishop of Canterbury, in 1165 concerning Eleanor's relationship with Ralph of Châtellerault, seigneur of Faye-la-Vineuse, her uncle and advisor, "Every day, many presumptions arise by which it seems possible to believe that her bad reputation [*infamia*] . . . approaches the truth."[23] The bishop is not sure whether to put credence in the rumors that Eleanor misbehaved elsewhere (presumably in Antioch). But because of the intimacy that he observes between the queen and Ralph now, he suspects that there may also have been intimacy between her and another man (perhaps another uncle) at an earlier date. Both ecclesiastics present their interpretations of Eleanor's behavior as worth believing, not because they are true, but because they *seem* true, given the moral character already attributed to this lady. Whatever Eleanor had done in Antioch, there was always someone like William or John who would remember the "bad reputation" she had acquired in her youth and interpret her present actions in light of those past allegations. For that reason, it is not that there was a historical Eleanor, primary, original, and defined by her own actions, and then a legendary Eleanor, secondary, supplemental, and constituted by other peoples' stories about her. Rather, the historical queen was always already defined in people's minds by the legendary queen, even during her lifetime, and she necessarily operated in reference to that persona.[24]

In evaluating a queen's (or king's) moral character, chroniclers were particularly interested in whether this ruler displayed *prudentia*. The modern English word "prudence" does not do justice to the medieval Latin *prudentia*, given our tendency to associate this concept with sound fiscal management or other arenas of narrow self-interest. In the Middle Ages, "prudence" is perhaps best understood as "good judgment," that is, as the ability to discern the most advisable way to act in a situation, both morally and politically. At times, "prudence" is compared to "wisdom" (*sapientia*) as both faculties allow one to distinguish good from evil,[25] but at other times it is contrasted to this companion virtue because it is practical, not speculative; applied, not theoretical; and particular, not universal. Encompassing not only thought but the application of thought to action, prudence was considered to be essential for effective leadership. Gerald of Wales, a diplomat and chaplain to Henry, writes of kings, "It is all the more becoming that a ruler be endowed with prudence . . . so that he may be able to distinguish the good from the bad, the true from the false, and the rightful from the useful and honorable, with the file of discernment."[26] Other authors stress the importance of prudence for queens as well. Turgot of Durham, Bishop of Saint Andrews, writes of Margaret of Scotland, in a work designed for the instruction of her daughter Matilda of Scotland, who was Queen of England and Henry's grandmother, "All things . . . were directed by this prudent queen. The laws of the kingdom were administered by her counsel. . . . The people rejoiced in the prosperity of their affairs. Nothing . . . was more just than her decisions."[27] Because prudence was regarded as the principal virtue necessary for those involved in public life, it is not surprising that it is the quality most referenced in discussions of the moral character of female as well as male rulers at this time.

Given medieval chroniclers' general interest in prudence, the question was always whether Eleanor possessed this virtue. As we have seen, William of Tyre writes, "She was . . . an imprudent woman [*mulier imprudens*]." By committing adultery, the archbishop believes, Eleanor failed to distinguish between good and evil counsel and, in doing so, failed to display the practical wisdom that earns a sovereign the respect of her subjects. Other sources offer more-mixed views. Peter of Blois, a diplomat and secretary in

Henry's service, chides Eleanor for her participation in her sons' rebellion against their father, claiming, "Though you are a most prudent woman [*mulier prudentissima*], you have turned away from your husband."[28] In general, Peter suggests, Eleanor is able to distinguish between good and evil, but in defying the man to whom she is married, she has not acted in accordance with this trait. Gervase of Canterbury attests of Eleanor, "She was an extremely prudent woman [*prudens femina valde*], originated from noble birth, but flighty [*instabilis*]."[29] He too sees the queen as capable of telling virtue from vice, but he also sees her as inconsistent in doing so. Yet while Eleanor was deemed imprudent as a queen consort, either in her overall moral character or in her occasional behavior, she was deemed surprisingly prudent as a queen mother. Richard writes to her from his captivity in Germany, "Your prudence and discernment [*prudentia et discretio*] is the greatest cause of our land remaining in a peaceful state until our arrival."[30] By ensuring that his barons remain faithful to him despite his lengthy absence from the kingdom and his brother's efforts to usurp his throne, Richard asserts, Eleanor has indeed exhibited the practical wisdom one needs in public life. Whatever may have been said about the queen's behavior during her youth, her prudence was generally perceived as helping Richard and then John to secure and retain dominion over their lands for as long as she lived.

In recent decades, historians and biographers, who have turned away from the study of moral character, have expressed interest, not in whether Eleanor possessed prudence, but in whether she possessed power. A biographer asserts of this queen, "Her whole life . . . became a struggle for the independence and political power that circumstances had denied her, although few of her contemporaries would realize this."[31] A historian maintains that it was always "power, and the interests of her native region"[32] that determined what Eleanor did, though such a "political explanation" of her behavior "did not apparently occur to contemporary commentators."[33] In particular, scholars have argued that when Eleanor went off on the Second Crusade, she did so, not merely as the consort of Louis, King of France, but as Countess of Poitou and Duchess of Aquitaine, leading her own vassals in a "joint venture" with her husband.[34] When she quarreled with Louis in Antioch, it was not because she was engaged in an extramarital dalliance with her uncle or anyone else but because, against her husband's objections, she was supporting her uncle's proposal that they unite the French and the Antiochene forces to attack local Muslim strongholds.[35] As modern historians and biographers see it, medieval chroniclers evaluated Eleanor as a moral subject, defined in large part by her susceptibility to love and sexual desire, and not as a political subject, defined by her involvement in affairs of state, and they did so because their assumptions about the frivolity and carnality of the female sex distorted their perception of the queen.[36] One biographer writes, "Only men were considered capable of acting rationally, and when they encountered women wielding power, they attributed their actions to irrational, passionate motives, not to practical political considerations."[37] In advancing this interpretation, modern authors recognize they are making an argument that is in no way supported by contemporaneous evidence about Eleanor, but they believe they are justified in doing so. Their task, as they understand it, is to take the facts that the original sources almost inadvertently convey about the queen's life and develop out of them a narrative that seems plausible to them, however much it may be at odds with the story the sources themselves are telling. Though the medieval chroniclers transmitted valuable information about Eleanor, these modern authors suggest, given the shortcomings of their culture, they failed to grasp the truth about this queen that was hidden in that information, a truth that we, from the superior vantage point of our more enlightened age, can now apprehend.[38]

Yet at the risk of stating the obvious, insofar as we know Eleanor, it is through historical texts. The chronicles of Gervase of Canterbury, William of Newburgh, John of Salisbury, Roger of Howden, and Richard of Devizes, all written during the latter part of the twelfth century and hence during Eleanor's lifetime, are as reliable as any from the Middle Ages. While their accounts of Eleanor are sparser than we might wish, they convey important facts about this queen, and more interestingly, they suggest interpretations of those facts, whether explicitly, through the judgments they make of her behavior, or implicitly, through the language they employ in reporting her deeds. The structure of a sentence, the diction of a phrase, or the nature of a simile can give us a greater understanding of the moral context within which Eleanor was operating than has been recognized heretofore. For even if modern scholars are right and Eleanor was, in some sense, drawn to what we would call "power" (and one can make the argument that she was), she would have spoken, not of her own desire to rule, but of her family's ancestral claim to Poitou or Aquitaine or of her sons' hereditary right to the English throne. Even today, people who seek power typically insist on the impersonal mandate imposed on them by lawful elections, not on their personal ambition to seize the reins of state. Whatever motivations Eleanor had would have been filtered, even in her own consciousness, through the cultural values available to her, and "power," divorced from family, inheritance, and justice, was not one of them. If we wish to know Eleanor as she truly was, we will come closest to achieving that goal, not by speculating about aspects of her life about which the medieval texts remain silent, but by listening to these texts as attentively as we can.

As we know Eleanor through historical texts, we also know her through what we might call "parahistorical" texts, which claim to be historical but do not satisfy medieval, let alone modern, criteria of historicity. These works include Andreas Capellanus's *De amore* (1186–96), in which Eleanor presides over the so-called Courts of Love with her daughter and other noble ladies; the anonymous "life" (*vida*) of the troubadour Bernart de Ventadorn (c. 1217–53), in which she grants her patronage and her love to this celebrated poet; and the popular chronicle of the so-called Minstrel of Reims (1260), in which she attempts to elope with Saladin; as well as love songs, ballads, romances, exempla, and literary epistles. There exists no absolute separation between historical and parahistorical writings about the queen. A story like the account of Eleanor's love affair with a Muslim during the Second Crusade first appears in the largely reliable chronicle of Matthew Paris, a Benedictine monk at Saint Albans Abbey in Hertfordshire active in the mid-thirteenth century, and is then embellished in the largely fantastical chronicle of the Minstrel of Reims shortly thereafter, only to return, in this elaborated form, in later histories and historical romances. Yet the distinction between history and parahistory is still useful for our purposes because it allows us to take seriously a set of texts about Eleanor that have traditionally been regarded by historians as too fanciful to be worthy of their discipline's attention and by literary scholars as too factual to fall under their purview. If people of the Middle Ages told these stories about Eleanor, it may have been because they were filling in the gaps in the historical record as best they could to make it correspond to what they thought to be the truth; it may have been because they were correcting that record to make it correspond to what they hoped or feared to be the truth; or it may have been because they were merely seeking to tell an entertaining story, all the more intriguing because it involved salacious anecdotes about a famous queen. If we wish to know Eleanor as she truly was, it may be hazardous to speculate about her ourselves, but it may be helpful to consider the speculations of those who lived during her lifetime or not long thereafter, whose interpretations of this figure provide access to the cultural context in which she existed.

While historical and literary writings from the twelfth and the thirteenth centuries deserve pride of place in any life of Eleanor, accounts from the Late Middle Ages and the Renaissance can also help us appreciate this high medieval queen. Sometimes the authors of these works take the information they have found in the earlier sources and develop its implications. For example, while medieval chroniclers mention in passing the attacks Eleanor launched against rebellious cities in Poitou during John's reign, Elizabethan historians and playwrights expand on these brief references to portray her as a three-dimensional political and military leader. These later authors do not perceive Eleanor in the same way her contemporaries would have done, but they are still closer to her culture than we are and, for that reason, they can help dislodge anachronistic assumptions that we might otherwise make about her motivations. In other cases, late medieval and Renaissance authors recount episodes in Eleanor's life of which no mention was ever made in the high medieval sources. In the sixteenth century, for instance, the story emerges that Eleanor seethed with jealousy toward Henry's mistress Rosamund Clifford and, tracking the young woman down in the bower where she had been concealed, forced her to drink poison. There is no reason to believe that this tale has any veracity at all, yet it helps us appreciate, by means of contrast, the far more sober contemporaneous accounts of Eleanor's life during her mature years. So much of the information we think we possess about Eleanor's life—information that has been repeated in even the most recent biographies and cinematic representations of the queen—is due to early modern historical, dramatic, and poetic texts that we need to recognize at what point these supposed facts first appeared in her story, so that we can appreciate what the story was before their interpolation. Whether this later literature echoes or diverges from the medieval chronicles, it puts into relief what we see in those chronicles and, in doing so, enables us to discern what is distinctive about them.

It is not that we will ever do away with the silence that enshrouds so much of Eleanor's life, like the lives of almost all her female contemporaries. In the only text we have that was written to Eleanor by a woman during her lifetime,[39] the great abbess and polymath Hildegard of Bingen advises her, "Your mind is like a wall which is covered with clouds, and you look everywhere but have no rest. Flee this and stand with stability with God and men, and God will help you in all your tribulations. Let God give you his blessing and help in all your works."[40] Hildegard clearly regards Eleanor as a person of consequence, but she feels that, in facing certain unspecified adversities, the queen needs to rely more on God's grace, which will aid her in both her outer actions and her inner meditations. In a life filled with political tumult, she believes that her correspondent must cultivate the spiritual tranquility that comes only from the Lord. From what we can tell, Eleanor never turned away from politics or from the men who dominated this sphere of activity. In the last few years of her life, however, she spent much of her time at the Abbey of Fontevraud, on the border of Poitou and Anjou. When the doors of that monastery closed behind her, she entered a world of women, embracing the female relatives and companions she had known throughout her long life but about whom so little was ever said. As we shall see, while few stories have survived about Eleanor's time at Fontevraud, tales have survived about some of the men she knew who were kept outside these walls and some of the women she knew who were admitted inside, and these tales give us a sense of the spiritual atmosphere in which she lived during these final years. In the very end, the silence that had veiled so much of Eleanor's existence conceals it almost completely.

It is with the goal of appreciating the texture of this rich and complex life that we now turn to its beginnings.

I

THE HEIRESS

Consent in Marriage

We do not know what exact form the marriage ceremony took when Eleanor wed Louis in Bordeaux in 1137 or Henry in Poitiers in 1152, but we do know what normally happened in weddings in the mid-twelfth century in what is now western France. On a Sunday morning, the bride and the bridegroom would each be led to the church by their family members and friends. The priest, wearing a stole and white vestments, would be waiting for them outside by the door of the church, and, in front of all who had gathered, he would ask them a series of questions establishing the legitimacy of this union. When he inquired whether each person consented to marry the other, the man would affirm, "I accept you as mine, that hereafter you may be my wife and I your husband," and the woman would echo, "I accept you as mine, that hereafter I may be your wife and you my husband."[1] The priest would ask whether the couple was barred from marrying by any impediment of consanguinity or affinity, and they would give responses to his satisfaction. The final arrangements for the woman's dowry would be made, the wedding ring would be placed on her finger, and everyone would enter the church for the nuptial Mass. After the ceremony was over, everyone would retire to a hall where the wedding feast would be held, to the accompaniment of jongleurs and jesters. That evening, after the dinner was over, the guests would proceed to an upstairs chamber and put the couple into the marriage bed, which the priest would then bless and cense over the couple's recumbent bodies. From the words at the church door to the church service, to the feast, to the bedding of the couple, the wedding was a public event held, as a pontifical from Evreux puts it, "before the testimony of many people."[2] At the same time, from the man and the woman's marital vows to their bodily intercourse after the door to the bedchamber was

closed, the marriage was also a private sacrament, uniting the bride and the
bridegroom before God. The tension between the roles of the family and
the individual in marriage is a constant in writings about this institution
during these years, especially when the individual in question is a woman,
whose volition in this matter was so often uncertain.

As a great heiress, Eleanor was in an ambiguous position when it came
to marriage. At the time when she was living, if a lord had no legitimate
sons, his daughter had a claim to inherit his lands and the titles that went
with them.[3] As a result, an ambitious man might seek to marry an heiress over whose lands he could rule "by the right of the wife" (*iure uxoris*), and if this woman or her guardians resisted his plans, he might abduct her and force her into this union. Because the Church considered
any marital or amorous relationship within seven degrees consanguineous,
if the man later found another woman he preferred, he might cast off his
wife on the basis of some distant kinship in order to wed her replacement.
As a young girl, Eleanor was sufficiently well guarded to have been transferred from her guardian's care to her first husband without incident. Yet
according to some sources from the time, after fifteen years of marriage
she was repudiated by this husband, and once she was removed from his
protection, was vulnerable to two separate suitors who attempted to seize
her and claim her as a wife. Whether bestowed in marriage, repudiated, or
subjected to attempted abduction, she was the passive victim of the men
around her. According to another contemporaneous reading of the situation, however, Eleanor engineered the annulment of her first marriage so
that she could wed a man more to her liking, and, with the help of her loyal
vassals, thwarted the men who threatened to abduct her. Whether plotting to divorce one husband or to marry another, she was an active player
in the spheres in which she operated. If she could act so independently, it
was because, even after her divorce, she remained Countess of Poitou and
Duchess of Aquitaine, and she was able to take her vast land holdings into
her second marriage, to the displeasure of her former husband. Given that
whatever agency Eleanor displayed in these marriages was necessarily co-
vert, those who write about her during these years use their imagination to
fathom what she was up to.

THE KING OF FRANCE

Eleanor was married for the first time in 1137, when she was thirteen years
old. In the spring of that year, her widowed father, William X, had de-

parted on a pilgrimage to Saint James of Compostela, leaving Eleanor and her younger sister Petronilla behind in the care of Geoffrey III du Loroux, Archbishop of Bordeaux. Far off in Galicia, a few leagues from his destination, William fell ill. On Good Friday, April 9 of that year, he passed away, at thirty-seven or thirty-eight years of age, having received the viaticum, and, in recognition of his high rank, was buried before the altar of the great church.[4] When messengers arrived before Louis the Fat at the Castle of Béthizy, about forty miles northeast of Paris, to apprise him of the death of one of his major vassals, the king was lying ill with dysentery and suffering from the oppressively hot weather. Learning that William had consigned his daughters to his care, he arranged for his son Louis the Younger, who was around seventeen years old at that time, to marry Eleanor, and he sent the youth to Bordeaux for this purpose. On or around July 25, Eleanor and Louis were united in the Cathedral of Saint Andrew, in the presence of the barons of Poitou, Gascony, and Saintonge and the prelates of Aquitaine. Less than a week later, on August 1, King Louis died, at the age of fifty-five, and was buried in the church of the Abbey of Saint-Denis.[5] In accordance with Capetian custom, Louis the Younger had already been consecrated as king, almost six years earlier, and Eleanor was crowned at the time of her marriage to him. The accounts of this royal wedding are concerned with the political sphere and, especially, with the successful transmission of an inheritance from one generation to the next. Insofar as the texts are concerned with the personal sphere at all, they are focused, not on the bride and the bridegroom, but on their fathers, that is, not on young people at the time of their marriage, as they are making the transition from the single to the wedded state, but on their elders at the time of their death, as they are making the transition from the temporal to the eternal realm. It is only once these newlyweds become actors in their own lives, and, especially, conflicted actors, that they become interesting to these authors.

It was not a foregone conclusion that on her father's death, Eleanor would become Countess of Poitou and Duchess of Aquitaine. Members of their "Ranulfid" lineage—that is, the descendants of the ninth-century Ranulf I, Count of Poitiers and Duke of Aquitaine—had been ruling Poitou, Aquitaine, Saintonge, and Angoumois without interruption for the past 175 years and Gascony for the past 85. Yet as long-standing as this family's dominion over these territories may have been, it was contested outside their borders by the neighboring Counts of Anjou, who claimed Saintonge, and the Counts of Toulouse, who claimed Gascony, and inside their borders by the Lusignan, Parthenay, and Taillefer clans, who periodically rebelled against their overlords. Just as it was not entirely

settled whether Eleanor's family should rule over all this territory, it was
not entirely settled which member of that family should do so.[6] Because
a daughter inherited land only in the absence of a legitimate son, if Eleanor's younger brother William Aigret had not died when she was eight
years old or if her father had not failed to produce another male heir after
his son's death, Eleanor never would have inherited and we never would
have heard of her. Because a deceased man's brother could claim his inheritance as well as his child, if Raymond, William's younger brother, had not
moved to Antioch to marry its heiress and to rule that principality *iure
uxoris*, Eleanor would likely have had a competitor for her lands. Even if a
daughter was able to inherit her father's territory, she customarily moved
to her husband's domain after she married, and her absence encouraged
the ambitions of potential usurpers. In 1094, when Philippa, the daughter
of William IV, Count of Toulouse, and Eleanor's grandmother, was in line
to inherit her father's city, her uncle, Raymond of Saint-Gilles, was able to
seize the domain in her stead. Despite the fact that Eleanor's ancestors had
ruled Poitou and Aquitaine for centuries, the line of succession would not
necessarily go unchallenged.

Faced with the tenuousness of Eleanor's claim to his lands, Duke William acted to strengthen her position. It is not clear whether it was the
duke or the king who first had the idea that the young heiress should marry
Louis the Younger. According to the chronicler of Morigny, "As [William]
realized that the inevitable exhalation of his spirit was impending, summoning the peers and the leading men of his land, he constrained them
with the coercive bond of an oath that they would unite his daughter to
Louis, the son of Louis."[7] While the king would obviously have to consent
to this arrangement, in this chronicler's view it was the duke who took the
initiative in affiancing the two young people. Alternatively, according to
Suger of Saint-Denis, who was with the king at this time, when the king
heard that the duke had given him responsibility for choosing Eleanor's
husband, he consulted with his advisors and, "with his customary magna-
nimity," decided that she should wed his own son.[8] Similarly, it is not clear
whether William expected Eleanor to rule his lands with her new husband
as her coruler or Louis the Younger to do so with his wife at his side.[9] The
chronicler of Morigny writes that William made his men swear, not only
that they would join his daughter to Louis, but that "they would transfer
his land to both,"[10] as joint rulers, yet other authors indicate that he gave
his daughter to Louis the Younger "with the duchy of Aquitaine,"[11] with no
expectation that she would share rule of the duchy with him.[12] William's
first concern was to link his duchy and his daughter legally to the French

king so that both would come under his protection, but whether he intended for her to rule in her own right or merely to transmit his lands to her husband is not clear.

Whatever the arrangements William made for Eleanor as he was dying, the chroniclers do not represent her as having any say in them. It is true that at this time, a woman was formally asked to consent to any marriage into which she entered. According to a commonplace cited by virtually every theologian and canonist of the twelfth century, including Yves of Chartres,[13] Gratian,[14] Hugh of Saint-Victor,[15] John of Salisbury,[16] and Peter Lombard,[17] "It is consent that makes marriage." The permission of the spouses' guardians, the espousal by their parents, and the bequest of a dowry merely give that union, as the Lombard put it, "decorum and solemnity."[18] If consent is so important in marriage, these clerics argue, it is because spouses are expected not just to unite two families' bloodlines in their children but to love one another. Scripture instructs, "Husbands, love your wives, even as Christ also loved the Church."[19] Like the bride and the Bridegroom in the Song of Songs, whose union was understood to prefigure that of the Church and Jesus Christ, the bride and the bridegroom in the world celebrate the mystical union of the soul and the Godhead in their consent to marry and their consummation of this marriage. It was only if a woman agreed to her marriage that she was thought likely to experience the affection she should feel for her spouse and, by extension, the blessedness she should find in the marital state. Yet while, theologically speaking, the woman was asked to consent to the marriage, socially speaking, she was expected to consent to any union her guardians arranged for her. The late eleventh- and early twelfth-century canonist Yves of Chartres cites with approval Justinian's assertion that "A daughter is always understood to consent to her father unless she manifestly dissents."[20] Indeed, a certain tradition held that it was only with her relatives' assent that her marriage could be valid.[21] If we hear nothing about Eleanor's views on her marriage, it is because, whether a bride eagerly sought to wed her betrothed or grudgingly acquiesced to her guardians' choice, she was expected to accept the decisions they made on her behalf.

Though the chroniclers display no interest in Eleanor's thoughts at the time of her marriage, authors of romances at this time express curiosity about the conflicted inner lives of young heiresses in her situation. In the *Roman de Thèbes* (c. 1150), the *Roman d'Enéas* (1156–60), and the *Roman de Troie* (c. 1165), the rulers of Thebes, Latium, and Troy have no sons who can defend their lands, so they seek to use their daughters to acquire sons-in-law who can play this filial role. If the heiresses in these romances are conflicted, it is, not because they resist the husbands their guardians find for them, but, on the contrary, because they long for these men so ardently. In the *Roman d'Enéas*, Lavinia has an arrow shot into Aeneas's camp with an attached letter in which she reveals her love for the hero. When Aeneas reads the letter and looks up at the tower where she is watching, she blows him a kiss. Yet later, the maiden worries that she has been too forward. A voice in her mind exclaims, "Foolish [*folle*] Lavinia,"[22] "A woman of your rank becomes so frenzied as to go speak to a foreign man in order to offer herself—to propose herself to him!"[23] Similarly, in the *Roman de Thèbes*, from the moment Antigone first meets Parthenopeus, it is said, "She coveted him strongly in her heart."[24] Yet this maiden (who is described as "very worthy and wise [*sage*]")[25] informs her eager suitor that she will not grant her love easily: "I am . . . the daughter of a king. I must not love lightly, nor must I love out of lechery, about which one could speak folly. This is how one should beseech shepherdesses and other light women. . . . If I now gave you my word that I loved you, you could hold me as a fool [*pur fole*]."[26] She takes pride in her high birth and believes that she should not act on carnal desire, as only girls of lower status behave in such a manner. While the maidens in these romances do not challenge their parents' decisions about whom they will marry, they do feel desire for these men in their own right, and that desire puts them at odds with the modesty expected of such princesses. Torn between "folly" or "foolishness" (*folie*), which makes them want to express their love for their suitors, and "wisdom" (*sagesse*), which makes them want to restrain and conceal this desire, these young women develop a complex inner life. What makes a heroine worth examining, as these poets see it, is when she is conflicted in her mind, as it is that psychomachia that makes her interesting.

If the chroniclers show such little concern about Eleanor's state at the time of her marriage, it is because they show so much concern about her father's state at the time of his death. William had been a sinner. During the papal schism of 1130, he had supported the antipope Anacletus II against Pope Innocent II, he had expelled bishops who refused to share his preference in the pontiff, and he had amended his behavior only after an intervention by Bernard of Clairvaux, the great Cistercian abbot. In addition, in September of 1136, he had supported Geoffrey "the Fair" Plantagenet, V Count of Anjou, who was claiming Normandy in the name of his wife, the Empress Matilda, and he had taken part in what was seen as an ill-advised military campaign against this province.[27] Yet, having been a sinner, William became a saint. The Monk of Saint-Maixent cites him as describing himself as "aware of my innumerable sins, which I committed with temerity, by the persuasion of the devil, and fearing, trembling, the judgment of God, seeing those things that are held by us as good to be like smoke in the air." He made a pilgrimage to Saint James, inspired, it was said, "by penitence for his wicked deeds,"[28] and he died there (according to hagiographic embellishment) on Easter Sunday, before the altar, after receiving Holy Communion.[29] William's contemporaries were much taken with the image of such a great lord expiring on a pilgrimage to such a holy shrine. The chronicler Richard of Poitiers, a Benedictine monk of the Abbey of Cluny, in a eulogy for the dead nobleman, writes, "As Christ lay a pauper in the grave abroad, the duke lay a pauper in a grave abroad, a foreigner in the land. The venerable duke died an exile for Christ."[30] The troubadour Cercamon, who had enjoyed William's patronage, sings, "It is the Count of Poiters I lament. . . . Lord, keep him far from Hell, for his end was most noble."[31] So strong an impression did William's death make on his contemporaries that the legend developed that he had not died at all, but had slipped away in disguise, become a hermit in Italy, and founded the Order of the Blancs Manteaux of Paris, whose monks were known as the Guillemins.[32] For that reason, Eleanor's father came to be remembered over time as Saint William.

As King Louis the Fat was dying, we are told, he too was concerned with the future of his kingdom and his son. Before Louis the Younger headed off to Aquitaine to marry Eleanor, Suger reports, the king gave him his blessing. "May the most powerful right arm of almighty God, through whom kings reign, protect you and your companions, my dearest son," he said. "For if by some misfortune I were to lose you and those whom I send with you, I would no longer care for myself and the kingdom."[33] King Louis indicates that he fears his son may encounter hostility in this region, presumably from residents unwilling to have a French prince marry their duchess and rule their lands, and that his life and the lives of his men may be in danger. For that reason, he arranges for high-ranking secular and ecclesiastical lords, including Suger himself, Louis's cousin Ralph I, Count of Vermandois, and Theobald II, Count of Champagne, to bring his son into Aquitaine, along with an escort of five hundred knights, or what Orderic Vitalis terms "the army of France," to accompany them.[34] The aim of young Louis's trip, this chronicler makes clear, was twofold: "to take as wife the daughter of the Duke of Poitou and to subjugate the whole duchy, as Duke William had ordained."[35] Like William, who acted to secure his child's inheritance through marriage, Louis acts to ensure his son's acquisition of this vast new territory through this union.

Again, if the chroniclers show so little concern about Louis the Younger's state at the time of his marriage, it is because they show so much concern about King Louis the Fat's state at the time of his death. The king is not represented as repenting of his sins, as William was, but he is depicted as undergoing a similar late conversion. Even as he was suffering from diarrhea and the foul medicines his doctors were imposing on him, he turned his thoughts to higher matters. Suger writes, "Despite the severe disturbance of his flux and the prolonged decline of his weakened body, he scorned the thought of dying shamefully or unready." Calling together his clerics, he bequeathed all his rich possessions to churches and the poor. He confessed his sins, and he had the viaticum brought into his presence, before which he knelt and recited the Creed. Calling his son to him, he gave him his ring and had him swear to protect the Church, the poor, and orphans and to administer justice fairly. At that point, Suger recalls, "With the deposition of his kingdom and his crown, . . . [he] professed the monastic way of life," exchanging his royal regalia for "the humble habit of Saint Benedict." It was common for noblemen and noblewomen to adopt religious life *ad succurrendum*, that is, on their deathbed, so that they could go to God in this holy state, but the abbot was greatly moved by the sight of a monarch doing so. He relates, "When he saw that I was weeping—as any man would for one who had been so great but was now so small, for one who had been so lofty but was now so humble—he said, 'Dearest friend, do not weep for me, but rather rejoice with great exultation. For, as you see, the mercy of God has allowed me to prepare myself before meeting him.'"[36] Like William, Louis seeks to turn from the temporal kingdom over which he has ruled to the eternal realm over which God presides and from the ephemeral duration of mortal existence to the lasting state of immortal blessedness. This shift, while expected of all dying Christians, is, as the chronicler sees it, all the more impressive on the part of a great king, given how much glory such a man enjoys on earth and, hence, how much humility he displays in rejecting that world for Heaven.

Eleanor and Louis's wedding was magnificent, the chroniclers agree, but it was also politically decisive in the way that their dead or dying fathers had intended. At Bordeaux, the chronicler of Morigny writes of the populace, "The common happiness, derived from the exaltation of their common lord, was declared by all. Without measure and number, all presented and exhibited themselves as if they had unanimously sworn to empty out the royal coffers."[37] So abundant and so varied were the delicacies offered at the feast and so distinguished were the secular and ecclesiastical lords in attendance at the celebration that, the chronicler attests, Cicero or Seneca would have failed to do them justice. Suger too writes, "The leading men of

Gascony, Saintonge, and Poitou having assembled, the prince joined himself in marriage to the previously mentioned maiden and had her crowned with the diadem of the kingdom."[38] From what these accounts say, the entire population of the duchy was united in jubilation at the union between their duchess and the young king, and they wished to be present at the wedding in order to partake in these festivities and to receive Louis as their new lord. At the same time, the wedding, in all its pomp, was a display of power, and the presence of the local lords at these festivities was a sign of their submission to the new duke, to whom they were now expected to swear fealty and homage. By being not only wed but crowned at this time, Orderic Vitalis writes, "The boy Louis . . . gained possession of the kingdom of France and duchy of Aquitaine, which none of his forebears had secured before him."[39] Even as the people of Aquitaine are seen as welcoming young Louis to their lands and celebrating his union with their duchess, they are also seen as potentially resisting the absorption of their lands into his domain which his army was ensuring. Though Suger praises the "exultation" with which the royal entourage were received in this region, he notes, "We returned through the district of Saintonge ready to put down any enemies we might encounter."[40] As joyful as the wedding was said to be, it represented the transfer of power over Aquitaine to the House of Capet, a prospect about which the locals were ambivalent at best.

While the Latin chroniclers never represent Eleanor as experiencing the conflicted inner life that the vernacular poets attribute to their classical heroines, they do represent Louis as undergoing such psychomachia. The wedding party was still celebrating the marriage of these two young people when news arrived of the death of King Louis. The chronicler of Morigny writes, "Having heard about the death of his father, this tender young spirit of a new bridegroom was bewildered beyond measure. The garment of happiness having been laid aside, he was clothed with the tunic of mournfulness, for the loss of the one struck him with great sadness while the gaining of the other had made him very happy." Louis must head back directly to France to assert power over his kingdom, but before he does so, he leaves his young bride in the care of Geoffrey II de Lèves, Bishop of Chartres. The chronicler continues, "Because conjugal affection troubled his mind, it pleased him to provide some outstanding man on whom he might impose the custody of his wife by an edict of royal power."[41] Torn between joy at acquiring his bride and sorrow at losing his father, between responsibility for this new wife and responsibility for his new kingdom, Louis becomes divided within himself in a way that makes him interesting to this author. In contrast, Eleanor, who had been transferred from her father to her new husband and is now left behind under the protection of the bishop, remains a pale figure in these accounts. There is no reference to her possible sorrow at her own father's death, which had occurred shortly before her marriage; no reference to her possible joy at her wedding to the king's son, even at this time of mourning; and no reference to her potential confusion at her new husband's rapid departure. What makes an individual worth discussing, as the chroniclers see it, is, not only when he is conflicted in his mind, but when he is conflicted in the decisions he must make about his life, as Louis is, and Eleanor is not in the position to make such decisions.

For the next eleven years, until she was twenty-four years old, Eleanor remained in her husband's shadow.[42] While she retained her own titles, Louis became Count of Poitou and Duke of Aquitaine, and the evidence from the charters suggests that he ruled these lands largely in her stead.[43] The only anecdotal evidence we have about her from this time appears, not in historical accounts produced at the royal court, but in the hagiographic records used to promote Bernard of Clairvaux's canonization. When Eleanor left her native lands to be with her new husband in France, she had in her company her sister Petronilla, just as Louis had in his company his cousin Ralph of Vermandois and his vassal Theobald of Champagne. Before long, Petronilla and Ralph determined to marry, despite the fact that Ralph was already wedded to Theobald's sister. Not surprisingly, the count took offense at the repudiation of his kinswoman, and between 1142 and 1144, he waged war against Ralph and Louis. During that time, Geoffrey of Auxerre writes of Bernard of Clairvaux, "The holy man was with the king, laboring to further the cause of peace, and the queen was putting her efforts in the opposite direction."[44] In October of 1144, Bernard had a conversation with Eleanor at the Abbey of Saint-Denis, during which, Geoffrey relates, "He warned her to desist from her undertakings and to suggest better things to the king." By the end of their exchange, the abbot had brought the queen into agreement with him. As a result, Geoffrey reports, "With her having been reformed, the said king, because the queen had conveyed the words to him, humbly executed what had been promised to the man of God."[45] As minimal as the evidence about Eleanor's role in the French court may be, this anecdote shows her to be capable of exercising influence over her husband, at least in a matter concerning her sister, to the point where someone like Bernard appeals to her to intervene on his behalf. Pope Eugenius III would eventually lift Ralph and Petronilla's excommunication at the Council of Reims,[46] but, for the time being, Louis and Theobald were reconciled, thanks to Eleanor's efforts. As was customary with queens, Eleanor's power lay, not in her ability to act, but in her ability to intercede on behalf of others and induce the king to act.

From what we are told, Eleanor was not happy in her marriage. While she was talking with Bernard about Petronilla's situation at Saint-Denis, Geoffrey of Auxerre informs us, "She began to bewail her sterility."[47] Though she had conceived a child during the first months of their marriage, as Geoffrey notes, she had had a miscarriage and had remained infertile afterward, "despairing of her fecundity." With Eleanor's abrupt change of topic from her sister's bigamous marriage to her own inability to have a child, it seems that her state of sin, as the promoter of an illicit union, is rooted in a state of despair, as a queen consort unable to bear a child and heir to the throne. She is described as "bewailing that the Lord had concluded that she would not bear from her womb,"[48] as if she saw God as responsible for her sterility, and "humbly asking [Bernard] if he could obtain offspring for her from God,"[49] as if she saw him as capable of interceding before God on her behalf. While Eleanor was originally positioned as the more powerful partner in the conversation with the abbot, given her presumed influence over the king, she now recognizes her holy interlocutor to be the more powerful of the two, with his presumed influence before God. In response, Bernard spoke "pityingly to the bewailing one," promising her that if she endeavored to establish peace between Louis and Theobald, she would have a child.[50] As a result of the agreement between the abbot and the queen, Geoffrey notes, in 1145, Eleanor conceived and gave birth—though not, he neglects to add, to the hoped-for son and heir to the throne, but to a daughter, the future Marie, Countess of Champagne. The unhappiness Eleanor expresses in her marriage, even if temporarily relieved by the birth of her first child, foreshadows the unhappiness that would, in time, bring about its dissolution.

THE DEMON WIFE

According to all reports, Eleanor's marriage to Louis started to unravel when they were away on the Second Crusade. As the couple was returning from this expedition, they stopped at Tusculum, south of Rome, on October 9 and 10, 1149, where they visited with Pope Eugenius III, who had retreated here to escape civic unrest in his capital. During this encounter, the pontiff urged the two to reconcile,[51] apparently with some success: Eleanor bore her second child, a daughter named Alix, in France nine months later. But relations between Eleanor and Louis only continued to deteriorate. In March of 1152, a group of prominent ecclesiastical and secular lords gathered in the Castle of Beaugency, in the county of Blois, to consider allegations that Eleanor and Louis were too closely related to remain

a wedded couple. Given the high rate of intermarriage among the aristoc-
racy at this time, it was not difficult for a restless husband to discover that
he was related to his wife through a distant ancestor and, hence, that their
union needed to be annulled. Among the kings of France, five out of the
six who ruled during Eleanor's lifetime had had at least one marriage dissolved on this basis. Among the recent dukes of Aquitaine, William VIII
had discarded two wives before taking up with Hildegard of Burgundy,
and William IX had cast off Philippa of Toulouse, the mother of Eleanor's
father, William X, in order to unite with "Dangerosa" de l'Isle Bouchard,
the wife of his vassal Aimery I de Rochefoucauld, Viscount of Châtellerault (and the mother, with her legitimate husband, of Eleanor's mother,
Aénor).[52] It is in the context of such widespread divorces on the grounds
of consanguinity that, on March 21, 1152, Eleanor and Louis's marriage was
pronounced invalid. Many sources represent the separation neutrally, as
something that simply happened between the two spouses because of what
was admittedly their close kinship.[53] Yet given that in losing his wife, the
king lost the vast territory of Poitou and Aquitaine, there was much speculation at the time about what had really happened that had led to the un-
doing of their union. While for some observers, Eleanor remained a passive
victim of her husband's rejection, to be pitied for having been cast aside,
for others, she was the active instigator of this rupture, to be celebrated for
having regained her freedom.

Pope Eugenius did not deny that Eleanor and Louis were too closely related to be a wedded couple, but he did not seek to dissolve their marriage.
According to John of Salisbury, who was present at the papal court in Tusculum when the king and queen stopped by, the pope felt so strongly about
the sacramental union of a husband and wife that he did whatever he could
to repair ties between quarreling couples. From what John indicates, Eleanor and Louis spoke frankly to Eugenius about their marital difficulties,
and the pope "listened to the grievances of each side." That night, John continues, "He made them lie down in the same bed, which he had adorned
with his own most precious hangings. Each day during their brief visit, he
strove by familiar conversation to restore love between them. He honored
them with gifts."[54] In his role as a priest, Eugenius repeated Eleanor and
Louis's marriage ceremony, preparing the marital bed and bestowing presents on them. He acted similarly a year later, when he met with Hugh II,
Count of Molise, who was also seeking to annul his marriage, and Hugh's
wife. He begged the count "to put aside all rancor and to receive his wife
kindly, not so much obeying the necessity of the law as exhibiting the trust
and affection of a spouse," and he again reenacted the couple's marriage
ceremony.[55] By the mid-twelfth century, theologians and canonists were

increasingly insisting on the sacramental nature of marriage. Scripture had commanded, "A man . . . will leave his father and mother and will cling to his wife, and the two will become one flesh. . . . What God has united, let no man put asunder."[56] Because God had made the husband and wife into one flesh, ecclesiastics now felt, it was wrong for men to allow them to be separated. The love that joins these spouses, Eugenius makes clear, is not simply the personal affection one individual may feel for another, but the impersonal commitment, sanctioned by God, a husband or wife must cultivate for a marriage partner; it is thus, not a transitory emotion, which may come and go, but a permanent orientation of one's affective life, which must persist.

In the absence of Eugenius's objection to Eleanor and Louis's marriage, it was thought to have been Louis who pursued their divorce. As far back as 1143, rumors had circulated that the royal couple was too closely related to be married. In the fall of that year, when Eleanor and Louis were attempting to have the union of Petronilla and Ralph of Vermandois legitimized, Bernard of Clairvaux remarked that Louis had nerve to claim that Ralph's previous marriage should be annulled "when it is openly known that he himself is living with his cousin within the third degree of consanguinity."[57] The Benedictine monk Stephen of Rouen writes retrospectively of Eleanor in *Draco Normannicus* (1167–69), "Rumor attested her to be relative to the king. . . . Peers, pontiffs, the crowd whispered. The sound was extended to the ears of both."[58] In the first months of 1153, we are told, Louis was informed (again) of these allegations, and he was troubled by them. The anonymous author of *Historia gloriosi Regis Ludovici VII* relates, "Certain kinsmen and relatives approached King Louis and gathered together with him, saying that there was a line of consanguinity between him and Queen Eleanor his wife, which they promised to confirm by oath. Hearing this, the king did not wish to have his wife any longer, contrary to Catholic law."[59] From what this author indicates, Louis (who was known by the epithet "the Pious") shrank from living in open defiance of ecclesiastical statutes. As a result, the chronicler of Tours attests that "Louis, King of France, . . . at the Castle of Beaugency, consanguinity having been sworn, repudiated his wife [*uxorem suam repudiat*],"[60] with a phraseology echoed by numerous authors.[61] The chroniclers identify Louis as the subject of the action, "repudiate" as the verb, and the queen as the object of the action; even more often, they use "repudiated" (*repudiata*) as a passive past participle modifying the queen.[62] As the man was commonly seen as the party who initiates a marriage, Louis is here seen as the one who brings it to an end, on his advisors' encouragement.

Yet if Louis pursued a divorce from Eleanor, it was not always clear to his contemporaries why he was doing so. Despite all the rumors about Eleanor and Louis's shared ancestry, when the topic came up during the king and queen's meeting with Eugenius, the pope forbade them from mentioning it. According to John of Salisbury, "Confirming their marriage, both orally and in writing, he prevented anyone assailing it from being listened to under threat of anathema and it from being dissolved under any pretext."[63] It is not that the pope denies the facts of Eleanor and Louis's consanguinity but that he resists having this fact used as an excuse for dissolving the marriage when the relationship had broken down. At this time, authorities in the Church were increasingly arguing that couples who had wedded in ignorance of their close relationship should be encouraged to remain joined.[64] Indeed, however pious Louis may have been, concerns about consanguinity did not prevent him from later marrying Constance of Castile, and after her death, Adela of Champagne, both of whom were even more closely related to him than Eleanor. If it was not qualms about consanguinity that motivated Louis to repudiate Eleanor, contemporaries speculated, it may have been bitterness about her alleged behavior during the Second Crusade. Still, four years had passed between the incident at Antioch and the couple's divorce, and chroniclers did not regard whatever lingering anger the king may have nurtured about it as sufficient to explain his actions now. In our time, it is taken for granted by modern historians—always eager to explain earlier rulers' behavior on rational, political grounds rather than emotional, personal ones—that Louis rejected Eleanor because, after fifteen years of marriage, she had provided no son to inherit the throne.[65] It is true that the Minstrel of Reims and the chroniclers who follow him cite Louis's barons as recommending that the king let her go because "You have no child from her."[66] Yet these late and generally unreliable authors are the only medieval sources to mention the lack of a male heir as a justification for the divorce, and they attribute this rationale to the king's barons, not to the king himself. It was because none of these possible explanations for the king's repudiation of Eleanor seemed to observers to be adequate to account for his behavior that they hypothesized about other motives.

As surprising as it may seem, one of the major medieval theories used to explain why Louis repudiated Eleanor was that he had discovered that she was a demon, like the mysterious wife in folkloric tales circulating at this time. While modern readers of the Minstrel of Reims have stressed the barons' argument that Louis should leave Eleanor because of her failure to furnish a son, they have ignored the rest of these vassals' words: "In faith, . . . the best counsel we can give you is that you let her go, for she is a devil."[67] In his *Chronica majora* (1240–59), Matthew Paris lists as the reasons for Eleanor and Louis's divorce the facts that "They were consanguineous in the fourth degree; . . . she was defamed for adultery; . . . and she was of the devil's race."[68] The Franco-Flemish poet Philippe Mouskés, in his *Chronique rimée* (1240–72),[69] and the anonymous authors of accounts in two mid-thirteenth-century manuscripts, one now located at the Cambridge University Library[70] and the other at the Bibliothèque de l'Arsenal,[71] also claim that Louis rejected his wife because of her diabolic affiliation. In the folkloric tales, a lady of unknown lineage meets a nobleman and agrees to marry him so long as he will adhere to a certain condition. The nobleman consents to this arrangement, and for many years the lady makes him happy, bringing prosperity to his household and providing him with children. Inevitably, however, the husband breaks the taboo and the wife departs in spectacular fashion. The many clerics who recount stories about demonic wives recognize that readers may hesitate to accept the existence of such creatures, but they remind such skeptics that the "marvels" (*mirabilia*) of God's creation are manifold and that it behooves us not to dismiss out of hand everything we do not understand. Authors like Walter Map,[72] Gerald of Wales,[73] Geoffrey of Auxerre,[74] Gervase of Tilbury,[75] and Jean d'Arras[76] cite eyewitness testimony, learned books, and "the common people" (*vulgares*) to justify credence in these popular tales.[77] Like urban legends today, stories about demonic wives existed in a gray zone between history and fiction or, to put it another way, between what was believed and what was not believed.

In the folkloric tales, the mysterious lady who turns out to be a demon is never identified as Eleanor per se, but she is often associated with the queen in some manner or other. She may be Eleanor's ancestor. Philippe Mouskés announces, "Now I will tell you the truth, without fail, about why the king claims [Eleanor] to be a devil" (vv. 18720–21). He relates how an unnamed lady once married an unnamed "Count of Aquitaine" (v. 18722) and had several children by him, and he asserts, "From these children issued heirs, of whom Queen Eleanor was one" (vv. 18815–17). In other works, this lady may be the possessor of Eleanor's titles or lands. In the lengthiest and most famous versions of this story, the "ancestral romances" of the House of Lusignan, namely, Jean d'Arras's prose *Roman de Mélusine ou Histoire de Lusignan* (1392–94) and Coudrette's verse *Roman de Mélusine* (c. 1401–5), this woman is a certain Mélusine, whose lands are located in the county of Poitou and the duchy of Aquitaine. Other versions of the story identify the woman as the wife of the Count of Anjou,[78] which Eleanor became after her marriage to Henry, or even as the wife of Henry and mother to

Richard and John.[79] It is not clear to what extent anyone actually believed that Eleanor was a demon, but the tale was told, and even her sons seem to have believed that their lineage was cursed because of a nefarious ancestor.[80] Far off in Germany, the Cistercian prior Caesarius of Heisterbach remarks, around 1230, during the reign of Henry III, Eleanor's grandson, "Even the kings now ruling in Britain, which we call England, are said to be descended from a phantom mother."[81]

In the folkloric tales, the husband of the demonic lady suffers from an excessive passion for his wife. In Philippe Mouskés's account, the Count of Aquitaine is hunting when he becomes lost in a forest and discovers a maiden sitting alone by a fountain. The author writes, "Never could nature have formed anything in the world so well" (vv. 18736–37). When the count greets her "loudly" (v. 18740), she responds "meekly" (v. 18741). Dismounting from his horse and sitting down next to her, he proposes that she marry him, to which she readily agrees. He brings her back to his lodgings, "and there was great joy there, for she seemed so fair that she stole heart and body" (vv. 18753–55). In general, in these tales, the man finds the woman in a forest or some other desolate setting, alone or with just one maidservant, and weeping because she has been left vulnerable to the predations of men. Bereft as she is of family and friends, she inspires his protective instincts, so that he feels he is helping her by taking her in and wedding her, even though he knows nothing about her origins. The lady's seemingly supernatural beauty and gentle manner inspire him with a desire for her so strong that it overcomes all rational considerations, including the customary evaluation of her lineage and negotiations about her dowry. Of the Count of Aquitaine, Mouskés writes that "the count . . . greatly coveted [the maiden]" (v. 18767). These tales represent the husband as going astray by allowing a sudden, intemperate, and lustful desire for this woman to dictate his actions.

Like the husband in the folkloric tales, Louis was said to suffer from a misbegotten love for his wife. He married Eleanor, not because he found her alone in a wood, but because their fathers arranged the match, but he too was said to succumb to an excessive ardor, as the Belgian chronicler Lambert of Waterlos puts it, for "the very beautiful daughter of the Count of Poitou."[82] John of Salisbury attests that when Louis first heard mention made of their consanguinity, "The king was very upset at this. Although he loved the queen with an immoderate affection [*affectu . . . immoderato*], he agreed to release her if his counselors and the peers of the French permitted it."[83] Later, when the pope refused to dissolve the marriage, John adds, "This ruling was seen to please the king, for he loved the queen vehemently, in an almost youthful way [*puerili modo*]."[84] In his *De spirituali amicitia* (1164–67), Aelred, the Abbot of the Cistercian Abbey of Rievaulx, identifies "youthful friendship" (*amicitiae puerilis*) with "carnal friendship" (*amicitia carnalis*), that is, with a love inspired by corporeal qualities "such as beauty"[85] and characterized by "the violence of affection"[86] without "the restraint of moderation."[87] If young people are prone to carnal friendship, he explains, it is "because it is mostly in young people that affection rules as something unfaithful, unstable, and always mixed with impure loves."[88] With his immoderate love of his spouse, Louis exhibits, not the calm, rational affection that a husband should feel for his wife, according to ecclesiastics of this time, but a tempestuous, emotional passion of the kind that young men experience for their mistresses. As with the men who love these mysterious ladies, the vehemence of Louis's attraction to Eleanor is seen as deeply suspect.

The folkloric husband realizes at a certain point that his wife is a creature of the devil. In some accounts, the lady arouses her husband's suspicions because she always leaves Mass before the consecration of the Eucharist. One morning as she is exiting the church, the husband has her seized by some of his knights and has the priest approach her with holy water or the Host, which causes her to react with horror. In other accounts, the lady arouses suspicion because she withdraws for a bath on a regular basis, on Saturdays or when the rest of the household is at religious services. Someone—perhaps the mother, perhaps a maidservant, perhaps the husband himself—peers through a peephole into the chamber where she is bathing and sees her transformed into a dragon,[89] a serpent,[90] or a creature who is a woman down to the navel but a serpent below. However the lady's demonic or bestial form is exposed, when her husband confronts her with his discovery, she flees the scene in a dramatic and often violent manner. Faced with holy water or the Eucharist in the church, she wrenches herself free from the knights who are holding her[91] and flies through the roof with loud shrieks,[92] breaking off the top of the building (18802–9). On being interrupted in her bath, she plunges into the bathwater, never to be seen again.[93] It is thus that the lady is revealed to be, as the authors put it, not a woman, but a "phantom" (*fantasia*)[94] in the shape of a woman, that is, a devil or some other spirit who assumes a woman's form in order to deceive a man. Saint Paul had warned that "The devil transfigures himself into an angel of light,"[95] and the lady who would become the Countess of Aquitaine, Mouskés attests, was something that had transfigured itself "into the guise of a woman" (vv. 18795–96), speaking to the count "with a covered smile and a false heart" (vv. 18746–47). He explains, "She was truly the devil, who sought to take and deceive the count" (vv. 18756–58). However meek and vulnerable the maiden had seemed to him when he found her by herself in the wood, she was actually bold and predatory.

Like this folkloric husband, Louis is said to have realized that Eleanor was a demon. According to Philippe Mouskés, if Louis discovered her nefarious nature, it was, not because he saw her recoil when confronted with the Eucharist or because he saw her transform into a serpent or a dragon, but because he learned of her descent from this demonic countess. Once the king discovered her parentage, the poet states, "He did not love her nor [could he] because he knew about these ancestors" (vv. 18826–27), and he rejected her, "as one who was very troubled" (vv. 18697–98). As Louis was said to have expelled Eleanor from his marital bed in the historical chronicles, he is said to have shunned her now foul-seeming body in this more fantastical account. After her husband has repudiated her, Eleanor informs her barons, "The king said that I was a devil and that I was in all ways something misshapen and unworthy of his bed" (vv. 18709–11), indeed, some kind of "beast."[96] Whereas he had once found her body good and attractive, now that he suspects it to be the apparition of a devil, he thinks it evil and repulsive. Whereas he had once loved her passionately, he now hates her passionately. As his feelings shift from one extreme to another, Lambert of Waterlos depicts "King Louis accusing the queen his wife in a youthful way [*pueriliter*]."[97] The vehemence of the king's love of his wife has been replaced by the vehemence of his hatred.

Even if Eleanor was a creature of the devil, it does not necessarily follow, according to the folkloric tales, that Louis should have repudiated her. In a fair number of the stories of demonic wives, the husband comes to regret having broken the conditions of their marriage and having thus discovered the truth of her demonic nature. In the anecdote Gervase of Tilbury tells, though the lady warns her husband that he will lose all his prosperity and endanger his life if he ever sees her naked, he will not be deterred. He writes, "She reminded him of the long-lasting happiness they had enjoyed by observing the condition, and she warned him of the unhappiness that would follow if it were despised. But the knight could not refrain from rushing headlong off a cliff."[98] In certain versions of the story, the demonic wife is not so much a demon as an accursed soul, condemned to do penance on the earth. Jean d'Arras writes of such women, citing Gervase of Tilbury, "It is because of some misdeed, hidden from the world and displeasing to God, that he punishes them with these afflictions so secretly that no one knows of it except himself."[99] Mélusine, who is easily the most eloquent of these demonic wives, is, not a sinner, but a penitent; not someone who has wronged her husband, but someone who has been wronged by him; and, hence, not someone who is to be feared, but someone who is to be pitied. Her husband is so remorseful at having broken their agreement and lost his beloved companion in doing so that he becomes a hermit at Monserrat in Aragon, where he will never laugh or rejoice again. In the Late Middle Ages, the descendants of the House of Lusignan took pride in their mythical foundress, to whose magical ability at construction they attributed their great castle as well as other fortresses, towns, and abbeys on their lands.[100] The *Très riches heures du Duc de Berry* (c. 1412–16), the famous Gothic illuminated book of hours, depicts the Castle of Lusignan with Mélusine flying overhead in her dragon form. Far from sympathizing with the husband, who rejects his wife after discovering her true, demonic nature, the authors of the tales ask us to sympathize with the wife, whose husband pries into a secret whose disclosure will only bring destruction on both of them.

Yet another tradition maintains that it was, not Louis who rejected Eleanor, but on the contrary, Eleanor who rejected Louis. According to John of Salisbury, in the course of the spouses' quarrel in Antioch, "Mentioning their kinship, [the queen] said it was unlawful for them to remain together any longer because a relation existed between them in the fourth and fifth degrees."[101] When Eleanor and Louis later met with Eugenius in Tusculum, she seems to have continued to make the case for the need of an annulment. (Someone is doing so at the time, and it is clearly not Louis, who is said to be delighted when the pope rejects this possibility.) By speaking of her excessively close kinship with her husband, in a way that was heard and passed along by observers, Eleanor took what had been an open secret, that is, something known but not acknowledged as known, and made it something that had to be acknowledged and, hence, acted on. Hugh of Saint-Victor had written that marriages in the upper degrees of kinship could continue to stand so long as they remain hidden, but "When they have been made manifest, they are not to be tolerated because they are against precept."[102] By making the illicit nature of her marriage manifest, Eleanor is making it something that can no longer be ignored. When Eugenius forbids any future mention of the couple's consanguinity and of the consequent advisability of their divorce, he attempts, through papal authority, to unsay what Eleanor had said. Yet the rumor of the couple's close relationship was now set loose on their kingdom, and the origin of this rumor is traced time and again to the queen. Gervase of Canterbury writes of Eleanor, "Lo, suddenly there began to stir up, under the pretext of consanguinity, the dissolution of matrimony. . . . It was said that her repudiation was contrived, having proceeded from her inclination."[103] As pressure accumulated in favor of the divorce, William of Newburgh states, "She, as it was said [*ut dicitur*], was most insistent, and [Louis] either did not resist or was remiss in his resistance. Thus, the bond of conjugal unity between them was loosened by the force of ecclesiastical law."[104] While Eleanor and Louis would remain together for another two and a half years, it would be the charge of consanguinity that she had raised in Antioch that would ultimately be used to justify the annulment of that marriage, an annulment to which Eugenius himself would, in the end, be obliged to consent.

If Eleanor brought about her divorce from Louis, the sources agree, it was, not out of concern for the consanguinity of their marriage, but out of disgust with her spouse. According to William of Newburgh, "When the king had returned from the East to his own land with his wife, with the ignominy of the unsuccessful enterprise behind them, the former love between them gradually grew cold, and reasons for a separation began to grow. She grew most irritated with the king's habits, and she said that she had married a monk, not a king."[105] The problem, William suggests, was in part the failure of the Second Crusade under Louis's leadership. The king had been admired for embarking on the holy war, but the expedition had proved a disaster, for which he had received a large portion of the blame. Yet the problem was also the fecklessness in Louis's overall character, which the failure of the crusade had only exposed. It was Louis's older brother Philip who had been expected to inherit the throne, while he had been sent to be trained by the monks of Saint-Denis and prepared to enter the Church. Even after Philip had died and the eleven-year-old Louis became heir to the throne, the boy continued to receive a monastic education. With a language similar to that attributed to Eleanor, the secular cleric Stephen of Paris writes about Louis, "He was so pious, so gentle, so Catholic, and so kind that those who saw the simplicity of his deeds and habits, if they did not know him, would believe that he was, not a king, but some religious man. . . . He was entirely ecclesiastical in his conversation and habits."[106] While Eleanor is said to have perceived negatively what Stephen perceives positively, both recognize a conflict between the monastic qualities observable in Louis and the regal qualities required of someone of his position. To be a monk, as Eleanor sees it, is to fail as a king, and she has no interest in being married to a man who fails as a king. However much someone like Eugenius may insist that the wedding vows create an impersonal commitment, sanctioned by God, uniting a man and a woman for their entire lives, Eleanor sees her marriage as a personal relationship and one in which, at a certain point, she decides she wants no more part.

Whatever she had felt on marrying Louis many years before had proved to be a transitory emotion, now replaced by contempt for his newly apprehended moral character.

Rejecting Louis, Eleanor returned to her own lands, which she continued to hold of her own right. It is said that "Eleanor repaired quickly to her land of Aquitaine"[107] or "She repaired to her land, namely, Aquitaine."[108] Though she is no longer Queen of France, she is still Countess of Poitou and Duchess of Aquitaine, and she is able to retain this high status and the wealth that comes with these positions even when cast off by the king. According to Gervase of Canterbury, "Eleanor, having been repudiated [*repudiata*] and returned to her own freedom [*propriae libertati reddita*], possessed as lady her land, that is, Poitou, Aquitaine, and other lands of hers which bordered on them, by hereditary right."[109] While Gervase's description of Eleanor as "repudiated" might suggest a grieving, cast-off woman, his depiction of her as "returned to her own freedom" evokes someone who experiences this rejection as a liberation. If Eleanor is "returned" to her freedom, it is because living on one's lands, either under one's own rule or under the rule of one's rightful lord or lady, is what medieval people most associated with freedom. Other chroniclers likewise stress the freedom Eleanor now enjoyed as a woman independent of her husband. William of Newburgh remarks, "She was now released from the legal authority of a husband."[110] Though she had been queen and she had remained countess and duchess, because she was a married woman, she had been required to obey her husband and to bend her will to his. Now, as a free woman, she is subject to no such constraints. As Stephen of Rouen writes, after the dissolution of the marriage had been announced, "The free star sought out the ancestral soil [*solum patrium libera stella petit*]."[111] However much Stephen and other authors perceive Eleanor as having freed herself through this divorce, it was her capacity to retain her own lands during and after her marriage, to return to these lands when she was separated from Louis, and to reclaim the power and wealth that went with them that made that sensation of freedom appealing. As the Norman poet Wace writes happily, "She suffered no harm from this separation. She went to Poitiers, her native estate. There was no closer heir to her lineage than she."[112]

On returning to her lands, Eleanor was welcomed by her vassals. According to Philippe Mouskés, when Louis cast her off, "She sent for her barons, some after others, the highest by name. Then she returned to Aquitaine, very angry, with a great company" (vv. 18700–18703). Far from the seemingly meek and submissive demonic ladies, Eleanor is the one in control of the situation, summoning her barons to her presence, giving vent to her

anger at the king's treatment of her, and requesting their counsel as to how
to respond. The poet continues, "At Saint-Jean-d'Angély [in Saintonge],
she took her rest one evening. And when it came to the *desfublar*, she said
to them, 'See, lords, is my body not delightful? The king said that I was a
devil, and that I was in all ways something misshapen and unworthy of
his bed'" (vv. 18704–10). Defending herself against this charge, she protests, "Lords, . . . I am not of the race of devils, which the King of France
has just called me."[113] The Baron de Reiffenberg, who edited this text, understands *desfublar* as a "reception of the great men of the country," but
Daniel Power has argued persuasively that the word should be translated as
a "stripping" of clothing and, in particular, as the removal of a single outer
garment.[114] According to this reading of the text, when Eleanor asks her
vassals, "Lords, what kind of beast am I?"[115] she exposes her body to their
appraisal, perhaps taking off a cape and revealing its shape—but perhaps,
given the sexual aggressiveness that is so often attributed to her and that
would make the episode especially piquant, taking off more and showing
them more. Her power as a lady, who rules the lands on which these men
live, is complemented by her power as a woman, who behaves seductively
with them, removing her clothing and asking them to admire her beauty.
The scene where the husband or someone else peers through a keyhole and
beholds the lady's half-serpentine form is here turned around, so that the
lady is, not passively and privately being spied on, but actively and publicly
exhibiting her beauty to her men. In response to this display, the vassals affirm, "My lady, . . . there is no one as attractive as you in all the kingdom"
(vv. 18712–13), and they promise her, "You will have a husband in few
days, rich and powerful. Remain on your domain, my lady, and wait" (vv.
18715–17). They support her, flatter her, and predict (correctly) that she
will win another suitable spouse. Now that the bond between Eleanor and
her husband is broken, she replaces it with the bond between a lady and
her vassals. "By my head," the queen replies, "my heart inclines toward you"
(vv. 18718–19).

   In the end, it was not Eleanor but Louis who was said to have ended
up worse after their separation. It is a commonplace for chroniclers of
Eleanor and Louis's divorce to remark on how much land Eleanor possessed and, hence, how much land Louis lost by repudiating her. The author of the *Continuatio Aquicinctina* writes, for example, "Louis, the King
of the French, . . . repudiated his wife Eleanor and gave up the duchy of
the province of Aquitaine. She was the daughter of the Duke of Aquitaine."[116] By juxtaposing Louis's repudiation of Eleanor with the loss of
this province, the author connects Louis's action and the unhappy result.

The political consequences of Louis's abdication of such great territories could not be denied. William of Newburgh states, "Afterward the duchy of Aquitaine, which extends from the borders of Anjou and Brittany to the Pyrenees Mountains separating Gaul from Spain, gradually withdrew from the control of the French."[117] The Minstrel of Reims openly criticizes Louis for ridding himself of a wife with such great land holdings: "He acted like a fool. It would have served him better to have immured her. Then her great lands would have remained his during her lifetime, and those evils which happened would not have happened."[118] In mentioning the troubles that befell France as a result of the loss of Eleanor's lands, the Minstrel of Reims is referring to the fact that Poitou and Aquitaine would become possessions of the English kings, the major rivals of the French rulers. In mentioning Eleanor's possible immuration, he is contrasting Louis with Henry, who, decades later, when angry at his wife for misbehavior, did not cast her off but, rather, imprisoned her so that her great lands could remain his.[119] Whether through their implicit or their explicit criticisms, no chronicler represents Louis's rejection of Eleanor as anything but to his detriment.[120]

All in all, authors of accounts of Eleanor's divorce from Louis express great ambivalence about this queen. There was some secret about her origins—whether an incestuous affiliation with her husband or a maleficent affiliation with a demon—which Louis discovered and which filled him with such horror that he cast her out of his bed. Everything that had once seemed attractive about her now seems to him repulsive, as the product of a purposeful deceit. The issue, as these authors depict it, is not so much what Eleanor has done. The phantom wives, whether understood as demonic or not, never harm their husbands; on the contrary, they only bring them prosperity and happiness. The issue is, rather, what Eleanor is capable of doing, even if she never does it. When Louis's barons warn their lord that Eleanor is a demon, they add, "If you keep her long we fear that she will cause you to be murdered."[121] Indeed, in the anonymous ballad "Queen Eleanor's Confession," Eleanor confesses that she has been, not only an adulteress, but an aspiring murderess: "I carried a box seven years in my breast, / To poison King Henrie."[122] Eleanor did not kill Louis, or Henry for that matter, but she seems to the barons to be someone capable of killing her mate, just as she was capable of betraying him, and for that reason she is to be spurned. The stories about this queen are thus grounded, not in the observation of her actual deeds, but in the imagining of her potential acts. At the same time, the authors of these accounts perceive Eleanor as sympathetic. They pity her for having been rejected by her husband, much as the authors of the accounts of the phantom wives pity these ladies for having been cast aside, and they celebrate her for having regained freedom and independence in her ancestral territories. Whatever concerns Louis may have had about her, whether because of her close kinship to him, because of her alleged adultery, or even because of her demonic ancestry, they are not in the end sufficient to warrant her repudiation, given the trouble France will suffer from the loss of her lands from the realm. However alarming and unsettling Eleanor may have been when she was in the kingdom, she is missed once she is gone.

THE KING OF ENGLAND

Well before Eleanor and Louis's divorce, the political developments that would culminate in her second marriage were set in motion. In 1150, Geoffrey Plantagenet renewed the claims of his wife, Empress Matilda, to England and Normandy against those of her cousin, Stephen of Blois, and he named his eldest son, Henry Curtmantle, Duke of Normandy, as his heir. Alarmed by the rise of Angevin power in lands north as well as south of his own, Louis sent forces to champion the right of Stephen's son Eustace IV, Count of Boulogne, to this duchy. It was in August of 1151, when Geoffrey and Henry arrived in Paris for the peace talks that would end this conflict, that Eleanor seems to have met the young man for the first time. Louis agreed to recognize Henry as Duke of Normandy so long as he did homage to him for this province; a month later, when Geoffrey died, he was obliged to recognize him as Duke of Anjou as well. In March of 1152, after the Council of Beaugency, when Eleanor left for her own lands, Henry was in Lisieux, in Normandy, preparing to sail to England on another mission, but, hearing of the turn of events, he quickly joined her in Poitiers. On May 18, less than two months after the divorce, the thirty-year-old Eleanor united in matrimony with the eighteen-year-old Henry in the cathedral of that city.[123] Though her marriage to Louis had been annulled because the spouses were related in the fourth and fifth degrees, she and Henry were related in the fifth degree as well.[124] For that reason, as William of Newburgh comments, they married "less solemnly than respect for their persons justified but with more cautious forethought, lest the solemn preparation of the nuptials provoke some impediment."[125] Given that there were clearly communications between Eleanor and Henry prior to their marriage, we may wonder who initiated this correspondence and who proposed the union. The authors of these works do not have definitive answers to these questions, but they have their suspicions. While to some observers,

Eleanor remained the passive object of Henry's predation, to others, she was, again, the active force behind the marriage.

During this time of continued social unrest, it was not uncommon for a man "to seize" (*rapere*) an heiress like Eleanor for the purpose of marriage. The term "rape" (*raptus*) referred not just to forcible sexual intercourse with a woman against her will but to any abduction of a woman by an un-approved suitor, even one to which she was a willing party.[126] In Eleanor's own family, three of the four preceding generations had been marked by such crimes. In 1052 or 1053, Ramon Berenguer I, Count of Barcelona, had abducted Almodis de la Marche, Eleanor's great-great-grandmother.[127] In 1115, Gerald of Wales writes, William IX "seized by force and abducted [*vi rapuit et abduxit*] the wife of the Viscount of Châtellerault, his vassal, . . . and made her his de facto wife,"[128] though other sources indicate that Viscountess Dangerosa had agreed to become his companion. In the 1130s, William X was intending to marry Emma, the daughter of the Viscount of Limoges, when William Taillefer VI, Count of Angoulême, "seized [*rapuit*]"[129] his betrothed. The violent abduction of an heiress could some-times be passed off as a consensual marriage in order to save appearances for both parties. In an otherwise unsupported account, Gervase of Til-bury claims that, following the death of the Emperor Henry V in Germany, "When [the Empress Matilda] was on her way to her father in England, she was captured in a secret ambush, and by an extension of the same furor, she was taken to wife by the most mighty Geoffrey, the illustrious Count of Anjou." If this commencement to Matilda and Geoffrey's marriage was not generally known, he explains, it was due to "King Henry of England dissimulating the seizure [*raptum*] of his daughter and representing what had been an act of violence to be what he wished."[130] Given the great lands Eleanor held, once she was outside the protection of her first husband, she became the target of ambitious suitors.

By this point, Eleanor was already said to have received the attentions, willingly or unwillingly, of Geoffrey Plantagenet, Henry's father. Gerald of Wales states, "Geoffrey, Count of Anjou, when he was seneschal of France, had abused [*abusus fuerat*] Queen Eleanor, for which reason he many times forewarned his son Henry, it is said [*ut dicitur*], warning him and forbid-ding him to touch her in any way, . . . because she had earlier been known [*fuit ante cognita*] by his own father."[131] The phrase "had abused" could indicate that Geoffrey had consorted with Eleanor improperly, given that she was a married woman and the wife of his lord, or that he had consorted with her against her will. In the Book of Judges, for example, when wicked men come to the Levite's house and rape his concubine, it is said that they "had abused" (*abusi essent*) her.[132] In both the phrases "Geoffrey . . . had abused Queen Eleanor" and "She had . . . been known by his own father," Geoffrey is the subject of the action and Eleanor is the object, whose degree of consent to their encounter is left uncertain.[133] It is not clear when this "abuse" of Eleanor would have occurred, if ever. As we have seen, Geoffrey fought by William X's side in Normandy in 1136, when Eleanor was twelve years old, so there was contact between the neighboring rulers of Anjou and Poitou, but we do not know that he spent much time at the French court after she became queen. While the Counts of Anjou were traditionally seneschals of France, we have no evidence that Geoffrey occupied this position.[134] But whatever happened to Eleanor and Geoffrey, if anything, would be seen as casting a shadow on her marriage to his son.

Geoffrey Plantagenet was not the only Angevin to whose brutality Eleanor appears to have been exposed. We learn from the chronicler of Tours that after her repudiation by Louis, "The queen returned to Blois, but, with Theobald [V], Count of Blois, wishing to marry her by force, she fled at night and, escaping, came to Tours." Eleanor was traveling to her native lands of Poitou when she stopped at Blois, apparently expecting to spend the night in that town. Discovering Theobald's intentions toward her, she departed under cover of darkness for Tours, forty miles southwest. Yet Eleanor was not yet out of danger. The chronicler continues, "When Geoffrey Plantagenet, the son of Geoffrey, Count of Anjou, Henry's brother, wanted to take her as his wife and seize [*rapere*] her at Port-aux-Piles, she, warned by her angels, returned to her region of Aquitaine by another route."[135] One historian, examining the topography of this area, hypothesizes that Eleanor heard of young Geoffrey's plot when she was in Tours and that, instead of stopping at Port-aux-Piles, where it was customary to cross the Creuse River into Poitou, she continued downstream to the river's confluence with the Vienne, where she was conveyed by boat into her county. Passing through the villages of Ports, Pussigny, and Antogny, she would have come to the castle of her uncle Hugh II, Viscount of Châtellerault, who would have given her asylum.[136] The chronicler thus indicates that during this brief stage of her life when she was between husbands, Eleanor was twice in danger from ambitious men who aspired to seize her lands by seizing her, but also that she twice had men on her side who were well informed enough to discover these plots, well intentioned enough to warn her about them, and intrepid enough to help her elude them. After Henry married Eleanor, the two failed suitors allied themselves with Louis in his subsequent wars against Henry, though young Geoffrey did attend his older brother's coronation in 1154, and Theobald resigned himself to marrying Alix, Eleanor's fourteen-year-old daughter with Louis, ten years later.

Just as most sources identify Louis as the one who brought about the divorce with Eleanor, most identify Henry as the one who brought about his marriage to this rejected woman. There is no evidence that Henry perpetuated his father's and brother's legacy of violence against Eleanor, but he too was active and energetic in taking her as his wife. Once he learned that Louis had repudiated Eleanor, sources suggest, he did not hesitate to take action. The Cistercian monk Hélinand of Froidmont states in his *Chronicon* (1211–23), "Henry, Count of Anjou and Duke of Normandy, later King of England, took the relinquished wife of Louis, King of the Franks, as his wife [*uxor . . . duxit*]."[137] The chroniclers commonly identify Henry as the subject of the sentence, "took her as his wife" (*duxit in uxorem*,[138] *duxit uxorem*,[139] or simply *duxit*[140]) as the verb, and the queen as the object. They are struck by how rapidly Henry moved to wed Eleanor after her divorce and even by how quickly he traveled from Lisieux to Poitiers for this purpose: he took the rejected queen as his wife, they say, "soon" (*mox*),[141] "without delay" (*sine mora*),[142] or "immediately, without an interval of time" (*protinus, sine temporis intervallo*),[143] with a speed that reinforces the impression of his energy in bringing about these second nuptials. Robert of Torigni, the Benedictine Abbot of Mont-Saint-Michel, refers to Henry taking Eleanor as his wife, "whether with unplanned or with premeditated counsel."[144] By referring to possible "premeditated counsel," Robert suggests that Henry may have approached Eleanor after her divorce because of a prior understanding between the two, but by referring to possible "unplanned . . . counsel," he also suggests that he may have acted impulsively, of his own initiative, in doing so. Whatever role Henry played in obtaining Eleanor as his wife, he was already Count of Anjou and Duke of Normandy by this point, with a claim on the English throne, and, hence, a good match for her.

Because Henry acquired great lands by marrying Eleanor, he is said to have sought her as his wife in order to acquire these territories. Gervase of Canterbury writes that when Henry received word that Eleanor's marriage to Louis had been annulled, "The duke, seduced by the nobility of the woman and especially by covetousness for the lands that came with her, impatient of love and all delay, having taken with him few companions, quickly ran the long way. Within a short time, he was able to bring about the coveted union."[145] Other chroniclers do not address Henry's motivations in marrying Eleanor, but they invariably recall who Eleanor was and, by extension, what lands he obtained by wedding her. Henry, the

Archdeacon of Huntingdon, notes, "Henry, the new Duke of Normandy, took [Eleanor] as his wife and, enriched through her, possessed the county of Poitou with all its great holdings."[146] Richard of Poitiers states, "After [Eleanor] was repudiated by Louis, Henry the Englishman associated himself with her in marriage, from which all of Aquitaine from the Loire River to the Pyrenees mountains became his."[147] As a result of his acquisition of this vast realm, Thomas Wykes, a canon regular from Oseney Abbey, near Oxford, writing in the second half of the twelfth century, observes, "He began to be reputed most famous among the first peers of the world."[148] Though none of the chroniclers use this language specifically, they suggest that Henry was stirred by what Aelred of Rievaulx terms "worldly friendship" (*amicitia mundialis*) in his attraction to Eleanor. While true friendship is sought, "not for consideration of any worldly advantage of for any extrinsic cause, but from the dignity of its own nature and the feelings of the human heart, so that its fruition and reward is nothing other than itself," Aelred states, "worldly friendship is born of a desire for temporal things or goods."[149] Aside from Gervase's passing reference to Henry as "impatient of love," which suggests his eagerness to join with Eleanor in sexual union, the chroniclers agree that it was not so much personal affection as ambition that drew him to her.

In taking Eleanor as his wife, Henry was not deterred by the fealty he owed Louis. Gerald of Wales claims that "King Henry presumed to pollute the Queen of France, so rumor has spread abroad, with an adulterous liaison, and he took her away from her lord and united with her in a de facto marriage."[150] Despite the judgment of the Council of Beaugency, Gerald alleges that Henry did not so much marry the wife Louis had abandoned as lure away the French king's rightful spouse. He quotes Geoffrey Plantagenet *père* as telling his son to avoid Eleanor, not only because she had been known by him, but also "because she [was] the spouse of his lord," that is, the king to whom he owed fealty for his continental domains.[151] Geoffrey made it clear that if Henry married Eleanor, he would be committing, not just incest, by sleeping with his father's mistress, and not just adultery, by sleeping with another man's spouse, but treason, by sleeping with his lord's wife. While other chroniclers criticize Louis for his foolishness in relinquishing Eleanor and her lands, Gerald criticizes Henry for taking advantage of Louis's naivete. He repeatedly refers to Henry "abusing to his advantage the holy King Louis's simple ways"[152] and "insolently and unfaithfully abus[ing] [Louis's] devout meekness and mildness."[153] Walter Map, a courtier and diplomat in Henry's service, likewise asserts of his lord, "This same king had done to the most pious Louis many wrongs."[154] In their accounts of Henry's marriage to Eleanor, these authors make no reference to any love Henry might have for the queen. If he married her, they suggest, this action was noteworthy, not for any affection he had for this woman, but for the hostility he felt toward Louis, whose rights both as Eleanor's husband and as his own feudal lord he was abrogating. His involvement was thus defined, not by any amorous bond he created with this mistress and then wife, but by the feudal bond he broke with his lord.

Yet once again, another tradition maintains that it was, not Henry who brought about the second marriage, but Eleanor herself who instigated this development. As it was Eleanor who sought, and obtained, her freedom from Louis, it was she, according to some accounts, who sought, and obtained, her union with Henry. William of Newburgh remarks that Eleanor was now not only freed of Louis's legal authority but, as a result, "in possession of the power to marry whom she wished." And the man she wished to marry, he makes clear, was Henry. The chronicler continues, "She eventually obtained the marriage she desired."[155] Once Eleanor was legally released from her earlier marriage, William states, "She quickly summoned him for marriage,"[156] and "She and the Duke of Normandy, coming together at an agreed-upon place, sealed the marriage-pact."[157] Other chroniclers also identify Eleanor as the party who not only pushed through her divorce from Louis but arranged for her marriage to Henry. Thomas Wykes states, "She worked insistently toward divorce, by which she fervently aspired to marriage with Henry, Duke of Normandy and future King of England. . . . Matrimony having been dissolved between her and the king, she flew to nuptials with the duke, which she strongly coveted."[158] Gervase of Canterbury likewise reports, "With messengers secretly sent to the duke, she announced herself free and unrestricted, and she urged the mind of the duke to the contracting of matrimony."[159] When speaking of this marriage to Henry, a series of chroniclers identify Eleanor as the subject, "marry" (*nupsit*) as the verb, and Henry as the object of the verb. An anonymous biographer of Louis writes, for example, "The said queen, having been abandoned by the King of the French, married [*nupsit*] Henry, Count of Anjou, who was later anointed King of the English."[160] The Minstrel of Reims states that after the queen's marriage was dissolved, "She immediately sent for King Henry of England," for the purpose of marrying him.[161] The juxtaposition of Eleanor's repudiation by the King of France with her marriage to the future King of England makes clear that she did not suffer from Louis's rejection. As the author of the *Continuatio Aqui-cinctina* writes, "Thus this woman crossed over from one kingdom to the other."[162] Like Henry, we are told, Eleanor only profited from this exchange of husbands.

If Eleanor sought to marry Henry, the chroniclers indicate, it was, not because she sought to acquire great lands through this union (though she did), but because she desired this man. William of Newburgh writes, "It is ... said [*dicitur*] that even during her marriage to the King of the French, she aspired to be wed to the Duke of Normandy, as one more congenial to her character, and that she therefore preferred and procured a separation."[163] A few authors interpret her attraction to Henry as explicitly erotic. While Gervase of Canterbury describes Eleanor as "disdaining [Louis's] decrepit Gallic embraces," he indicates that "Duke Henry of Normandy was spending time in that region during those days, and he was appealing to the eyes in all things."[164] Walter Map observes, "Eleanor, Queen of the French, the wife of the most pious Louis, cast her unchaste eyes upon him."[165] The marriage with Henry is described as "desired"[166] and as something she "coveted,"[167] with no explanation as to why she desired or coveted this union beyond her raw longing. As these chroniclers represent Eleanor's interest in Henry, it is not a sentimental love. In contrast to what we see in the romances of Thebes, Troy, and Aeneas, the bride is not a tender maiden, overwhelmed by the first stirrings of passion, but a mature woman, attracted by a man and using the legal ploys available to her to free herself to marry him. In contrast to what we later see in the romances of Lancelot and Guinevere or Tristan and Yseut, the heroine is not a lady who engages in an exalted and secretive love affair with a knight, but a married woman who divorces one man in order to marry another more to her liking. Eleanor is depicted as drawn to Henry's looks and moral character, but this attraction is interpreted as lust rather than love and, hence, as coarse rather than courtly. Once again, Eleanor sees her marriage, not as an impersonal commitment sanctioned by God, but as a personal relationship between herself and a man and, preferably, a man she desires.

In taking Henry as her husband, certain chroniclers suggest, Eleanor was not deterred by the duty she owed Louis. Just as Gerald of Wales and Walter Map chastised Henry for having taken Eleanor from her proper spouse, they chastise Eleanor herself (albeit in a more passing manner) for having abandoned her husband for another man. Map writes, "Having contrived an unjust divorce, she married him."[168] Adam of Eynsham, in his *Magna vita Sancti Hugonis* (c. 1212), quotes Hugh, Bishop of Lincoln, as referring to she "who repudiated the unspotted marriage bed and, unchaste, attached herself to his rival, the King of the English."[169] While Henry is seen as having betrayed his lord by marrying his wife, Eleanor is seen as having betrayed her husband, not only by absconding with another man, but by absconding with his primary political opponent. William of Newburgh recognizes that Eleanor did not brazenly commit adultery but, rather, was "released by law from her earlier husband," yet he too judges her as having acted "in defiance of the Church, by a certain lawless license."[170] Even if the Council of Beaugency did dissolve Eleanor and Louis's marriage, William suggests, it was Eleanor who arranged matters to satisfy her desire. Her role in these events was thus defined, not by the amorous bond she created with her new mate, but by the marital bond she broke with her former husband and lord or, in other words, not by affection for her adulterous lover, but by disrespect for her lawful spouse.

The outrage at Eleanor's action in leaving Louis and marrying Henry brings us back to the role of a woman's consent in marriage. Consent, while increasingly expected of a woman in wedlock, was never the same thing as choice. In another account of Empress Matilda's marriage to Geoffrey Plantagenet, radically different from that of Gervase of Tilbury, the empress is represented as having meekly agreed to marry her second husband because her father wished her to do so. In 1144, Gilbert Foliot, Abbot of Gloucester Abbey and later Bishop of Hereford and London, praises Matilda for returning to England after the death of her husband the emperor, "not impelled by any urgent necessity or, frivolously, by the impulse of some womanly will, but called back by a father who had sent for her." There, he writes, she comported herself as a daughter "subjected to the will of her father in every command, having undergone second nuptials by his counsel."[171] Foliot suggests that because Matilda had possessed the most elevated of titles, that of empress, she might have been expected to exhibit willfulness toward her father, but, as a properly obedient daughter, she submitted herself entirely to him. A woman should not be forced to marry unwillingly, ecclesiastics increasingly agreed, but she should willingly acquiesce when her parents arrange a match for her. She should not be treated as an object, passed from one man to another, but she should act as a subject, choosing to submit to her parents when they select her husband. It is this submission of her will that makes her a rational, virtuous partner in this union. A man can also be led astray by passion. Louis, for example, is criticized for loving Eleanor too vehemently. But given the perceived need of the female sex for greater direction, a woman was deemed especially susceptible to "folly." It was in the course of the Second Crusade, to which we turn now, even more than in her divorce and remarriage, that Eleanor was thought to have succumbed to this vice.

THE CRUSADER

Infidelity, Marital and Religious

Famous for her marriages to the kings of France and England, Eleanor is famous, as well, for her participation in the Second Crusade. It seems that Louis had long been contemplating a pilgrimage to the Holy Land. In the summer of 1145, news arrived of the fall of Edessa—one of the four states of the Latin Kingdom of the East, along with Antioch, Tripoli, and Jerusalem—to Zengi, the Turkish Atabeg of Mosul and Aleppo, and he decided to take action. At his Christmas court in Bourges that year, he announced his plan to go on crusade. In the spring of 1146, on the bidding of Pope Eugenius III, Bernard of Clairvaux undertook a preaching campaign throughout France and Germany, persuading Conrad III, King of Germany, and his nephew, the future Emperor Frederick Barbarossa, to join in this expedition. That Easter Sunday, as the saintly abbot espoused the crusade to a vast crowd at Vézélay, in Burgundy, we are told, "King Louis, inflamed and inspired by divine grace, accepted the cross, and after him Eleanor his wife."[1] It is to be expected that the chronicler would emphasize the king's public declaration of his intention to undertake this campaign, yet it is striking that he mentions the queen's identical action as well. We catch sight of Eleanor again in June of 1147, as the royal couple stopped for a blessing at the Abbey of Saint-Denis en route to the Holy Land. Before proceeding to the religious house, the king made a detour to a nearby leper colony as an act of piety. According to Odo of Deuil, "His mother, his wife, and innumerable others went on ahead to Saint-Denis. . . . What with the press of the crowds, the king's wife and mother—who, between the tears and the heat, almost gave up their spirit—could not bear with the delay."[2] After Louis finally arrived at the abbey, he received from the pope the pilgrim's staff and scrip, as well as the oriflamme, the standard that French kings carried into battle. It was the first time a crowned monarch was participating in a crusade, and he was doing so in the company of his wife.[3]

In short order, the Second Crusade experienced the series of disasters that would mark its history. As the French army made its way through Germany, Hungary, Bulgaria, and Constantinople, it encountered various difficulties, which only increased as it entered into Asia Minor. En route to Ephesus, a band Louis was leading became lost in the mountains and had to be redirected by local inhabitants. As the army continued on along the Anatolian coast, it suffered from the mountainous terrain, the harsh winter weather, and a lack of provisions. While the soldiers were crossing Mount Cadmus, the advance guard, under the command of one of Eleanor's vassals, ignored the plans they had made with the rest of the army to stop at the summit and wait for the others. Seljuk forces had been harrying the French troops ever since they had arrived in Asia Minor, and now, seeing the army dispersed across this mountainside, they swept down on the main forces and plundered the baggage train. For ten more days, the army struggled on through the mountains before arriving at the port city of Attalia, where they had difficulty securing the ships necessary to transport them farther. When the royal couple arrived in Antioch in March of 1148, it was with less than half the men-at-arms they had started out with.[4] The French forces reached the Holy City in June of that year, but more setbacks ensued. The Haute Cour of Jerusalem decided that, instead of attempting to regain the lost county of Edessa, Louis and Conrad's combined armies should attack Damascus, the major seat of Muslim power in the region. They marched on this capital in July, but they set their camp in an unfavorable spot and, as a result, were forced to abandon the siege after only five days. Discouraged by this series of setbacks, the French army melted away. Eleanor and Louis remained in the Latin Kingdom of the East for another year, visiting sacred sites and making gifts to monasteries, but they had accomplished nothing and, indeed, had only harmed the crusader cause through their ineffective campaign.

As the Second Crusade faded into an unpleasant memory in western Europe, its failure became entwined with the recollection of Eleanor's role in it. A woman, as a woman, was outside the feudal system. Though modern historians have frequently argued that the knights on the crusade from Poitou and Aquitaine were following Eleanor on this campaign, no medieval chroniclers represent them as doing so.[5] On the contrary, from what these authors indicate, any relation Eleanor had to the political and religious aims of the crusade was mediated by her husband, to whom she owed fidelity not so much as a vassal but as a wife.[6] Yet as external to the feudal system as a woman may have been, she was also internal to it. Eleanor was in Louis's presence as much as if not more than his principal advisors and, hence, had a perspective on his behavior as privileged as anyone in their camp. Seeing him as he was, we are told, she judged him to be contemptible, and she acted on that judgment, though how exactly she did so remained unclear. Given the disastrous outcome of the crusade, the chroniclers share Eleanor's low opinion of her husband's leadership, but they cannot condone her for having had this opinion, let alone for having broken faith with him. If Eleanor's participation in the Second Crusade was considered a problem, it was because her apparent personal infidelity to her husband represented a political and religious infidelity to Christendom as well, for which she could not be forgiven.

THE PRINCE OF ANTIOCH

When Eleanor and Louis arrived in Antioch on March 19, 1148, the royal couple were welcomed by Raymond, the prince of this city. Raymond was Eleanor's uncle—her father's younger brother—and he had already led an adventuresome life. Thirteen years earlier, he had been living at the court of Henry I, King of England, when he had received a secret invitation from the Latin patriarch of Antioch and the noblemen of this city to marry Constance, the young daughter and heiress of the late Bohemond II, Prince of Antioch. He is said to have traveled to the Holy Land in disguise in order to avoid notice by those who would seek to thwart this match. Once married and installed as prince of this city, Raymond established himself as one of the most noteworthy Christian rulers of the Latin Kingdom. He clashed with Joscelin II, Count of Edessa, and failed to come to his aid when his lands were attacked by Zengi's forces. Yet after Edessa fell and his own principality became more vulnerable to attack, he sought to strengthen its position by conquering adjacent Muslim-held cities. We are told that "Lord Raymond was . . . handsome in appearance far beyond the kings and princes of the world, praiseworthy in conversation and affability" (XIV, 21, p. 659) and that "It was said that he surpassed in chivalry all those who had ever been in the land overseas and all those who afterwards were there" (XIV, 18, p. 28).[7] Just as Raymond had acquired his principality through his marriage to a young girl, he is now reported to have angled to fortify it through his relationship with a young woman.

What exactly happened between Raymond, Louis, and Eleanor in Antioch was an object of speculation even in the mid-twelfth century. The major chroniclers of the Second Crusade say nothing about this incident. Though Odo of Deuil was by Louis's side throughout the campaign, he mentions Eleanor only half a dozen times in his chronicle without ever naming her, and he stops writing altogether abruptly, and, some believe, tellingly, as the French forces were approaching Raymond's city.[8] Otto of Freising, who accompanied Conrad on the crusade, never refers to Eleanor at all. The three chroniclers who do speak of the incident at Antioch were all living in western Europe during the crusade. Gerhoh of Reichersberg, the author of *De investigatione Antichristi* (1158–62), and John of Salisbury, the author of *Historia pontificalis* (1164–66), were both in attendance at Pope Eugenius's court when Eleanor and Louis stopped by in October of 1149 on their return to France, and they may have based what they wrote on what they had heard from members of the royal entourage. William of Tyre was studying in France and Italy during the 1140s, and he seems to have derived his account of what happened either from French crusaders who had returned from Outremer or from Levantine Christians who spoke with him when he returned to the Holy Land twenty years later. The popular French translation of his Latin *Chronicon* (1170–84), which was known as the *Estoire de eracles* or *Eracles* (1219–23), became the foundation for all subsequent accounts of the incident at Antioch.[9] Yet if Gerhoh, John, and William all speak so mysteriously about what happened in this city, it seems to be, not so much because they were ignorant of what happened, but because nothing really occurred. There was some sort of violent quarrel between Eleanor and Louis. Shortly thereafter, the French camp left Antioch in a manner so sudden, so secretive, and so marked by discord that it provoked widespread speculation. The king and queen remained on bad terms for the rest of the crusade, and several years later, they divorced. Instead of recording an event that happened and was observed by eyewitnesses, these chroniclers relate what *could have* happened behind closed doors or what *would have* happened if it had not been prevented from doing so.

When Eleanor and Louis arrived in Antioch, Raymond was eager to take advantage of his kinship with the queen and his access to their army in order to wage war against neighboring Muslims. From what William of Tyre tells us in his Latin chronicle, when the royal couple was approaching Antioch, Raymond had his noblemen and principal citizens lined up outside the city to meet Louis, "exhibiting to him all reverence," and he then had them escort him "most magnificently" inside the walls. Once the king's men were settled in their lodgings, he visited them there, gave them presents, and chatted with them in order to get to know them. Given the hospitality, generosity, and friendliness he is reported to have showered on the king and his entourage in an effort to win them over to his side, William writes, Raymond experienced "most great hope" that he would obtain their military assistance and would thus be able to subject the neighboring cities to his rule (XVI, 27, p. 754).[10] Indeed, William's French translator tells us, "He trusted so much in the king's help that he was already of the opinion that the cities of Aleppo and Shayzar and the other fortresses of the Turks that were near him would come easily into his hand" (XVI, 27, p. 133). If Raymond was so confident that Louis would respond favorably to his appeal, the chronicler makes clear, it was in large part because he thought that the queen would affect the king's decision. According to William's Latin chronicle, "He counted greatly on an intervention before the lord king by the queen, who was attached to the king as his inseparable companion during his pilgrimage. She was the niece of the lord prince, namely, the daughter of William, Count of Poitou, his older brother" (XVI, 27, p. 754). The other local Christian lords also sought to profit from Louis's presence in the Latin Kingdom of the East at this time, but, we are told, they too expected that Raymond would be favored among them because of his connection to Eleanor. Though these lords were glad that the king was coming to their kingdom's aid, William describes them as "fearing that he would be detained around Aleppo by the lord prince, to whom he was related and to whom he seemed tied by the firmer bond of love, and most of all by the intervention of the queen, which seemed probable" (XVI, 16, vol. 2, p. 757). As Eleanor first appears in this narrative, she is someone presumed to enjoy influence over her husband and to be ready to use that influence for the benefit of her kinsman.

Yet despite Raymond's expectations of military assistance, Louis was disinclined to go to war immediately. When John of Salisbury begins his account of the episode at Antioch, he observes, "The most Christian King of the Franks, his forces having been destroyed in the East, came to Antioch. . . . They remained there to console, heal, and restore the survivors from the wreck of the army."[11] In order to understand what happened in this city, John suggests, one must keep in mind the military disasters that preceded Louis's arrival in its walls. While Raymond perceived Louis as the head of a great army that was ready to help him conquer lands, Louis perceived himself as the head of decimated forces that needed to recuperate from their recent losses. William of Tyre confirms John's interpretation of the situation, especially in the French translation of his text. When Raymond asked Louis for military aid, he writes, "The king . . . responded that he was vowed to go to the [Church of the Holy] Sepulcher, and he had taken up the cross in order to go there. Since he had come from his country, he had encountered many difficulties. For this reason, he had no desire to undertake any wars until he had accomplished his pilgrimage. After that, he would willingly listen to the prince and the other barons from the land of Syria. On their counsel, he would do what he could for the profit of the business of Our Lord" (XVI, 27, p. 134). If Louis turns down Raymond's request, he explains, it is because, at this time, he needs to fortify himself spiritually by traveling to Jerusalem, as a pilgrim, before he can apply himself militarily by leading forces in battle, as a king. He sees himself, not in a position of strength, given his still-considerable army, as the prince does, but in a position of weakness, given his recent troubles, and, as a result, in need of divine succor before he can provide human assistance. Even after Louis has visited the Church of the Holy Sepulcher, he plans to take up arms, not to assist his wife's uncle in the battles he chooses, but to support the Christian barons of the Latin Kingdom of the East in whatever theater of war they decide is most important. Insofar as his priorities are, not just spiritual, but military, they are focused on the kingdom as a whole and not on one principality, even one to whose ruler his wife is related.

Once Raymond realized that he would not be receiving military assistance from Louis after all, he decided to use his intimacy with Eleanor to turn her against the king. From what the chroniclers indicate, he may have done so through "force" (*vis*), that is, by removing the queen physically from the set of rooms she and her ladies were occupying and confining her in another set of rooms, to an uncertain fate. Alternately, he may have done so through "fraud" (*frauda*), that is, by leading her astray her verbally, so that she allied herself with him against her husband. Gerhoh of Reichersberg writes that, though Louis did not suspect any evil among his compatriots in Antioch, "He was deprived of the company of his own wife, whom he had brought with him, by the prince of this city, through fraud as well as through force [*fraude simul et vi*]. After some time, having been restored to freedom, she did not wish to be with him since, conscious as she was of having served wifely faith, she was not believed."[12] As Gerhoh understands the situation, Raymond first used force to separate Eleanor from Louis and then used fraud to make her want to remain apart from him. Whatever influence the prince brought to bear on the queen, Eleanor claimed to have remained faithful to Louis during her absence from his company and only became embittered with her husband when he refused to place credence in her words. In contrast to Gerhoh, William of Tyre hesitates as to whether the prince employed force or fraud. When Raymond saw that he was having no success at persuading Louis to lend him his army, he writes, in the original Latin text, "Frustrated in his hopes, his plan having changed, he began to detest the king's ways, to openly devise plots against him, and to mobilize to do him injury. He undertook to seize [*rapere proposuit*] his wife, either violently or through secret plotting [*aut violenter aut occultis machinationibus*]" (XVI, 27, p. 755). As we recall, "to seize" (*rapere*) a woman at this time was to take her from her lawful guardian, with or without her consent, and this is what Raymond intends to do with Eleanor. A late thirteenth-century chronicler from Saint-Denis states that "Queen Eleanor, having been deceived through the fraud of her uncle [*fraude patrui sui . . . decepta*], Prince of Antioch, wanted to remain there,"[13] as if Raymond employed fraud alone, but a fraud with which Eleanor collaborated. However these chroniclers represent what happened, they agree that Raymond was the instigator of the plot and Eleanor his accomplice. He may have physically overpowered her, compelling her to submit to a wicked action; he may have mentally overpowered her, persuading her that this wicked action was a good one; or he may have subjected her to some combination of physical and mental coercion in order to achieve this end.

Though Raymond attempted to use Eleanor as a means by which to harm Louis, the chroniclers never blame him for what happened in Antioch. Gerhoh of Reichersberg and John of Salisbury cite allegations that Eleanor committed adultery during this time, and John quotes one source who makes a veiled suggestion that her partner in adultery may have been Raymond himself, but neither chronicler asserts in his own voice that she was guilty of this crime, whether with her uncle or any other man. Alone among the three, William of Tyre unequivocally represents Eleanor as having been unfaithful to her husband in his Latin chronicle, but he declines to name her lover. Though he speaks of Raymond extensively, and though he describes his close relationship with the queen, he pointedly does not state that he entered into a criminal liaison with her. On the contrary, he writes of the prince, "After his marriage, he was careful to observe and maintain faithfulness in the conjugal relation" (XIV, 21, p. 659). Later chroniclers regularly refer to Eleanor as having committed adultery on the crusade, but Raymond largely disappears from the story. Before long, Eleanor's marriage to Louis would be dissolved on grounds of consanguinity, but the possibility that she had committed incest, not just with a third cousin once removed to whom she was married, but with her own uncle, is never raised, even by her harshest critics. In accordance with the medieval logic of *raptus*, what is important in a man's seizure of another man's wife is, not the offense he is committing against the woman, whose volition in this situation is typically unclear, but the offense he is committing against another man, to whom he may or may not owe fealty. The issue, as the chroniclers see it, is not whether Raymond raped Eleanor, but whether he broke faith with Louis (to whom, John wrote, "he owed . . . loyalty, affection, and respect for many reasons")[14] by taking his wife, or whether Louis broke faith with Raymond by refusing him military assistance (which, William feels, he had a right to expect). Whatever Raymond did or did not do with the queen, it is clear that, when he could not triumph by claiming lands with Louis's help, he attempted to triumph by claiming Louis's consort, alienating her affections from her rightful lord, and that he did so more to avenge himself on the king than to spend more time with the young woman.

If Raymond is not to be blamed for what happened in Antioch, the chroniclers agree, it was because, whatever happened with Eleanor, he was such a great prince. It is true, William of Tyre concedes in his Latin chronicle, that Raymond could be vindictive. By declining to aid the Count of Edessa against the Muslim forces that were endangering the kingdom as a whole, Raymond forgot "that personal hatred should not cause harm to the public weal" (XVI, 4, p. 720). There are several possible reasons why the local Christian lords advised Louis and Conrad to set their camp outside Damascus in an unfavorable location, but, William acknowledges, one was that Raymond, still seeking to avenge himself on Louis, incited them to do so. Yet in the end, Raymond was remembered, not for having sabotaged Louis's efforts on the Second Crusade, but for having ridden out bravely against the crusaders' enemies. Once Louis and Eleanor had left the Holy Land, Nureddin, the son of Zengi, began to ransack the territory around Antioch. In response, William writes, Raymond rushed "imprudently" to Nureddin's fortress of Inab, northwest of Aleppo, with only a few men, without waiting for the cavalry he had ordered to arrive (XVII, 9, p. 771). Though Raymond fought valiantly, he was slain in June of 1149, and his head was sent back to the caliph of Baghdad in a silver box, William notes, "as a sign . . . that the great persecutor of the heathen could be believed to have been killed." Imprudent as Raymond may have been in taking on such a great force with such a small army, he was also courageous in exposing himself to such danger in the hope of defeating his enemy. Back in Antioch, Raymond's subjects mourned his death, remembering "the outstanding deeds of that man." So extraordinary a warrior was Raymond, William relates, that "The many deeds he wrought vigorously and magnificently in his principality require special treatment" (XVII, 10, p. 772). The prince may have treated Louis treacherously by seeking to separate his wife from him and to undermine his military campaign, but he fought gloriously against Muslims and died a martyr of the faith, and for that sacrifice of his life on the field of battle, his memory was cherished.[15]

As it is unclear how Raymond attempted to turn Eleanor against Louis, it is unclear why Louis ordered the French party to depart so suddenly and unexpectedly from Antioch. It may have been that Louis feared that Eleanor was in danger of remaining with Raymond. John of Salisbury writes that Thierry Galeran, a knight among Louis's secretaries and a eunuch, recommended that Louis take her from Antioch immediately "because it would be a lasting disgrace to the kingdom of the Franks if, among all the other misfortunes, the king was said to be despoiled of his wife or abandoned by her." Thierry is unsure whether Eleanor is about to be taken from Louis or to leave him of her own accord. But whatever is going on with Louis's wife, he suggests, it is happening in the context of Louis's recent military losses at Mount Cadmus and his army's discouragement at the state of their campaign. The king must act quickly in order to prevent the shame of his military defeat from being compounded by the shame of losing his wife, he argues. Alternatively, if Louis left Antioch abruptly, it may have been because he worried that he himself was in mortal peril. William of Tyre indicates that after Louis rejected Raymond's request for military aid, the situation in Antioch became so tense that he feared for his life. In the Latin text, he speaks of Louis conferring with his magnates "about his life and his safety" (XVI, 27, p. 755). In the French translation, he relates, "Many people made known to the king that the prince was taking this badly, so that he secretly took counsel with his men. By their agreement, he left the city of Antioch at night so they would not all know about it" (XVI, 27, p. 134). If it remains unknown what danger Louis was seeking to escape when he had his entourage leave Antioch under cover of darkness, it is because the king had escaped it. Gerhoh of Reichersberg states that Raymond separated Eleanor from Louis, yet William of Tyre suggests that the prince merely *attempted* to bring about this separation, without accomplishing it: in the Latin chronicle, he "began" (*cepit*) to construct plots against the king, and he "undertook" (*proposuit*) to seize Eleanor (XVI, 27, p. 755), while in the French translation, "He brought the queen his wife to such a pass that she wanted to leave and separate from him" (XVI, 27, p. 134). Because Raymond never took action against Louis, we do not know what form this action was going to take, if, indeed, it was ever going to take any form at all, let alone what degree of complicity Eleanor had in it.

While Raymond is not to be blamed at all for what happened in Antioch, as the chroniclers see it, Louis is partly to be blamed. It was Louis, after all, who had brought Eleanor on the crusade. William of Newburgh writes, "She had so constrained and subjugated the heart of the young man with the beauty of her appearance that, when he was about to embark on the journey of that most famous expedition, he was so vehemently jealous of his young wife that he decided that she was definitely not to be left at home, but should depart with him for the field of combat." Attracted as Louis may have been to the Holy Land and the spiritual benefits he would accrue there, he was also attracted to his wife and the carnal delight he took in her beauty. Because Louis brought Eleanor on the crusade, William relates, other noblemen brought their wives, their wives brought their maidservants, and consequently, "In that Christian camp where chastity should have prevailed, a multitude of women was milling about,"[16] with scandalous results. It was these crusaders' lustfulness, aroused by the presence of all these women, that was blamed for the dismal results of the campaign. Henry of Huntingdon states, "The armies of the Emperor of Germany and the King of the French, which had marched out with great pride under illustrious commanders, came to nothing, because 'God spurned them.' Their incontinence, which they practiced in unconcealed fornications, rose up in the sight of God. In adulteries [*adulteriis*] as well they greatly displeased God."[17] Henry does not identify those "adulteries" with any particular ladies, but, like William of Newburgh, he sees sexual impropriety as rife in the camp and as leading to the crusade's lack of success. Having failed to apply himself militarily to the crusade, according to Raymond, because he prioritized what he saw as his duty toward God over his duty toward his wife's kinsman, Louis failed to apply himself to the crusade, according to the chroniclers, because he prioritized his lovely wife over this spiritual purpose.

If Louis is partly to be blamed for what happened at Antioch, the chroniclers concur, it is also because he was such a mediocre king. For his comportment on Mount Cadmus, he comes in for little praise. Odo of Deuil claims that the king escaped the attack by scrambling up a rock with the help of tree roots and that he cut off the heads and hands of the Turks who were pursuing him, but other chroniclers make no reference to any such heroics on his part. During this nighttime battle, when the enemy was everywhere, William of Tyre reports in his Latin chronicle, "The king escaped by chance rather by effort in the great confusion and peril" (XVI, 26, p. 752). He eluded harm, his French translator attests, only through others' intervention: "There were I know not how many knights who took the king by the reins and drew him away from the press" (XVI, 26, p. 130). It was only thanks to God's assistance, William writes in his Latin text, that this small group caught sight of the fires that the advance guard had set in their camp and were thus able to rejoin their side. Later, at the siege of Damascus, the chronicler praises Conrad, the other king on the crusade, for performing "a memorable feat" (XVII, 4, p. 765)—he struck a Turkish knight with a blow so strong that he severed the entire left section of his body—but he attributes no such deeds to Louis.[18] Instead, he writes of the disastrous outcome of this campaign, "There are those who impute it to the king's excessive cowardice [*maliciam*]" (XVI, 27, p. 755). From the beginning to the end of the expedition, according to these chroniclers, Louis was reluctant to attack, whether as an individual or as the leader of an army, and reluctant to take on the risks that might earn him or his nation glory. While chroniclers commend the king's decision to go on crusade, they attribute this decision to his "almost childlike joy in the propagation of the faith,"[19] and they criticize his failure to advance the political and military interests of the Latin Kingdom of the East.[20] In contrast to his remarkable account of Raymond's death, when Louis expired in 1180 of a stroke, William notes merely in his Latin text that "Louis, the most pious and Christian King of the Franks, a prince of many virtues and immortal memory, laid aside the burden of the flesh, and his spirit fled to the skies to enter upon its eternal reward with the elect princes" (XXII, 4, p. 1011). The chronicler acknowledges Louis's devotion to God and (vaguely) his other good qualities, and he speaks of the abode that awaits him in Heaven, but he makes no reference to "outstanding deeds" he accomplished on earth or to the "special treatment" that is required to recount them. While Raymond had exemplified what a prince is supposed to be like, Louis, pious as he may have been, was not much of a king.

As it is unclear how Raymond and Louis acted in Antioch, it is unclear how Eleanor comported herself in this city. It was observed that niece and uncle were in close contact during this visit. John of Salisbury writes, "The attentions paid by the prince to the queen, and his constant, indeed almost continuous, conversation with her, gave rise to the king's suspicions."[21] While Louis is said to have been concerned about the intimacy between his wife and her uncle, as John tells the story, it was Thierry Galeran who convinced him to put an end to this relationship. The chronicler explains, "He boldly persuaded him not to suffer her to remain longer at Antioch, . . . because 'guilt can be covered up by the name of kinship.'" With this suggestion, Thierry is quoting the words of Phaedra in Ovid's *Heroides*, a collection of letters allegedly penned by tragic heroines from Greek and Roman mythology, including Ariadne, Medea, and Dido, which had been popularized by Baldric of Dol, Abbot of Bourgueil, in the late eleventh century. In this particular epistle, Phaedra addresses her stepson Hippolytus and encourages him to join her in love. While other lovers of married women must wait in the darkness for a gate to her house to be unbarred, she points out, Hippolytus, as her kinsman, will be welcomed indoors and allowed to kiss and embrace her openly. If Eleanor's relationship with Raymond seems innocent, Thierry implies, it is only because, like Phaedra, she contrives to make it seem that way, passing off the intimacy between lovers as that between relatives. It is not certain that John means for us to share Thierry's concerns about Eleanor and Raymond. He describes Thierry as "a eunuch whom the queen had always hated and mocked, but who was faithful and had the king's ear like his father before him."[22] He may mean for us to understand that Thierry acted less to serve the appreciative king than out of a desire to avenge himself on the disdainful queen. Eunuchs at this time were commonly regarded as "perfect servants"[23] by emperors and kings in the East[24] and to some extent in the West,[25] but the very trust in which they were held by rulers not infrequently provoked the hatred of other members of court.[26] Yet while John does not assert in his own voice that Eleanor was having an affair with her uncle, he invites us to entertain the possibility of a guilty liaison between niece and uncle, as Thierry invited Louis to do, and, indeed, he is the only chronicler to take this incident in this direction. He and Thierry ask us, not so much to observe the guilty interactions of his wife and her uncle—there is nothing particularly guilty to see—but, with the help of this literary analogy, to imagine what these individuals might be up to.

With Raymond not to be blamed for what happened in Antioch and Louis only partly to be blamed, it is Eleanor who is seen as bearing primary responsibility for this episode. All the chroniclers refer to the queen's assertion of her desire to remain with her uncle in this city even if her husband is to continue on to Jerusalem. As we recall, Gerhoh of Reichersberg states that once Eleanor was released from imprisonment by Raymond, "She *did not wish* . . . to return to [Louis]."[27] As William of Tyre's French translator puts it, Raymond "brought the queen . . . to such a pass that *she wanted* to leave and separate from him" (XVI, 27, p. 134). As Louis was residing in Antioch with the surviving remnant of his army, John of Salisbury writes, "The queen *wished* to remain behind, although the king was preparing to depart, and the prince made every effort to retain her if it could be done with the king's leave." As John represents the situation, while Raymond aimed to retain Eleanor in Antioch, he deferred to Louis, whose permission he recognized as necessary for such an arrangement. It was the queen, the chronicler indicates, who insisted on staying in this city and who, when Louis refused to allow her to do so, upped the ante. John continues, "When the king hastened to tear her away, [the queen], mentioning their kinship, said it was unlawful for them to remain together any longer because a relation existed between them in the fourth and fifth degrees."[28] Whatever Raymond may have said or done, it is Eleanor who speaks out here, and it is Eleanor who raises, for the first time, consanguinity as a ground for divorce, to Louis's evident distress. Raymond may have sought to bring about a separation between the king and the queen—whether temporary or permanent we do not know—yet it is Eleanor who proposes the dissolution of their marriage and who continues to pursue this course of action long after she and Louis have left Antioch. As we have seen, when she and Louis met with Pope Eugenius in Rome a year and a half later (by which point Raymond was dead), she brought up the consanguineous nature of their marriage, and, according to some sources, she ultimately succeeded in having the marriage terminated on these grounds. However much Raymond attempted to remove Eleanor from her lawful husband, whether through "force" or through "fraud," and however much Eleanor may have been a victim of his violence, clearly at some point the queen supported this separation or even pursued it on her own.

If Eleanor is to be blamed for what happened in Antioch, the chroniclers suggest, it was because she did not act like a queen. In the Latin version of his chronicle, William of Tyre writes of Eleanor, "Contrary to regal dignity [*regiam dignitatem*], she neglected her marital vows, the faith of the marital bed having been forgotten" (XVI, 27, pp. 754–75). In the French translation of this passage, it is related, "She was greatly blamed in the land, nor did she consider at all (as it was said of her) the highness of her crown or the fidelity of marriage" (XVI, 27, p. 134). Just as William criticizes Eleanor for having acted "contrary to regal dignity," he criticizes Arda of Armenia, the spurned wife of Baldwin I, King of Jerusalem, who abandoned the religious community she had entered and pursued a dissolute life: "Having set aside the religious habit, she spread herself out to all who were passing by, sparing neither her own reputation nor the regal dignity [*regiam . . . dignitatem*] for which she had once been honored" (vol. 1, XI, 1, p. 496). As he sees it, a queen possesses a certain dignity insofar as she is chaste, observing either the vow of fidelity to her husband that she took on getting married or the vow of celibacy that she took on becoming a nun. It is on account of that chastity, he indicates, that she is respected by her subjects. If William criticizes Eleanor (and Arda), it is not simply because he is a cleric and clerics are traditionally misogynistic. He speaks highly of Melisende, Queen of Jerusalem, whom he judges as having governed the kingdom well for the thirty years she served as regent, and he reproaches

her son Baldwin III for attempting to remove himself from her tutelage
and to rule in his own right. Melisende was, he writes, "a prudent and cir-
cumspect woman, having a virile heart in no way whatsoever inferior in
wisdom to any prince" (XVII, 1, p. 761). Instead, if William criticizes these
other queens, it is because, in their unchastity, they forsook the "regal dignity" that made their subjects respect them and want to submit to their authority.[29] To be a prince, William suggests, is to be bold and courageous in
military affairs, to the point where even an imprudent charge in battle can
enhance one's glory. But to be a queen is to be wise and self-restrained in
one's sexual behavior, always avoiding an imprudent dalliance that would
destroy one's reputation. Because Eleanor fails to exhibit such wisdom and
self-restraint, she is not comporting herself like a woman of her rank.

Instead of acting like a queen at Antioch, the chroniclers indicate,
Eleanor acted like a whore. Hélinand of Froidmont writes of Eleanor
sometime between 1211 and 1223, "Louis relinquished her on account of
the incontinence of this woman, who acted, not like a queen, but like a
whore [*meretrix*],"[30] in a phrase that was echoed by important Cistercian[31]
and Dominican[32] chroniclers. In the Middle Ages (as today), a whore was
understood to be not so much a prostitute, who took money for sexual
favors, as a licentious woman, who indulged excessive sexual appetites.[33]
The opposition these chroniclers set up between the queen and the whore
may seem perplexing, given that so many famous queens—Phaedra, Dido,
Jezebel, Potiphar's wife, and Cleopatra, to name just a few—did not display the chastity William of Tyre associates with "regal dignity." Even
Queen Melisende, for whom this chronicler professes so much admiration, was accused by her husband of infidelity with Hugh II of Le Puiset,
Count of Jaffa, though William discounts this tale. The queen who takes
advantage of her power to make sexual overtures to attractive young men
and then accuses them of rape if they refuse became a stock character of
medieval romance.[34] Yet the point is not that queens were "wise" and sexually restrained, in contrast to "foolish" and wanton lower-class women,
but that they were expected to act prudently, in accordance with their status, in a way in which less exalted women were not. Like the eunuch, who
makes sense of Eleanor's behavior by interpreting it through the prototype
of Ovid's Phaedra, William and his followers make sense of her comportment by interpreting it through the prototype of the *meretrix*.

Whatever happened in Antioch and whoever was at fault, the acrimony
between Eleanor and Louis persisted, becoming general knowledge. After
the royal couple quit the city, John of Salisbury writes, "Their mutual anger ascended higher in each of their hearts, and, though they dissimulated

it as best as they could, it remained."[35] Even back in France, Abbot Suger, who was governing the kingdom in Louis's absence, caught word of the wrath between the king and queen. He wrote to Louis in 1149, "Regarding the queen your spouse, we dare to advise (if it is, however, pleasing), that you conceal the rancor of your mind (if it exists), until, God willing, you have returned to your own kingdom and can act with caution regarding these and other matters."[36] Yet after Eleanor and Louis returned to France, the antipathy between the spouses only worsened. As we have already seen, William of Newburgh writes, "When the king had returned from the East to his own land with his wife, with the ignominy of the unsuccessful enterprise behind them, the former love between them gradually grew cold. . . . [The queen] grew most irritated with the king's habits, and she said that she had married a monk, not a king."[37] As this chronicler sees it, if the love between husband and wife cooled off, apparently especially on Eleanor's side, it was because the crusade had turned out to be a disaster and because Louis's pious rather than warlike character had seemed to produce this result. As other authors see it, the problem was not only that Eleanor had become contemptuous of Louis, but that Louis was upset that his wife thought so little of him. An anonymous chronicler writes, "During this journey, the aforesaid queen gravely offended [*graviter offendit*] the king in many ways. . . . The king, when he had returned to his own kingdom, chose to vindicate himself."[38] The author of the *Ex libro III historiae Regum Francorum* states, "His wife Eleanor . . . was disagreeable and insulting [*ingrata et injuriosa*] on this journey,"[39] or, in the French translation of this work, "She was rebellious, wicked, and disloyal [*rebelle et mauvese et desloial*] on the pilgrimage."[40] The imputation that Eleanor was "offensive," "disagreeable," and "insulting" may relate to the queen's sexual infidelity toward her husband, but it may also refer to the low regard in which she held him. Even back in France, Eleanor looked down on Louis, and Louis resented that fact.

In the final analysis, the chroniclers see Eleanor as having been punished for her infidelity toward Louis. William of Tyre concludes the account of the Second Crusade in his Latin chronicle, not with the end of Louis's military campaign—in the previous year, there had been no such campaign to speak of—but with the end of his marriage: "The Lord King of the French, the course of a year having been completed among us, Easter having been celebrated in Jerusalem, at the time of the spring crossing, returned to his own lands with his wife and his noblemen. Arriving there, mindful of the injuries his wife had imposed upon him during the journey and, in fact, during the entire prolongation of the pilgrimage, in the presence of the high prelates of his kingdom, the charge of consanguinity having been raised, he separated himself from his wife" (XVII, 8, p. 770). Though two and a half years would transpire between Louis and Eleanor's return to France and the annulment of their marriage, it was Louis's bitterness about Eleanor's misbehavior during this campaign, as William sees it, that ultimately led him to divorce his wife. Other chroniclers also link the alleged adultery and the divorce. One author states, "The queen having offended him in many ways, once he had returned, he relinquished her."[41] The author who stated that Eleanor was "rebellious, wicked, and disloyal on the pilgrimage" goes on to report that, "When [Louis] had returned from the pilgrimage, . . . he abandoned her on the advice of his barons and with the assent and authority of Pope Eugenius."[42] In order for Eleanor to function as an exemplary figure illustrating a moral lesson about the vice of women's infidelity, it is necessary for her story to end in a way that shows her being punished for her sins, and, these authors suggest, it did conclude in this way, with the king's repudiation of his consort.

Yet Eleanor's story did not end there. Despite all the rumors about her infidelity that were circulating, Eleanor was never officially charged with adultery, and her marriage with Louis was dissolved at the Council of Beaugency on the grounds of consanguinity alone. When other women of her time found themselves repudiated, they customarily returned to the guardianship of their male kinsmen. But Eleanor's father was dead, she had no brothers, and it was she who exercised authority over her uncles, not vice versa. She held Poitou and Aquitaine in her own right and thus had wealth and power independent of any man's supervision. Once she was released from the conjugal bond, she was released from the control of any man and was free to act as she wished. Having been cast off by Louis, she was able to quickly marry Henry. Having been stripped of the crown of France, she was able to acquire, in short order, the crown of England. Indeed, as we have seen, things turned out so well for Eleanor that various chroniclers claimed that she was the motivating force behind the divorce and remarriage. The meaning of Eleanor's choice of Raymond over Louis would only become clear to the chroniclers years later, when she chose Henry of Anjou over Louis. William of Newburgh writes, we may recall, "It is . . . said that . . . she longed to be wed to the Duke of Normandy as one more congenial to her character, and that she therefore preferred and procured a separation." Just as chroniclers retrospectively trace the reason for Louis's rejection of Eleanor to the incident at Antioch, they also retrospectively trace the reason for Eleanor's rejection of Louis to his behavior on this crusade. She had always wanted to rid herself of the pusillanimous Louis in order to attach herself to a more virile companion, whether that partner was to be Raymond or the man who became her second husband. Given that Eleanor was never truly made to suffer for her misdeeds—given that she may even have gotten what she wanted all along—her tale did not rest easily with many of these authors.

THE SULTAN OF BABYLON

In 1148 and 1149, when Eleanor and Louis were on crusade in the Holy Land, a boy of ten to eleven years of age was growing up in Damascus, which Louis so unsuccessfully besieged. Brought to Egypt by his uncle, the general Shirkuh, Saladin (Salah ad-Din) rose high in the Fatimid government, becoming vizier and then sultan by the time he was thirty-six. During the next two decades, he emerged as the principal opponent of the crusaders in the Latin Kingdom. In July of 1187, he brought about a major defeat of the crusader forces at the Battle of Hattin, which constituted a turning point in the Latin fortunes in the Holy Land. Over the course of the following weeks, he gained possession of a series of coastal fortresses, including Acre, Sidon, Beirut, and Ascalon. Within three months, he had conquered Jerusalem itself. Yet, if Saladin impressed his Christian opponents, it was not only through his triumphs over them in battle, but also through his magnanimous acts. When the crusaders took the Holy City in 1099, they massacred the entire Muslim population. Now that he had gained possession of this site, Saladin permitted the resident Franks to leave the city for a moderate ransom, granting them safe-conduct to other Christian territories, and he allowed the Eastern Christians to remain. During the Third Crusade (1189–92), which Richard the Lionheart and Philip Augustus launched to halt Saladin's incursions in the Latin Kingdom, the sultan once again amazed Christian observers with his chivalrousness and courtesy. When Richard's warhorse was killed underneath him during a battle, Saladin gallantly sent him a replacement. When crusaders' wives were separated from their husbands, he allowed them free passage through the lands he had conquered to rejoin them. In historical records, in the West even more than in the East, Saladin was commended for his many virtues, while in literary texts, he became the model of the "noble heathen." Eleanor never met Saladin, either during the Second Crusade, in which he played no part, or during the Third Crusade, in which she appeared only peripherally. Yet, given the reputations the queen and the sultan acquired over the course of the twelfth and thirteenth centuries, it is not surprising that their stories came to be intertwined.

From the mid-thirteenth century on, reports circulated that, when Eleanor was in the Holy Land for the Second Crusade, she consorted with a Muslim and even attempted to elope with him. Around 1253, Matthew Paris alludes to "Eleanor, who, in addition to another adulterous relationship, mingled with a Saracen."[43] While chroniclers would occasionally identify that Muslim as "a certain Turk,"[44] "the Sultan of Babylon"[45] (that is, the Sultan of Cairo), or "Sultan Renaudin,"[46] in 1260, the Minstrel of Reims was the first to speak of him as the great Saladin himself.[47] In the north of France and Flanders, where historical writing was flourishing during the Late Middle Ages, at least half a dozen chroniclers repeated the Minstrel's account, including the anonymous *Chronique de Flandres* (1300s); the *Anciennes chroniques de Flandres* (1300s); the *Chronique abrégée* (1300s); *Ly myreur des histors* (1350–1400) of Jean d'Outremeuse, a notary at the episcopal court of Liège; the *Chronique normande* (1400s) of Pierre Cochon, a notary at the archiepiscopal court of Reims; the anonymous *Histoire et chronique de Flandres* (1400–1450s); and an anonymous *Abrégé de l'histoire des Rois de France* (1400–1450). The Minstrel of Reims and these followers filled in the gaps of the historical narrative with imaginative reconstructions of what must have happened in the royal household during the Second Crusade. From the accounts of John of Salisbury and William of Tyre, they knew that there was a military leader who wanted to enter into combat and that he clashed with Louis, who was hesitant to engage in battle; that Eleanor was attracted to this valiant military leader and disgusted with her cowardly husband; that she wished to leave her husband in order to be with this other man; that she was prevented by her husband from doing so; and that she was later repudiated by this husband for her aborted infidelity. In these chroniclers' versions of the story, however, the military leader is now, not a Christian ally, but a Muslim opponent, so the marital conflict between the queen and her husband is mapped onto the martial conflict between the Franks and the infidel. Eleanor is regarded as justified in judging a political and religious enemy to be superior to her husband, but she is harshly condemned for making this judgment and especially for acting on it.

As Raymond was depicted as eager to wage war against neighboring Muslims, Saladin is depicted as eager to wage war against the Christian crusaders. The Minstrel of Reims represents Louis as staying with Eleanor, now not in Antioch (which had declined in importance by the time of his writing), but in Tyre, outside whose walls "Saladin . . . challenged him many times to battle." In the Christian camp, the crusaders are said to be impressed, not only with the sultan's boldness in battle, but with his "goodness, prowess, intelligence, and generosity" (II, 7, p. 4). Elsewhere in his chronicle, the Minstrel refers to "Saladin . . . , who was a man wise man and generous" (VI, 33, p. 17), "Saladin, [who] was wise and chivalrous" (XXXI, 209, p. 110), and "Saladin, the best prince there ever was in Paynimry" (XXI, 213, p. 112). In a rare self-reflective moment, he recalls how once, when there is a truce between the Christians and the Saracens in the Holy Land, John of Brienne, the early thirteenth-century King of Jerusalem and Constantinople, learns that his people are holding a noble Saracen prisoner, and he has this man brought before him. Discovering that he was uncle to Saladin, "who was so valiant," he asks through a dragoman about "the adventures of Saladin" (XXI, 196, p. 103). This king recognizes that Saladin is someone one tells stories about, and, like the Minstrel's audience, he is eager to hear them. The "adventures" that this chronicler recounts about Saladin end up occupying 14 percent of his work. According to Jean d'Outremeuse, "The noble knights of France" in the Christian camp greatly praised Saladin, "who was worth esteeming, for he was the most valiant, chivalrous, strong, and bold man that could be found, and the wisest and the most generous. They attributed . . . many fair virtues to him."[48] A military leader is supposed to be eager to enter into combat and strong enough to vanquish his foes, and, in the context of these stories, Saladin epitomizes those values more than any other man on either side of the war.

Given his greatness, the chroniclers do not blame Saladin for how he behaved with Eleanor. In the Minstrel of Reims's account, the sultan receives a letter from the queen, informing him of her desire to flee to him. It is said, "When Saladin understood this, he was very happy about it, for he knew well that she was the noblest lady of Christendom and the richest" (II, 7, pp. 4–5). He sends a galley to Tyre to transport Eleanor to Ascalon. Wealthy as she is, the queen has two coffers filled with gold and silver, which she prepares to have carried onto the ship. In contrast to Raymond, who acted to separate Eleanor from Louis, whether by force or by fraud, Saladin merely accommodates Eleanor's action as she attempts to leave her husband for him. For this reason, the Minstrel's account of Eleanor's attempted flight with Saladin can be read as an interpretation, not so much of her interaction with Raymond during the crusade, but of her interaction with Henry of Anjou four years later. There, too, Eleanor was said to have preferred another man to her husband[49] and to have sent him secret messengers, asking him to join with her,[50] and the man was said to have responded positively to this invitation, complying with her wish. Like Gervase of Canterbury, who depicts Henry as "attracted by this woman's noble rank, and above all desirous of possessing the lands that came with her,"[51] the Minstrel depicts Saladin as "very happy, for he knew well that she was the noblest lady of Christendom, and the richest." If Saladin differs from Raymond, it is because he passively receives the queen's love instead of actively seeking it and because he appreciates her own status, as a rich and noble woman, instead of aiming to use her to increase his own power.

Just as Louis was reluctant to wage war in the original chronicles, he is represented as reluctant to meet Saladin in battle. Neither the twelfth-century chroniclers nor the Minstrel of Reims indicate whose idea it was that Eleanor accompany Louis on crusade, but the chroniclers who follow the Minstrel suggest that it was the queen who made this decision. According to the *Chronique abrégée*, when Louis decided to go on crusade, "Queen Eleanor went with him, nor could the king deter her,"[52] as if Louis wished to stop her from coming along but did not have the strength of character to do so. By bringing Eleanor on crusade with him, Pierre Cochon indicates, Louis proved himself to be, not only a weak husband, who bows to his wife's wishes, but a stupid one, who does so even when it is to his disadvantage: "He took his wife with him, for which he was foolish."[53] Once Eleanor and Louis arrived in the Holy Land, these chroniclers agree, this king did little to deliver these territories from the Saracens. The Minstrel of Reims writes, "He remained there all the following winter. He stayed in Tyre, and he did nothing but waste his sustenance. . . . The king did not want to join in combat" (II, 6–7, p. 4). If Saladin challenges Louis many times to battle outside the walls of Tyre, we are told, it is because "Saladin perceived his softness and simplicity" (II, 7, p. 4). Whatever struggles the historical Louis had experienced in leading his army along the Anatolian coast, in crossing Mount Cadmus, or in reaching Antioch are forgotten, and whatever desire he might have had to complete his religious pilgrimage in Jerusalem before beginning his military campaign is pushed to the side. Only his resistance to Raymond's plan of attack is remembered, as this resistance is seen as reflecting his essentially pusillanimous character. Whether Louis is contrasted to the Christian Raymond or the Muslim Saladin, he is distinguished, not by energy and bravery, as his opponent is, but by lassitude and cowardice. Elsewhere in his chronicle, the Minstrel characterizes Louis as "the base king" (*mauvais roi*) (III, 25, p. 13). Even Louis himself is said to recognize the justice of this poor opinion later on. We are told, "He knew that he himself was simple and old, little esteemed in his realm, and little feared by his enemies" (III, 15, p. 8). While Saladin epitomizes the bravery, boldness, and fortitude in battle expected of a leader, Louis represents the antithesis of these qualities.

In contrast to Saladin, Louis comes in for partial blame for how he behaved with Eleanor. In the Minstrel of Reims's version of the story, Louis

does not know that his wife is attempting to leave him, and he only becomes aware of this fact thanks to the intervention of one of her damsels.
On the night when Eleanor is preparing to flee, this maiden slips out of
her chamber as quietly as she can and goes to the king, rousing him from
his slumber. "Sire!" she warns him. "It goes badly. My lady wants to go to
Ascalon, to Saladin, and the galley is even now waiting in the harbor. In
God's name, sire, make haste!" Hearing her words, the king leaps up, gets
dressed, and rushes to the port. There, it is said, "He found the queen, who
was already with one foot on the galley" (II, 8, p. 5). According to some of
the Minstrel's followers, Louis is away besieging Ascalon at this time, but
once alerted to Eleanor's planned departure, he gallops all night back to
Tripoli, where she is staying, and, again, stops her just as she is boarding the
ship.[54] On approaching her, the Minstrel of Reims relates, "He took her by
the hand and brought her back to his chamber" (II, 9, p. 5) and there, we
are told, "asked the queen why she wished to do this" (II, 10, p. 6). In response to his wife's attempted elopement, Louis does not beat or even berate her. Instead, he gently takes her hand and asks why she wants to leave
him. What upsets him, it appears, is, not *that* she has tried to forsake him,
but *why* she did so. He is concerned, not that she has tried to shame him,
but that she has ceased to love him. When Eleanor responds to his question defiantly, insulting his character and threatening him with continued
misbehavior, he again does not beat or berate her. It is said simply that "The
king left her and had her well guarded" (II, 10, p. 6). If the Louis here differs from the earlier Louis, it is because he is weak, not only in his reluctance to meet the Muslim host in combat, but in his reluctance to stand
up to his wife.

Seeing that Saladin is brave and Louis cowardly, Eleanor decides to flee
to the sultan and abandon the king. After noting how Louis refuses to meet
Saladin in battle, the Minstrel of Reims continues, "When Queen Eleanor saw how the king had failed her, and when she had heard spoken of
Saladin's goodness, prowess, intelligence, and generosity, she loved him in-
tently in her heart" (II, 7, p. 4). Jean d'Outremeuse writes similarly, "The
noble knights of France blamed [the king] strongly and said so much that
Queen Eleanor . . . heard how they blamed the king and esteemed Saladin,
who was worth esteeming. . . . They attributed to him so many fair virtues
that the queen fell very much in love with him."[55] In a culture where it was
common for men and women to be said to fall in love with someone because of the good they hear told of that person,[56] Eleanor falls in love with
Saladin for that reason. When Louis asks Eleanor why she wants to leave
him, she replies, "In God's name, . . . because of your baseness [*mauvestié*],

for you are not worth a rotten apple. And I have heard such good said of Saladin that I love him more than you. Know well and truly that you will never have joy in keeping me from now on" (II, 10, p. 6). Just as Eleanor's love for Saladin is grounded, not in a subjective affection for his personality, but in an objective evaluation of his character based on a standard set of criteria, her disgust with her husband is grounded in her appraisal of his quality as a king and a husband. She falls out of love with Louis, we are informed, "when [she] saw how [her] king had failed her." By refusing to fight Saladin, Louis not only lowered himself in her eyes and the eyes of others, but he lowered *her* in the eyes of others as well. A woman cannot prove her worth by venturing out and vanquishing her opponents in battle, but she can do so by affiliating herself with a man who performs such feats, and Louis is not that man. Given that Eleanor is the finest lady in Christendom, she cannot bear to be with someone who is not the finest knight.

Eleanor is right that Saladin is brave and Louis cowardly, but, these chronicles make clear, she is wrong to think so poorly of her lord and husband, let alone to act on that low regard. When the Minstrel of Reims begins his account of the incident, he introduces the queen by telling how Louis's barons had arranged for him to marry "Duchess Eleanor, who was a very . . . evil woman [*mout . . . mal famme*]" (II, 6, pp. 3–4). It was she who instigated her flight from her husband, sending a dragoman to inform Saladin that, "If he could arrange to take her away, she would take him as her husband and would relinquish her religion" (II, 7, pp. 4–5). When the servant returns secretly one night, she asks him, "What news?" "My lady," he replies, "see here the galley which awaits you all ready. Now make haste so that we are not perceived." "By faith," she answers, "it is well done" (II, 8, p. 5). While in the earlier accounts of the incident at Antioch, Eleanor had been largely a passive victim of Raymond's machinations even as she was held responsible for her role in them, in these rewritings she is the active instigator of the infidelity. As the Minstrel depicts her, Eleanor is right that Saladin exemplifies prowess, boldness, and generosity. She is right that Louis, in contrast, is not worth a rotten apple. Like the queen, who condemned the king's "baseness" (*mauvestié*), the Minstrel himself characterizes Louis as "the base king" (*mauvais roi*). Yet in attempting to flee her husband, Eleanor has herself become base. A later chronicler refers to the fact that "She, like a base woman [*comme mauvaise*], intended to go to the Sultan Saladin and leave the said Louis when they were in Syria overseas."[57] As we recall, chroniclers referred to "the injuries [Louis's] wife had imposed upon him during the journey," "[the] many ways [the queen] gravely offended the king," and the many ways in which she was "disagreeable and insulting on this journey" and "disloyal on the pilgrimage." However contemptible Louis may have been, Eleanor was wrong to have treated him as contemptible, let alone to have attempted to leave him for someone better.

As a general rule, in the twelfth century, a woman was expected to love and esteem her husband, and she was seen to err if she failed to fulfill that expectation. In the *Pèlerinage de Charlemagne* (mid-1100s), Charlemagne asks his unnamed queen if she has ever seen a man wear a sword or a crown better than he does, and she replies that Hugh the Strong, the (fictional) Emperor of Greece and Constantinople, is superior to him in this regard.[58] In Chrétien de Troyes's *Erec et Enide* (c. 1170), Erec asks his lovely bride Enide why she is weeping, and she answers that his fellow knights are criticizing him for having given up feats of arms ever since he married her. Both of these women speak truthfully. Charlemagne *is* inferior to Hugh the Strong; Erec *has* become recreant. Situated as she is outside the system of masculine values, a woman is able to detect when a man falls short of those criteria. At the same time, both Charlemagne's wife and Enide speak "foolishly" insofar as they offend and insult their husbands.[59] Charlemagne tells his wife, "By my faith, . . . you have entirely lost my love and my good will. . . . My lady, you ought not to have doubted my power."[60] Erec complains to Enide, "I knew all the time that you did not hold me in esteem."[61] These women have not demonstrated "providence" or "foresight" (*providentia*), that is, the ability to anticipate the consequences of their actions, to decide on the appropriate actions as a result, and to say "the right things at the right time."[62] Though they speak the truth, they are tactless in doing so. By the end of *Pèlerinage de Charlemagne*, the queen falls at Charlemagne's feet in repentance for her misbehavior, and he forgives her. Enide laments, "God! why was I so forward as to dare to utter such folly?"[63] and "Alas, . . . how I rue my pride and presumption!"[64] Even if a woman sees the truth about a man, she should not utter that truth, let alone act on it by setting herself above him and scorning him.

Like these other women, Eleanor is said to speak truthfully but wrongfully. In the accounts of the Minstrel of Reims and his followers, the queen is depicted as perspicacious enough to recognize excellence in men and magnanimous enough to want to reward that excellence. These chroniclers invite the audience to see Saladin as the queen sees him, to share in her evaluation of him, and to acknowledge his superiority to other men. At the same time, like these other women, Eleanor is said to speak foolishly and pridefully. In one late medieval manuscript, when Louis refuses Raymond's request for military assistance, it is said that "Queen Eleanor, who was a very wicked, proud, and haughty woman [*femme moult di-*

verse, fiere et haultaine], had great disdain that the king did not grant the prince's request" and that "She responded proudly and with great arrogance [*fierement respondy et par grant orgueil*] that truly she wanted to leave him on account of his great cravenness and cowardice."[65] Though the chroniclers share Eleanor's judgment of Louis, they feel that she should not have expressed that judgment. When Eleanor perceives Louis to be unworthy and when she acts on that perception by trying to leave him for someone worthier, she shames her husband in a way that no good wife should ever do. To consider more fully a passage we have already addressed in part, an anonymous chronicler writes that "During this journey, the aforesaid queen gravely offended the king in many ways, most gravely in that, plotting to relinquish the king, she wanted to attach herself to a certain Turk."[66] Whereas in the original sources, it had been Raymond who secretly plotted against Louis in order to deprive him of his wife, now it is Eleanor who secretly plots against him, with the aim of going over to the enemy side. Given that Louis is king and leader of the crusade, Eleanor shames, not only her mate, but the French and the crusading armies, in a humiliation that reverberated over the course of the late twelfth and the thirteenth centuries, as the disaster of the Second Crusade was followed by the gradual loss of the Latin Kingdom of the East.

A KNIGHT OF POITOU

Like Saladin, the Poitevin knight Andrew of Chauvigny was a historical figure whose story became embroiled with Eleanor's. Chauvigny was a first cousin to Eleanor, the son of her maternal aunt Haois of Châtellerault and Pierre-Hélie, the hereditary provost of Chauvigny, and, in time, a member of Richard's household. As a reward for his service, when Richard ascended to the throne in 1189, he gave Chauvigny Denise of Déols, the widowed Countess of Devon, the heiress to Châteauroux, and a member of Eleanor's entourage, as his wife and, in doing so, made him one of the principal landholders in Berry. When Richard then embarked on the Third Crusade, Chauvigny accompanied him, fighting by his side at the Siege of Acre and the Battle of Arsuf, and he remained faithful to his lord during the long wars he undertook with Philip in later years. In August of 1199, after Richard's death, when Eleanor was attempting to shore up support for John's reign, she granted him a fiefdom in a charter where she refers to him as "our dearest friend and relative, Andrew of Chauvigny."[67] Appearing in numerous twelfth-century historical records, Chauvigny also appears in several fifteenth-century parahistorical works, where he is described as "the most valiant of the valiant, as much among the lords of Christendom as among those of Saracenerie" (Prologue, p. 220).[68] While these works do not feature Eleanor per se, they continue to represent a French queen who engages in a love affair with Saladin during a crusade. In these rewritings of the Minstrel of Reims's tale, Chauvigny finally corrects the behavior that earlier observers had found so objectionable in the queen.

By the Late Middle Ages, it was recognized that if a French queen had attempted to elope with Saladin, it must have been, not Eleanor, the wife of Louis, who was involved in the Second Crusade, but the wife of Louis's son Philip, one of the leaders of the Third Crusade. From the thirteenth century on, tales had been circulating that Saladin was the scion of the counts of Ponthieu, in the north of France.[69] Between 1465 and 1468, an anonymous author composed a continuation of the Second Crusade Cycle, known as *Saladin*, which tells the story of this noble family "and of the valiant and courageous Turk, Sultan Saladin, who descended from them and their lineage" (Explicit, p. 170). At a certain point in this account, Saladin travels in disguise to Western Europe, where he competes in a tournament at Cambrai, sparks the passion of the French queen, and accepts her sexual advances.[70] After he returns to his lands, the queen accompanies her husband Philip on crusade, with the hope of reuniting with her lover. Sometime prior to 1482, Jehan de La Gogue, a master in theology and prior of the Benedictine Abbey of Saint-Gildas of Déols, included a version of this story in his history of the princes of Déols, which he composed for Chauvigny's descendant Guy III of Châteauroux.[71] The unnamed queen is identified in the anonymous *Saladin* as "the daughter or the sister of the King of Aragon" (XIV, p. 93) and, in the version by Jehan de La Gogue, as this Spanish king's sister.[72] (Because Philip was a widower when he was in the Holy Land and because he never married a woman of Aragonese lineage, this queen has no historical foundation.) Though Chauvigny benefited from an advantageous marriage that Eleanor presumably helped arrange and a fiefdom that she granted him, in these fifteenth-century rewritings of his story, he is represented as asserting mastery over her fictional descendant. In this rewriting of history, the Poitevin knight emerges as a new, forceful model of Christian masculinity, in contrast to the weak and uxorious King of France, and the queen he prevents from eloping is harshly punished for her misbehavior on crusade.

Once again, in these late medieval accounts, Saladin is a great warrior, outstanding in his chivalry. According to the author of *Saladin*, while the King of France is staying with the queen in Acre, Saladin arrives before the city, "demanding if there is a valiant Christian or up to four of them who would dare fight with him" (XXVII, p. 147). None of the Christian knights are willing to enter into combat with him. Finally, a certain William Longsword comes forward but is quickly dispatched by the sultan. Four more knights sally forth against him, but they are overcome as expeditiously as their predecessor. Just as Saladin distinguishes himself through his valor at arms, he distinguishes himself through his courtesy. When he breaks William Longsword's lance and throws him off his horse, it is noted that, "By his graciousness, he helped William to remount and sent him back to the city" (XXVII, p. 148). This courtesy is evident in his behavior, not only with men, but with women. When he first becomes the object of the queen's attention at Cambrai, where he is disguised as a simple knight, he protests that he has not merited her love, as he is of such humble rank and, as he puts it, she is "a highly placed and esteemed queen." He initially attempts to deflect her passion out of reluctance to consort with a married woman, but he speaks "very courteously" to her in doing so, assuring her that he will protect her honor so that she will never be blamed on his account (XV, p. 96). Throughout their love affair, Saladin employs the language of courtly love in speaking to the queen and of his beloved to other men. He chides Chauvigny for taking offense at the attention he is paying her, "for you have learned little if you do not know that princes have the custom of welcoming ladies above everything, for from them comes all honor and joy" (XVIII, p. 152).

Once again, the French king is not of the same stature as Saladin. While the king in these accounts is Philip, not Louis, and hence not as much of a coward in battle as his father, he too is represented as unable to stand up to his wife. According to the author of *Saladin*, not only is it the queen who decides that she will accompany her husband on the crusade, but it is she who decides that they will take up the cross in the first place: "She did so much toward her husband King Philip of France that he undertook the voyage to Jerusalem" (XXVI, p. 146). Once they are in the Holy Land, the queen declares before the king and his men that she has heard a voice commanding her to go to Saladin and convert him to their faith and assuring her that she alone would be able to accomplish this feat. The king's men are reluctant to escort her to the enemy's city so that she can fulfill her alleged mission because they are of the view that, as Jehan de La Gogue puts it, "The words of women are little to be esteemed" (XXVIII, p. 252). But the king grants the queen's wish, "fearing to anger God and thinking that the lies of his wife were true" (XXVIII, p. 151). Just as he agreed to go on crusade because she urged him to do so, he agrees to let her travel to Jerusalem because she persuades him of this plan. If the king is as mistaken about his wife as he is, it is because his judgment about her is swayed by his excessive love. He is described as "her husband, who loved her for her great beauty, like someone who has lost his mind" and "who never took guard against her wickedness" (XVIII, p. 150). Given the high mission he believes her to have been assigned by God, he announces to his men that "He had the best wife that could be found in the world" (XVIII, p. 252). Like Louis, who was allegedly besotted with the beautiful Eleanor, this French king is besotted with his beautiful wife.

Once again, the queen flies to the worthy Saladin, abandoning her less-worthy husband, but she now employs "fraud" in plotting her escape. In her address to the king and his men, she says, "I tell you that . . . when sleeping I have twice heard a loud voice preciously calling out, which admonished me to go to Jerusalem to visit the Sepulcher and the holy places as I had vowed and which charged me to go to Saladin to preach the points of our religion—that is, the birth, life, Passion, miracles, Resurrection, and Ascension of our sweet Savior Jesus Christ—saying that I alone, if I accomplish this, will convert the Turk and his company" (XXVIII, p. 150). It is not that the queen wishes to go to Saladin, she claims; it was that the voice has twice ordered her to do. And it is not primarily the man she wants to see, but the Church of the Holy Sepulcher and the other sacred sites. Her aim is not amorous, she insists, but pious: to proselytize the tenets of their faith. With these words, the queen is not only deceiving her husband in order to rejoin her lover; she is deploying the language of piety in order to indulge her lechery and, in doing so, conspiring to make a wicked action seem good. She is thus committing "fraud" (XXIX, p. 255). We are told that "The queen fraudulently gave the king to understand that, if she could speak to the said Saladin, she would have him converted" (XXVIII, pp. 251–52). According to Saint Paul's First Letter to the Corinthians, just as Jesus Christ is the head of the Church, a Christian husband should be the head of his wife. Instead of presuming to speak out about the faith, she should direct any questions she has to him. In this account, the queen's abandonment of her faith takes the form, not of an abandonment of Christian beliefs and rituals, but of an abandonment of her Christian husband, whom she clearly no longer regards as her head.

However chivalrous Saladin may be, these chroniclers make clear, the queen acts wrongly, not only in choosing another man over her husband, but in choosing a Muslim over a Christian. In the Minstrel of Reims's chronicle, we already saw Eleanor send word to Saladin that, in relinquishing her husband, "She . . . would relinquish her religion."[73] Now the ramifications of her attempted elopement with the sultan have become all the more stark. In *Saladin*, the queen has already taken Saladin to her bed by the time she discovers that he is a "pagan." She is taken aback by this information, but after some reflection, we are told, "Considering that she had abandoned herself to him, remembering his beauty, alerted to his great nobility and high chivalry, she left her heart where it was" (XVI, p. 109). While she is disconcerted to learn that the man she loves is not a Christian, she ultimately decides that she has gone too far to withdraw her attachment from him now and that, given his great virtues, that attachment was not misplaced. At Acre, when she watches Saladin triumph over her husband's men, she finds her judgment confirmed. Seeing him cast William Longsword to the ground, it is said, "The queen . . . was very joyful" (XXVII, p. 148). Watching him defeat four more knights, she continues to cheer on her lover in her mind. Winter approaches, and Saladin, realizing that he will not be able to take the city, breaks camp and returns to Jerusalem. While the rest of the Franks are pleased with the end of the siege, the queen is distressed because she will no longer be able to see her beloved. She perceives Saladin, not as a political or religious opponent, as her husband and his men do, but as an amorous partner. When she ultimately leaves to be with him, the author suggests that she is leaving the Christian faith, given "the evil will she had to want to live among the Turks" (XXIX, p. 156). In Jehan de La Gogue's account, it said that "The queen wished to betray the noble king her spouse and to destroy all of Christianity" (XXIX, p. 257). For a queen to leave a Christian king for his Muslim counterpart is for her to be unfaithful to both her husband and her religion.

In general, in the Middle Ages, it was not accepted that a Christian woman should marry a Muslim man. Women of royal status were often wedded to foreign potentates and were therefore obliged to move to their new husband's court, to adopt its language, and to assimilate to its culture. A man like Fulk V, Count of Anjou, or Raymond of Antioch may travel to a foreign land to marry an heiress and rule *iure uxoris*, but a woman who made such a journey and married such an heir would be expected to subordinate herself to her new spouse. Eleanor's daughters with Henry—Matilda of Saxony, Eleanor of Castile, and Joan of Sicily—were praised for adapting so well to populations that were "in lifestyle, clothing, manners, and habitation so far from England."[74] We are told that "The three daughters of the king and Eleanor endure with equanimity alienation from their native soil."[75] Yet there was a point beyond which such cultural assimilation was no longer considered desirable. In October of 1191, during the Third Crusade, the widowed Joan accompanied Richard to the Holy Land with the assurance that she would be provided with an appropriate new husband. While they were staying in Jaffa, Richard, controversially, became friends with Saladin's brother, Al-Malik al-Adil Saif ad-Din (known in the West as Saphadin), and entertained the possibility of making a match between his sister and this young Saracen.[76] According to the twelfth-century Kurdish jurist and scholar Bahā' al-Dīn Ibn Shaddād, who knew Saladin well and who was Saphadin's representative in these negotiations, the couple was to possess the entire coastal plain, and their capital was to be Jerusalem.[77] This author represents Joan as swearing that she would never consent to this marriage and exclaiming, "How could she possibly allow a Muslim to have carnal knowledge of her!"[78] Yet another Muslim chronicler relates that Joan had at first been intrigued by this possible match and had only changed her mind about it when she was reproached by her fellow Christians: "The young woman feared after having desired; she withdrew herself after having sought out; . . . she abhorred what she had coveted. After having covered her eyes with kohl, she preferred to leave them without sparkle."[79] Even if a Christian woman initially felt herself attracted to a Muslim man, she would be taught to hold such an alliance in horror. While royal women were expected to cross national lines and even confessional lines within Christianity through their marriages, for a woman to leave a Christian spouse for a Muslim one, let alone a Christian king for a Muslim sultan, would have been a scandal for the faith.

In the late medieval accounts of Saladin, the chroniclers commend Chauvigny's forcible and even brutal return of the French queen to her lord. In Jehan de La Gogue's version of the story, when the crusaders are gathered before embarking on the campaign, Chauvigny is limping due to a recent wound, and he sees the queen mocking him for this defect. He strikes her so harshly across the mouth that blood flows over her clothing. Later, in Jerusalem, when Saladin tells Chauvigny to leave him alone with the queen, the knight replies, "Sire, . . . I will be present when the queen is speaking to you . . . for I am in charge of her. If there is good there, I will have great joy from it, but if there is evil, I will be upset about it, for I will set it right" (XXVIII, p. 254). Though she is a queen and he a mere knight, he regards himself, not as serving her by escorting her to this city, but as supervising her; his responsibility is, not to the queen, to do as she wishes, but to the king, to ensure that his consort does not misbehave. Later, when the queen makes clear to Chauvigny that she will not return with him to her husband in Acre, but, on the contrary, will remain with Saladin in Jerusalem, he responds to her in what is represented as an appropriately virile manner. He pretends to accept her decision, but as he is leaving on horseback, he suddenly asks to speak with her about a secret matter. Bending down, he acts as if he wants to whisper into her ear, but instead he seizes her, hoists her onto his mount in front of him, and gallops away with her. While she cries out and struggles to be free of him, he draws out his sword and causes her such fear that "She let herself be man-handled and carried like a sheep a butcher carries in front of him" (XXIX, p. 155). In contrast to Saladin, who was courteous and loving toward the queen, and the king, who was submissive and loving toward her, both admiring her beauty and force of character, Chauvigny is brutal, beating her and asserting his dominance over her, with no respect for her superior status as ruler.

Throughout these works, the chroniclers contrast the queen's disloyalty toward her husband with Chauvigny's loyalty toward his lord. Assigned the task of escorting the queen to Saladin, Chauvigny discovers her plan to remain with her lover, and he determines to bring her back to her rightful husband. In *Saladin*, he kneels before the king and swears to him, "Noble king, . . . I will conduct her to Jerusalem to speak with the sultan, as she said to you she would do, and I will bring her back by the faith that I owe God and you" (XXVIII, p. 253). Whatever Chauvigny may think of the king as an individual, he respects him as his lord, and he takes great pride in the loyalty he shows to him. He affirms, "Every good knight must accomplish that which is agreeable to his lord" (XXIX, p. 256). While the queen seeks to shift her allegiance to the best of men, even if he is not her husband, "Chauvigny, the loyal knight" (XXVIII, p. 254), recognizes that it is necessary to remain loyal to one's lord, whatever his merits. He feels that the queen should display a similar loyalty to her "husband" and "lord" (both signified in the Old French by the word *seigneur*). In a conversation with the king once he returns to court, Chauvigny reports that, when the queen had arrived before Saladin, "She granted herself entirely to his will, nor did she speak more of you or of anything else except her pleasure. . . . I saw well that she was inflamed with love of the sultan" (XXIX, pp. 256–57). In recounting how the queen behaved at Saladin's court, he urges the king, "Lord, listen to the trickery of the queen and the disloyalty she had conceived" (XXIX, p. 256). Chauvigny will also use trickery, namely, by enticing the queen to approach his horse, so he can seize and abduct her; he will also show disloyalty, namely, to Saladin, whose safe-conduct he betrays by stealing this woman; he will also later allege a vision from God, namely, one that inspires him to attack Jerusalem, though he is only taken captive during the battle; and he will also later engage in adultery with a Saracen, namely, Gloriande, the wife of the Sultan of Damascus (who is keeping him prisoner), and even have a child with her. Yet Chauvigny differs from the queen because he does not ally himself with his Muslim paramour against his lord. On the contrary, when the French forces arrive outside Damascus, he persuades his mistress to set him free so he can fight with them against the Saracens. While the queen breaks faith with her husband because she recognizes his inferiority to Saladin, Chauvigny understands that what matters is, not the merits of one's lord, but one's own merit, as a loyal servant of that lord.

In contrast to Eleanor, who, though repudiated by Louis, never really suffered punishment for her alleged misbehavior, the French queen in these tales is put to death for her crimes. Brought back from Saladin's residence in Jerusalem to Acre, she is exposed, weeping, to the king and his men. As Chauvigny recounts to all what happened, we are told, "She was screaming, but she was led into a chamber in order that she not trouble the company" (XXIX, p. 256). Her words, which had once been listened to so attentively by the king and his men, are now so disregarded that we are not even told of what they consist. Her presence, which was once so dominant in the court, is now so dismissed that she is placed in another room. In contrast to Eleanor, this queen possesses a living kinsman who is King of Aragon, and it is to his jurisdiction that she is ultimately returned. When this king gets the queen back, Jehan de La Gogue informs us, "It was recounted to him how the queen had wished to betray the noble king her spouse and to destroy all Christianity. The King of Aragon had her burned and delivered to justice, to the honor of the noble King of the French. He acted wisely, for war could have been engendered between him and the Aragonese, by which Christianity would have been greatly diminished" (XXIX, p. 257). Irrespective of what is happening on the battlefield between the Christians and the Saracens, if the queen had succeeded in leaving the Christian king for the sultan, if her French husband had not repudiated her for this infraction, or if her Aragonese kinsman had not punished her when she was sent back to him, Christendom would have been weakened. The source of the danger to the land of this faith is not the Muslim sultan (who is represented as generally admirable) but a Christian queen who shows disdain for her husband. By representing the French queen as suffering from the end of their marriage, to the point where she was subjected to among the cruelest of deaths, these authors are following, not the chronicles about Eleanor or any other contemporaneous queen, but their own sense of rectitude. This story was meant to teach a moral lesson, and in order for it to do so, it was not possible for this wicked queen, once rejected by her indignant husband, to marry another king and to live a long and prosperous life, blessed with many children. Instead, it was necessary to replace Eleanor's happy ending with the appropriate punishment for an adulterous wife and unfaithful ruler.

In the end, it did not matter that the Franks failed in the Second Crusade or that they eventually lost the entire Latin Kingdom of the East. The stories of the crusades would be retold for centuries, and the Christian knights who fought in these battles would be remembered as paladins of the faith. What was remembered as humiliating about the crusades was not Saladin, who exemplified the culture's chivalric and courtly ideals and who was even alleged to have converted to Christianity on his deathbed. It was not the crusader forces, who, despite an occasional weak king, were seen as having fought heroically, with warriors like Chauvigny in their ranks. It was the French queen, who despised her weak husband and who distanced herself from him over the course of the campaign. So troubling was her behavior that the story had to be rewritten and the queen had to be suitably punished for her misdeeds. Yet however harshly Eleanor was criticized for evaluating the men around her and rewarding those she found deserving with her love when she was on a crusade in her youth, she would be celebrated for these same actions on her own lands in her later years.

THE COURTLY LADY

Love and Patronage

In addition to her marriages to the kings of France and England, Eleanor is remembered for the court over which she presided in Poitiers. In the last months of 1151, she and Louis made a circuit around Aquitaine, and they held a Christmas court at Limoges in the Limousin. While Louis returned to the Ile-de-France after the holidays were over, Eleanor seems to have remained in her native county of Poitou, already acting as the independent woman she was about to become with her divorce. After she married Henry in May of 1152, she shifted her base of operations to Normandy, and, in October of 1154, she moved to England in preparation for her coronation as queen of that nation. While she remained on Henry's lands for many years thereafter, bearing their many children and overseeing their education, in 1167 she returned home to Poitiers. During these two periods of her life, when Eleanor was living apart from any husband—for a few months when she was twenty-seven years old and then for six years when she was between forty-six and fifty-two—she functioned as Countess of Poitou and Duchess of Aquitaine, with her own vassals and her own court. She was clearly powerful in the medieval sense of the word, that is, a ruler whose wealth and status made her a force to be reckoned with. As such, she found herself surrounded by men who sought to serve her, whether knights who fought under her pay and protection, clerics who celebrated religious services for her and her entourage, or poets who composed verse in the hope of her patronage. Once again, there are rumors of love affairs. As much as one might want Eleanor's private life to be documented as positively as her public life, in chronicles, charters, and court records, we hear about it only in lyric poems, "lives" (*vidas*) of poets, a treatise on love, and a verse history, whose testimony is questionable at best. In the historical texts we have considered so far, clerical authors spoke critically of Eleanor's alleged liaisons, condemning her for succumbing to lust and neglecting her marriage vows. Yet in these parahistorical genres, courtly authors commend such dalliances, praising her for recognizing and rewarding men of merit.

The evidence of Eleanor's literary patronage in Poitiers is ambiguous. As we recall, she was the granddaughter of William IX, the first troubadour, and the daughter of William X, a noted patron of Cercamon, Marcabru, and other troubadours, many of whom hailed from his lands. As we shall soon see, one of the most famous of the troubadours was said to have enjoyed Eleanor as his patron. In addition to these Occitan lyric poets, several French narrative poets invoke the queen in their works, including Wace, in his *Roman de Rou* (1160/90),[1] Benoît de Sainte-Maure, in his *Roman de Troie* (1165–70),[2] and a rededicator of Philippe de Thaon's *Bestiare* (1121–35),[3] in the apparent hope that she might reward them for their efforts or intercede with Henry on their behalf. Yet when William X died in April of 1137, Cercamon expressed distress at the loss of his lord,[4] and he declared his intention to seek patronage from King Alfonso VII of Castile,[5] not from the new duchess. Marcabru likewise gave voice to his unhappiness at the subjection of Poitou to France, which came about with Eleanor's marriage to Louis.[6] On the only occasions in which these poets seem to refer to the queen, they criticize a "false woman"[7] who "committed that fault which is spoken of all the way to Poitou,"[8] in an apparent allusion to her adultery in Antioch. While Eleanor's power was based in Poitou, in the north of her duchy, many of the poets from her lands received patronage beyond its southern borders, such as in Toulouse, Narbonne, or Aragon. For whatever reason, there are far more references in the troubadour corpus to other historical noblewomen, such as Ermengarda, Viscountess of Narbonne, and Maria, Viscountess of Ventadorn, than there are to her. This scattering of authors who speak of Eleanor as someone who enjoys and supports the production of literary works offers some sign of her interest in vernacular poetry, but not much.

Given this mixed evidence, some scholars have magnified the importance of Eleanor's role as a patroness of literature, while others have downplayed it. Gaston Paris, the great nineteenth-century scholar of French medieval studies, writes of this queen, "She summoned to her several troubadours, and one can believe that it was she who made their complicated art imitated and known among the poets who wished to please her."[9] Alfred Jeanroy, the dominant specialist in troubadour poetry in the first part of the twentieth century, describes Eleanor as the "hyphen" who brought together Occitan and French literary traditions.[10] He states, "Though we know only one of her protégés, we can affirm that poets and jongleurs proliferated around her."[11] Rita Lejeune, the prominent Belgian scholar of medieval French literature, sees Eleanor as the center of virtually all the literary innovations of the twelfth century, including troubadour "love songs" (*cansos*), *romans antiques*, *chansons de geste*, and Arthurian romances: "At the juncture of these different literary currents, which converge about 1150 around the idea of the woman, the figure of one very real woman shines forth: that of Eleanor of Aquitaine."[12] For these critics, if troubadours are known to have come from Eleanor's lands, then she can be assumed to have supported them. If she is known to have supported one such poet, then she can be assumed to have supported many of them. If she supported many such poets, she can be assumed to have shaped their literary creations through her tastes. In more recent years, however, scholars have emphasized that, when one considers the eighteen works associated with Eleanor's patronage,[13] there is no proof from either an author's prologue or household accounts that she sponsored any of them and, hence, no proof that she sponsored literature at all.[14] For these critics, if we cannot convincingly demonstrate that Eleanor supported the troubadours from her lands, then, for all intents and purposes, she did not support them. If she is said to have supported only one troubadour—even one of the most important among them—that is equivalent to her having supported none. And if she supported no such poets, she could have had no influence on the works they ended up composing. If one cannot establish something positively and absolutely, one cannot establish it at all. Lauded as "the queen of the troubadours,"[15] Eleanor has also been dismissed as someone with no known interest in literature,

Like the evidence of Eleanor's literary patronage, the evidence of her involvement in the type of love relationships extolled in the poetry of her day is ambiguous. As we shall see, a troubadour *vida* claims that she engaged in a least one such love affair. When Chrétien de Troyes composed his *Chevalier de la charrette* (c. 1177), the first account of the *amours* of Queen Guinevere and Lancelot of the Lake, he did so at the behest of Marie de Champagne, Eleanor's daughter,[16] and, hence, it is often thought, with Marie's mother in mind.[17] When Béroul and Thomas of Britain sang of the love of Queen Yseut and Tristan, they were working in lands under Eleanor and Henry's control, and therefore, it is alleged, with the queen as their inspiration. The number of women of high rank who were implicated in extramarital affairs in the twelfth century, including Eleanor's grandmother Dangerosa, Bertrade of Montfort, Matilda of Tuscany, Ermengarda of Narbonne, Melisende of Jerusalem, and Eudoxia Comnena, the wife of William VIII, seigneur of Montpellier, makes clear that such dalliances were by no means unthinkable, nor were they always punished. At times, when the allegedly adulterous lady abandoned her husband and attached herself to another man, as Dangerosa and Bertrade did, there is little doubt of her guilt. At other times, when the woman did not take such drastic action, it is unclear what she was up to.[18] In 1175, Elizabeth of Vermandois, the daughter of Eleanor's sister Petronilla and the wife of Philip I, Count of Flanders, was said to have had a love affair with a certain Walter des Fontaines, "a knight," Roger of Howden notes, "arisen from noble stock and distinguished in military arms before all of his kinsmen."[19] When the liaison came to light, Walter ended up, in decidedly uncourtly fashion, being beaten with clubs and dangled head down in a privy until he died,[20] but Elizabeth seems to have escaped unscathed. However strict the ecclesiastical and secular laws may have been, at a time when women could inherit great property and retain that property during and after marriage, a lady who was rich and powerful in her own right might exercise considerable freedom in her private life.

Those scholars who have perceived Eleanor as a great patroness of literature have seen her as transforming the amorous mores of her time through the works she encouraged, while skeptics have denied that she had any such effect. In the same essay in which Gaston Paris spoke highly of Eleanor's support of the troubadours, he coins the term "courtly love" (*amour courtois*), which he defined as the passion a man feels for a married lady of higher social status, in whose presence he feels fearful and anxious and for whose admiration he performs great knightly deeds. While Paris refrains from alleging that Eleanor herself engaged in courtly love relationships, he affirms that she was "one of the principal instigators of a societal movement . . . which had for its principal characteristic . . . the conception of a refined and learned love, intimately tied to courtesy and prowess, and giving to the lady, as mistress, an importance that she had not had before."[21] Paris's theory of courtly love, including its connection to Eleanor, was further elaborated through the 1970s by many of the most important critics of medieval Occitan and French literature, such as Alfred Jeanroy,[22] Reto Bezzola,[23] Denis de Rougemont,[24] and Moshé Lazar.[25] Rita Lejeune summarizes these scholars' views when she writes, not only that "it is quite evident" that Eleanor "reigned . . . over an entire group of poets . . . originating in her states," but that "it is even highly probable that several of these troubadours celebrated Eleanor under pseudonyms or with allusions that we have not been able to decipher."[26] At the same time, other scholars have expressed caution about how much the social norms of a time can be discerned from its literary works. The "Robertsonian" thesis, which contended that courtly love was never praised unironically in literary works let alone practiced in real life, has long been refuted, but historians remain reluctant to view courtly literature as a reflection of lived experience.[27] John F. Benton, for example, warns scholars against relying on lyric poems and romances, "works which may often be difficult to understand, or at least are subject to controversial interpretations,"[28] for their conception of medieval society, instead of "secure historical sources,"[29] such as chronicles, penitentials, and court cases. Yet it is doubtful that affairs of the heart can be documented in the same way as affairs of state and, if Eleanor were as amorous as her contemporaries claimed, that she would have acted so indiscreetly that her infidelities could be established by standard historical sources.

If there is any merit to the old interpretation of Eleanor as a great patroness of poetry and courtly love — and I am arguing here that there is — it is because the ambiguous evidence to this effect remains nonetheless evidence. In the past, maximalist scholars assumed that the legendary tales about Eleanor were true. If she was alleged to have done something, it was possible she had done it; if it was possible, it was probable; and if it was probable, it was certain. Everything that may have happened must have happened and therefore did happen. More recently, minimalist scholars have assumed that the legendary tales about Eleanor were false. If we do not have firm proof that she did something, it is not certain that she did it; and if it is not certain, then for all intents and purposes, it did not occur. Everything that cannot be established to have happened did not transpire. Yet as readers of the love stories about Lancelot and Guinevere or Tristan and Yseut will recall, courtly literature of the twelfth century consistently delights in love affairs which the court "slanderers" (losengiers) suspect but can never demonstrate are going on. It has been argued that this literature was "intentionally enigmatic"[30] and that its authors employed a vocabulary whose purposeful vagueness thwarted any efforts to determine what exactly was occurring between the lovers.[31] "Ambiguity was," as one scholar puts it, "not a problem to be surmounted, but a poetic value."[32] If we are to respond to allegations of Eleanor's love affairs in the way in which the authors of courtly literature invite us to, we must resist the temptation to transform an ambiguous suggestion into either an affirmation or a denial. Instead, it behooves us to dwell, not in the actuality of a love affair, but in the *possibility* of such a relationship, as the *cansos* and romances of this time suggest.

THE TROUBADOUR

It was in the vicinity of Ventadorn (or Ventadour in modern French) in the Limousin, in the Duchy of Aquitaine, in an eleventh-century castle whose ruins survive to this day, that troubadour poetry first surfaced. William IX was the first troubadour whose songs have come down to us, but his vassal and companion Ebles II "the Singer," Viscount of Ventadorn, may have been the first such poet.[33] According to Geoffrey du Breuil of Vigeois, the Benedictine Abbot of Saint-Martial of Limoges, who was writing just a few years after the viscount's death, "Ebles . . . was very graceful in his songs. . . . He delighted in gay songs until his old age."[34] From what we are told, Bernart de Ventadorn hailed from the Castle of Ventadorn, the son of servants who toiled in the kitchens, gathering twigs and heating the furnace in which the bread was baked.[35] However humble Bernart's origins may have been, he would later refer to himself as having been "a singer . . . of the school of Lord Ebles,"[36] which suggests that he learned his craft from the viscount or from members of his entourage. By the time Bernart was a young man, the viscount's eldest son and heir, Ebles III of Ventadorn, had inherited his father's lands, which he ruled together with his wife, Azalaïs of Montpellier.[37] With the support of this pair, Bernart began to compose the *cansos* that would make him famous. At a certain point, for reasons that will soon become clear, he is said to have been forced to quit this court and seek out new patronage. If this departure occurred between May of 1152 and December of 1154, he could have found Eleanor residing either in Aquitaine (which encompassed Ventadorn) or, more likely, in Normandy, of which she had recently become mistress, thanks to her marriage to Henry.[38] In the "turning" (*tornada*), or final stanza, of his *canso* "Pel doutz chan que·l rossinhols fai," Bernart addresses his jongleur and tells him to whom he should deliver his song: "Hugh, my courtly messenger, sing my song gladly to the Queen of the Normans" (*Huguet, mos cortes messatgers / chantatz ma chanso volonters / a la reina dels Normans*).[39] With this allusion to Eleanor as the *destinataire* of his song, he makes the sole explicit reference to this queen in the entire troubadour corpus.

If audiences of Bernart's songs believed this troubadour to have had a love affair with Eleanor, as they seem to have done, it was because of the context within which his works would have been performed. It is likely that the jongleur who sang Bernart's *cansos* would have prefaced his recitation with an account of their author's life, including a brief explanation of the love affairs that had inspired him to compose these songs. As a result, when the works of troubadours like Bernart were collected into songbooks in the thirteenth and fourteenth centuries, they were often introduced with a "life" (*vida*) of the poet, which placed the lyric poems within such a narrative framework.[40] Of the thirty-eight songbooks that contain Bernart's poems, eight, or a little over a fifth, contain a *vida* of the poet, either the shorter, more common Vida A or the lengthier, rarer Vida B, which develops the same narrative as Vida A, but in greater detail.[41] Both versions of the *vida* recount that, when Bernart was living in his native region, he entered into a love affair with an unnamed "Viscountess of Ventadorn" (Vida B, p. 27) and that, having been expelled from her court when the liaison came to light, he entered into a similar relationship with his new patroness, the "Duchess of Normandy" (Vida A, p. 24), which lasted until she moved to England. However skeptical modern critics may be of the veracity of information included in the *vida*, the author of Vida A attests, "Now everything I have told you about him Viscount Ebles [IV] of Ventadorn, who was the son of the viscountess Sir Bernart loved so greatly, recounted to me" (p. 30). The author of Vida B identifies himself as Uc of Saint-Circ, a troubadour and a prolific author of *vidas* who would have been especially knowledgeable about Bernart's life. Between 1211 and 1219, Uc was active in the Limousin, where he could have heard tales about the poet from Ebles IV, the brother-in-law of Ralph of Faye, Eleanor's uncle and close advisor, and where he is known to have participated in debates with the brother of Maria of Ventadorn, Ebles V's wife. If we are to read the *cansos* as the compilers of these manuscripts intended us to do, we should interpret the love songs in light of this *vida*'s love story and, by extension, the seemingly abstract, universal lady of whom Bernart sings in the light of the concrete, particular person of our queen.[42]

According to Bernart's *vida*, Eleanor was a lady of high aristocratic status who welcomed the troubadour to her court. The author of Vida A relates that, after Bernart quit the Viscountess of Ventadorn, "He left and went to the Duchess of Normandy, who was young and of great merit [*valor*], and she attended to esteem [*pretz*], honor [*honor*], and good words in her praise [*bendig de sa lausor*]. And the *cansos* and verses of Sir Bernart pleased her greatly" (pp. 24–25). The author of Vida B adds that the duchess was "of great power" (*de gran poder*) (p. 27). Not only Eleanor, but the ladies depicted in *vidas* in general are said to welcome the attention of troubadours, who promise to enhance their reputations. In particular, they desire praise for the "merit" (*valor*) they have achieved, the "esteem" (*pretz*) they have earned for this merit, and the "honor" (*honor*) they have acquired. We are told of a certain Alamanda de Stanc, for example, "She permitted the beseechments and attentions of Sir Giraut de Bornelh for the great enhancement he brought about of her esteem and honor and for the good *cansos* he made about her" (p. 193). We are informed of Lady Loba de Pennautier that she welcomed Raimon de Miraval's attentions "because she knew that Sir Miraval could more give esteem and honor than any man in the world" (p. 296). If a troubadour enhances a lady's reputation through his songs about her, he wins for her the admiration and friendship of both noblemen and noblewomen. It is said of Uc de Saint-Circ's Lady Clara that "She had a great desire for esteem, to be heard about far and near, and to have the friendship and intimacy of good ladies and noble men" (pp. 333–34). As the *vida* represents the situation, Eleanor wanted to be admired by the society in which she lived, like many of the noblewomen of her time, and she valued Bernart's poetry because she saw it as the means by which she might acquire such a good reputation.

In recompense for the service he offered, the author of the *vida* relates, Eleanor granted honor to Bernart. Because the troubadour's verses and love songs pleased Eleanor greatly, he tells us, "She received him, welcomed him, honored him, and did him a great many kindnesses. For a long time he was at her court" (pp. 24–25). Noblemen as well as noblewomen could offer a troubadour honor, yet they more often offered "honors" (*honor*) in the sense of material gifts. Well before Bernart arrived at Eleanor's court, we are told, he had received "great honor" from the Viscount of Ventadorn, at whose castle "He was honored and esteemed by all people. . . . And he was seen, heard, and received most willingly, and the great barons and the great men gave him great honors and gifts, on account of which he went about in great equipage and in great honor" (Vida B, p. 27). The "honors" Bernart receives from these lords take the form of clothes, arms, horses, and the equipment for horses, like the "honors" that other troubadours are said to have received from such men.[43] Yet when noblewomen offered a troubadour "honor," it was typically more in the form of personal attention and encouragement than of material goods. After Raimbaut de Vaqueiras had enhanced Lady Beatriz's reputation, it is said, "She did him great honor in welcoming him" (p. 272). When Eleanor's daughter Matilda of Saxony met Bertran de Born, we are told, "She did him great honor through her welcome and her noble speech" (pp. 44–45). For a woman of high status and great worthiness, as Matilda was said to be, to address a man of lower status like Bertran, to converse with him in a kindly way, and to make him feel welcome in her presence, is for her to bestow on him a great gift. Though a woman of Eleanor's great wealth could easily have rewarded Bernart with possessions, as his male patrons are said to have done, it is her courteous reception that is said to have mattered the most.

By welcoming and honoring Bernart, as the *vidas* represent her doing,

Eleanor elevated his social status. In both versions of Bernart's *vida*, Eleanor is said to love the poet for his merits, despite his low rank.[44] It is reported that "He was a man from a poor family" (Vida A, p. 23; Vida B,
p. 26), but he was not defined by this origin. As Vida A puts it, "He became
a handsome and clever man, and he knew well how to sing and to compose.
And he became courtly and well-taught" (p. 24). As Vida B states, "But
whoever's son he was [*Mas de qi q'el fos fils*], God gave him a handsome
and charming person and a gentle heart [*gentil cor*], whose origin was in
gentility [*gentilessa*], and he gave him reason, knowledge, courtliness, and
noble speech [*sen e saber e cortesia e gen parlar*]. He had subtlety [*sotilessa*]
and the art of composing good words and gay tunes [*art de trobar bos motz
e gais sons*]" (p. 27). Either implicitly, through the juxtaposition of his parentage and his individual qualities, or explicitly, through the conjunction
"but," the *vidas* contrast who Bernart was thanks to his lineage and who
he was thanks to his character and talents. Considering the original con-
notation of *gentil* as "noble" and *gentilessa* as "of noble birth," the *vida* suggests that Bernart may not have been of gentle birth, but he was of "gentle
heart" and "gentility," as could be seen in his "courtesy," that is, his display
of the refined manners appropriate to someone at court. And it is noble
ladies who recognize his nobility and who respond to him accordingly. It
is said of the Viscountess of Ventadorn, "On account of his good manners
and his gay composing, she wanted him beyond measure" (p. 27). And it
is said of Eleanor, "She was very happy with his arrival, and she made him
lord and master of all her court" (p. 27). In other *vidas*, ladies recognize
the virtues of their troubadours, despite their low birth.[45] Guillem de Mur
maintains that a lady is more honored if she loves a man of lower rank than
higher because "The gift will be more praised and the gratitude greater."[46]
By recognizing the noble heart of a low-born poet and loving him for this
nobility, Eleanor, like other high-born women, allows the son of a servant
to run her court and, in doing so, enables him to attain the position in society that he deserves.

Yet after Eleanor had received and honored Bernart and raised his status in doing so, the *vida* continues, she married Henry, who cut short this
pleasant interlude in their lives. Bernart is said to have been driven from
Ventadorn when the viscount noticed his liaison with his wife, whom he
then locked up and kept under guard. We are told, "He made the lady give
leave to Sir Bernart so that he would depart and go far away from that
region" (Vida A, p, 24). There is no indication that Eleanor and Bernart's
love affair was discovered in a similar manner or, if it was discovered, that it
was punished. Still, a man of higher status, who can marry her, does so and

asserts his rights over her. According to Vida A, "King Henry of England took her for his wife, and he took her from Normandy and brought her to England. Sir Bernart stayed behind there, sad and sorrowful" (p. 25). According to Vida B, "For a long time [Bernart] had great joy and great benefit from her, until she took King Henry of England for a husband and he brought her across the Arm of the Sea of England, so that he did not see her again, nor her messenger" (p. 28). Whether Henry is said to take Eleanor as his wife or Eleanor is said to take him as her husband, Henry is the one who forces a separation between this lady and the poet. In both cases, Bernart is left behind on the Continent, grieving for her departure. In other *vidas*, Peirol is driven from Dalfi d'Auvergne's court when this lord suspects him of having become too intimate with his sister, and Peire Rogier is forced to leave Ermengarda of Narbonne's court when "the people of that region" (pp. 231–32) blame the viscountess for her conduct toward him. Whereas in a relationship with a social inferior, like a troubadour, the lady imposes her will on the man, in a relationship with a social equal or superior, like her husband, the man imposes his will on the lady and, by extension, on those serving her, like her poet. The troubadour Raimon refers to the fact that, in a marriage, "the husband, if he has but a little forcefulness, is . . . the lord and master" and that he may therefore "confine"[47] the lady and forbid her heart's desire. From the troubadour's perspective, while the lady may upend the social hierarchy, raising the poet to her level, the husband to whom she is bound restores that hierarchy, to the poet's detriment.

From what the *vidas* tell us in general, a troubadour and a lady may merely pretend to love each other, but they may also genuinely feel and act on such passion. It is said of Uc de Saint-Circ that "He knew well how to feign being in love to [ladies] with his fair speech"[48] and of Folquet de Marseille that he was suspected of harboring a passion for a lady "for whom he did not wish well, if not out of courtliness [*si no per cortezia*]."[49] As the troubadour may praise the lady's beauty and merit, he may present himself as having succumbed to her charms in order to please her and encourage her patronage. Elias Cairel informs his lady, somewhat brutally, "If I have uttered your praise, it was not for dalliance, but for the honor and profit I expected from it, as a jongleur does with a lady of worth" (p. 101). Just as the poet may pretend to be in love with the lady, she may pretend to be in love with him. She may say pleasing things to him (p. 296), kiss him and embrace him (p. 291), and even give him the ring from her finger "as a token and guarantee" (p. 284) of her affection. She may coyly hint that further favors will be forthcoming. Like the troubadour who feigns love for a lady in order to flatter his patroness, the lady may feign love for the

troubadour in order to reward him for the fame he has given her. Though
Maria of Ventadorn was served by Gaucelm Faidit, it is said, "She did not
love him if not out of courtliness [*si no per cortezia*] and in return for the
great praise he had given of her and the exalted reputation he had made
for her throughout the world" (p. 113). Yet the love that a troubadour and
a lady profess to each other is also depicted, on occasion, as sincere. While
Folquet pretended to love one of the ladies at court "out of courtliness,"
he is also said to have loved another of them "more than anything in the
world" (p. 101). And while most often the lady is said to lead the troubadour on, promising him sexual favors that she will never grant, occasionally
she is said to succumb. According to the *vida* of Peire Rogier, "He fell in
love with [Lady Ermengarda], and he composed his poems and his songs
about her. . . . For a long time he was with her at her court, and it was believed that he had the joy of love from her" (pp. 231–32). Eleanor's courteous reception of Bernart reflects, we are told, not only the affection a patroness may feel for her protégé, but the affection a woman may feel for a
man, whether as a kind of playacting or as an actual emotion.

According to his *vida*, Bernart sincerely loved Eleanor. When the Viscountess of Ventadorn fell in love with this troubadour, we are told, she
did not hold back: "She wanted him beyond measure, so that she did not
keep to reason [*sen*], nor gentility, nor honor, nor merit, nor shame, but
she fled her reason [*sen*] and followed her will. As Sir Arnaut de Mareuil
says: 'Attending to joy and forgetting folly [*foudat*], I flee my reason [*sen*]
and follow my will,' and as Gui d'Ussel says, 'Thus it happens with courtly
lovers [*fin aman*], that reason [*sens*] does not have power against desire'"
(Vida B, p. 27). As we have already seen in the *romans antiques* and the
chronicles, a lady is often represented as torn between "reason" (*sen*), which
would keep her behavior within the bounds appropriate to a noblewoman,
and "folly" (*foudat*), which compels her to act in a manner exceeding those
limits, even to her shame, and the viscountess succumbs to folly. She differs
from Maria de Ventadorn, about whom it is said that, as the most highly
respected lady of the Limousin, "Her reason [*senz*] always helped her, and
folly [*follors*] never made her do foolish things" (p. 213). It is not stated
that the love affair between Eleanor and Bernart was expressed in physical
terms. When Bernart met Eleanor, it is said in Vida A, "He fell in love with
her and she with him, and he made many good *cansos* about her" (p. 25).
After his tumultuous love affair with the viscountess, we are told in Vida
B, "As he had fallen in love with the wife of his lord, so did he now fall in
love with the duchess, and she with him" (pp. 27–28). There is no indication that Eleanor succumbed to "folly" in her dealings with Bernart, yet

her love of this poet is depicted as parallel to that of the viscountess, who did fall prey to such madness.

If one turns from the Bernart's *vida* to his *cansos*, one finds much that seems to support the view that they are about Eleanor. Bernart speaks of his beloved as a high lady of aristocratic status and himself as her "man" or "vassal" (*om*) or her "servant" (*servidor*).[50] He describes himself as receiving honor from a distinguished lady in a way that makes him comparable to Henry. In a *tornada*, he instructs his messenger to go to "my lord the king"[51] and to inform him that "I wish, as it is appropriate for him, that he have all the world in his power, just as he has Touraine, Poitou, Anjou, and Normandy."[52] Though Henry was ruling these lands at the time when Bernart was writing, and though Bernart suggests that he deserves to hold, not only those lands, but the whole world, the poet does not envy him. He declares, "I am a courtly lover [*fis amans*] with such a love that I envy neither a duke nor a count. There is no king or emir in the world who, if he had such [a love], would not enrich himself as I have done."[53] With these words, Bernart may be boasting that his beloved is a lady of high rank, courted by a king, a duke, and a count (and Eleanor was courted by all three, as well as, allegedly, an emir). He acknowledges what might seem to be the unsuitability of his beloved's affection for such a poor man as himself, but he claims that, far from lowering herself to his level by loving him, she has raised him to her level and would raise him still further if she could: "And I tell you that if it were in her power, I would be King of France, for as much as she can, she advances me."[54] Yet after having been raised up and brought near his lady, Bernart relates, he was cast down and separated from her. In a *canso* that is often identified with Eleanor, he relates, "This verse has been completed . . . beyond the Norman land, across the fierce, deep sea. And if I am far from milady, she draws me to her like a magnet [*azimans*], the beautiful one—God protect her! If the English king and Norman duke wish, I shall see her before winter overtakes us."[55] Whereas elsewhere in his verses, it was the lady who was in power, here, it is Henry who is in control of Eleanor's movements, retaining her in Norman England while Bernart is on the Continent or keeping her in Normandy while the troubadour is in England or possibly elsewhere on the Continent.[56] Though Bernart's *cansos* do not praise Eleanor by name, they do praise someone *like* her, that is, a lady of high status, who has honored him but from whom he is now separated across the sea, and they do so in the midst of a series of allusions to Henry, this lady's husband.

At the same time, there is also much in Bernart's songs that indicates that his lady was not Eleanor or, indeed, any historical woman. As often as

Bernart refers to his beloved as a lady of high status, he refers to her with epithets like "the beautiful one" (*la bela*) or "the lovely one" (*la genta*) or, even more vaguely, with personal pronouns like "you" (*vos*) or "she" (*ela*) or relative pronouns like "the one who" (*so que*), so that her identity can never be stabilized and localized. Just as the lady's excellence may be due to her personal qualities, not her social rank, his distance from her may be psychological, not geographical. He asserts, "I am here [*sai*], not elsewhere, and I do not know how she is. And so I am dying of grief, for I seldom have a chance to go there [*lai*]."[57] The point is not that his lady is in England while he is on the Continent; the point is that, essentially speaking, she is "there" (*lai*) while he is "here" (*sai*). To love is to suffer from the distance between the self and the beloved, which can be expressed in spatial terms, and to long to span that distance mentally if not physically. As Bernart bids in a *tornada*, "Messenger, go and run. Speak for me to the loveliest one of the pain and sorrow I suffer for her, and the torment."[58] The very form of the *tornada*, which locates the singer in one spot and the *destinataire* of the song in another and which appeals to the messenger to bring the song from one site to the other, reflects the spatial imaginary of troubadour verse. Just as Bernart's lady may not be Eleanor, his lady's husband may not be Henry. If he mentions this king, it may be, not because the object of his love is his wife, but because the manner in which he loves makes him superior to even the most exalted of men. He writes, "Man can only achieve worthiness in the love and service of ladies. . . . No man is worth anything without love, and therefore I would not want lordship over the whole world if I could not have joy."[59] It may seem that a man who rules over many countries has achieved the greatest merit, but, the poet claims, it is the man who serves and loves ladies, as he does, who has done so. As a result of love, Bernart experiences, not power, like a king, but lack of power. Since his lady let him look into her eyes, he writes, "I never had power over myself, and I was not mine."[60] And it is right for a lover to feel this lack of power. He explains, "A man does not have lordship in love."[61] While Bernart's *cansos* may seem to be praising Eleanor or someone like Eleanor, this lady's high status, distance from him, and power over him may be, not literal, but figurative.

For several centuries, critics accepted the *vida*'s claim that Bernart had a love affair with Eleanor. Jean-Baptiste de La Curne de Sainte-Palaye, in a work edited by the abbé Claude-François-Xavier Millot, writes in 1774 that, after Bernart was expelled from the court of Ventadorn, he found asylum with Eleanor: "This princess, too well known for her gallantries, welcomed the troubadour with a kindness filled with esteem and consideration. He soon dared to sigh for her. Although the language of love was often nothing more than a game of imagination or wit, it seemed truly serious in the songs where Bernart celebrates Eleanor."[62] These authors acknowledge that the declarations of love between troubadours and their patronesses were often only playful, but they allege that, in Bernart and Eleanor's case, they were made in earnest, and they may have been acted on: "To judge by some places in his pieces, the princess did not disdain the vows of this bold lover."[63] Not only the belletrists of the eighteenth century but the scholars of the nineteenth century accepted the veracity of the *vida*'s account of this love affair, including Friedrich Diez, a professor at the University of Bonn who produced the first major critical study of the troubadours in 1829,[64] and Claude Fauriel, the first chair in foreign literature at the Sorbonne, who followed up on Diez's study with his own in 1846.[65] Though Eleanor is alluded to explicitly in only one of Bernart's songs, several scholars proposed that she was referenced as well by the "code name" (*senhal*) "Magnet" (*Azimen*), which appears in three of Bernart's *cansos*. Carl Appel, who prepared the first major edition of Bernart's poetry in 1915, deems "Pel doutz chan que·l rossinhol fai," "Lancan vei per mei la landa," and "Tant ai mo cor ple de joya" to have been composed for Eleanor, as well as four other songs.[66] As these scholars see it, Eleanor's reputation for "lightness of morals"[67] makes it easy to believe the *vida*'s allegation of her love affair with a troubadour.

Yet, other critics have maintained, there is no evidence that Bernart ever really did feel such passion, let alone for Eleanor. While Gaston Paris accepted that Bernart composed songs for Eleanor in 1883, he later warns that scholars should not rely on the *vidas* in reconstructing the troubadours' lives. The love story advanced by the *vidas* may seem to be supported by the love songs, but Paris states, "The confirmations of their accounts often believed to be found in troubadour verses are only illusory: it is these verses, more or less understood, which gave birth to the accounts."[68] Stanislaw Stronski, following Paris, judged the authors of the *vidas* to be, not biographers of these poets, about whose love affairs he believes they knew little to nothing, but commentators of their poems, whose details they transposed into their narratives. "In order to explain, they invent," he announces.[69] In the reading of the poems so far, I have cherry-picked certain themes that correspond to the *vida*—the poet's love for a lady of high rank; the honor he received from this lady; the social elevation this honor led to; and the separation from her—but there are many other themes that could have been emphasized instead, such as his jealousy over a rival for his lady's love, which find no echo in the relationship in the *vida*.[70] As one

critic has observed,[71] in the absence of any consistent, distinguishing char-
acteristics that would identify the lady as Eleanor or anyone else, it is not
clear if Bernart is singing about one lady, about three ladies, or about ten
ladies. Indeed, it is not clear that he is singing about a lady at all. Despite
efforts to identify "Magnet" (*Azimen*) as Eleanor, one critic has pointed
out that Folquet de Marseille and Bertran de Born both use this *senhal* to
signify their fellow (male) troubadours.[72] Given the impossibility of attain-
ing true, historical information about Bernart's love affairs, many scholars
have insisted, instead, on a purely formal approach to his poems. Alfred
Jeanroy writes, "We must resign ourselves to not knowing anything about
the man and not considering anything but the artist."[73] Instead of "Seek
the woman" (*Cherchez la femme*), Stronski advises, "Appreciate the poet's
art" (*Appréciez l'art du poète*).[74]

Yet to abandon the notion that Eleanor and Bernart loved each other
is more easily said than done, In many of his poems, Bernart pivots from
the first-person "I" (*ieu*) to the third-person "Bernart"[75] or "Bernart de
Ventadorn,"[76] a shift that encourages us to perceive the speaker, not as a
generic poetic voice, but as a specific historical figure. Whether or not
the speaker of these poems can be identified with a "Bernart," let alone a
"Bernart" who has experienced the love his poems portray, he asks us to
believe that he felt love and that, inspired by this emotion, he composed
these love songs. By the same token, in many of his poems, Bernard indicates that his lady is, not a generic beloved, but a specific individual, whom
he declines to name only out of concern for her privacy. "Our love is not
known through me. You may be sure of that," he asserts.[77] "I would swear
to her, by her and by my faith, that any good that she might do me will
not be known through me."[78] Indeed, Bernart was well known for his dis-
cretion regarding his love life. According to the *vida* of the Catalan troubadour Guillem de Cabestaing, when Guillem was confronted by someone who demanded to know the name of his beloved, he cited Bernart's
verses to justify his refusal to respond (p. 168). At the same time, Bernart
gives us hints, such as ambiguous references to a place that may or may not
be where the lady resides, a *senhal* that reveals her identity even as it conceals it, or a detail about her that may or may not be identificatory, and
these hints allow us to apprehend the silhouette of that which we cannot
apprehend fully. As futile as it may be to attempt to decipher any single,
coherent narrative from his poems, Bernart does refer to "the Queen of
the Normans" and to the king who holds Anjou, Normandy, Touraine,
and Poitou. While his poems may exist outside time, many of them do
exist within space, and that is the space of the Plantagenet domain, ruled

by this family's king and queen. As much as modern critics dismiss Bernart's *vida* for imposing a narrative on the lyrics, the lyrics themselves call out for such an imposition through such references. Even in our own day, it is common for fans to interpret a popular song as a commentary on the singer's girlfriend or boyfriend. However much formalistic critics may urge us to seek, not the woman, but the art, and hence, not the narrative, but a pure lyricism, audiences of poetry did not limit themselves to such purely literary concerns in the Middle Ages, nor do we do so today.

If we can accept the love affair between Eleanor and Bernart, not as something that did or did not occur, but as something that *may* have occurred, we gain access to her private life at court, at least as it was understood at the time. We can see what may have attracted a great lady to a love affair with a troubadour. Bernart represents himself as recognizing and respecting his lady's great nobility and wealth, but ultimately as loving her, not for these extrinsic advantages, but for her intrinsic merit. Though she lifts him up and grants him honor, she does so, not by making him lord of Poitou and Aquitaine, as she did with Henry, but by granting him her love, which makes him *feel* that he has achieved an even greater status. In his relationship with her, it is not that he dominates her (as Henry did, by taking her to England), but, rather, that she dominates him, through the empire she gains over his heart, and he willingly and gladly submits to her power. Yet even as we can see what would have been appealing in a dalliance with a troubadour, we can also see why the nature of that dalliance would have best been kept ambiguous. Bernart's *vida*, it can be remembered, represented the Viscountess of Ventadorn as the poet's great love, not Eleanor. It was the viscountess who inspired his passion in his youth, who, having given into "folly," suffered the consequences of her actions, and whose sad story, from what the *vida* represents, became the stuff of family legend, passed down from generation to generation. In contrast, the Eleanor of the *vida* was never exposed as guilty of the same infraction, just as the Eleanor of history was never punished for her alleged infidelity. The absence of positive knowledge about the queen's private life, though a source of frustration for historians, is what protects her from reprisals.

THE COURTS OF LOVE

In the last half of the twelfth century, when troubadours were singing the love of their ladies, they not uncommonly depicted themselves as turning to another lady for advice or assistance with their love affair. According to the anonymous author of a prose "cause" or "reason" (*razo*), which can preface a song and explain the circumstances of its composition, when Bertran de Born's lady cast him off, "He went off to Saintonge to see Lady Tibors de Montausier, who was one of the most esteemed women in the world in beauty, merit, and learning,"[79] and he complained to her about his lady's mistreatment of him. In response, Lady Tibors, "like the wise lady she was,"[80] offered to try to help, so long as Bertran was not at fault. "I will do my best to restore and make concord between you and her," she promised.[81] When Giraut de Bornelh was likewise rejected by his lady, he consulted with another woman, requesting her insight into the situation: "I seek your counsel, my fair friend Alamanda. . . . What do you advise me to do?"[82] A troubadour who cannot get through to his lady turns to other members of her sex whom he expects to intervene on his behalf or at least to shed light on what has happened. Over time, the story developed that these noblewomen not only agreed to be consulted on an ad hoc basis about such liaisons but served on Courts of Love, where they would hear and pass judgment on these cases. These tribunals were associated with several noblewomen of this time and place, but, as the legend developed, none was deemed more central to their operations than Eleanor.

Though troubadours provided the initial evidence of these Courts of Love in their poems, Andreas Capellanus, a chaplain in the service of Marie de Champagne[83] or possibly Philip,[84] Marie's half-brother, offers the fullest description of their operation in his *De amore* (1186–96). While primarily a scientific treatise, this Latin work contains within it a medley of literary genres, including a romance about a British knight who undertakes a series of feats to win the love of his lady; a set of "Rules of Love" (*Regulae amoris*) that this knight discovers at King Arthur's court in the course of his adventures; allegorical accounts of the King (or God) of Love, who was said to have dictated these rules for the benefit of all lovers; and nine dialogues between men and women of different social classes where the man beseeches the woman for her love, with uncertain success. Most importantly for our purposes, the treatise contains accounts of a series of cases in which ladies consider "doubtful matters" (*dubitationes*) regarding love, that is, points of debate on which there are two reasonable but opposing points of view. There had long been a tradition in both classical and medieval Latin literature of lovers having recourse to the King or God of Love for his opinion on their love affair,[85] yet Andreas represents the judges who deliberate on these cases, not as an imagined, allegorical ruler or deity, but as actual, historical ladies. Of the twenty-one judgments he records, seven were pronounced by Marie de Champagne, five by Ermen-

garda, two by "the Countess of Flanders" (perhaps Eleanor's niece Elizabeth de Vermandois),[86] and one by "a court of ladies … in Gascony" (II, 18,
p. 266). And six of the judgments are attributed to Eleanor herself, three as
"Queen Eleanor of England" (I, 6, p. 92) or "Queen Eleanor" (II, 2, p. 252;
II, 6, p. 256; II, 7, p. 256) and three as "the Queen" (II, 17, p. 266; II, 19,
p. 268; II, 20, p. 269), who is most likely, if not definitely, the subject of our
study. Like the authors of the *vidas* who claim that troubadours loved identifiable noblewomen, Andreas affirms that lovers had their cases judged by
identifiable viscountesses, countesses, and queens.

In the course of her deliberations in *De amore*, Eleanor applies the Rules
of Love to particular cases. "The Queen" is told about a knight who sought
in love a woman already bound to another man and who received the assurance that, should she ever be deprived of her current lover, she would grant
him her favors. When the woman's lover became her husband, she refused
to let her suitor take his place as her paramour, claiming that she had not
been dispossessed of her earlier attachment. Was the woman obliged to
comply with the earlier agreement? The Queen answers, "We do not dare
to oppose the sentence of the Countess of Champagne, who ruled by her
judgment that Love cannot extend his force over conjugal partners. And
so we approve that the aforesaid woman should bestow the promised love"
(II, 17, p. 266). With this response, the Queen refers to Marie de Champagne's most famous Rule of Love: "No married woman can be crowned
with the prize of the King of Love unless she is perceived to be joined to
Love's Army outside the pact of marriage" (I, 6, p. 156). As the Queen, and,
by extension, the Countess represent it, a Rule of Love is descriptive, based
on the observed behavior of lovers. A woman who is married to a certain
man is legally bound to grant him her favors whenever he wishes. Because
love, as the ladies understand it, can only be experienced in a state of freedom from such obligations, it cannot be experienced in wedlock. But a
Rule of Love is also prescriptive, based on the codified behavior of true
lovers. A woman is not required to accept a suitor, but once she has given
him reason for hope of success, based on the fulfillment of certain conditions, she is forbidden to disappoint him. While lovers will not be condemned for having broken their marriage vows—while, on the contrary,
they will be celebrated for having joined "Love's Army" in doing so—they
must adhere to the strictures of this alternate moral code.

In addition to applying the Rules of Love to particular cases, Eleanor
applies her understanding of the "nature of love" to such instances. At
times, the nature to which she refers is that of love in general. In a case on
which she was consulted, a man requested and obtained his lady's permis-

sion to enjoy another woman's embraces. Later, he returned to his lady, claiming that he had not availed himself of this woman's consolation, or even attempted to do so, but had merely sought to test his partner's response to this plan. Was the lady right to reject his love on the grounds that the mere request for such permission was unacceptable? "Queen Eleanor" decrees, "We recognize that it proceeds from the nature of love [*amoris . . . natura*] that partners often feign, with false simulation, to long for fresh embraces, by which they will perceive the partner's fidelity and constancy. Therefore, she who withdraws her embraces from her partner or refuses to love him for this reason offends against the nature of love [*naturam . . . amoris*] itself, unless she knows her lover to have manifestly broken faith with her" (II, 2, p. 252). It is to be expected that a man who is uncertain of his lady's devotion will pretend to be attracted to another woman in order to arouse his lady's jealousy and, hence, revive her flagging feelings for him. On other occasions, the "nature" to which Eleanor refers is that of lust in particular. When asked whether the love of a young man is to be preferred to one of advancing years, "the Queen," speaking with what Andreas terms "marvelous subtlety" (II, 20, p. 269), deems a man attractive on the basis of his capacity to arouse sexual interest, which a young man is more likely to do. "The natural instinct of lust [*naturali . . . instinctu . . . libidinis*] having been considered" (II, 20, p. 269), she states, women of all ages seek the consolations of younger men. Once again, the code the Queen is applying is descriptive, based on lovers' observed behavior. As it is natural for them to play games to test a partner's interest, it is natural for them to feel attracted to partners of a certain age over others. But once again, the code the Queen is deploying is also prescriptive. Whatever is natural, whether it affects the emotional or physical aspect of a relationship, has to be tolerated by all parties. While lovers will not be condemned for toying with their partners or for seeking bedmates of certain ages, they cannot complain when their partners indulge in this behavior.

Finally, turning from the Rules of Love and the nature of love, Eleanor judges the cases she is considering in terms of social mores. "Queen Eleanor" is told about a woman who was courted by two men, one a mature man of considerable honesty of character and the other a young man of none. While the older man argued that his merits made him more deserving of the woman's love, the younger man pointed out that, "If his lack of honesty were transformed by her into honesty of manners, the praise for the woman would not be minimal" (II, 6, p. 256). Which lover should the lady choose? Eleanor decides that, while the lady might indeed improve the younger man through her love, she would be acting incautiously in choosing him over the older suitor, as she has no assurance that her efforts will bear fruit. The deciding factor in making Eleanor choose the older man over the younger one, interestingly enough, is not any private pleasure the lady may experience in her relationship with one of these potential lovers, but the "praise" she may enjoy as a result of one dalliance or the other. Though the woman may possibly earn plaudits if her involvement with the younger man results in his improvement, she can be sure that her involvement with the older, already meritorious man will earn her the respect of her peers. In other cases as well, the Queen advises women on how to act in love in order to enhance their reputations. When faced with a woman who, "having been bound by the chain of love," resisted abandoning a lover who turned out to be related to her within the prohibited degrees, she affirms, "This woman seems to contend sufficiently against what is lawful and permitted. . . . We are bound for all time to loathe incestuous and damnable acts, which we know human laws themselves to oppose with the gravest punishments" (II, 7, p. 256). When faced with a woman who gave a knight hope of her love by accepting small gifts from him but then rejected him in the end, the Queen rules that this woman should either repay these gifts or grant the knight her love or, alternatively, "she should patiently support being classed with companies of whores" (II, 19, p. 268). No longer descriptive of how men and women behave in love, when it comes to how a woman should enhance or preserve her honor in society, Eleanor, or the Queen, has become rigorously prescriptive.

If a pattern is to be found in Eleanor's judgments on love, it is that, even as she encourages ladies and gentlemen to pursue their attachments "outside the pact of love," she rules that they must comport themselves, not with folly, but with wisdom. She accepts that men and women will only experience love with partners outside their marriage; that women in particular will seek younger lovers from whom they will receive more sexual pleasure; and that lovers of both sexes may pretend to be unfaithful to their partners (though they should not actually be unfaithful). She believes that the influence of an older woman on her younger lover may be so beneficial that he will become a better man under her tutelage. At the same time, Eleanor, or the Queen, denies that men and women should pursue their desire wherever it leads them. The very fact that she is so often depicted deciding which of two potential lovers a lady should select shows that the choice of a lover should depend, not on the lady's personal preference, but on an impersonal evaluation of their merits and on the effect her association with someone of such merits will have on her own reputation. In this context, a lady will be disgraced, not if she is discovered to have engaged in an adulterous love affair, but if she is discovered to have engaged in such a love affair with an inferior or otherwise inappropriate man. In her emphasis on what lovers should do, not on what they want to do, Eleanor argues that, unlike the Viscountess of Ventadorn, they should follow reason and not just desire.

Still, it is not at all clear that a pattern is to be found in Eleanor's judgments. Andreas names the ladies who pass judgments in love as "Queen Eleanor of England," Marie de Champagne, and Ermengarda of Narbonne, but he makes no allusion to any identificatory details about these women, such as their parents, their husbands, or their lands,[87] and he never names "the Countess of Flanders" at all. So little definition is given to Eleanor or her colleagues that, when a certain Drouart la Vache translated *De amore* into French in 1290, he attributed Eleanor's judgments to an unnamed Queen of Germany and did not appear to appreciate the historical significance of any members of this tribunal.[88] Indeed, not only none of the ladies of the Courts of Love, but none of the men and women who appear in any section of *De amore* possess a distinct personality, let alone consistency in speech or behavior. In the Eighth Dialogue, for example, a woman claims to reject her suitor because she is a damsel, desirous of maintaining her virginity for a future husband; because she is a married lady bound by a previously established relationship with another lover; and because she is a widow and is in mourning for her husband.[89] Andreas is trying out different arguments a woman might make in response to a suitor, but he has no more qualms about attributing this series of contradictory self-descriptions to one speaker than Bernart de Ventadorn had about attributing an assemblage of divergent traits to his beloved. Modern readers, influenced, perhaps, by modern novels, with their unified and coherent characters, expect to see a unity and coherence in these ladies, and what they have expected to see, they have seen. Whatever attention we have paid to Eleanor's judgments in the cases that came before her, the other ladies who deliver judgments on the Courts of Love express views about the Rules of Love, the nature of love, and the effect of love on one's reputation whose substance is no different from her own.

Without any pattern to be found in Eleanor's judgments or in those of the other ladies, it is not at all clear that the Courts of Love were historical events, as normally conceived. In historical writings of this time, it was customary for authors to provide the Aristotelian "circumstances" that were seen as defining an event, including the time when it occurred, the place where it happened, and the names of those in attendance, yet Andreas never furnishes these details about the ladies' deliberations. Eleanor could possibly have met Marie in the spring or summer of 1173, in March of 1191, or before Christmas of 1193,[90] but he does not indicate that she did so, nor do we have any independent evidence that she ever saw her eldest daughter after her divorce from her father. Instead of emphasizing the circumstances in which Eleanor and the other ladies delivered their judgments, Andreas stresses the substance of these verdicts. When recounting those cases in which Eleanor was involved, he summarizes the lovers' situations and then relates, "The sentence of Queen Eleanor, who was consulted [*consulta*] on this case, seemed to be against this woman" (II, 2, p. 252); "This . . . case of love [was] delivered [*defertur*] to the same Queen's arbitration" (II, 7, p. 256); or "It was asked [*fuit . . . quaesitum*] of this Queen which love was to be chosen" (II, 7, p. 269). With his use of the passive voice, he stresses the philosophical statement that is being made about love, not the historical context within which it was supposedly uttered. He is representing, not the judgments that were made by Eleanor in cases of love, but judgments that could have been made by someone *like* Eleanor, that is, by someone of her social status, connected (as Marie and Ermengarda also were) to the courtly love literature of her time.

While it is not clear that the Courts of Love, as represented in Andreas's *De amore*, ever took place as historical events, something like these judgments did indeed transpire on Eleanor's lands at this time. In poems known as *tensos*, *partimens*, or *jocs partis* in Occitan, two troubadours enter into an argument about a "doubtful matter" concerning love and, after an exchange of stanzas, propose certain noblemen or noblewomen who might be able to resolve their dispute. In a recent collection of 157 such debate poems, the poets propose ladies as judges roughly half the time.[91] The editors of this volume consider the possibility that these disputes were purely literary inventions, but they ultimately decide that they were representing historical events. The ladies who are nominated as judges, including Maria of Ventadorn; Matilda, the wife of Hugh IX "le Brun," seigneur of Lusignan; and Margarita, the wife of Rainaut VI, Viscount of Aubusson; were actual, identifiable individuals who lived in the neighborhood of the poets while they were composing these poems. For that reason, they are thought likely to have been present at the performance and involved in the discussion of the song afterward.[92] The disputing poets recommend that a particular lady be invited to judge because she is someone who, through her graciousness, can alleviate the tension between them, because "what she may decide to say on the matter ought to be pleasing to all,"[93] or because she is "the best at reproving one who argues falsely, in a more agreeable fashion than would another woman who would accept his view."[94] They seek to have a "courtly debate" (*cortes plaitz*)[95] or a "pleasant discussion" (*plaszen solatz*),[96] and this lady is the one who will ensure that this congenial tone is preserved in the conversation. We have no record of any such poetic debate in which Eleanor took part, but the ladies involved in these exchanges were members of her social class, in the time and place in which she was living. Because the choice of a judge was based on the two poets' respect for an individual's merits, a high noblewoman like herself could be selected.

Just as ladies of Eleanor's social standing adjudicated debates about love, ladies of this time, including Eleanor herself, adjudicated disputes about more commonplace matters on their lands. Both civil and canon law codes of the Middle Ages declared that women were not allowed to occupy public offices and, hence, serve as judges,[97] but the women Andreas names as sitting on the Courts of Love nevertheless did so.[98] According to a charter of Péan de Rochefort, Seneschal of Anjou, in the course of a dispute between the Abbey of Fontevraud and the nearby town of Saumur in 1190, the abbess and the brethren of Fontevraud appealed to judgment "before us and the queen."[99] Péan and Eleanor summoned the previous mayors of Saumur to give testimony on this matter, and they ruled in favor of the abbey. At other points, Eleanor intervened in disagreements involving the monks of Reading,[100] the monks of Bourgueil,[101] and the monks of Canterbury Cathedral.[102] During the fifty years in which Ermengarda of Narbonne ruled her city, she too served as a judge in trials.[103] Around 1164, Louis wrote to the viscountess that, though the law of the Holy Roman Empire prevents women from serving as judge, "The custom of our kingdom is far kinder, whereby, if the better sex is lacking, it is conceded to women to succeed to and to administer their inheritance."[104] Even more relevantly, when two parties of this time were attempting to settle a dispute privately, through arbitration, they could choose a woman to serve as "arbitratrix" (*arbitratrix*) between them.[105] It was because arbitrators were not proper judges, appointed to civil office by public authorities, but mediators, selected by private disputants on an ad hoc basis, that they could occasionally be a local female dignitary.[106] In 1202, Pope Innocent III confirmed that Adela of Champagne, Queen of France, had the authority to serve as arbitratrix between a Cistercian abbey and a group of Knights Hospitaler in resolving their quarrel, as these parties had asked her to do. He decreed, "Although, according to the rule of the civil law, women are removed from this kind of public office, . . . nevertheless, in accordance with approved custom, which is regarded like law in Gallic regions, excellent women of this kind are known to have ordinary jurisdiction."[107] Like Louis, the pope recognizes that it is the tradition in France to allow women to serve as arbitratrixes, and he respects that tradition. In *De amore*, when a case is brought to Eleanor's attention, Andreas writes, "This . . . case of love was delivered to the same queen's arbitration [*arbitrium*]" (II, 7, p. 256). Because the selection of an arbitrator was based in the litigants' mutual recognition of an individual's good judgment, in history and in Andreas's treatise, distinguished women could, again, be nominated to play this role by those who valued their opinion.

For centuries, belletrists and even scholars believed that the Courts of Love had taken place, with Eleanor as one of the judges. In 1575, Jean de Nostredame, *procureur* at the Parlement at Aix-en-Provence (and brother of the notorious prophet Nostradamus), became the first to argue that, between the twelfth and the fourteenth centuries, there were "Court[s] of Love" in various locales in Provence, all dominated by "illustrious lady *présidentes*."[108] Though Nostredame's evidence for such courts was at least partly invented, over the course of the seventeenth,[109] eighteenth,[110] and early nineteenth[111] centuries, his claims were repeated and embellished by various authors, all of whom represented the Courts of Love as an actual tribunal, like ordinary civil and canonical courts. Along with the "right of the lord" (*droit du seigneur*) and animal trials, the Courts of Love were considered one of the "bizarre" but intriguing legal curiosities of feudal Europe.[112] After Andreas's treatise was rediscovered by François-Juste-Marie Raynouard in 1817[113] and then publicized by Stendhal in 1822,[114] its depiction of the Courts of Love seemed to confirm what Nostredame and his followers had been saying all along. By this point, the Courts of Love were regarded, not simply as a practice, but as a "remarkable institution,"[115] over which Eleanor and Marie de Champagne presided.[116] In a 1937 article, Amy Kelly, Eleanor's most popular Anglophone biographer, hypothesized that when the queen was living in Poitiers in the 1160s and 1170s, she held "those famous assemblies . . . to which lovers brought their complaints for the judgment of the ladies."[117] Kelly paints a vivid tableau of sixty or so noble ladies, aged between twenty-five and thirty years, mounting a dais in a grand hall and seating themselves around Eleanor, while their male companions settle down on stone benches along the walls. The advocate for an anonymous young lover approaches the ladies with a question about a point of conduct in a love affair, and the ladies deliberate about his case and pass judgment. Neither the troubadours nor Andreas had ever represented the Courts of Love as a standing tribunal, let alone one with such elaborate procedures, but they had become what Rita Lejeune calls "those feminine assizes over which Eleanor was, both literally and figuratively, the sovereign."[118]

Yet all along, other belletrists and scholars denied that the Courts of Love ever existed and, hence, that Eleanor played any part in them. As far back as 1780, Jean-Pierre Papon, a historian of Provence, claimed that there was never a Court of Love that decided questions in matters of the heart.[119] As the fictional nature of Nostredame's writings was readily evident by the early nineteenth century, Friedrich Diez focused on Andreas's *De amore*, asking how we are to believe historical claims made "in a work so fabulous and containing so many contradictions."[120] The Courts of Love are no more credible, he argued, than are the Castle of Love or the discovery of the Rules of Love that Andreas also depicts in these pages. The issue for most scholars was not so much whether the Courts of Love existed as what one meant by the Courts of Love. Critics acknowledged that there were discussions at courts about love in which ladies were involved, but they insisted that these discussions were nothing more than a frivolous game. As Diez put it, the Courts of Love were "nothing but occasional invited societies, in which questions of love or quarrels of love were tried as cases more with social pleasure than with judicial seriousness."[121] According to other scholars, they were "only . . . *jeux d'esprit*";[122] "only diversions of society";[123] "only a society game";[124] and "never anything but a society pastime of society, without juridical importance, without legal effect."[125] The troubadours themselves had referred to these discussions as "games" (*jocs*), but they had not described them as "only" games, nor is there any indication that, because these ladies' influence was cultural, affecting "only" the mores of their society, they had regarded it as trivial. When Socrates and his disciples took part in debates (including on love) in Athens, when medieval scholastics participated in disputations at the University of Paris, or when Renaissance humanists engaged in dialogues at the Court of Urbino, these events were not regarded as "only" a game, despite their lack of judicial consequences, but as serious philosophical discussions. In their efforts to rebut maximalist claims about the Courts of Love which neither the troubadours nor Andreas ever made, critics have minimized the importance of the debates about love that were in fact taking place.

If we can accept Eleanor's involvement in discussions of love, not as something that did or did not occur, but as something that *may* have occurred, we gain insight into the courtly culture this queen inhabited. In Andreas's *De amore*, Eleanor is treated, not as the patroness who decides whether she will grant her favor to a particular troubadour, as she did in Bernart de Ventadorn's *vida*, but as the judge or arbitratrix who will decide how another lady should grant her favor. Her name is first mentioned in the treatise by a nobleman who is considering a "doubtful matter" regarding love and who recalls the resolution of this matter "according to the opinion of Queen Eleanor of England" (I, 6, p. 92). Though the nobleman's own view on this issue differs from that of the queen, he considers her to be sufficiently authoritative on matters of the heart to be worth quoting. If Eleanor's views carry such weight, it is because she is someone of lofty social status but also because she is someone of real political and judicial clout. It is possible that Eleanor did share her thoughts during a dispute on amorous topics, perhaps after a troubadour *joc partit*, as Maria of Ventadorn, Matilda of Lusignan, and Margarita of Aubusson, all wives of her vassals, were said to have done. It is also possible that, as in a work of historical fiction, she is a historical figure brought in to play a role with no historical basis. In either case, the ambiguity of Eleanor's appearance in this treatise, like the cameo appearance of a celebrity in a television program today, gives a contemporary edge to the work that the appearance of the God of Love never would have done.

THE KNIGHT ERRANT

Among the knights with whom Eleanor had dealings when she was living on the Continent, William Marshal (1146/47–1219) was the most noteworthy. Marshal was a historical figure. The son of a minor Anglo-Norman nobleman, he inherited from his father the title of "Marshal," which became the cognomen for him and his family, but, as a younger son, he came into no lands. In order to support himself, he attached himself to the entourage of his maternal uncle, Patrick, Earl of Salisbury, who, in 1163, had been appointed commander of Henry's forces in Aquitaine, and after this uncle's death, to Eleanor and a succession of Plantagenet kings, including the Young King, Henry, Richard, and John. As a result of this service, at the age of forty-three, the Marshal was granted the hand of the seventeen-year-old Isabel de Clare, Countess of Pembroke and Striguil and the heiress of Earl Richard de Clare (alias "Strongbow"), a major figure in the Anglo-Norman conquest of Ireland. With his wife's vast holdings in Ireland, Wales, and England, he became one of the wealthiest men in the Angevin realm. A historical figure, the Marshal nevertheless resembled a literary hero. As he did not marry until middle age, he spent much of his life as a knight errant, traveling throughout England, Normandy, France, Flanders, and Anjou and competing in tournaments wherever he could find them. So extraordinary were his feats in jousts and in other battles that Stephen Langton, Archbishop of Canterbury, termed him "the best knight who ever was in our time."[126] If there was any knight who lived in the latter half of the twelfth century and who seemed to his contemporaries to embody the virtues of the chivalric romances, it was this man who was, for a time, this servant of our queen.

The Marshal is well known to this day thanks to the *Histoire de Guillaume le Maréchal* (1224–26), a lengthy Anglo-Norman verse account of his life written just a few years after his death. From what the poem's author tells us, he was a professional trouvère named John (vv. 19195–96), probably from Anjou, the Touraine, or another region south of the Loire, who wrote at the bidding of William Marshal II, the Marshal's eldest son, in the hope that the members of his family would take pleasure in "the great qualities and the honor they will hear of their ancestor" (vv. 19209–10). Surviving in only one copy from the mid-thirteenth century, the poem does not seem to have been read outside the immediate circle of the Marshal's household. As the author of a "history," John makes clear that he relies on what had long been recognized as the two legitimate sources of information for such a work: the testimony of eyewitnesses, including the Marshal's squires Eustace de Bertrimont and John of Earley, who were by his side during many of his adventures, and the evidence of written records, including the family archives of accounts, rolls, charters, and correspondence in South Wales and Gloucestershire. For many scholars, it is because of this "historical" orientation that the author says very little about women, whom they deem as marginal to the world of this poem—"a man's world, a world of violence, comradeship, and high politics"[127]—as they were to the real feudal world it depicts, and what he does say about them appears at first glance to have little to do with courtly love.[128] As one critic remarks, "Eleanor... is almost the only woman named in the text, the only one whose character is analyzed,"[129] and there is no indication of a liaison between this queen and this hero. Yet even as the poem refrains from portraying the Marshal as engaged in a courtly love relationship with Eleanor, it provides a kind of palimpsest of such a relationship, which later readers would not fail to detect.

In the *Histoire de Guillaume le Maréchal*, Eleanor is represented as vulnerable in war and, hence, in need of the Marshal's protection. In the winter and early spring of 1168, the Poitevins, including the brothers Geoffrey and Guy de Lusignan, rebelled against Henry, their overlord, laying waste to his lands. In retaliation, Henry moved into this region, and, we are told, "He brought with him his wife and select barons, and he brought Earl Patrick too" (vv. 1591–92), as well as the earl's nephew. That April, when Henry was away in Normandy negotiating with Louis, who was supporting the rebels, it is said that "The King . . . asked for Earl Patrick. He commanded him and his knights to conduct the queen" (vv. 1615–18), from where and to where we are not told. Patrick replied, "Willingly" (v. 1618), to the assignment of the task. Yet the author remarks, "It grieves me that he conducted her, for there was no safe-conduct to be had there" (vv. 1619–20). At a certain unidentified spot en route, the traveling party appears to have been taking a rest, with the men unarmed and apart from their horses, when the Poitevins suddenly sprang out. In the first instants of this attack, it is said, "Come what may, [the earl] sent the queen on to the castle" (vv. 1632–33). As Patrick was preparing to mount his charger, "a traitor, an assassin" (v. 1648), pierced him through the back with his lance. In this account of the episode, the men function as the subjects and Eleanor as the object. Henry brought his wife to Aquitaine with him, along with his barons and Patrick. He entrusted her to the earl, to accompany her from one place to another, a responsibility the earl gladly accepted. When the band came under attack, Patrick sent the queen to a nearby castle. Whether these actions were decided on by one man alone (Henry or Patrick) or by two men (Henry and Patrick), Eleanor had no say in them. Though she escaped to safety, she was clearly in danger, from which only the earl's quick action saved her. As someone caught in the fray between Henry and the Poitevin rebels, she depended on her husband's vassals to keep her safe from his enemies.

Like Eleanor, other women in this poem are depicted as vulnerable in war and in need of men's protection. Twenty-seven years earlier, when England was in the midst of the civil war known as the Anarchy, John Marshal, William's father, ensured that the Empress Matilda remained safe. In September of 1141, our author relates, "The empress besieged Winchester" (v. 168), which was allied with King Stephen against her. When news arrived that Stephen was sending a vast army to defend this site, we are told, "It did not seem to [Matilda] either fair or good" (v. 194). It is John Marshal who recommended that she abandon the siege and who "had her set off forthwith straight for Ludgershall" (vv. 197–99), his castle on the road from Winchester to Marlborough. In the course of this flight, John chastised the empress for riding sidesaddle, urging her to place her leg over the saddlebow so they could make faster progress. It is said, "She did this whether she liked it or not, since their enemies, who were harrying them close by, were causing them trouble" (vv. 222–24). He ultimately put her into the care of another man so that he could stay behind and hold off their pursuers, an act of bravery that ended up costing him an eye. In this incident, Matilda functions as a subject in a way that Eleanor does not. She is the one besieging Winchester, and she is the one who, on the counsel of her advisor, makes the decision to retreat from the town. Yet, as in Eleanor's journey, a man assumes the task of guiding the lady, he sends her off toward safety when they are attacked, he attempts to hold off the assailants in order to protect her retreat, and he is harmed in the process. Vulnerable as these royal ladies may be in the midst of civil strife, other women were even more at risk. The author speaks of the hazards women without guardians face when he refers to a battle where "many a maiden [was] orphaned, who, failing to get married, eventually went and shamed herself" (vv. 160–66) and "many a lady was left a hapless widow" (v. 163). As Eleanor and Matilda depend on their husband's and their own vassals to keep them safe from other knights, women overall depend on their fathers and husbands to protect them from other men's lust and ambition.

Yet in the *Histoire de Guillaume le Maréchal*, not only Eleanor, but the Marshal himself is represented as vulnerable, and he is in need of the queen's protection. During the battle with the Lusignans, the Marshal flew at the assailants to avenge his uncle Patrick's death, but more than sixty soldiers turned against him as he was pinioned against a hedge. One man stabbed him from behind, through the hedge, wounding him through the thighs with his lance. Taking him captive, the attackers compelled him to mount an ass and to ride off with them at a trot, despite the pain this brisk gait caused him, and they left his wound untreated. The author relates, "They were very wicked and mean-minded men, who knew the great pain he was in and yet had no pity for him" (vv. 1739–40), though one of their women, when hearing of his great merit, managed to secretly send him bandages. Eleanor may have been the object of Henry's and Patrick's actions, brought into the region, entrusted to the earl for a journey, and sent to a nearby castle, but it is also true that Patrick and the Marshal are the objects of the Poitevins' actions. They are ambushed and either killed in battle or wounded and taken prisoner. In the same passage in which the author expresses regret at how a battle left maidens orphaned and ladies widowed, he expresses regret at how, during this conflict, "Many a good knight of reputation was there wounded, killed, or taken prisoner" (vv. 162–63). While Eleanor had been in need of Patrick's and the Marshal's protection during her journey, the Marshal is in need of Eleanor's protection during his later captivity. The author relates, "The queen paid the ransom when she could for the Marshal, who had suffered much pain and tribulation in the wicked prison. . . . When the Marshal was delivered from prison and handed over to the queen, it was very pleasing to him, for no one from the time of Abel . . . had ever escaped from such cruel hands" (vv. 1859–69).

While the knights stand to rescue Eleanor when their party is attacked, Eleanor stands to rescue this knight when he is taken captive.[130] While the knights are able to rely on their superior physical prowess to protect the queen, she is able to rely on her superior financial resources to redeem them from prison.

As the *Histoire de Guillaume le Maréchal* continues, we see that Eleanor not only raises the Marshal from captivity to freedom but raises him from obscurity, in his uncle's service, to celebrity, at her own court. Our poet writes of the Marshal, "He reckoned that he was now living well [*en l'or*, literally, 'in the gold'], for Queen Eleanor [*Alienor*] arranged his affairs as she should for such a bachelor: horses, arms, money, and fine clothes she readily gave him, whoever might object, for she was very valiant and courtly" (vv. 1870–77). Later in the poem, the author will refer to "Queen Eleanor, who has her name from 'pure [*aili*]' and 'gold [*or*]'" (vv. 9507–8), as if her excellence of character is presaged in her very name. Eleanor is generous in providing the ransom that freed the Marshal, and she shows herself to be generous again in providing the accouterments he needs to distinguish himself. Though Eleanor is the first to recognize the Marshal's merit and to reward him for it, soon many others of the highest social rank follow her example. It was at this time, the author observes, that "His prowess, virtue, and largesse multiplied, so that kings and queens, dukes and earls, held him in great account" (vv. 1901–4). The Marshal would remain in Eleanor's service until 1170, when Henry had the fifteen-year-old Young King crowned and appointed this outstanding knight to take over his heir's education. As Georges Duby notes, Eleanor gave the Marshal his first break, drawing this landless knight to the attention of the king and, by extension, to the three sons of theirs who also became kings.[131] Years went by, but the bond between the queen and this knight remained strong. In 1189, when the Marshal returned to England following Henry's death and Richard's ascension to the throne, Eleanor, who had just been released from captivity, was delighted to see him: "Queen Eleanor, the king's mother, who was loyal to him and never wished his harm [*qui enterine / li fu, unques ne volt son mal*], gave the Marshal a most joyous welcome" (vv. 9911–14). While Eleanor may at one point have depended upon Earl Patrick's and the Marshal's physical protection, she now offers the Marshal her social patronage, from which he will greatly benefit.

Eleanor is not the only woman in this work who recognizes and rewards worthy men. As knights arrive at a castle in Joigny, in north-central France, for a tournament, a beautiful countess—presumably Adela or Adeliza, wife of William, Count of Joigny—and her ladies and damsels emerge and entertain their visitors, dancing and singing with them. We are told, "With her were ladies and damsels, so beautiful and well adorned that, as regards their beauty there was nothing to reproach, nor had they anything to learn about courtliness or good sense. The knights rose up from the ranks to meet them, as they should. It was their opinion that they had been improved through the ladies' arrival, and so they had, for all those there felt a doubling of strength in body and soul, and of their boldness and courage" (vv. 3459–70). When the fighting starts, it is said that, though all the knights sought to increase their reputation by dealing fine blows, "Those who had been at the dance with the ladies put their bodies, hearts, and souls into performing well" (vv. 3538–40) and that all were emboldened by the knowledge that the ladies were watching their feats of arms. At another tournament, this time in Pleurs in the northeast of what is now France, an unnamed lady bestows an enormous pike in prime condition on Hugh III, Duke of Burgundy, who decides to pass it on to another competitor "in order to double the honor of the lady who was in body and soul so worthy, courtly, and knowledgeable" (vv. 3050–54). The duke sends the pike to Philip I, Count of Flanders, who sends it to Ralph I, Count of Clermont, who in turn sends it to Theobald V, Count of Blois and Chartres. Finally, the Count of Flanders proposes that the pike be given to "the most worthy man" (vv. 3073–75), whom they all agree is the Marshal, given his superlative performance at the day's contest. While the tournament is an event at which knights like the Marshal strive to increase their "honor" (*enur*) and "reputation" (*pris*), it is also an event at which the lady strives to increase her "honor" (*enor*). While the men triumph by defeating opponents in battle, the lady too will triumph, she and the duke believe, by having her pike given to the man who has proved himself to be the best of them all. Both these men and this woman pride themselves on possessing the ability to identify men of worth. Like Eleanor, the ladies who socialize with the knights at the one tournament and the lady who donates the pike at the other recognize the merit of these men and reward them for it.

Having rescued Eleanor from potential abductors and having received her favor as a result, the Marshal is later accused of an extramarital affair with a queen. From what the author tells us, in 1182, five members of the Young King's entourage, including Adam d'Yquebeuf and Thomas de Coulonces, were envious of the Marshal, who, they felt, had risen too high, and they spread the rumor that he was conducting a liaison with Eleanor and Henry's daughter-in-law, Margaret of France, the Young King's wife.[132] A knight who was being recruited for their plot, when told of the love affair, exclaims, "Upon my soul! It could well be so; the Marshal

makes himself too much the master" (vv. 5393–94). If this man is inclined
to deem the Marshal guilty of this intrigue, it is because he regards him as
having too high an opinion of himself in a way that might make him aspire
to the affections of a royal lady. One of the Marshal's supporters later refers
to these conspirators as "slanderers [*losengiers*], who spoke ill of him out
of envy" (vv. 6428–30). While the Marshal at first attempts to ignore the
rumor about himself and the Young Queen, after the Young King grows
cool toward him, he offers to defend himself against the charge in a trial
by battle, but he is refused this opportunity. Throughout all this discussion, the alleged affair between the Marshal and the Young Queen is envisioned, not as a love relationship between a man and a woman, but as the
fracturing of a feudal relationship between a lord and a vassal. The Marshal insists that, if he had committed such a deed, he would have betrayed
the Young King, and such an act of treason would have been inconceiv-
able to him: "Never for one single day, hour, or moment did I have a mind
or a heart to commit such a foul outrage as those wicked men have attributed to me, who by their treason have undertaken this" (vv. 6591–99).
The bond of fealty that binds a lord and a vassal together is considered far
more significant than any potentially amorous bond between a man and a
woman, which is envisaged as a purely physical connection. No attention is
given to the Young Queen, who is never named, who is designated instead
only as the person to whom the Marshal is "doing it" (vv. 5243–44), and
whose sufferings as a result of this calumny are never mentioned. Though
the Marshal consorted publicly and joyfully with Eleanor, he was charged
falsely, we are told, with consorting privately and wretchedly with her
daughter-in-law.

Like the Marshal, Lancelot and Tristan are accused of adultery with a
queen in contemporaneous Arthurian romances. Just as the Marshal found
himself defamed by fellow knights, who resented his success, these two romance heroes suffer from their peers' envy. After Lancelot triumphs over
all his opponents at a tournament and earns King Arthur's praise, we are
told, "Those of the Round Table were so aroused by these words of King
Arthur that they hated Lancelot with a mortal hatred,"[133] to the point
where they plot to accuse him of an illicit relationship with Guinevere.
Tristan's enemies at court accuse him of adultery with Yseut, not out of
genuine concern for the king's honor, but "out of hatred for his prowess"[134]
and "out of envy."[135] Like the Marshal, who finds himself the victim of conspirators who spread lies about this knight and the Young Queen, these
two knights fall prey to "slanderers" (*losengiers*) who tell similar tales.[136]
Just as the Marshal attempts to exculpate himself from the charges levied

against him through a trial by battle but is refused the opportunity to do so, these two romance knights make a similar offer and receive a similar rebuff. And just as, throughout this episode in his life, the Marshal speaks with horror of the crime of which he is accused, Tristan and Lancelot express outrage at being charged with such a felony. If they were to abscond with their queen, they recognize that, as Lancelot tells Guinevere, "There is no one who would not openly know your shame and my great disloyalty,"[137] and, as Tristan puts it, "There would be no worthy man in the world, if he knew the truth, who would not hold him as a traitor and a disloyal man."[138] For these knights, as for the Marshal, the most important bond in society is that between a lord and a vassal, and the breaking of that bond through a vassal's liaison with his lord's wife would constitute an unforgivable act of treason. Yet, as any reader of these romances will remember, however Lancelot and Tristan may present themselves to their fellow knights at court, they *are* secretly engaged in love affairs with their queens. Because the *Histoire de Guillaume le Maréchal* was most likely recited to the Marshal's household on the anniversary of his death,[139] it focuses exclusively on the public aspects of this knight's career, including his glorious deeds in battles and tournaments, and not on his private love life, including possible extramarital affairs, which would be inappropriate to mention in such circumstances. While these romances give us insight into both the outer and the inner aspects of their heroes' lives, this history stays on the outer level.

The *Histoire de Guillaume le Maréchal* would not have the last word on the relations between Eleanor and the Marshal. The traditional English ballad "Queen Eleanor's Confession," which has been dated to anywhere between the thirteenth and sixteenth centuries,[140] builds on the alleged affection of the queen for the Marshal, representing the knight, no longer simply as her protector and her protégé, but as her lover. As the ballad begins, Eleanor is ill and afraid of dying, and she sends for two friars from France in order to make her final confession. When the king hears of the queen's intention, he summons the Marshal to him, and he proposes that they disguise themselves as these friars so that they can hear what she will have to say. The Marshal only consents to this proposal when the king swears that, whatever the queen may confess, he will not suffer repercussions from it. Eleanor initially suspects that these friars are actually English lords and threatens to hang them if that turns out to be the case, but she finally accepts that they are who they say they are and confesses to them a long series of grievous sins, including the loss of her virginity to the Marshal. She relates, "Oh, the first vile sin I did commit / Tell it I will to thee; / I fell in love with the Earl Marshal, / As he brought me over the sea / . . . / Earl Marshal had my virgin dower / Beneath this cloth of gold." She gestures at two children playing nearby, one of whom she identifies as the Marshal's, whom she says she loves most of all, and one of whom she identifies as Henry's, whom she loves far less. Enraged by his wife's confession, Henry pulls off his friar's gown and reveals himself to be her husband, at which point, we are told, "The Queen . . . / Cried that she was betrayed." Looking over his left shoulder with a "grim look,"[141] the king asserts that, if he had not made the oath to the Marshal, this man would be dead. The ballad is, needless to say, not historically accurate. Despite her alleged predilection for younger men, Eleanor is not likely to have had an affair with the Marshal, who was twenty-four or -five years her junior, let alone to have had an illegitimate child with him.[142] Yet if the author suspects more to have happened between the Marshal and Eleanor than was generally perceived, it is because it makes a kind of literary sense for the most notable knight of the day, already rumored to have dallied with a Plantagenet queen, to have had a liaison with that dynasty's most notable lady.

In the final analysis, the Eleanor we see at court provides an important counterbalance to the Eleanor we saw on crusade. When the queen was in the Holy Land, she was represented as recognizing and rewarding men of great merit, whether her uncle, Raymond of Antioch, or the great Saladin, but she was condemned for betraying her husband, the French king, in doing so. In Bernart de Ventadorn's *vida*, in Andreas's *De amore*, and in the *Histoire de Guillaume le Maréchal*, she is again depicted as recognizing and rewarding men of value or as advising other ladies on how to do so. With the help of her patronage, Bernart will go on to become one of the most celebrated troubadours of his day and the Marshal one of the most famous knights of history, just as the Eleanor of Andreas's treatise imagines that men in general are improved through their ladies' affection. A woman's love take the form, not of a subjective, sentimental feeling, but of an objective, rational evaluation of the suitor in question, which ascertains his excellence or at least potential excellence. Its purpose is, not to provide her with sexual or emotional gratification, but to cultivate her lover's best qualities through her favor and encouragement. It is a kind of philanthropy, in which she aspires to raise a man up personally and professionally through her financial and social resources at the same time that she increases the esteem in which she is held by her peers through her generosity. Yet though the accounts of Eleanor's interactions with men of her own social status echo the accounts of her interactions with the men who serve her, they could also not be more different. Whereas Raymond of Antioch and Geoffrey Plantagenet were said to have abused and possibly raped the queen, these more lowly ranked men treat her gently, even, in the Marshal's case, rescuing her from other men's assaults. Whereas Henry was said to have been attracted to her wealth and lands, these men are said to appreciate her own excellence. In the reprieve they offer from her relationships with her masculine peers, Eleanor's interactions with her protégés look ahead to her relationships with her sons.

THE QUEEN MOTHER

Authority, Maternal and Seigneurial

When Eleanor was in her fifties, sixties, and seventies, with her children grown, she found herself the mother of four sons who were generally regarded as exceptional in their abilities but cursed. Henry the Young King was widely praised for his accomplishments on the tournament circuit, where he stood out for his knightly prowess and his generosity toward his men as well as for his beauty, grace, and charm, yet he would die at twenty-eight without ever having ruled. Richard was one of the principal leaders of the Third Crusade, regarded by Christians and Muslims alike as among the greatest warriors of his age due to his personal courage and strength in battle, yet after ten years on the English throne, he would be killed at forty-one by a freak crossbow shot at the siege of an insignificant castle. Geoffrey, the only one among the brothers never to be crowned king, was often considered the most intelligent and eloquent of them all as well as a formidable military and political tactician, yet he passed away at twenty-seven. Neither the Young King nor Richard would leave a legitimate heir, and Geoffrey's only son, Arthur, would be dead by the age of sixteen. Only John would live long enough to ascend to the throne, produce a prince to carry on his legacy, and survive his mother, but he was generally regarded as the worst of the lot. Among his various wicked deeds, he was believed to have killed Arthur in order to eliminate his claim to the crown. As the sons were unfortunate individually, the family was unfortunate as a whole. The sons clashed with their father, the brothers with the brothers, and the uncle with the nephew, to the point where Richard of Devizes compares the clan to "the confused house of Oedipus."[1] Yet, as antagonistic as these sons may have been toward their father and each other, they were united in their common affection for Eleanor.

Eleanor's sons had reason to cherish her as much as they did. As we shall see, her influence on them was said to be so great that, when the Young King rose up against Henry, it was with her encouragement, and when Henry imprisoned her for as long as he lived, it was because he feared her continuing sway over their children. Indeed, in some of his last words, the Young King requested that his father treat his mother more kindly. As soon as Richard became king, he released Eleanor from prison and endowed her with considerable wealth independent of the crown. When he was absent from the kingdom, he counted on her to keep the realm under control. Though John was notoriously capricious in his behavior toward his vassals, he was loyal to Eleanor, whose help he depended on as he consolidated his hold on his kingdom. The one outstanding act of military leadership he ever performed—the relief of the siege of Mirebeau—was designed to rescue her when she was in danger. If Eleanor was as valuable to her sons as she was, it was because she could advise and support them, but, as a woman, and one without Angevin blood, she could never supplant them on the throne. For that reason, their self-interest was her self-interest and their success was her success. Whichever one among them might be king, she remained the queen, recognized and respected as such by all, and she provided a continuity between one man's reign and the next.

Because whatever power Eleanor enjoyed in England was dependent on her sons, her political role was intensely personal. In the early nineteenth century, the literary critic William Hazlitt recalled how, when William Shakespeare's Coriolanus finds himself rejected by the people of Rome, his mother Volumnia cries out for pestilence to strike the city. Hazlitt comments, "This is but natural: it is but natural for a mother to have more regard for her son than for a whole city. . . . The great have private feelings of their own, to which the interests of humanity and justice must courtesy."[2] This being the case, he continues, "The city should be left to take some care of itself. The care of the state cannot . . . be safely entrusted to maternal affection."[3] As a mother, Volumnia indulges her private feelings for her child at the public expense. For that reason, Hazlitt proposes, she should have no role in politics, which should be the realm, not of particular values, like one's child's well-being, but of universal values, like "humanity and justice." If one accepts this critic's way of thinking, it was "but natural" for Eleanor to be more concerned for the Young King, Richard, or John than for England. When a king dies, she would not suggest, as William Marshal is said to have done to Hubert Walter, Archbishop of Canterbury, after Richard's death, "My lord, we should be thinking of choosing quickly . . . a man to make king,"[4] and then go on to consider the merits of different claimants to the throne. She would always advocate to have her son in this position, however promising or unpromising he looked to be. As a mother, it may seem, Eleanor must love her child, not the kingdom.

Yet in the Middle Ages, a political role was necessarily a personal one. The opposition William Hazlitt sets up between the mother and the state, the private good and the public good, was not recognizable in the twelfth century in the same way that it would be today. The public bond between lord and vassal or king and subject that structured so much of political life was also a private attachment defined, not just by duty, but by love. As we shall see, what was good for the king was assumed to be good for his people, and what was a source of suffering for the people was assumed to be a source of concern for their ruler. One's status in society was determined, not by "rights," bestowed by God on humanity, in all their impersonality and universality, but by "privileges," granted by a ruler to this monastery or that town, to this guild or that family, in all their personality and particularity. Insofar as Eleanor functions as a public figure, it is, not only because she is the mother of the country's kings, but because she is the ruler of the kingdom's subjects, including the imprisoned and the poor, with whose sufferings she commiserates. When she acts to defend her son, as she sees it, she does not overlook "humanity and justice," as Hazlitt imagines someone like her to do, but, on the contrary, appreciates these principles more than the ambitious and self-interested men around her do. Maternal love does not blind her, but rather, enables her to apprehend a moral truth that those who are supposedly impartial cannot see.

THE YOUNG KING

In June of 1170, when Henry *fils* was fifteen years old, King Henry had his eldest son crowned, an action he was soon to regret. As his heir, the Young King was expected to succeed to his father's titles as King of England, Duke of Normandy, and Count of Anjou. If Henry had him recognized as king during his own lifetime, it was to ensure a smooth transition between his own reign and that of his son, in contrast to the years of turbulence that had preceded his own assumption of the throne. But Henry had arranged for Richard to become Count of Poitou and Duke of Aquitaine through his inheritance from his mother and for Geoffrey to become Duke of Brittany through his marriage to Constance of Brittany, the heiress to that duchy. Though the Young King was due to inherit far more lands than his brothers, for the time being he had none to call his own, and he could expect to have to subsist on an allowance from his father for the foreseeable future. In November of 1172, when he was eighteen years old, the Young King and his wife, Margaret, met with Louis, Margaret's father, who is said to have encouraged his son-in-law to press his case for his own lands, but Henry proved unbending. In February and March of 1173, when he was accompanying his parents in a tour of their continental territories, he is alleged to have become so angry with his father that he could not converse with him peaceably on any topic.[5] At a certain point during their travels, Raymond V, Count of Toulouse, who was in their company, took Henry aside and warned him that "His sons and his wife were conspiring against him."[6] Around March 8, perhaps at Chinon, perhaps at Alençon, perhaps at Argentan, the Young King escaped from the royal party at night, eluding the guards Henry had assigned to watch him, and fled to Louis, who was then at Chartres. He had decided to claim by force the lands he could not obtain by paternal bequest, and he would enjoy his mother's support in doing so.

In the accounts we possess of the sons' rebellion against Henry in 1173 and 1174, the chroniclers articulate two competing political theories. According to the first theory, what is most important in the state is the preservation of a fixed, stable social order with a single center of power. In marriage, the authority of a husband is to be promoted over his wife just as, in a family, that of a father is to be promoted over his son, and in society, that of a lord is to be promoted over his vassals. In all these cases, the dominant party is expected to treat the subordinate party with love and consideration, so that he will experience that domination, not as oppression, but as caretaking. According to the second political theory, however, what is most important is the recognition of multiple poles of power, even if that recognition destabilizes the social order. The authority of a husband over his wife becomes complicated when that wife is a duchess and a countess, with her own lands and her own court. The authority of a father over his son becomes complicated when that son is a crowned king with his own retainers. The authority of a lord over his vassals becomes complicated when those vassals are themselves minor lords, desirous of ruling over their own territories. What looks like an intolerable insubordination from the perspective of the husband, father, or lord looks like a laudable desire for freedom and independence from the point of view of the wife, son, or vassal.

The major chroniclers depict Eleanor as having instigated her sons' rebellion against Henry. During the court's circuit of Henry's continental lands, Eleanor's advisors, Ralph of Châtellerault, seigneur of Faye-la-Vineuse, her uncle and seneschal, and Hugh II, seigneur of Sainte-Maure, acted "on the counsel, as it is said [*sicut dicitur*], of this queen" when they encouraged the Young King to assert himself against his father.[7] Returning to Poitiers, Eleanor rejoined the fifteen-year old Richard and the fourteen-year old Geoffrey, who were living in her custody at this time. It may have been she who sent these younger sons to join their elder brother at Louis's court, "so that they would be against the king their father,"[8] or it may have been her eldest son who doubled back to the Poitevin capital to retrieve them, "conniving, it is said, with their mother [*conivente ut dicitur matre*]."[9] Whoever induced the younger sons to leave for Louis's court, Ralph of Diceto, a dean of Saint Paul's cathedral, states, "Richard, Duke of Aquitaine, and Geoffrey, Duke of Brittany, the king's younger sons, on the counsel of their Queen Mother, that is Eleanor, as it is said [*consilio matris suae reginae, scilicet Alienor, sicut dicitur*], chose to follow their brother rather than their father."[10] Throughout the spring of 1173, we are told that the Young King and his brothers acted "on the counsel of their mother, it was said, Queen Eleanor [*consilio matris suae, ut dicebatur, Alineor reginae*]."[11] The princes function as subjects, in the nominative case, while Eleanor, though the instigator of their actions, is subordinated to them, with her "counsel" (*consilium*) introduced in the ablative. Equally strikingly, Eleanor's participation in the plot is referred to, not as a fact, but as an allegation: it is, not that the sons acted on her counsel, but that they acted, "as it is said" (*ut dicitur*), on her counsel.[12] Louis is also alleged to have influenced the Young King and his brothers,[13] but he is typically depicted as a subject of the plot, and his involvement is represented, not as a rumor, but as a fact. Roger of Howden, who was a clerk in Henry's service, writes, for example, "The nefarious authors of this treason were Louis, King of France, and even, as was said by some [*ut a quibusdam dicebatur*], Eleanor, Queen of England, and Ralph of Faye."[14] Though Roger attributes agency to both Louis and Eleanor, he distinguishes between Louis, whom he portrays without hesitation to be one of the originators of the conspiracy, and the queen, whom he represents only tentatively as the Young King's partner in crime, along with her chief advisor. While Louis functions as a principal player, Eleanor acts, grammatically and substantively, as an accessory to her sons' deeds, and only a possible accessory at that.[15]

Though the chroniclers qualify their depiction of Eleanor's role in these events, Peter of Blois, a diplomat in service to Henry and the author of the most celebrated collection of letters of the Middle Ages, does not hesitate to charge the queen with rebelling against her husband. In an epistle addressed to Eleanor in the name of Rotrou, Archbishop of Rouen, presumably at the behest of the king,[16] Peter imagines the union of husband and wife to be corporeal. He recalls how in the Book of Genesis, woman was created out of man's rib, united to man "in one flesh" as of Creation and subjected to him after the Fall, and how, in Saint Paul's Letter to the Ephesians, "The man is the head of the woman."[17] As Peter sees it, the physical union of man and woman in Creation and the sacramental union of husband and wife in marriage bring about a kind of moral union, whereby the two spouses are joined in one will (which is the husband's will): "Since conjugal parties are made into one flesh, it is necessary that the union of the bodies be accompanied by a unity of spirits and equality in consent." Yet Eleanor, Peter warns, has failed to recognize that, in marrying, she became one with her husband and that, as a result, she must submit her will to his. He informs her, "Though you are a most prudent woman, you have turned away from your husband, side has receded from side, and the limb does not serve the head" (ep. 154, col. 448). The wife who fails to obey her spouse is like an arm or a leg that fails to recognize the body of which it is a part and the head to which it should be subjected. In order to repair this disruption of the biblical ordering of the sexes, Peter urges her, "Return . . . to your husband, whom you are bound to submit to and live with. . . . Return, . . . illustrious queen, to your husband and our lord." He recalls that, even as Saint Paul had enjoined wives to obey their husbands as their head, he had enjoined husbands to love their wives as they love their own bodies: "Whoever loves his wife, loves himself." For this reason, if Eleanor returns to Henry, he assures her, "We are most certain that he will exhibit to you every kind of love and the fullest assurance of safety" (ep. 154. col. 449). The relationship Peter imagines between these two spouses is not equal, insofar as one party obeys the other, but it is complementary, insofar as the party that obeys will be cherished and treated well by the party to which it submits.

While the chroniclers offer little comment on Eleanor's incitement of her sons to rebellion, they do condemn the sons for rising up against their father. So unnatural is the rebellion of the sons against their sire, as they see it, that, again, it resembles the rebellion of a body against itself. The chronicler of Melrose writes that "A dispute and a war, which may almost be styled inexorable, arose between the belly and the viscera, between the parent and the child, between Henry the Elder and Henry the Younger of England."[18] Roger of Howden cites a letter that William II, King of Sicily, wrote at this time to Henry, his father-in-law, where he expresses astonishment that "The order of humanity having been forgotten and the law of nature undone, the son has risen up against the father, the begotten against the begetter, the viscera have been moved to intestine war, the entrails have had recourse to arms, and—a new prodigy taking place, unheard-of in our times—the flesh has raged against the blood, and the blood has sought means to shed itself."[19] Unprecedented as this attack of son on father, body on body, and self on self may be, chroniclers such as Walter Map[20] and William of Newburgh[21] nevertheless compare the Young King's revolt against Henry, with the encouragement of the French, to Absalom's revolt against David, with the encouragement of Ahithophel. Dante Alighieri echoes this analogy when he represents Bertran de Born, one of the Young King's allies, carrying his severed head about like a lantern in the Circle of the False Counselors in Hell. The head addresses the shocked Dante Pilgrim, saying, "Know that I am Bertran de Born, the one who gave to the Young King bad advice. I made the father and the son enemies. Ahithophel did not do more with Absalom and David through his wicked goading. Because I severed persons thus conjoined, I carry my own brain, alas, severed from its starting-point, which is in my trunk."[22] For a man to separate father and son is akin to him separating the head from the body, as Bertran's mutilated form reflects. The sons' defiance of their father, to which Eleanor has goaded them, is envisioned as the part's defiance of the whole.

Just as Peter of Blois reproaches Eleanor for rebelling against her husband, he reproaches her for encouraging her sons to rebel against their father. In a letter to the Young King, again in the voice of Rotrou, Archbishop of Rouen, Peter imagines the union of father and son, like that between husband and wife, to be corporeal. The son was not created from the father's rib as the wife was created from her husband's side, but he does derive "from his flesh and blood, . . . by the benefit of seminal origin" (ep. 33, col. 110). The son who fails to recognize the unity of the child and his father is, again, like flesh and blood that fail to recognize the body of which they are a part. In his letter to Eleanor, Peter complains, not only that "You have turned away from your husband, side has receded from side, and the limb does not serve the head," but, "what is far worse, you allow the viscera of your lord king and yourself to rise up against their father" (ep. 154, col. 448). In order to repair this disruption of the biblical ordering of the generations, Peter not only recommends that Eleanor return to her husband, but he urges, "Return with your sons to your husband. . . . Turn back, so that neither you nor your sons may be suspect. . . . Warn your sons, I ask, that they be subject and devoted to their father" (ep. 154, col. 449). The very fact that Peter writes this letter to Eleanor shows that he deems her to have influence over her sons, which she has used badly in urging them to rebel against their father, but which she might use well in making them obey him. As he assumes that should Eleanor return to her husband, Henry will welcome her back, he assumes that should the Young

King return to his father, the king will embrace him with the affection that fathers naturally bear toward their children. For that reason, in his letter to the Young King, he advises, "Be subject to him, and he will subjugate his will to you in all things" (ep. 47, col. 137). The relationship he imagines between father and son is, again, not equal, insofar as one party must obey the other, but it is, again, complementary, insofar as the party that obeys will be loved and be taken care of by the party that commands.

In rebelling against her husband and inciting her sons to rebel against their father, Eleanor overlooked, it is alleged, the effects of this insurrection on the existing political and social order. Henry is not only her husband and the father of her sons, but the king. The chroniclers do not mention the political effects of Eleanor's disobedience, but Peter of Blois reminds her that when she rebels against him and encourages her sons to do the same, she is fanning, not just a family squabble, but a civil war, whose conflagration will cause death and destruction throughout their lands. Urging her to reconcile with Henry, Peter adds, "If our pleas do not stir you to this, may at least the affliction of the people, the threatened pressure upon the Church, and the desolation of the kingdom stir you. . . . Unless you return to your husband, you will be the occasion of general ruin." As the negative effects of her and her children's rebellion are now felt, not only by themselves, but by the people over whom they rule, the positive effects of their submission will be felt throughout the kingdom. He expresses hope that "By your reconciliation, quietude may be restored to those who labor, and, by your return, happiness may come back to all" (ep. 154, col. 448). The result of this restored relationship, he believes, will be, not oppression, as we might imagine it nowadays, but peace and, as a result of that peace, contentment. Richard FitzNeal, Henry's treasurer, also links the rebellion of Eleanor, the sons, and the vassals when he asks in his *Dialogus de Scaccario* (1176–83), "Since without cause a wife was angry with her husband, sons with their father, and menials with their lord, might you not well say that a man was in rebellion against himself?"[23] The resistance of a wife to a husband, children to a father, and subjects to their lord was again seen to be as contrary to their own interests as would be the resistance of the parts of a body to the whole. The patriarchal order is ultimately regarded as beneficial, not just to the patriarch, but to everyone under his natural jurisdiction, as that order ensures the integrity and harmony of society.

Yet when Henry took Eleanor prisoner, he did not treat her with the forgiveness and affection that Peter of Blois had anticipated. At the beginning of May 1173, just two months after the Young King had fled to Louis, Eleanor learned that Henry's men were in pursuit of her, and she attempted to escape them by adopting a masculine disguise, though in vain. Gervase of Canterbury relates, "When Queen Eleanor, her [women's] clothes having changed, followed her sons, she was captured by those following them."[24] Brought to Rouen, she was kept in the Norman capital for a year. In July of 1174, as the theater of the war was shifting across the Channel, Henry set sail for England, and he brought Eleanor back with him. The royal couple's youngest children, John and Joan, and the Young King's wife, Margaret, were on the ship with them, but the atmosphere on board was hardly amicable, accompanied as they were by other noble rebels being transported across the sea in irons. By September of that year, the princes' uprising had collapsed and the Young King, Richard, and Geoffrey were obliged to seek terms with their father. Geoffrey du Breuil of Vigeois writes, "After the sons, humbling themselves with their mother in the presence of their father, submitted themselves to the king, [Henry] enclosed his own wife, the mother of his sons, in England, in Salisbury Tower, for many years, fearing a renewed plot."[25] Though it had been the Young King and, to a lesser extent, Richard and Geoffrey who had waged war against Henry, and though Eleanor as well as her sons is represented as seeking his forgiveness, the king did not forgive his wife, given that, from what this chronicler represents, he held her responsible for his sons' rebellion and worried that if free, she might lead them to rise up again. Gervase of Canterbury likewise refers to "the king having loathing of his queen, whom he had held in custody in well-guarded strongholds, for it was said that the aforesaid sedition emanated the queen's counsel"[26] and to Eleanor as "kept in harsh custody for many years."[27] Gerald of Wales suggests that Henry would have liked to have had the queen confined to an abbey.[28] As the years went by and Henry allowed his sons and many of their fellow rebels to live in freedom and prosperity, the contrast between his leniency toward his children and his continued severity toward his wife became all the more stark. Far from aiming to restore their relationship in a way that would bring peace and happiness to all, as Peter of Blois had promised, Henry punished Eleanor more severely than he did his enemies at arms.

Ten years into Eleanor's incarceration, the Young King was dying, and he sought to reconcile with Henry. The twenty-eight-year old prince had fallen ill with dysentery in his camp near Limoges, where he was once again waging war against his father. Struck with remorse now that he was in extremis, he sent word to Henry, begging his forgiveness for his misdeeds and requesting that he visit him. The king was tempted to accede to his son's appeal, but his advisors persuaded him not to do so out of fear of treachery, if not from the Young King himself, then from his men. Instead, Henry sent his son a ring, it was said, "as a token of regard and forgiveness . . . [and] as a pledge of his fatherly affection."[29] Meanwhile, back in his own camp, the Young King was confessing his sins and exchanging his fine clothing for the hairshirt of a penitent. He placed a cord around his neck, beseeched Jesus Christ to have mercy on his soul, and had himself laid on a bed of ashes. It was either after he had received the viaticum[30] or after he had kissed his father's ring[31] that he expired. According to Robert of Torigni, in a letter the Young King sent to his father before he died, he asked "that he take pity [*misereretur*] upon his mother, the Queen of the English; his wife, the sister of Philip, King of the French; and his knights and servants, to whom he had promised many things."[32] While some chroniclers expressed skepticism at the Young King's deathbed conversion,[33] Henry is said to have been greatly grieved at the loss of his son, despite all his misbehavior. According to the *Histoire de Guillaume le Maréchal*, a captain from the Young King's mercenaries came to Henry and demanded payment of a debt incurred by his late lord. Though Henry was at first indignant at this petition, he finally replied, with tears in his eyes, "My son has cost me much more than that, and would that he were still costing me."[34] Though Henry settled the Young King's debts and though he eventually reimbursed his widow for her dowerlands in England, he did not fulfill his son's request that he take pity on Eleanor, whom he continued to keep imprisoned.

Having sought to reconcile with Henry as he was dying, the Young King, it is said, sought to console Eleanor once he was dead. After the Young King expired, his confessor, Thomas Agnellus, Archdeacon of Wells Cathedral, traveled to Salisbury, where Eleanor was being kept at that time, to inform her of her eldest son's demise, but she had already heard this unhappy news. He relates, "In the days when the blessed man migrated to the Lord, he appeared in dreams to his mother (as we have learned through her report) with a face happier and an expression more serene than [mortal] men." In Eleanor's dreams, the Young King was wearing two crowns, the one above of inestimable splendor and brightness, which his mother understood to represent the celestial realm, and the one below darker and dimmer, which she knew to signify the earthly realm. Crowned during his life but never able to rule, the Young King is now doubly crowned after death, with the celestial diadem of someone assured of eternal blessedness overshadowing the mere terrestrial diadem, whose authority he was never able to exercise. Thomas states, "The mother, exhilarated by this vision, as a matron perspicacious in intelligence, understood the mystery of the vision, and supported with patience the death of her son . . . more quickly in mind, having hope and faith in Christ himself that he was crowned in celestial glory."[35] However distressed Eleanor may have been to learn of her eldest son's death, the archdeacon indicates that she was gladdened to discover through this vision that he had ascended into Paradise and that, having been deprived of kingship during his life, he was now glorying in this position after death. In a life generally not distinguished by great piety, it is telling that the one mystical experience Eleanor is said to have undergone took the form of a vision of her eldest son returning to reassure her of his salvation and his heavenly coronation.

Even as many of Eleanor's contemporaries blamed her for her role in her sons' rebellion, others admired the eagle-like ferocity of character she showed at this time. According to Merlin, whose prophecies were collected in Geoffrey of Monmouth's *Historia regum Britanniae* (1134–36), "The eagle of the broken covenant [*aquila rupti foederis*] will gild the bridle and rejoice in a third nesting."[36] During these years, Eleanor was regularly identified as the eagle of the broken covenant of which Merlin spoke because both of her marriages were broken, that with Louis through their divorce and that with Henry "through carceral custody."[37] Her only hope was held to lie in her sons, who are the eaglets she has nested.[38] Richard of Poitiers addresses Eleanor as "bipartite eagle [*aquila bispertita*]" because her power was based on both sides of the English Channel. Now that she has been taken prisoner, he asks her, "Tell me, bipartite eagle, tell me, where were you when your eaglets, flying from their nest, dared to raise their talons against the King of the North Wind [*Regem Aquilonis*]?"[39] He sees Eleanor as sufficiently attached to her sons to incite them to rise up against their father, the "North Wind" (*Aquilo*), and these sons as sufficiently attached to Eleanor to come to her aid during this time of distress.[40] Ralph of Diceto similarly interprets Eleanor as the eagle "because she spread her two wings over two kingdoms, that of the French as well as that of the English."[41] Matthew Paris, building on Ralph's chronicle, would later describe the queen as "Eleanor, . . . an eagle because rapacious and regal [*Alienora, . . . aquila quia rapax et regalis*]."[42] As the queen is a figure of imperial majesty, a soaring bird of prey who extends her wings over two realms through her two marriages, she expects her eaglets to be similarly dominant in their realm. When Ralph of Diceto mentions how Ralph of Faye and Hugh of Sainte-Maure encouraged the Young King's revolt on Eleanor's counsel, he adds that they did so by "suggesting it to be unseemly for a king to be seen not to exercise appropriate dominion in the kingdom."[43] Once the Young King was crowned, the chronicler suggests, Eleanor felt that it was appropriate for him to seek a kingdom over which to rule and even that it would be shameful for him not to do so. Acting on Eleanor's encouragement, her eldest son did not defer to his father or to the social order that such filial deference reflects, as Peter of Blois would have had him do, but only because he sought to pursue his own, laudable ambition. As Eleanor would dream of the Young King wearing a crown, she wanted her son to be able to rule.

When the few chroniclers sympathetic to Eleanor at this time mention her role in her sons' insurrection, they stress, not her rebellion against Henry's authority, but the loss of her own authority, as Countess of Poitou and Duchess of Aquitaine. Richard of Poitiers reminds Eleanor, "You stirred [your sons], as we hear [*ut audimus*], to afflict their father vehemently. For this reason you have been carried away from your land and taken to a land you do not know." If Eleanor suffers in captivity, he imagines, it is not so much because she is being kept in poor conditions (for she was not), but because she is being kept in exile from her native lands and deprived of the court that had surrounded here there. Richard continues, "The notes of your lyre have changed into lamentation and your flute into the sounds of mourning. Formerly you lived in luxury and refinement, you enjoyed the taste of royal freedom and numerous riches, and your young maidens sang their sweet songs to you with the music of tambourine and harp. You rejoiced in the melodies of the flutes and delighted in the rhythm of drums."[44] By contrasting the sound of music, with which Eleanor was formerly soothed, and the sound of laments, with which she now grieves, Richard stresses, not the behavior that led to her captivity, but the captivity itself, where she is deprived of the pleasures she once enjoyed. Having once presided over her own court, where she had been able to spend her wealth as she pleased on skilled jongleurs and sweet-voiced maidens, she is now no longer able to exercise patronage and to surround herself with courtly entertainments. Thomas Agnellus likewise complains that, as her incarceration stretched out for many years, "Much time passed away in her soul with bitterness and anguish."[45] Eleanor's supporters shift the focus from what the queen had done to what was done unto her, from her offense to what they perceive as the excessive punishment of that offense, and from the few months of her rebellion to the many years of her imprisonment.[46]

As the sympathetic chroniclers had predicted, it became clear that Eleanor's release from captivity would come, not from Henry, but from her remaining children. In the years after the Young King's death, her situation gradually improved, perhaps because she seemed less of a threat to her husband. Though she remained under house arrest,[47] between 1184 and 1186, she enjoyed occasional visits in Winchester, Windsor, or Argentan in

Normandy with her daughter Matilda of Saxony and her family, who had been exiled from Germany as the result of a conflict with Emperor Frederick Barbarossa. Yet Eleanor's liberation would ultimately come, not from her daughter, but from Richard, who was the "third nesting" in whom the eagle was said to rejoice. After her first two sons had died, Ralph of Diceto writes, "Richard, having been indicated as the son of the third nesting, strove in all things to exalt the maternal name."[48] Richard may have vied against his father in a way that tarnished his reputation among good men, Ralph continues, "but he took care to show to his mother all the honor he could, so that by obedience to his mother he could atone for the offenses he committed against his father."[49] Indeed, in April of 1185, when Richard had fortified Poitou against Henry, the king ordered Eleanor to be brought to a family conference in Alençon, in Normandy, and there he demanded that Richard restore this county to his mother, including all its castles, "because they were her inheritance." According to Roger of Howden, he warned that if Richard did not do this, "The queen his mother would empty out his land with a great army, in order to devastate it,"[50] though a later version of the chronicle clarifies that this threat is coming, not from Eleanor, but from himself,[51] as one would expect at this time. In any event, Richard is said to have given Poitou "to his mother" and to have returned to his father "like a gentle son."[52] Having been made Count of Poitou and Duke of Aquitaine in 1169, "by the will of his mother,"[53] he is willing to relinquish this land, but only to Eleanor, who seems to hold it in escrow for him. Whatever other chronicles might indicate, it is clear that the sons were, in fact, filial—but to their maternal, not their paternal, parent.

In July of 1189, after sixteen years of imprisonment, Eleanor was finally freed. It is not clear where in England she was when the information arrived of Henry's death, but by the time William Marshal arrived in the country, having been sent by Richard to release her, "He found Queen Eleanor . . . in Winchester, now delivered and more at ease than she was used to being."[54] Roger of Howden writes that Eleanor, having been released after many years of imprisonment, "proceeded as it pleased her [*sicut ei placuit*], leading a queenly court from city to city and from castle to castle."[55] As Richard was still making his way from the Continent to England, it was Eleanor who traveled about the kingdom and received oaths of fealty from its notable citizens "to Lord Richard, King of England, son of Lord King Henry and Lady Queen Eleanor [*dominae Alienor reginae*]."[56] (The wording of the oath could also be interpreted as "to Lord Richard, King of England, son of Lord King Henry, and *to* Lady Queen Eleanor.") Together with a great crowd of bishops, abbots, and noblemen, she awaited Richard's arrival at Winchester, where he appeared on August 14, to great acclaim. While the new king was tempted to travel up to the border between England and Wales in order to subdue some unrest that had broken out on the marches, Eleanor advised him to continue directly to London for his coronation: "Truly he was recalled by the counsel of his mother, that is, Queen Eleanor."[57] The group proceeded to London, where Richard was crowned on September 3, at Westminster Abbey. By the king's order, there were no women allowed at the coronation, yet over one hundred pounds were spent on the clothing, furs, and horses for Eleanor and her entourage so that they might make a magnificent impression. At the time of Richard's accession to the throne, chroniclers saw the prophecy that the third nesting would give the eagle joy as being fulfilled.[58] As Matthew Paris explains, "Richard her third son, signified by the 'third nesting,' was his mother's joy, who, as it is said, freed her from the squalor of prison."[59] However much Eleanor may have been seen as disrupting the political and social order when she supported her sons against her husband, now that her son has inherited the throne, she is seen as confirming that order.

Insofar as Eleanor's defenders believed that the queen should play a public role in the Angevin domain, it was, not as a supporter of the existing political and social order, but as a liberator of those subjected to oppression. When Roger of Howden is describing Eleanor's procession through England after her release from prison, he writes, "Messengers having been sent throughout all the counties of England, she ordered that all captives be set free from prison and confinement for the soul of Henry, her husband, inasmuch as she had learned by experience in her own person that confinement is repellent to men and that it is a most delightful refreshment of the spirits to emerge from it."[60] It was common for a ruler to set prisoners free in the course of such a procession as an impersonal act of munificence, but Roger represents Eleanor's liberation of these captives as a personal expression of her joy at having been cast loose from a similar confinement. She perceives her past sorrow in captivity and her present happiness in freedom, not as unique to herself, despite her uniquely exalted status as queen, but as common to all captives, and she wishes to extend her happiness to all. As a result, Roger continues, "She gave directions, by the command of her son, the duke,"[61] that various parties who had been treated harshly by her late husband's judicial procedures should be reprieved. The patriarchal order is not beneficial to people under the patriarch's jurisdiction when it leads to excessive or irregular punishment of those who rebel against that order; for that reason, Eleanor suggests, this new order, in which she will play such a prominent role, will be distinguished, not only by justice, but by mercy.

RICHARD THE LIONHEART

While Eleanor ruled alongside Richard as queen dowager, the early years of his reign were not without their challenges. In response to Saladin's conquest of Jerusalem, Richard and Philip, the current King of France, resolved to embark on what would become the Third Crusade. Taking leave of their kingdoms, they spent the winter of 1190–1191 in Messina, in Sicily, along with Richard's sister, Joan, the widow of William II, King of Sicily. William of Tyre's continuator observes, "There was great love between the King of England and the King of France on the journey, as they had sworn together to be loyal companions and keep good faith with one another.... Had their love lasted, they would have been honored for all time, and Holy Christendom would have been exalted by it."[62] Yet by the time the kings left the island for the Holy Land at the turn of March and April 1191, dissension had arisen between them. They were able to retake Acre together that July, but Philip left for home shortly thereafter and, once back in France, allied himself with John, who had already been causing trouble in his brother's absence. By late 1192 the threat the two men were posing to his lands was serious enough that Richard too felt the need to return, but one misfortune followed another. Around December 10, off the coast of Istria, between Aquilea and Venice, his ship was wrecked, forcing him and his men to continue on by land. Sometime before Christmas, he was taken captive by Leopold V, Duke of Austria, and imprisoned in Dürnstein Castle on the Danube River. After much haggling, he was transferred into the custody of Emperor Henry VI in mid-March of 1193 and moved to Trifels Castle in Germany. The emperor gleefully informed Philip of the seizure of their mutual enemy, "knowing [the news] to be to your pleasure and to bring a most fruitful happiness to your heart."[63] After nearly two years away fighting in the Holy Lands, Richard spent sixteen months in captivity before Eleanor and her associates were able to raise and deliver the sum for his ransom. It was during this period, when the kingdom was weakened by Richard's absence, that Gervase of Canterbury refers in passing to "Queen Eleanor, who was ruling England at that time."[64]

In the accounts we possess of Richard's years on crusade and in captivity, two models for Eleanor's behavior stand out. According to one model, Eleanor is a faithful vassal to her lord. She repeatedly swore oaths of fealty to him. In 1192, for example, we are told, "Eleanor, the Queen Mother, and almost all the princes and magnates of England came to London and swore fealty to the King of England and his heir against all men."[65] Though Eleanor is queen and, hence, of higher rank than the princes and magnates with whom she takes this oath, she performs the same public profession of allegiance that they do and, in doing so, positions herself on their level. Exemplifying the behavior that she wishes them to adopt, she appeals to their sense of duty to their lord. According to another model, however, Eleanor is a loving mother to her son. She is regularly identified as "Eleanor, the Queen Mother" or "Eleanor, the King's Mother," as if these were her official titles. With this nomenclature, Eleanor situates herself apart from the other princes and magnates of the kingdom, who do not occupy the same privileged relation to the king. In addressing these men as the mother of a captive king, she appeals to their sense of compassion for her son and herself. Yet whether we are to see Eleanor as wise in the advice she gives her lord or as pitiable in the sufferings she endures for her son, those around her recognized and respected the love she manifested for Richard and deferred to her on that account.

When Richard was staying in Sicily, during the early months of 1191, as the chroniclers relate, the sixty-eight-year-old Eleanor followed him to this island kingdom, bringing him a young woman she intended him to wed. According to some sources, it was Richard who decided to marry Berengaria, the twenty-five-year-old daughter of Sancho VI, King of Navarre.[66] He was attracted by "the refinement of the maiden's manners and the suitability of her birth,"[67] and, having confided his infatuation to Eleanor, "He had his mother bring her straight to Messina."[68] According to many more sources, however, it was the queen who decided that Richard should marry this maiden and who negotiated with the King of Navarre for this purpose. As William of Tyre's continuator tells the story, she sent word to her son "that he must marry her, and that he should not delay for anything this marriage to the damsel she had brought him," and she arranged matters overall so that "It would be more certain that the marriage would take place all the sooner and that her will would be accomplished."[69] The facts of the continuator's account are not always to be trusted,[70] but his depiction of Eleanor as the active, even vigorous party here is seconded by other sources. We are told that "Eleanor, the mother of the King of England, . . . brought with her Berengaria, the daughter of the King of Navarre, whom the king was to take as wife [*quam rex in uxorem ducturus erat*]"[71] and that "She came to her son in Sicily, bringing with her the daughter of the King of Navarre, whom he was to marry [*nupturam*]."[72] The use of future active participles suggests that Eleanor not only escorted Berengaria to Sicily but brought the maiden there with a clear purpose in mind, in a manner that would brook no dissent. Regardless of whose idea it was to unite Berengaria and Richard in wedlock, Eleanor functions as the subject, traveling to Sicily and bringing the maiden to this man, with the intention that he take her as his wife.

Given the difficulty of Eleanor's voyage from Poitou to Sicily, the chroniclers are impressed with the maternal love she showed Richard by escorting Berengaria to him. William of Newburgh writes, "Queen Eleanor, having forgotten her old age, not pondering the length or the difficulty of the journey or the rigors of the wintry season, was led, or rather impelled, by maternal affection, to the ends of the earth."[73] Richard of Devizes states similarly, "Queen Eleanor, . . . still tireless in all labors, at whose ability her age might marvel, having taken up with her the daughter of the King of the Navarrese, . . . followed the King, her son."[74] The challenge Eleanor undertook in traveling such a great distance, at such an advanced age and during such a harsh season, was seen as a testament to her concern for her child. Receiving word of Eleanor's approach, on March 30, Richard crossed the short strait to Reggio, in Calabria, where the queen had arrived with Berengaria, and brought the women back to his palace in Messina. It is said that "His Queen Mother . . . was received with all the honor that was fitting and, after [the king's] affectionate embraces, was gloriously led in a procession."[75] The arrival of the Queen Mother with Richard's intended is represented as a great public spectacle, given the presence of the crusader fleet looking on, and the reunion of mother and son as a joyous event. Richard de Templo, a canon of the Augustinian Church of Holy Trinity in London and the supposed author of the *Itinerarium peregrinorum et Gesta Regis Ricardi* (1220s), reports, "All were happy at their coming."[76] With the spectators so favorably impressed by the devotion the queen had shown her son in traveling so far, there was no doubt that this match must now go ahead. As it was Lent, the wedding would have to wait until after Easter, so Eleanor ended up leaving Sicily on April 2, after only four days on the island. Entrusting the Navarrese princess to Joan's care, she departed by barge for Salerno and then continued on back to England. Again, regardless of whose idea the marriage between Richard and Berengaria had been, the energy Eleanor showed in making this journey was seen as a reflection of her determination to do whatever she could for her son.

Before Eleanor left Sicily, Richard entrusted her with the task of running the kingdom by advising the new de facto chief justiciar and his colleagues. When she was staying with the king in Messina, mother and son had discussed politics with Walter of Coutances, Archbishop of Rouen, who had accompanied the king thus far on the crusade. First in their mind was the disastrous performance of William Longchamp, Bishop of Ely and lord chancellor, whom Richard had appointed chief justiciar, with the authority to act on his behalf while he was away, along with a council of a half dozen or so other justiciars to assist him, but whose high-handed manner had deeply offended the English barons. When Eleanor returned to England, it was in Walter's company, with instructions from Richard to set the realm aright. Richard de Templo states, "[The king] gave his mother the queen leave to go, and he asked her to take custody of his kingdom jointly with the aforementioned Walter, Archbishop of Rouen, a man of great virtues."[77] Ambroise, whose *Estoire de la guerre sainte* (c. 1195) typically parallels Richard's chronicle, writes, "He sent back his mother to look after his land, which he had left, so that his holdings would not diminish. Walter, Archbishop of Rouen, who is a very wise man, looked after England with her."[78] These chroniclers identify both the queen and the archbishop as the people Richard appointed to run the kingdom in his stead, and they name Eleanor first, presumably because of her higher status, and Walter as someone looking after the kingdom "with her." Still, it was Walter who received documents from Richard authorizing him to restore order; it was Walter who, by October of that year, brought about Longchamp's deposition as chief justiciar and his exile; and it was Walter who, as head of the council, replaced Longchamp in function, if not in title. The author of the *Histoire de Guillaume le Maréchal* writes approvingly of Walter's appointment, "Following the counsel of the Marshal and the barons together, he acted well and wisely, and by the counsel of the queen, who was [in England] at this time."[79] Walter is identified as acting, and Eleanor is identified as advising him on how to act, together with the other justiciars. As a woman, Eleanor is not granted a formal position in the government in the way that Longchamp and Walter are, but she is given the responsibility of directing the country through the counsel she gives them.

When Eleanor responded to John's misbehavior in Richard's absence, she functioned in large part, if not entirely, as the king's representative, along with the justiciars. In February of 1192, her youngest son made plans to travel from England to see Philip, who had invited him to France to discuss matters to their mutual advantage. According to Roger of Howden, it was Eleanor who learned that John was intending to cross the Channel for this purpose. At that point, Roger states, "His mother, Walter, Archbishop of Rouen, and other justiciars of England prohibited him, on the part of the King of England and his men, from crossing over, saying that, if he crossed over, they would seize all of his lands and castles by the hand of the king."[80] The queen and the justiciars act together as agents of the king in his absence, all warning John not to depart for France and all threatening to confiscate his territories if he does so. The chronicler continues,

"Having been admonished by them and by others, John, Count of Mortain, acquiesced to his mother, and, the mandates of the King of France having been postponed, altered his undertaking to the better."[81] Though John is reproached by the justiciars and his mother, he relents to his mother alone, as if she exercises a power over him that the others do not. According to Richard of Devizes, "With difficulty, through her own tears and with the pleas of the nobles, she was able to obtain his assurance that he would not cross over for the time being."[82] While the justiciars can plead with John, it is Eleanor alone who can weep, and those tears appear to be what changes his mind. Later, when Richard was still away, John would gain control over the Castles of Windsor, Wallingford, and the Peak, but he would finally be persuaded to release them "into the hand of Queen Eleanor, the said Count of Mortain's mother, and of other guardians, who took them into hand."[83] Just as, during Henry's reign, Richard had agreed to withdraw from Aquitaine only when Eleanor assumed control over this land, John agrees to withdraw from these three castles only when his mother and her allies occupy them. Eleanor is clearly acting in Richard's interest, aiming to preserve his kingdom as he asked her to do. At the same time, John trusts her. With her tears and her pleas, she is the only figure who can persuade him, even for a time, to abandon his rebellious impulses and into whose custody he feels comfortable releasing his fortresses.

Even as Eleanor is functioning as a representative of the king, she is seen as functioning as a mother. When she was returning from Sicily in the spring of 1191, Peter of Blois, who was returning from the Holy Land,[84] seems to have attached himself to her entourage. In 1193, when Richard was being held captive, he composed three letters in her voice to Pope Celestine III. It can be debated whether Peter's letters were a literary exercise, never sent or intended to be sent to Celestine,[85] or a historical expression of Eleanor's actual state at this time, perhaps commissioned by the queen herself.[86] In either case, the letters reflect a view of Eleanor as a suffering mother whose authority lies in her ability to appeal to the reader *ad misericordiam*. In one of these epistles, the queen writes, "I, pitiable and pitied by no one, why have I come to the ignominy of this detestable old age, who have been the lady of two kingdoms and the mother of two kings?" In the past, Eleanor indicates, she had been happy. She had been Queen of France and then Queen of England, and she had been the mother of the Young King and of King Richard. She had been able to glory in the lands over which she had ruled and the powerful sons to whom she had given birth. But now, she recounts, two of her sons have died—the Young King and Geoffrey—leaving "their most unhappy mother" behind.

She continues, "Two sons have remained to me for my solace, who today remain to me—pitiful and condemned—for my punishment. King Richard is held in chains. John, his brother, despoils the captive's kingdom with iron and lays it waste with fire. . . . This is a conflict where one is afflicted and restrained in chains. The other, adding sorrow to sorrow, endeavors to usurp the exile's kingdom by cruel tyranny." Of her two surviving sons, she points out, one suffers in prison in a foreign land, while the other contributes to his brother's suffering by ravaging and laying claim to his territories. Though John might seem to be the one in the wrong in this case, Eleanor's point is not to blame him, but, rather, to draw attention to the suffering *she* endures as a result of both children. Whether she is considering Richard's captivity or John's misbehavior, she sees God as chastising her. Echoing the words of Job, she laments, "In all things, the Lord has turned cruel toward me, and he opposes me with the harshness of his hand" (ep. 4, col. 1269). Just as her tears before John were said to have contributed to his change of heart, her laments in this letter recenter the situation on herself and inspire compassion, she hopes, in her audience.

After Richard was taken captive, the chroniclers relate, Eleanor continued to function as the representative of the king along with the justiciars. In the beginning of 1193, when the news arrived in England that Richard had been taken prisoner, the author of the *Histoire de Guillaume le Maréchal* writes, "His mother was distressed about this, but it did not grieve his brother."[87] The emperor demanded a ransom of 150,000 marks, with an initial deposit of 70,000 marks to obtain Richard's liberation in exchange for hostages. So enormous was this sum, Roger of Howden writes, that, on April 19, 1193, "The king's mother and the justiciars of England determined that all the clergy as well as the laity ought to give the fourth part of the present year's revenue for the ransom of our lord the king and to add as much from their chattel property."[88] This twenty-five percent tax on both income and movable property would be imposed with no exceptions for anyone, whether layman or cleric, secular or religious clergy. For seven months, Eleanor and Walter of Coutances applied themselves to collecting the ransom, which was stored in chests at Saint Paul's Cathedral in London, "under the seal of our lady the queen and the seal of the Lord Archbishop of Rouen."[89] What made the greatest impression on contemporary observers was the fact that gold and silver religious vessels were confiscated from churches and monasteries, with the result that Masses would have to be celebrated for years to come with pewter or wooden chalices and patens. Yet Eleanor was not undiscriminating in collecting this wealth. When the monks of the Abbey of Bury Saint Edmund contributed an expensive golden chalice Henry had once given them, Jocelin of Brakelond relates, Eleanor redeemed it with her own money and returned it to them,[90] requesting that they preserve it in perpetuity "for the salvation of our most dear son King Richard."[91] The queen wants Richard's subjects to help him, not just by paying his ransom, but by praying for his soul, especially if they are monks, and she hopes that the return of their chalice will inspire these religious to do so. With the material and spiritual benefits she and Walter have solicited from their subjects, she hopes to free the king.

Even as Eleanor acts as a representative of the king, in securing his release from captivity, she is still seen as acting like a mother. As she presents herself in her letters to Celestine, she is not just Eleanor, Queen of England, but a mother whose sufferings she expects the pope to pity and to attempt to alleviate. She asks him "to show himself a father of pity to her, a pitiable mother" (ep. 4, col. 1269), reminding him, "You are the father of orphans and judge of widows" (ep. 3, col. 1263). So intense is Eleanor's sorrow that she cannot but cry out, even if in doing so she is breaking the rules of decorum. She relates, "I had determined to be silent, lest I be reproved for insolence and presumption if perhaps the overflowing of my heart and the vehemence of my sorrow drew out some less than cautious word against the Prince of Priests. Truly, sorrow is not very different from insanity, for, in the impetus of its arousal, it does not recognize lords, it does not respect confederates, it does not spare anyone, not even itself" (ep. 2, col. 1262). In her sorrow, she cannot control her speech, which bursts out in lamentations that defer to no authority (not even that of the pope) and adheres to no rules of protocol. Throughout these letters, Eleanor speaks as if the sorrow of a mother for her son is a cultural motif which her audience will recognize and respect and to which they will respond with appropriate compassion. As readers of this time would remember, conflating two stories from the Gospel of Luke, when an importunate widow beseeched Jesus Christ, he revived her dead son.[92] When a poor widow whose son had been murdered appealed to Emperor Trajan and a mother whose child had been abducted by soldiers sought out Saladin, these rulers gave the women justice, even though they were preoccupied with military affairs at the time when they received their petitions.[93] While a mother's grief is personal, rooted in her love for her child, her demand that the ruler take action to protect her child is also impersonal, based in the sense of rectitude that underlies her maternal affection. The grieving old widow, bereft of the sons who should have supported her in this stage of her life, "the staff of my old age 'and the light of my eyes'" (ep. 4, col. 1269), as Eleanor is said to put it, is someone who breaks social hierarchies, to the point where she can berate the pope, but she does so in a way that is ultimately sanctioned because it reflects the natural love of a mother for her child. Her weakness becomes a kind of strength, which authorizes her wild speech.

While Eleanor was defending Richard's kingdom on his behalf, she received three letters from her imprisoned son, dated March 30, June 8, and April 19, 1193, each of which recognizes her as a faithful supporter of his realm. In his first letter, the king writes, "First to God and then to your serenity, sweetest mother, we give thanks as much as we can—though we cannot give sufficient thanks for actions so worthy of thanks—for the fidelity [*fidelitate*] with which you are serving us and the faithful care and diligence you are giving so devotedly and effectively to our lands for peace and defense. Indeed, we have learned a great deal, and we know that, through the mercy of God and through your counsel and help, the defense of our lands is and will be in great part provided for. For your prudence and discernment [*prudentia et discretio*] is the greatest cause of our land remaining in a peaceful state until our arrival." Richard is grateful first to God, due to whose "mercy" his lands have remained as peaceable as they have so far. But after God, he is grateful to Eleanor, due to whose "counsel" and "help" his kingdom has been defended during this period. He commends her "fidelity" or "loyalty" (*fidelitas*), that is, her constancy in supporting him as king and in preserving his right to rule (in contrast, presumably, to the infidelity and disloyalty John has displayed). As Richard sees her, Eleanor is not passively suffering as a bereft mother during his absence from the kingdom (as Peter's letters would have it), but is actively shoring up his reign during this difficult time. For that reason, he expresses, not pity for her suffering, but only respect and gratitude for her service. In representing Eleanor as a faithful supporter, Richard describes her in terms no different from those he uses in describing loyal male subjects. The archbishopric of Canterbury had fallen vacant around this time, and the king is concerned to ensure that this high position will be filled by Hubert Walter, Bishop of Salisbury, who had accompanied him on the crusade and who had visited him in his captivity. Writing to Eleanor, he justifies his support of Hubert "because we have had sufficient experience of this bishop's discernment [*discretionem*], fidelity [*fidelitatem*], constancy of sound mind, and the sincerity of love with which he embraces us."[94] Just as he had commended Eleanor for her "fidelity" and "discernment," he commends Hubert for the same qualities. And just as Eleanor's personal attachment to him had made him trust her, Hubert's personal attachment to him has produced the same effect. He treats his mother as an ally, like the ecclesiastics who are also sustaining his kingdom.

Even as Eleanor is seen as a faithful supporter of Richard in defending his kingdom, she is also seen, again, as a mother, outraged at her son's captivity. In Peter of Blois's letters, she expresses anger at the Duke of Austria, who, contrary to all Christian custom, has taken prisoner a crusader returning from the holy wars, and at the emperor, who bought this prisoner from the duke and keeps him a captive in his castle. She rages, "O impious, cruel, terrible tyrant, who did not fear to lay your sacrilegious hands on the anointed of the Lord, neither the royal unction, nor reverence for holy life, nor the fear of God kept you from such inhuman action" (ep. 4, col. 1270). In addition to these two secular rulers, she expresses anger at the pope, who has taken no action against the emperor for this crime, neither excommunicating him nor laying his lands under interdict.[95] As Eleanor presents herself, she is the one party who remembers that ecclesiastical law prohibits a crusader from being seized or his lands from attacked when he is engaged on this holy campaign and who demands that this law be enforced.[96] If the pope has hesitated to protest the scandal, she hypothesizes, it is because he sees that he has little to gain materially from doing so. He has not traveled to Germany or sent his legates there, she writes, because "Profit makes legates today" (ep. 2, col. 1264), and there is little profit to be gained from helping a captive. With these words, Eleanor pivots from focusing on her suffering, as the mother of quarreling brothers and an imprisoned son, to focusing on that imprisoned son, as the victim of unchristian Christians who have no respect for the rights of an anointed king and returning crusader. Shifting from lamentation to indignation, she suggests that, it is not she who is blinded by her maternal love, but the duke, the emperor, and the pope who are blinded by their self-interest. It is precisely because she acts, not as a ruler, distracted by worldly concerns, but as a mother, focused on her son, that she is able to grasp a principle these men cannot. Her love for her own flesh does not distort her perception of a moral truth; it is what enables her to grasp it.

In the accounts of Eleanor's arrive in Germany with Richard's ransom, the queen functions both as an advisor and as a mother. Though the emperor's agents had transported the bulk of the wealth to Germany by the end of the summer, Richard requested that Eleanor and Walter of Coutances travel to Germany to finalize arrangements for his release. By the middle of January 1194, this party had arrived at Speyer, where Richard was then being held. An anonymous Salzburg annalist observes, "The Queen of England, with the Archbishop of Rouen and many peers, barons and nobles of her land, came to the emperor, desiring to free her son, whom she loved to an extraordinary degree."[97] Eleanor is represented as the dominant figure in this party, and her love for her son is represented as the animating force of her efforts to release him from captivity. Though the emperor had set January 17 as the date for Richard's release, emissaries from Philip and John arrived, attempting to bribe him if he would retain Richard in custody. ("Behold how they loved him!")[98] Roger of Howden comments ironically.) On February 2, when Richard met with the emperor at Mainz, with Eleanor and Walter in attendance,[99] this ruler was still prevaricating, and he told Richard that he was tempted to accept his enemies' proposal. Even after the Archbishops of Mainz and Cologne shamed their lord into keeping his word and releasing his prisoner, the emperor imposed a last-minute condition, namely, that Richard grant him England as an imperial fiefdom. The king was offended by this final, unexpected, and exorbitant demand, yet he agreed to it, Roger of Howden writes, "on the advice of Eleanor, his mother, in order that he might escape from this captivity."[100] However irritated Richard may have been at this additional condition, Eleanor focused exclusively on securing her son's release, at a point when the emperor was wavering as to whether to grant it or not, and she counseled her son to do whatever was necessary to achieve this end. Finally, on February 4, after all these negotiations, Richard was allowed to depart. Roger relates, "The Archbishops of Mainz and Cologne delivered him, free and released by the emperor, into the arms of his mother Eleanor. . . . When the king was set at liberty, all who were present shed tears of joy."[101] Though many important officials from Richard's kingdom were present at this time, Eleanor is recognized as the person who was most concerned about the king's well-being and, hence, as the person into whose custody he should be placed.

From the perspective of her contemporaries, Eleanor's love for Richard went hand in hand with her love for the people. In the letters Peter of Blois writes in her name, Eleanor laments, not only that she and Richard suffer as a result of his imprisonment in Germany, but that their subjects suffer as well. Though she yearns to go to her son in Germany, she hesitates because of her duty to her country: "If I go, deserting my son's kingdom, which is laid waste on all sides with grave hostility, it will be deprived of all counsel and solace in my absence" (ep. 4, col. 1270). While she has the responsibility to bring about Richard's liberation, she also has the responsibility, she believes, to offer advice to those who are ruling the kingdom and comfort to those who are suffering in the king's absence. One could argue that Richard's subjects were suffering at this time primarily from the enormous taxes they had been obliged to pay, first, to fund his crusade and, then, to supply his ransom. Yet when Eleanor argues that the pope should send his legates to Germany, she asks, "What more glorious profit could there be than to free a captive king, to return peace to his people, tranquility to the religious, and joy to all?" (ep. 4, col. 1271). If one frees Richard, she suggests by this series of appositions, one is returning peace and happiness to the king's subjects. However much the people must sacrifice in order to fund the king's ransom, the presence of a strong monarch ensures the stability of his kingdom, so his return will be to the benefit of all. According to the *Histoire de Guillaume le Maréchal*, when Richard thanked William Marshal and others who remained loyal subjects to him during his absence, the Marshal objected: "Sire, . . . we did no more than our duty, for all men of good birth should suffer hardship and great pain for their rightful lord."[102] In a world where the ruler and his subjects are so intimately connected, there is no conflict, not only between Eleanor's private concern for Richard and her public concern for their subjects, but between those subjects' concern for their king and their concern for themselves.

Eleanor's care for the people during Richard's absence from the kingdom was especially evident in her handling of the crisis in the diocese of Ely. In 1192, when Walter of Coutances took action against William Longchamp, he confiscated the revenues of the latter's diocese, and Longchamp, in retaliation, laid an interdict on these lands. As a result, the people were impoverished, no religious services could be celebrated, and the bodies of the dead could not be buried in consecrated ground. According to Richard of Devizes, Eleanor, "that matron worthy of being remembered so many times," was making a tour of her dowerlands in Cambridgeshire, in this diocese, when she discovered the sufferings the parishioners were experiencing as a result of this quarrel. The chronicler writes, "There came before her from all the villages and hamlets, wherever she passed, men with women and children, not all of the lowest conditions, a people weeping and worthy of being wept for, with bare feet, unwashed clothes, and unkempt hair. They spoke through their tears, by which, on account of sorrow, words failed them. There was no need for an interpreter, for more than what they wanted to say could be read on the open page [of their faces]."[103] Eleanor is a foreigner to these lands, unable to understand the English speech of these villagers, but, the chronicler conveys, the visual impact of the poverty and suffering is such that it has no need of verbal explanation. "As one who was very merciful, commiserating with the misery of the living because of their dead,"[104] it is said, she immediately took action. Returning to London, "She requested [*egit*], indeed commanded [*exegit*]" that Walter repay those funds he had confiscated from Longchamp's revenues, which had so impoverished these people. She then went to Longchamp, and "She compelled [*coegit*] him to revoke the sentence [of interdiction] he had laid," which had prevented them from burying their dead. Richard of Devizes represents Eleanor as appealing to these men to act ("She requested"), but also as compelling them to do so ("She . . . commanded" and "She forced"). He asks rhetorically, "And who would be so savage or cruel that this woman could not make him bend to her wishes? Thus the manifest acrimony between the warring parties was appeased with the queen mediating [*mediante regina*]."[105] If Eleanor induces Walter and Longchamp to relent, it is not because they have compassion for the people they are harming, but because, through her combination of gentleness and sternness, pleading and ordering, she induces them to act in accordance with her own compassion. These ecclesiastics have the official power to excommunicate and to interdict, but the queen has the interpersonal skill to get them do what she wants.

After all this trouble during his absence from his kingdom, Richard finally arrived back in England, in Eleanor's company, on March 13, 1194. As the king then made a circuit around the country for the next month, reasserting his presence in his kingdom, Eleanor continued to attend upon him. At a great council in Nottingham where he reorganized his administration, we read first in the list of those present, "Queen Eleanor his mother was there."[106] At a solemn ceremony at Winchester Cathedral, on April 17, Richard appeared, wearing his crown and dressed in his royal attire, carrying a scepter in his right hand and a golden wand in his left, with four earls bearing a silken canopy over his head. Led up to the altar, Richard knelt before it, received a benediction from Hubert Walter, now Archbishop of Canterbury, and then went to his place for the Mass. At that time, Roger of Howden tells us, "Eleanor, the Queen Mother, was seated with her maidens on the northern side of the church, opposite the king."[107] While women had been excluded from Richard's original coronation at Westminster Abbey, his mother and her ladies are now seated in the place of honor. Given John's betrayal of Richard, it is understandable that he was not present at this ceremony in Winchester. Still, William of Newburgh relates that "When John saw that his brother had not only returned in safety to his own country but was even prospering, he deigned at length to be reconciled to him."[108] Before Richard left his kingdom, he had compelled John to swear that he would not enter England for three years,[109] though he later relaxed this prohibition "through the counsel of Queen Eleanor his mother"[110] or "at his mother's pleas."[111] Now, William continues, "With their mother mediating [*mediante matre*], he returned as a suppliant and was received with sufficient fraternal affection, and afterwards he faithfully and valiantly performed military service for him against the King of

France. He thus expiated his former errors by his recent services and completely recovered his brother's love."[112] As Walter of Coutances and William Longchamp had called a temporary truce in their quarrel, according to Richard of Devizes, "with the queen mediating," Richard and John reconciled, according to William of Newburgh, "with their mother mediating." For the remaining years of Richard's reign, John showed his brother a surprising loyalty, in return for which his lands and titles were restored to him. In the years after his liberation from captivity, Richard devoted himself to reconquering the lands he had lost to Philip during his absence.

Richard's luck came to an end on March 26, 1199, when he was besieging the small castle of Châlus-Chabrol in the Limousin. As he was supervising the work of the sappers on the castle wall, without having taken the precaution of donning his chain mail, an archer from inside the castle shot at him with his crossbow, wounding him on the left shoulder near the neck. The author of the *Histoire de Guillaume le Maréchal* laments, "A Satan, a traitor, who was servant to the devil, who was up on the castle walls, shot a poisoned arrow. It wounded the best prince in the world, so that he had to die from it. All the world grieved at this."[113] Mercadier, an Occitan mercenary who had fought for Richard during the Third Crusade and his later campaigns, had his own physician attend to him, but the man so botched the job that the wound festered. It was at this point, the Cistercian chronicler Ralph of Coggeshall tells us, that "The king, greatly uncertain as to his subsequent health, summoned by letter his mother, who was staying at [the Abbey of] Fontevraud."[114] He passed away by her side on the evening of April 6. Eleanor speaks of the death of her favorite son in a charter dated April 21: "Know . . . that we were present at the death of our said son the king, who, after God, placed all his faith in us, so that we would provide, with maternal solicitude, for his salvation in these and other matters to our full ability."[115] With a language that reflects Richard's own letters, she makes clear that, after God, he trusted her more than anyone else. Aware of the "maternal solicitude" that drove her to seek his best interest, he counted on her to help him preserve his kingdom when he was alive, and, she indicates, he counts on her now to help him attain God's kingdom after his death. Despite the chroniclers' claim that Richard loved Berengaria, he did not have his wife attend his coronation at Winchester after his release from captivity, he did not have her come to him often in subsequent years, to the point that ecclesiastics repeatedly chastised him for this neglect,[116] and he did not summon her to his deathbed, though she was nearby. The couple never had children, nor is it clear that their marriage was ever consummated. Instead, as he was dying, Richard called Eleanor to him so that he could be comforted by her presence, and she took charge of making the arrangements that were necessary at that time for his physical interment and his spiritual salvation.

KING JOHN

After Richard's death, John's claim to his brother's lands did not go uncontested. While John was now Henry's only surviving son, his elder brother Geoffrey had left behind a twelve-year-old heir, Arthur, Duke of Brittany. Given Arthur's young age, Geoffrey's widow Constance promoted her child's interests on his behalf, and she did so with the support of Philip, who for a time took Arthur under his wing. In the first stage of this conflict, in the months following's Richard's demise in April of 1199, the English and the Normans recognized John as king, but the barons of Anjou, Maine, and Touraine recognized Arthur as their liege lord. It was only after Eleanor made a tour of her territories between April and July, granting her vassals' privileges and obtaining from them oaths of allegiance in return, and only after she attacked Angers and Le Mans later that year, quelling resistance to her son in these two cities, that they agreed to profess loyalty to her son. In the second stage of the conflict, in August of 1200, John provoked his continental vassals by impulsively marrying young Isabella, the daughter of Aimery, Count of Angoulême, though she had already been promised to Hugh IX "le Brun," seigneur of Lusignan. It was only in July of 1202, when John relieved the siege that Arthur and the Lusignans had set before the Castle of Mirebeau in northern Poitou, where Eleanor was staying, and took the prince and over two hundred knights prisoner that he was able to quiet unrest in these regions a second time. It seemed that John had finally appeased the fractious continental barons, but by April of 1203, Arthur had vanished, and he was widely rumored to have been murdered by his uncle. Disgusted with John's wickedness, the barons became even more hostile toward his rule and more inclined to side with Philip against him. Throughout this tumultuous period, when the barons were shifting their allegiances back and forth between the English and French kings, Eleanor was the one figure whom the notoriously suspicious John consistently trusted. Yet precisely the qualities that enabled John to count on her—her attachment to him as his mother and the advantages she accrued through this affiliation—were what made her judgment of his claim to the throne seem doubtful as time went on.

In accounts of Eleanor's relationship with John, it is not clear whether mother and son are driven by the "natural" love of family members for each other or by an "unnatural" ambition, which makes them turn against these blood relatives. According to one interpretation of the events, Eleanor loves her son and champions his claim to the throne out of maternal affection, while John loves his mother and rushes to her aid when she is under attack out of filial devotion. In contrast, Arthur, who is deficient in natural love, rebels against his uncle and besieges the castle where his grandmother is staying, with no regard for her advanced age and the fragility of her sex or for the closeness of their kinship. Yet according to an alternate interpretation, it is Eleanor and John who are lacking in natural love, making war against their young relative and even, in John's case, putting him to death, with no consideration for his youth, his noble blood, or their familial ties. Though Eleanor is originally represented as taking no part in John's dark deed, over time she comes to be seen as complicit in it. The medieval chroniclers, including Ralph of Coggeshall, Roger of Wendover, and Matthew Paris, convey how Eleanor advanced John's claim to the throne between 1199 and 1204, but they are relatively restrained in their commentary. In the sixteenth century, however, the humanist Polydore Vergil, an Italian who lived and worked in England, provided an account of John's reign in his *Historia Anglica* (1512–54), which Raphael Holinshed then translated and adapted in his *Chronicles of England, Scotland, and Ireland* (1577, rev. ed., 1587). The playwright George Peele relied on the second edition of Holinshed's *Chronicles* when he wrote *The Troublesome Reign of King John* (1589–91), as did William Shakespeare in his *The Life and Death of King John* (1594–96). These Renaissance historians and playwrights base what they say about Eleanor, John, and Arthur on the medieval chronicles, but it is they who suggest for the first time that Eleanor's ambition for John was indistinguishable from her own ambition and her goal that he be recognized as king was indistinguishable from her own desire to continue to be recognized as queen. It is here that we see the origin of modern historians' view that Eleanor "sought power."

According to the medieval chroniclers, during the strife over the inheritance of Richard's kingdom between 1199 and 1202, Eleanor was crucial in advancing John's claim to the throne. In England, as Roger of Howden tells the story, the barons resisted John's rule until John sent Hubert Walter, Archbishop of Canterbury, and William Marshal to the country to establish calm. With the archbishop threatening to excommunicate rebels against John's rule, the two men demanded that the chief citizens swear oaths of homage and fealty to the new king, which they eventually did. Meanwhile, on the Continent, the people of Maine, Anjou, and Touraine

pledged themselves, not to John, but to Arthur. Here, John relied on Eleanor to reestablish order, with the help of Mercadier, who had joined forces
with the queen in her efforts to suppress her son's rivals. After the citizens
of Angers resisted John, Roger writes, "Queen Eleanor . . . and Mercadier,
with his band, entered Angers and devastated it because its people had received Arthur."[117] In retelling this story, Roger of Wendover, a monk of
Saint Albans Abbey in Hertfordshire, states that John sent Eleanor, with
Mercadier, to Angers, but he also writes of the queen and the mercenary's
approach to the city that, "descending upon it hostilely, they devastated it,
and they foully took away the citizens as captives." As Eleanor destroyed
Angers for its failure to recognize her son as king, she destroyed this other
city. Roger continues, "Count John and his mother Queen Eleanor, surrounded by an abundant army, coming to the city of Le Mans, took the
castle. They reduced the houses in it to stones because [their inhabitants]
had adhered to Arthur, and they confined the leading citizens as captives in
carceral custody."[118] Now in the company of her son, Eleanor again acts severely, razing the city and taking its leaders captive. In depicting her armies
as having "devastated" these cities, the chroniclers stress the violence she
and her ally perpetrated, and, by characterizing these conquerors as having
"foully" taken their leading citizens captive, they condemn this unchival-
rous deed, though they acknowledge that it was prompted by the citizens'
rejection of John. Whether acting on her own initiative or on John's instructions, with the mercenary or independently, Eleanor brings some of
the major cities of her lands under her son's control.

The efforts that Eleanor made to advance John's claim to the Angevin
lands can be seen, not only in the chronicles, but in her own charters.[119] A
woman's husband or son traditionally received homage from her vassals or
gave homage to an overlord for her lands, and, in the past, Henry or one of
his sons had performed this task on Eleanor's behalf. Now, in 1199, as she
travels throughout her lands, Eleanor receives homage from her vassals,[120]
and she gives homage to Philip for Poitou.[121] At some point in 1200,
Aimery VII, Viscount of Thouars, one of Eleanor's Poitevin kinsmen and
subjects, who had given homage to John but had failed to stand up to fellow vassals who had not proved so loyal, was summoned to her presence.[122]
In a letter to John, Eleanor reports that, together with Guy of Dina, Con-
stable of Auvergne, "We showed him that he ought to feel great shame and
guilt because he allowed your other barons to disinherit you unjustly. He
listened, and understood our words, and because we spoke justly and reasonably to him, he freely conceded to us with an open heart that he and his
lands and castles were from this time forth subject to your will and com-

mand, whatever he had done before." Eleanor does not address Aimery angrily and injuriously but, rather, calmly and rationally. She does not dwell on "whatever he had done previously," but, rather, stresses what he might do differently in the future. She thus allows him to save face. As a result, Aimery promises to oppose friends of his who had seized John's lands and castles. Eleanor concludes, "And since he agreed benignly to the things we asked, namely, that he will be in your service, true and faithful against all mortals, I, who am your mother, and your faithful Guy of Dina urge you to be to him as a lord should be to his liege man."[123] Favorably impressed by the candor with which Aimery spoke with her and by the renewed fidelity of which he assures her, she vouches for him. As evidence of his loyalty, Aimery welcomed John to the Castle of Thouars in February of 1202, and he fought with him at Mirebeau that July. In recognition of the assistance Eleanor had provided in establishing his rule, in a decree issued sometime before mid-May of 1200, John acknowledges his mother's right to hold Poitou during her lifetime, and he adds, in a remarkable passage, "We wish her to be the lady [*domina*], not only of our said lands, but also of us and all our lands and possessions."[124] While John expects to come in to these territories after Eleanor's death, for the time being, he bows to her as his feudal "lady," with authority over him and all he owns. Like Richard, who bestowed considerable wealth on Eleanor on his accession to the throne, John is appreciative of his mother and generous toward her.

Just as the chroniclers represent Eleanor as acting vigorously in order to strengthen John's claim to the throne, they depict John as for once acting vigorously at the siege of Mirebeau in order to protect his mother. John was generally regarded as reluctant to wage war, even to defend his own interests. Gervase of Canterbury attests, "Because, out of prudence, he preferred to obtain peace rather than to fight, malevolent detractors and envious mockers called him 'John Softsword.'"[125] Yet when Eleanor found herself besieged by Arthur's army at Mirebeau, she wrote to John, who had been recruiting an army in Normandy, and asked him to come to her aid. Ralph of Coggeshall relates, "The queen, fearing to be captured, sent word to the king her son that he bring help with the siege, and the sooner the better."[126] While Ralph depicts Eleanor as bidding her son to come and relieve the siege, Matthew Paris represents her as "asking, insistent and imploring, that, upheld by piety, he would succor his desolate mother,"[127] and, hence, as appealing to his filial concern. Despite his reputation for indolence, John responded to this call with energy and determination. To cite ·the language of various chroniclers, he set off "immediately"[128] with his army from Le Mans and crossed the seventy miles "in a rushed flight,"[129] "more quickly than one would believe it to be possible,"[130] until he arrived at this castle less than two days later. The Breton and the Poitevin soldiers at Mirebeau, confident in their numbers, were sleeping[131] or eating[132] when he arrived and were thus caught off guard by his surprise attack. The result of the battle was an utter triumph for John, enabling him to take Arthur, Hugh IX of Lusignan, and many of their chief allies prisoner. Yet as momentous as this battle would be for his cause, chroniclers are clear that he acted so quickly, not in order to advance his political aims, but in order to rescue his mother from peril. Though William the Breton was a chaplain and diplomat in Philip's service, he cites, with apparent approval, John's justification of his actions: "No one will judge it an unjust war where a son frees his mother from a faithless enemy."[133] Everyone who writes about the relief of the siege of Mirebeau agrees, not only that Eleanor was in a perilous situation and that John acted well in rushing to her defense, but that the incident cast John in a positive light, as a son who rescues his mother from a disloyal grandson.[134]

Though the chroniclers represent Eleanor as devoted to John, they depict Arthur ambiguously, perhaps as concerned with her welfare, perhaps not. Given his youth, Arthur is commonly portrayed as the pawn of older political leaders and, especially, of Philip, who dubbed him a knight in April of 1202 and engaged him to marry his young daughter Marie. Ralph of Coggeshall suggests that Arthur rose up against his uncle and then besieged the castle in which his grandmother was staying only because he had come under the sway of the French king, who had bound him to him and who had directed him to take this path of action.[135] In some sources, Arthur is said to have meant no harm to Eleanor in the attack on Mirebeau. An anonymous chronicler from the first half of the thirteenth century writes that, when he besieged Mirebeau, "Arthur . . . requested that she exit the castle, take all her things, and go into a good country wherever she would like, for he did not want to do anything to her that was not to her honor." His aim was to take the castle, not to take Eleanor captive, the chronicler indicates, and, given the opportunity to imprison her, he would set her free to go where she would like. Yet this chronicler also relates that "The queen responded that she would not leave, but that, if he wished to be courtly, he would depart from here, for he could find enough castles to besiege aside from the one she was in."[136] No matter how politely Arthur treats her, Eleanor asserts, the very fact that he is attacking the castle in which she is located means that he is not treating her well. Just as feudal ties should prevent the Poitevins from rising up against their countess, so should family ties prevent the grandson from attacking his grandmother.

In other sources, Arthur is portrayed, not only as besieging Eleanor, but as intending to take her hostage. William the Breton cites the boy's Poitevin allies as advising him, "In Mirebeau, the queen ancestress of John, by whose utterly wicked suasion John acts, sits in the tower. . . . Let us besiege her."[137] It is Eleanor, these allies suggest, who stirs John to wage war on him. By taking the castle, they propose, they will be able to take Eleanor hostage and, "in exchange for the mother,"[138] to regain for Arthur the lands they have lost. With these words, William implies, they aroused the illustrious youth and stoked his boldness and desire for triumph. While John, consistently supported by Eleanor in his claim to these lands, consistently supports her in turn, young Arthur, whose ambitions the queen does not condone, exhibits doubtful loyalty toward her.

According to the Renaissance chroniclers no less than medieval predecessors, Eleanor played a crucial role in retaining the Angevin lands for John during these years. In England, Polydore Vergil and Raphael Holinshed report that it was, not Hubert Walter and William Marshal, but Eleanor herself who, encouraged by these men, ensured that the people would remain faithful to John. As Vergil writes, "John's mother Eleanor, whose authority was supreme among the English, at the persuasion of Hubert of Canterbury, with no small number of other men, less wise than noble, arranged for an oath to be given to John by all England."[139] As Holinshed puts it, Eleanor traveled throughout the country and received oaths of allegiance to her son from the principal citizens. Insofar as the kingdom submitted to John's rule, he writes, "All this was done chiefly by the working of the king's mother, whom the nobility much honored and loved. For she, being bent to prefer her son John, left no stone unturned to establish him in the throne."[140] Such was the esteem and affection in which Eleanor was held in England, he indicates, that she succeeded in establishing John's base of support in this country. On the Continent, these chroniclers likewise relate, it was Eleanor who, having heard how the people of Anjou, Maine, and Touraine were recognizing Arthur as their king, crossed the Channel "quickly"[141] or "with all possible speed" and "wasted"[142] these lands. More explicitly than the medieval chroniclers, these Renaissance writers represent Eleanor and John as harsh in their treatment of these cities, but also as regaining their obedience through this harshness. Vergil relates that, "Arms having swiftly been taken up, they either slaughtered the citizens or delivered them into custody as captives, but they punished most cruelly those who had helped Arthur,"[143] and they thereby put people of this region into such fear that, "of their own accord, they turned to their wonted obedience."[144] While the medieval chroniclers, in their more sober, factual accounts of these events, simply recorded what Eleanor did to support John's claim to these lands, the Renaissance chroniclers accentuate the initiative, energy, and brutality of her actions, as well as their effectiveness.

The Renaissance playwrights followed the chroniclers of their time in representing Eleanor as powerful, but they expressed even more qualms about this power. At times, they say, the queen goads John into war. In Shakespeare's *King John*, Chatillon, the French ambassador, describes Eleanor as "An Ate, stirring [John] to blood and strife,"[145] that is, as an inhuman, hellish force which stirs men to ruinous acts of violence.[146] At other times, they indicate, she encourages him to pursue diplomacy. When it seems to her more advantageous to have Philip as an ally rather than an enemy, she recommends that John return the lands that Richard had spent years reconquering from him in order to purchase his support for her son's shaky claim to the throne. When there is talk of having her granddaughter Blanche of Castile marry Philip's son Louis, she urges John, "make this match,"[147] as ". . . by this knot thou shalt so surely tie / Thy now unsured assurance to the crown."[148] As she states elsewhere regarding the conflict between England and France, "We must with policy [i.e., diplomacy] compound [i.e., settle] this strife."[149] At times bloodthirsty and at times conciliatory, Eleanor nevertheless possesses a political philosophy. When John affirms that he will depend on his right to the contested lands to establish his claim to them, she replies, "Your strong possession much more than your right."[150] Instead of putting stock in principle, she looks to ownership as that which will enable him to hold this territory. Critics have been struck by the "Realpolitik"[151] implicit in Eleanor's words, which locates God, not on the side of a political legitimacy defined by bloodline, but on the side of "de facto power."[152] As Phyllis Rackin observes, "[Eleanor] is . . . a tough, Machiavellian dowager."[153] Whatever is necessary to establish John as king, she is depicted as ready to do, without concern for the justice of her cause.

As the Renaissance playwrights depict John, he was devoted to the powerful Eleanor. He repeatedly asks his mother's advice. When the possibility arises of his niece Blanche of Castile marrying the dauphin Louis, he inquires, in Peele's play, "Mother, what shall I do?"[154] Eleanor answers, "Son John, follow this motion, as thou lovest thy mother."[155] Instructing him, she appeals, not just to his reason to see the wisdom of the match, but to his filial affection. Both Peele and Shakespeare portray John as overcome by grief at Eleanor's death. In Peele's play, John is reproached for raving like a madman at the loss of his mother. He mourns, "Dame Eleanor, my noble mother-queen, / My only hope and comfort in distress, / Is dead."[156] In Shakespeare's play, when he learns that a vast French army is headed to

English shores, he does not understand why Eleanor has failed to send him word about this development until a messenger explains that she has died. Left alone, he exclaims again, in his only soliloquy in the play, and, indeed, the only evidence of his inner life, "My mother dead!"[157] Eleanor was the only person in John's life whose loyalty and whose competence he entirely trusted in running the kingdom, and his love for her was the love of the one person on whom he could utterly rely. Modern scholars of Shakespeare's play, even of a supposedly feminist bent, have often interpreted John's dependence on Eleanor as a sign of the weakness of his character. One critic writes, "John and Arthur appear as men excessively dominated by their respective mothers,"[158] and another refers to "the astonishment which the audience feels at seeing a man so tied to his mother's apron strings."[159] But there is no evidence that anyone in the Middle Ages or the Renaissance ever perceived John's reliance on Eleanor's assistance or, indeed, any man's reliance on his mother's assistance, as unseemly. However many flaws John was held to possess during these centuries, his attachment to his mother was never regarded as one of them.

Even as Eleanor consistently sought John's best interest, for which she earned his gratitude, she may have sought Arthur's downfall, the Renaissance playwrights speculate. In Peele's play, when John and Eleanor meet with Arthur, John offers him Brittany, Richmond, and Angers, and Eleanor adds, "And if thou seek to please thine uncle John, / Shalt see, my son, how I will make of thee."[160] Both uncle and grandmother insist upon their affection for the boy as a result of their kinship, and both urge him to place his trust in them, given that affection and that family tie. Eleanor in particular holds out hope that, as she tells John, ". . . soon shall we teach him to forget / These proud presumptions and to know himself."[161] While Constance, Arthur's mother, and, at times, Philip seek to inflame the boy's ambitions by making him think he is greater than he is, she presents herself as his true friend by limiting the scope of his aspirations. In the original chronicles, there is no indication that Eleanor had played any role in Arthur's murder, though she may have been informed about it after the fact.[162] Yet in Shakespeare's play, when John is plotting with Hubert de Burgh, Arthur's jailor, to kill the boy, Eleanor is on the stage, apparently not hearing what her son is saying, but (whether consciously or unconsciously) collaborating with it. Before John orders his vassal, "Come hither, Hubert. O my gentle Hubert,"[163] she urges her grandson, "Come hither, little kinsman; hark, a word,"[164] distracting Arthur from the murderous plot that is being hatched within his earshot. The parallel syntax of the son's and the mother's words suggests that their actions are synchronized. While some performances of

Shakespeare's play have represented Eleanor as ignorant of her son's brutal plans,[165] others have depicted her as steeling John in his resolve to have the boy killed.[166] Given the play's ambiguity about Eleanor's feelings toward her grandson, it is left up to individual directors to decide how to represent her role in his death.

Whatever Eleanor felt toward Arthur, the Renaissance playwrights represent her as driven by ambition, not just for John, but for herself. Polydore Vergil writes, "Envy alone stirred Eleanor, for she foresaw that, if Arthur were to obtain the kingdom, his mother Constance would do everything by her own judgment until her son came to reign of his own right."[167] If Eleanor opposed Arthur, Vergil suggests, it is, not only because she wanted John to occupy the English throne instead of Arthur, but because she herself wanted to wield power in the kingdom instead of Constance, who would rule in her son's minority. Though modern historians have become accustomed to referring to the hostility between Eleanor and Constance as an established fact,[168] there is no record of it in the medieval sources (and, indeed, precious little about Constance at all). In Peele's play, however, when Eleanor claims that she possesses "a will" proving that Richard left his kingdom to John (as indeed he did), Constance retorts, "A will indeed, a crabbèd woman's will, / Wherein the Devil is an overseer, / And proud Dame Eleanor sole executress,"[169] a phrase that Shakespeare rewrites as "... a will! a wicked will: / A woman's will; a canker'd grandam's will!"[170] As Constance sees it, Eleanor insists that John be recognized as king, not because an impersonal document establishes that he is entitled to this position, but because her own personal inclination decrees that he should be in this place. This will is "a woman's will," that is, an instrument originating in a woman and, hence, illegitimate and even diabolical. For the first time, Eleanor is represented as "seeking power," as modern historians have so often interpreted her as doing, yet given how her ambition undermines the legitimacy of the monarchical system, it is not a positive trait in her, or in anyone.

As the Renaissance playwrights suggest that Eleanor harmed Arthur through her own ambition, they suggest that she harmed him through the accursed legacy she has passed on to him. According to Gerald of Wales, a holy hermit, unable to persuade Eleanor's father (in reality, her grandfather) to relinquish his mistress, warned him that he foresaw "offspring never to be begotten by you on her or their progeny never to have any fortunate fruit to follow them." Gerald himself refers obliquely to "how Eleanor, Queen of France, ... behaved both toward her first husband and toward the second, and how her sons, for whom there was such hope in the flower, withered without fruit,"[171] as if their shortened and childless lives were the product of generations of adultery. In Peter of Blois's letters, Eleanor herself expresses fear that punishment for her sins was being visited on her sons (ep. 4, col. 1271). In his play, Shakespeare alludes to this tradition of the queen's misdeeds bringing misfortune on her children and, now, her grandchildren. At one point, when Constance is addressing Eleanor, she gestures toward Arthur and says, ". . . This is thy eldest son's son, / Infortunate in nothing but in thee. / Thy sins are visited in this poor child; / The canon of the law is laid on him, / Being but the second generation / Removèd from thy sin-conceiving womb."[172] As a fulfillment of the Book of Exodus 20:5, where sins are said to be punished through the third or fourth generation, young Arthur has been made to suffer, not as a result of any wrongdoing on his part, but as a result of Eleanor's distant crimes. The queen's most significant legacy, as Constance would have it, is, not her bloodline, which could elevate either John or Arthur to the throne, but the cosmic retribution for her sins, which infects one generation of her descendants after the next.

Yet the legacy Eleanor is seen as passing on to her descendants is not unmixed in these dramatic works. When Arthur is taken captive by John in Peele's play, he defies him, announcing, "Uncle, my grandam taught her nephew this, / To bear captivity with patience. / Might hath prevailed, not right, for I am king / Of England, though thou wear the diadem."[173] In contrast to Eleanor, Arthur cares, not just about "might," which permits one man to gain power over another man's kingdom, but about "right," which determines which man should gain power over a particular realm. Though John possesses might, which has enabled him to take his nephew prisoner, Arthur declares that he himself possesses right, and his confidence in this right—his pride, as Eleanor puts it—is what makes him refuse to submit to him. Arthur did not learn the principle of right from Eleanor, but he did learn from her, he claims, "to bear captivity with patience." For sixteen years, Eleanor awaited release from imprisonment, until Henry's death brought her freedom and power. For a long time, Arthur suggests, he too will await release from imprisonment, until John's death will bring him freedom and the throne. Accursed and accursing as Eleanor may be, she is also a model of perseverance in tribulation for her progeny. And when all but the worst of her sons has passed away, she will be the one who survives and ensures that they will be commemorated both in their mortal remains and in their immortal souls.

THE OLD WOMAN
OF FONTEVRAUD

The Cloister and the World

In the last years of her life, Eleanor spent much of her time at the Abbey of Fontevraud, near Chinon. Founded almost a century beforehand, between 1099 and 1101, the abbey had become famous for the piety of its virgins. As at other monasteries, a nun would spend her days attending religious services; gathering regularly with her sisters to pray, sing hymns, and listen to psalms; and devoting her solitary hours to private orisons and reading. She would never venture outside the walls of this abbey or even interact with visitors inside the enclosure except under the most strictly regulated conditions. At the same time, Fontevraud became well known for its "converts" (*conversae*) or "widows" (*viduae*), onetime married women who also found refuge in its walls. While the virgin occupied herself exclusively with contemplative matters, the *conversa* not infrequently concerned herself with the active administration of the compound, especially in its dealings with the outside world. Because she typically had experience running a household or an estate prior to her entry into religion, only a *conversa* was eligible to lead the community. If elected abbess, she would travel to confer with Fontevraud's priories, represent the order at councils, and visit potential donors. Most remarkably, she would wield power, not only over the nuns, but over the religious brothers who were brought in to serve the women's needs. Until its dissolution at the time of the French Revolution, Fontevraud constituted, not only the largest and most prosperous confederation of monasteries for women in Western Europe, but one where, as Voltaire remarked with astonishment, "One sees the male sex . . . serve the female."[1] Once attached to this abbey, Eleanor was able to affiliate herself with a spiritual community, as was thought appropriate for women after a certain age, but one that respected women's authority.

When Eleanor began to spend significant amounts of time at Fontevraud, she was, in effect, living in two worlds. She was existing in historical time in the lands ruled, at least nominally, by her sons, with their ceaseless political tumult. She was employing her considerable skills and experience to ensure that Richard and then John preserved the power and wealth that was their due. Yet Eleanor was also existing "under the aspect of eternity" (*sub specie aeternitatis*) in an abbey governed by an abbess and given over to the daily *opus dei*. When she thought of Henry, their children, or any members of her family in these last years, she was thinking of them, not just as historical figures in the world, but as eternal figures, all of whom but John and young Eleanor had by this point migrated from this world. This late husband and these late sons and daughters, who once eagerly strove to accomplish their political ambitions in the secular world, were now quietly awaiting the end of time and the Resurrection of the Flesh it would bring in the hereafter. At that future moment, it was believed, their bodies, having been buried in splendid royal vestments, would reassume their original flesh, now glorified thanks to the heavenly beatitude they would then be enjoying. If there was a spirituality specific to Fontevraud at this time, it lay in the simultaneous recognition of the earthly political life in which women as well as men were deeply engaged and the heavenly spiritual existence to which the abbey could serve as a portal.

Because the nuns of Fontevraud sought to live, not in the world of present-day Angevin politics, but in the world to come, if we are to understand the spiritual life into which they welcomed Eleanor, we must appreciate their silence. The nuns have left us some of their psalters, their breviaries, and a legendary, which they used in their daily devotions, but they did not leave behind records about their lived experience. In the early years of the twelfth century, Petronilla of Chemillé, the order's first abbess, sponsored the writing of *vitae* of their founder, Robert of Arbrissel, by Baldric of Bourgueil and Andreas of Fontevraud, prior of the brothers' cloister at Fontevraud, in the hope of obtaining his canonization.[2] By the time we get to the mid-twelfth century, when Eleanor was beginning to be associated with the abbey, narrative histories of the order were no longer being produced, nor would they be produced again for another four hundred years. In the late sixteenth and the seventeenth centuries, Fontevraud witnessed a significant resurgence thanks to the patronage of the Bourbon family, which led to the sponsoring of the histories of the order by the Franciscan Yves Magistri in 1586,[3] the Benedictine Laurent Pelletier in 1586,[4] the Jesuit Honorat Nicquet in 1642,[5] and the secular priest Baltazar Pavillon,[6] with the assistance of Dom Jean Lardier, a prior from Fontevraud and the first archivist of the order, in 1666.[7] At the end of the seventeenth century, the priest Jean de La Mainferme assembled a collection of many of the most important documents of Fontevraud, including its necrology.[8] Abbesses of Fontevraud thus commissioned histories from a wide range of secular and religious clergy, but no nuns appear to have been involved in writing these works. As Father Nicquet observes, "It seems . . . that the former abbesses of Fontevraud have sacrificed to silence, so much have their deeds remained unknown to us."[9] It is only by piecing together texts written from the perspectives of the men surrounding Eleanor, who do speak of Fontevraud; texts written from the perspectives of women attached to this abbey, insofar as they exist; and the tomb sculptures that still adorn the abbey's main church that one can glimpse what it meant for Eleanor to be a member of this extraordinary community. And what that membership meant was that royal and aristocratic women who affiliated themselves with this order at the end of their lives could balance their longterm attachment to the outer, political world, with all its vicissitudes, with an increasing attachment to the inner, spiritual world, with its promise of eternal serenity.

OUTSIDE THE WALLS

From the earliest years of Fontevraud, Eleanor's menfolk had dealings with this abbey, though not without ambivalence. At first, stories circulated that the women and men in Robert of Arbrissel's entourage mixed freely and that Robert himself ate with women at a common table, engaged with them in private conversations, and, most scandalously, slept next to them at night, so that, by subjecting his flesh to temptation, he might overcome physical desire.[10] He is said to have preached repentance to "women fornicators and sinners,"[11] even "whores,"[12] and he built residences at Fontevraud where these women could atone for their sins—and where William IX jeeringly suggests they continued to ply their trade,[13] apparently not without some justification.[14] After Robert died in 1115, Fontevraud became more like a traditional monastery in which women were largely separated and hidden from male view. While the initial mingling of Robert's female and male followers had been a source of ribald suspicion among both ecclesiastical and secular lords, the later cloistering of the nuns left the men left outside the abbey's walls ignorant of what was going on inside. Cut off from the world Eleanor's kinsmen dominated, the women could seem to these men irrelevant to its functioning, but they could also seem disconcertingly independent of their jurisdiction.

Despite its future as a royal necropolis, Robert of Arbrissel acknowledged that it could seem undesirable for a great man to be buried at Fontevraud. According to Andreas of Fontevraud, when Robert was dying, he spoke of the possibility of being buried either at "the holiest places" (33, p. 254), that is, Bethlehem, where Jesus Christ had been born; Jerusalem, where Jesus had died; Rome, where so many martyrs had undergone their passion; or "the supreme monastery" of Cluny, "where every day there is such good service by God's grace" and "where gorgeous processions take place" (32, pp. 250–51). In doing so, he acknowledged that it was customary for someone to prefer to be interred in a place rendered prestigious either by its association with a divine or holy individual or by its wealth and splendor and that Fontevraud offered neither of these benefits. Yet Robert insisted that he wanted to be buried, as he put it, in the "mud" (33, p. 252) of his poor and obscure abbey. He explains, "There sleep my good nuns, by whose merits I believe I will be helped before God" (33, pp. 252–53). During his life, he had assisted these women by founding the abbey in which they would cultivate their virtues, and after his death, he believed they would assist him by ensuring his salvation.[15] Buried among the nuns at Fontevraud, he hopes that, "on the day of Resurrection, I will be able to go with them in this same flesh to God's judgment" (33, pp. 254–55). Companions in death as well as in life, the nuns and brothers of the abbey will, he believes, regain their bodies together at the Resurrection and gather in Heaven as one community. In all the religious institutions he had created, it is said, Robert dedicated the churches built for the nuns to the Virgin Mary, who is "placed next to her Son in Heaven, . . . alone without precedent" (11, pp. 339–40), and the churches built for the brothers to John the Evangelist, who "diligently served that same Virgin Mother as a devoted minister," regarding his service, not as a burden, but as a "pleasurable . . . obedience" (11, pp. 210–11). Though the brothers of Fontevraud would never be as close to God as the brides of Christ, Robert promised them that if they served these nuns well, "You will be rewarded for it in the blessed realm of Paradise" (11, p. 56), as he expected that he would be rewarded. The weaker sex benefits from receiving the solicitude of the strong, but the stronger sex benefits from giving this solicitude insofar as it becomes an occasion for charity.

When Henry died, he underwent many indignities prior to his burial at Fontevraud. After he expired in Chinon in July of 1189, it is said that his body was stripped of all its clothing, so that he was left stark naked until a young boy covered him with his short cloak and thus fulfilled the meaning of his nickname, Henry "Curtmantle."[16] His men finally arrived and ensured that he was properly attired in royal garments,[17] but even then no proper crown could found for his head, no proper scepter for his hand, and no proper ring for his finger "fitting such a great king as he was."[18] On the day after the king's death, his barons carried his body in a bier on their shoulders for the fifteen miles between Chinon and Fontevraud. Though Henry had made significant donations to Fontevraud during his life,[19] there is no evidence that he had chosen to be buried at the abbey after his death; it was presumably William Marshal and Henry's illegitimate son Geoffrey, the future Archbishop of York, the most authoritative figures present at this time, who made this decision on his behalf.[20] As Henry was lying in state in Fontevraud on July 7, Richard arrived, displaying, according to some sources, the grief one would expect a son to show at the sight of his dead father,[21] but, according to others, an inscrutable, perhaps pensive, visage.[22] When the cloth that was covering Henry's face was removed for him to see his sire, Richard was said to have been taken aback by the ferocity of his expression,[23] as well as by the blood that flowed from his nostrils,[24] in the corpse's traditional signal that his assassin is in its vicinity. Stripped naked, deprived of the emblems of royalty, and gazed on by the mortal enemy who was now replacing him on the throne, the great and powerful Henry was cast down at the end.

As some of his contemporaries saw it, the indignities Henry suffered after his death included the fact that he was interred at Fontevraud. Gervase of Canterbury writes, "He . . . was miserably interred at Fontevraud."[25] At this time, the defining marker of religious life for women was the wearing of the veil, which is what distinguished a nun from secular women in the eyes of her contemporaries. In the charters from Fontevraud, when a man brings his sister or daughter to the cloister to become a nun, it is commonly said that he brings her "to be veiled with the holy veil [*sacro velamine velandam*],"[26] which would be blessed by the bishop at the time of her consecration. In this context, Roger of Howden cites an unnamed Cistercian monk who had predicted of Henry that, "among the veiled women, he will be veiled [*inter velatas velabitur*],"[27] a prophecy that was fulfilled when the king was buried in the nuns' choir at this abbey. Gerald of Wales comments on the prophecy: "Where [Henry] had striven with such great desire and such great efforts to shut up [*includere*] Queen Eleanor in a nun's habit, there, quite to the contrary and as if through divine vengeance, he deserved to be shut up [*concludi*], enclosed in his last piece of earth, and brought to naught in an obscure spot, quite unfitting for such great majesty, while she lived on afterwards."[28] The issue is not simply that, in being buried at Fontevraud, Henry is being treated like a woman. As Gerald sees it, in being buried at this abbey, he is being treated like a woman who is cloistered, unseen, and, hence, in some sense, inexistent. To be a nun at Fontevraud, he suggests, is akin to being a corpse, locked away as if in a tomb, covered as if by a shroud, and separated permanently from the outside world, which is the only world that matters on earth. Because Henry had tried to consign Eleanor to obscurity in life, divine justice ensured that he was consigned to obscurity in death even as his wife reemerged into the light. For these commentators, Henry has been humiliated by ending up among these nuns.

Yet others of the king's contemporaries believed that Henry was buried "honorably"[29] or even with "royal magnificence"[30] at Fontevraud. The author of the *Histoire de Guillaume le Maréchal* writes of the cortège that transported his body, "When they reached Fontevraud, the nuns of that holy order, as it behooved them, came forth in a great yet simple procession to meet their lord, who had supported them and done them much honor. And once the body was inside the church, with plainchant and a fine service, they received him as their master, as a mighty king ought to be received. That night the nuns kept vigil over the body, reciting the verses in their psalters, with many weeping bitter tears as they prayed that the Lord our God (so it please him) have mercy upon King Henry."[31] However Henry's men or his son may have treated his dead body, the nuns of Fontevraud showed the departed king the respect he was due by emerging solemnly from their cloister to greet him, by accompanying him inside, and by keeping a tearful vigil over his body that night.[32] Because Henry had been generous to Fontevraud during his life, we are told, the grateful nuns were generous to him after his death. On account of his munificence to this abbey, William of Newburgh states, "It was fitting he should there receive, in preference, a place of rest for his body in the expectation of the Final Resurrection."[33] Many centuries later, the author of the necrology of Fontevraud lists the donations that Henry made to this abbey and then adds, "Let us say finally—and it is a thought that breaks our heart—that, leaving aside other churches that he possessed in the extent of his domains, although of a dignity superior to our own, he wished that his body rest after his death in our church, among the poor, the virgins, and the female servants of Christ. This is why we implore the infinite clemency of God, with eyes filled with tears, that the soul of this beloved father may rest in peace."[34] This author acknowledges that the nuns of Fontevraud are lowly, but, for that reason, he attests, they are all the more appreciative of the honor that Henry has paid them in choosing to be buried in their precincts, and they pray all the more ardently for his salvation. Fontevraud is here a place, not of women whose obscurity makes their abode unworthy of such a great king, but of holy nuns whose devotions on Henry's behalf do him honor. For these commentators, Henry has not been humiliated by ending up among the nuns; rather, he has humbled himself by choosing to be buried among them, and for that he deserves praise.

When Richard was buried at Fontevraud in March of 1199, the fact that he was interred at this abbey was no longer seen as an indignity because he was buried near his father. In contrast to Henry, whose wishes regarding his burial were unrecorded close to his death, Richard chose to be interred in this spot. As he was dying, Roger of Howden attests, "The king commanded that . . . his body be buried at Fontevraud, at the feet of his father."[35] Roger of Wendover comments that his body was buried the feet of the father "whose traitor he confessed himself to be."[36] Like the Young King, who repented of his sins toward Henry as he was dying, Richard acknowledges that he has sinned against his father, and, by setting himself at his feet until the Resurrection, he hopes to atone for that misdeed. Hugh, Bishop of Lincoln, was summoned to Fontevraud to say the funeral Mass, at which were present Eleanor; the Bishops of Poitiers and Angers; the Abbots of Le Pin and Turpenay; Aimery, Viscount of Thouars, and his brother Guy; and William des Roches, one of Richard's close companions-at-arms.[37] Adam of Eynsham writes of the late Richard, "He was most buried honorably, in accordance with royal magnificence." For three days after the interment, Hugh went to the monastery and said Masses in which he "prayed for pardon and the happiness of everlasting light for the souls of the kings buried there and of all the faithful who had fallen asleep in Christ."[38] There is no longer any concern that Fontevraud is "an obscure spot, quite unfitting for such great majesty," because it is the spot where the magnificent Henry has been buried, which makes it appropriate for his son's repose as well. While Richard may humble himself by lying at his father's feet, this is the humility of repentance; it is not the humility of self-abnegation.

Over the centuries, the story developed that Richard chose to be buried at Fontevraud, not because his father was already interred there, but because he bore a special affection for this abbey. The author of the *Histoire des Ducs de Normandie et des Rois d'Angleterre* states, "The good king was buried in Fontevraud, the good abbey of nuns that he had so loved."[39] It is true that Richard had been generous to this monastery, making seven donations to it, including one on June 24, 1190, when he was heading off on the Third Crusade.[40] As time went on, it was said that he had made this gift to ensure the nuns' prayers on his behalf during this expedition.

In the seventeenth century, historians of Fontevraud claimed that while Richard was being held captive in Germany, "He placed confidence only in the prayers of the holy monastery of Fontevraud, and he beseeched it by letters not to forget him before God." If he was released from captivity, it is implied, it was because of the nuns' prayers. "Having felt the power of such a religious company"[41] once he was freed and grateful for its aid in delivering him, these authors assert, Richard visited the abbey and endowed it with relics, including wood from the Holy Cross and the hair of the Virgin Mary. In the early twentieth century, it was said that when Richard returned from captivity, Abbess Matilda of Flanders remarked to her sisters, "You see now . . . that the prayers of the poor servants of the Lord count for something in the destiny of kings and peoples."[42] Richard may have been off fighting for the faith and may have suffered captivity, but, the abbess insists, the nuns of Fontevraud were praying for him all that time in their cloister and enabling him, through their orisons, to return safely to his own lands. It was because of the service Richard had received from the nuns of Fontevraud during his absence on crusade, Honorat Nicquet writes, that when he was asked where he would like to be buried many years later, he replied, "There is no salvation for me if the mercy of God does not halt the arm of justice. My sins are so great that my damnation is inevitable if I do not have powerful intercessors. I choose no others but the nuns of Fontevraud. I have tenderly loved them during my life. In dying, I give myself to them."[43] Richard may have labored to rescue the Holy Land from Saracen domination, but the nuns have labored, and still labor, to rescue him from the infernal damnation he otherwise deserves. Far from irrelevant—far from cut off from political life—the nuns of Fontevraud provide a contemplative counterpart to Richard's active life, and their virtues will offset his sins before God.

Though Fontevraud was now recognized as a worthy site for the burial of the Angevin rulers, the nuns were reluctant to allow secular men—even the new king, John—into their cloister in the absence of their abbess. According to Adam of Eynsham, shortly after Richard's funeral, John traveled to the abbey with Hugh of Lincoln and a large number of noblemen, with the intention of visiting his father's and brother's tombs and commending himself to the prayers of the community. Yet when he knocked at the door, "two nuns of respected gravity" informed him that their abbess was away on a journey and that no one was allowed to enter the inner enclosure of the convent in her absence.[44] The nuns advised John, "Your Excellency must not repute it harsh that we do not break the statutes of our order out of consideration for you. Rather, it is to be recommended that your father, of divine memory, should be imitated, who most respected religious men who observed strictly and with inviolable devotion the customs passed down to them by their predecessors."[45] The nuns recognize that John may be insulted by their refusal to admit him to their abbey, so they justify their position by setting up the authority of Henry, the old king and John's father, who had reigned for many years and had honored the rules of religious orders, over that of his son, who has just become king and has not even been crowned. Just as they follow the rules they have inherited from earlier nuns at Fontevraud, they imply, so he should follow the example that he has inherited from his predecessor.[46] With these remarks, Adam relates, "These 'prudent virgins' curbed and excluded the prince who had knocked and, the doors having been shut, diligently returned to their companions."[47]

Surprisingly, given the bad character generally attributed to him, John does not take offense at the nuns' refusal to admit him to Fontevraud. It was expected that wealthy and powerful men like him might be angered at being shut out of a women's cloister. Heloise, Abbess of the Paraclete and apparently the daughter of Hersende of Champagne,[48] Robert's closest associate in founding Fontevraud, cautions, "If we admit only women, men having been excluded from our hospitality, who would not see that we will offend with great exasperation men whose favor is needed by a monastery of the weaker sex, especially if little or nothing at all seems to be given to those from whom most is received?"[49] The Rule of Fontevraud itself acknowledges that, at times, "some wealthy man or Christian pilgrim"[50] may want to see the cloister in the absence of the abbess, and it allows for him to be given a tour by the prioress, cellaress, and two or three brothers, so long as the other nuns are hidden from view. Yet, despite the abbey's own recognition that it was not expedient to refuse entry to men like John, Adam of Eynsham reports, the new king deferred to the nuns' authority and abandoned his intention to visit the tombs. The chronicler writes, "Having turned to the bishop, he asked him to convey his request to the handmaids of Christ to obtain their intercessory prayers before God on his behalf and to divulge the many benefits he was disposed to confer upon them."[51] Hugh of Lincoln expresses skepticism that John will carry through on his promise to grant favors to the abbey, but John swears that if it is possible, he will do even more for the nuns than he has indicated—and he fulfilled these assurances. According to the necrology, he had been given to Fontevraud as an oblate when he was a child, and he had spent his first five years at the abbey, so that, later, when he became king, he showed it great generosity.[52]

It is striking that none of these stories of Henry's, Richard's, and John's experiences at Fontevraud have to do with Eleanor. She was imprisoned in England when Henry expired, so she took no part in his burial at Fontevraud. Yet she was present at Richard's burial and played a major role in the event, though the primary account of the ceremony—that of Adam of Eynsham—says nothing about her. As we have seen, when Richard was wounded at Châlus, he summoned his mother, who came to him from Fontevraud.[53] According to Adam, Hugh of Lincoln was traveling when "The venerable Abbess of Fontevraud [Matilda of Bohemia] came to him, indicating to him privately that the king, having been struck by a shaft from a crossbow, had passed some days in great pain. His fate uncertain, he was wavering between the limits of death and life."[54] Given the accurate and at that point exclusive information the abbess possesses about Richard's condition, she had presumably accompanied Eleanor to the king's camp, and she had presumably been bidden—perhaps by Eleanor—to continue on to find this holy bishop, whose presence would be requested at the funeral service. When Hugh arrived at Fontevraud, Eleanor was there, making the most generous series of bequests of her life "in pious remembrance of King Henry and good memory of our son King Henry" (338),[55] "for the salvation of the soul of his most dear lord King Richard, our son, so that he might swiftly obtain mercy from the Lord" (334), and for "our other sons and daughters" (338). It seems to be around this time that she founded and endowed the chapel dedicated to Saint Lawrence at Fontevraud (339–40). From the charters recording these bequests, we see her surrounded by numerous secular and ecclesiastical officials, who are serving as witnesses of her donations. If Eleanor is omitted from Adam's account of Richard's death, funeral, and burial, it is because she was left out, not because she was absent from these occurrences.

The silence about Eleanor's role at Richard's funeral and its aftermath does not reflect indifference toward the women affected by this man's demise. En route to Fontevraud, Hugh of Lincoln made a detour to visit with Berengaria of Navarre, who was staying at the Castle of Beaufort, in order to console her for the loss of her husband. Adam of Eynsham writes, "His words went straight to the heart of the mourning widow and as far as her soul, which had been overwhelmed by pain, and soothed her spirit in a marvelous way. With outstanding words, he informed her of the need to have forbearance in adversity and caution in prosperity."[56] The bishop knows that Berengaria has received little attention from her husband over the years, having himself reprimanded Richard for this neglect, yet he still expects her to grieve at his death, and he sympathizes with her sorrow. But

Hugh expresses no similar compassion for Eleanor, who was well known to have loved this son and to have been loved by him. Despite the many pages Adam devotes to describing Richard's funeral and its aftermath, he refers to Eleanor only once, elsewhere in this work, where he alludes to the woman "who repudiated the unstained marriage-bed with [Louis] and, shameless, attached herself to his rival, the King of the English."[57] While Hugh provides spiritual sustenance for the virtuous widow Berengaria, he has no interest in Eleanor, whose bad reputation from so many years before he cannot overlook. Though the men of Eleanor's family all supported Fontevraud with bequests, the chroniclers who describe their interaction with the abbey situate them outside its walls, like John when the nuns close the door in his face. Whether Fontevraud is denigrated or praised, it remains regarded by these men as an "obscure spot," shut off from the world and from them.

LIVING AT THE ABBEY

Whatever Fontevraud meant to Eleanor's menfolk, the abbey was a place to which her female relatives regularly turned. It was common for noblewomen of the twelfth and thirteenth centuries to affiliate themselves with religious houses as they grew older.[58] Some of these women took the veil as *conversae*. Others, like Ida of Lorraine, the widow of Eustace II, Count of Boulogne, Beatrix, the mother of Rotrou II, Count of Perche, and Elizabeth of Hungary, pursued lives of great sanctity in proximity to a religious community without ever taking vows. Devout but less heroic noblewomen also resided in the vicinity or perhaps even in the enclosure of a religious institution,[59] made bequests for its upkeep, and attended its religious services as they wished without submitting themselves to the austerities of consecrated life. They thus occupied what one scholar sees as a liminal space between the monastery and the surrounding, secular community at this time.[60] Berengaria of Navarre, for example, founded the Cistercian Abbey of L'Épau in 1229, but she continued to reside nearby in Le Mans, according to Rodrigo Jiménez de Rada, Archbishop of Toledo, "in praiseworthy widowhood, . . . turning her attention to almsgiving, prayer, and pious works [and] inspiring the emulation of women with her example of chastity and religion."[61] Given the succor a monastic environment could provide an older noblewoman, it makes sense that the anonymous author of a thirteenth-century *razo* should refer to Fontevraud as "an abbey where all the rich old women retire [*une abadia on se rendon totas las veillas ricas*]."[62] Yet even though the abbey could seem cut off from the outside, political world, it constituted the base from which Eleanor continued to operate as regally as ever before.

For Eleanor's female relatives, Fontevraud appears to have functioned as a place of retreat. In 1114, Eleanor's grandmother Philippa, Countess of Toulouse, was said to have heard Robert of Arbrissel preach in her city, whereupon she followed him to Fontevraud and there took religious vows.[63] On Philippa's encouragement, Robert constructed the Fontevrist priory of Lespinasse in the Toulousain, to which she then withdrew.[64] It may have been that William IX repudiated Philippa so that he could live with Dangerosa. William of Malmesbury writes, "His legal wife having been driven off, he carried off the wife of a certain viscount for whom he burned."[65] Or it may have been that Philippa made the decision to leave William on her own, perhaps as a result of his bad behavior. It was said at the time that "If any noblewoman wanted to follow [Robert], . . . all were received into his company,"[66] even if they were fleeing their husbands in doing so.[67] Sometime after 1136, Audiarda (or Agnes), Queen of Aragon, Philippa's daughter and Eleanor's aunt, having given her husband Ramiro II "the Monk," King of Aragon, the required heiress to the throne, abandoned secular life and became a nun at Fontevraud, while Ramiro returned to the monastery he had been forced to abandon in order to become king.[68] Audiarda would eventually be followed by a granddaughter, the child of a child from an earlier marriage. As Philippa may have lived until the 1130s,[69] it is possible that Eleanor visited her at Lespinasse as a girl, and as Audiarda lived until around 1159 and her cousin once removed until at least 1199, it is probable that she saw them when she began to frequent Fontevraud. During Eleanor's first visit to the abbey, she refers to having attended a chapter "in the presence of Lady Matilda, the abbess,"[70] by which she indicates Matilda of Anjou, the daughter of Fulk V, Count of Anjou, and hence Henry's aunt, whose young husband, William Adelin, the son and heir of Henry I, King of England, had drowned in the sinking of the White Ship in 1120. While the king was said to have been kind to Matilda and to have intended to provide her with another highly ranked husband, we are told, "She followed a better counsel when she attached herself to a heavenly Bridegroom, the Son of God and the Virgin."[71] These women had all turned away from marriage, whether because their husbands were notoriously licentious, famously pious, or tragically dead. Their decision to become *conversae* rather than continue to live in the world was widely regarded as holy and admirable, though it was not one Eleanor herself would make.[72]

In her first contact with Fontevraud, Eleanor represents herself, not as a potential convert to the nuns' ranks, but as their wealthy benefactress. Her grandfather, William IX, and her father, William X, had both made donations to this abbey over the years, and Louis had made an annual donation of five hundred Poitevin sous in 1146, "with Queen Eleanor, our cohabitor, assenting."[73] In 1152, shortly after she had separated from Louis and married Henry, Eleanor paid her first recorded visit to Fontevraud. At this transitional moment in her life, as she was shifting from one powerful husband to another, she relates in the charter that resulted from this visit. "I entered the chapter of the said virgins, where, my heart having been touched, I praised, granted, and confirmed whatever my father and my ancestors had given to God and the Abbey of Fontevraud, and especially the alms of five hundred Poitevin sous that my lord Louis, King of the French (at that time my husband), and I once gave."[74] Having examined the monastery to determine whether it was worthy of her support, she decided that it was, thus ensuring a continuity of patronage across generations of her family and across her own marriages. The emotional language Eleanor uses at this time echoes the language her father had used when he visited the Abbey of Saint-Jean de Montierneuf in Poitiers shortly after his assumption of the dukedom of Aquitaine. Seeing his late father's sepulcher, he had stated, "Myself having been touched by sorrow of the heart, all of my viscera were stirred within me on account of my father."[75] While Eleanor is allegedly moved by the nuns' chapter and her father by the sight of his own father's tomb, they both see the religious house as a place that brings together the different generations of their family, and they both wish to support it for that reason. It is with her financial contributions, not with her presence, that Eleanor at first sees herself as contributing to this institution.[76]

Even after Eleanor began to reside at Fontevraud, she remained involved in worldly affairs. She continued to be surrounded by her usual, secular entourage. From the witnesses to her charters, we see in her company high secular officials, such as the seneschals of Poitou (338), Anjou (338), and Gascony (338), as well as high churchmen, such as the Bishop of Poitiers (334, 338–39, 340) and the Archbishop of Bordeaux (338–39). In these documents, Eleanor makes reference to the presence of secular men, including "our kinsman" Ralph of Faye (340) and "our knights" Hamelin of Brolio and Peter Capicerio (340–41), and secular women, including her ladies-in-waiting "A[delina? Ala?], Duchess of *Borbonie*" (339); "M[atilda], Countess of *Tonnerre*" (339); and "Matilda, Viscountess of *Oenaic*" (340–41). These attendants enable Eleanor to act on her wealth and power, as she had always done. Having founded the chapel of Saint Lawrence at Fontevraud and endowed funds to support its chaplain, she speaks of Roger, the original holder of this position, as "our chaplain" (339), in the same way she speaks generally of "our clerics" (339–41) and "our servants" (340–41). Though the chapel belongs to Fontevraud, she refers to Roger, "who will celebrate divine services in our chapel" (339), as if she is retaining the building as a personal possession during her lifetime. In residence at the abbey, she remains queen, with her own staff and her own spiritual attendants.

When Eleanor was away from Fontevraud, as she was for much of 1199, traveling through her lands and attempting to bring them under John's control, Fontevraud came with her. A charter from Poitiers was written "by the hand of Roger, our chaplain at Fontevraud" (339, 341) and witnessed by "Matilda, Abbess of Fontevraud" (339), who was evidently in her company. In early 1200, at the age of seventy-seven, Eleanor trekked to Spain to arrange a match between her eleven-year-old granddaughter Blanche of Castile and Philip's son Louis. Roger of Howden writes that it was only on the return voyage, after she had handed the young girl over to Hélie de Malemort, Archbishop at Bordeaux, that "Queen Eleanor, being fatigued with old age and the labor of the length of the journey, took herself to the Abbey of Fontevraud and remained there."[77] Eleanor is old, she is tired, and, after the exertion of this lengthy voyage across the Pyrenees in winter, she desires, not to forge on to John's court in Normandy to attend her granddaughter's wedding, but to rest at the monastery—yet we know that when Arthur of Brittany rose up against John's rule two years later, in the summer of 1202, Eleanor sallied forth to the Castle of Mirebeau to oppose him. We have almost no further information about Eleanor after John rescued her from the siege Arthur set before this castle, but there were sightings of her at Poitiers as well as Fontevraud, so she seems to have continued to move around.

The meeting between Eleanor and Aimery VII, Viscount of Thouars, illustrates how the queen continued to exercise power over her vassals when she was in residence at Fontevraud. As we recall, in a letter to John in 1200, she recounts how she "summoned" Aimery, whose loyalty to the new king was suspect, "to come to visit us in our sickness at Fontevraud, and he came." In his own letter to John, Aimery reiterates Eleanor's account of their meeting: "Queen Eleanor, my mistress and your mother, struck down by sickness at Fontevraud, summoned me to hurry and visit her while she was gravely ill. With a devoted heart I rushed to her presence." Both Eleanor and Aimery represent the queen, the more highly ranked of the two, as leaning on that status to call him to her and Aimery as bowing to her command. Both represent Eleanor's illness as giving urgency to this request, which makes Aimery hurry to her presence. Both connect their conversation, which ended on a positive note, with the queen's recuperation from her illness, as if the health of her body were dependent on the health of her and her son's realm. "While I was in attendance, she greatly recovered her spirits, and I agreed with her on all points in our conversation concerning you,"[78] Aimery relates. Though Fontevraud may have been a hospice for old women, it was also a place where Eleanor could use her health as a pretext on which to summon a wayward vassal and bring him back into line.

Whether in residence at Fontevraud or traveling about, Eleanor continued to be perceived as a powerful and even dangerous figure. Back in 1183 or 1184, Bertran de Born had written of Alfonso II, King of Aragon, in his *sirventes* "Qan vei pels vergiers despleiar," "He knew how to shortchange Peire the minstrel, . . . since the old woman who runs Fontevraud [*la vella, que Fons-Ebraus / atent*] had him cut all to pieces. Even the badge that the king gave him, made with a band from his pourpoint, could not keep him from getting hacked up with knives."[79] The minstrel Peire, it appears, had received patronage from Alfonso, including a long tabard adorned with this king's coat-of-arms, which should have protected him against attack.[80] Yet an "old woman [*vella*]" of Fontevraud, who was formidable in her defiance of the King of Aragon's protection and in her access to paid assassins, took no notice of this patronage and had him stabbed to death. It is not clear who this woman was, if she ever existed at all,[81] but she was not Eleanor. At this date, the queen was still imprisoned in England; she would not be in residence at the abbey for at least another ten years. Yet the anonymous author of the thirteenth-century *razo* cited earlier comments about this *sirventes*, "Peire the Jongleur had said many evil things about the old Queen of England, the one who was holding Fontevraud [*la veilla reïna d'Englaterra, la quals tenia Font-Ebrau*], which is an abbey where all rich old women retire. So she had him killed with the consent of the King of Aragon."[82] What is interesting here for our purpose is that the author of the *razo* evidently perceives a powerful old woman at Fontevraud to be Eleanor and, conversely, that he perceives Eleanor to be a powerful old woman when she is at this abbey. Given the queen's long-standing reputation, it is not surprising that she should be regarded as someone sufficiently notorious to inspire a jongleur to compose a *mala chanso* about her, sufficiently vindictive to arrange for his murder, and sufficiently persuasive to get her kinsman Alfonso to permit this assault. Although Fontevraud may have been a place of retirement for an old woman, it was also a place where Eleanor was seen as remaining involved in the world, including in the killing of someone who had spoken ill of her.

DYING *AD SUCCURRENDUM*

For the noblewomen who retired to Fontevraud, the abbey was important, not just as a place where they lived, but as a place where they died. When noblewomen who resided in the precincts of a religious house came to the end of their lives, they not uncommonly took the veil *ad succurrendum* so that they would die as *conversae* and thus enjoy the spiritual benefits of this status. In 1192 or 1193, for example, Amicia Pantulf, a onetime "damsel" of Eleanor, bequeathed half the manor of Winterslow in Wiltshire, which she had received from the queen, to the nuns of the Fontevrist Priory of Amesbury, "having notified [them] that she will die in the house of Amesbury and there assume the habit of religion at the end of her days."[83] Having expired as a nun of Fontevraud, this *conversa* of the last moment would be buried in the abbey's cemetery and remembered in its prayers like any other member of the community. After Eleanor had lived for at least five years in association with Fontevraud—whether the last months, the last days, or the last hours of her life, we are not sure—she is said to have taken the veil and died a nun. Yet if Eleanor did move in this religious direction at the very end of her life, from what we are told, it was less out of love of God than out of love of the nuns, including her daughters and granddaughters, to whose community she wished to belong.

Not long after Richard's death in the spring of 1199, Eleanor was joined at Fontevraud by her daughter Joan of Sicily, whose fortunes had taken a turn for the worse. Since her return from the Third Crusade, Joan had married Raymond VI, Count of Toulouse, to whom she had born a son, the future Raymond VII, in 1197. Sometime in the winter of 1199, she attempted to quell an insurrection among her husband's vassals that had been instigated by the brothers Raymond and Bernard of Saint-Félix, the lords of the Castle of Les Cassés, about twenty-four miles southeast of Toulouse. Joan had recently given birth to a daughter,[84] but the chronicler William of Puylaurens writes, "As she was a spirited and provident woman [*mulier animosa et provida*], zealous to avenge the injuries with which many magnates and knight were offending her husband, she took up arms against the lords of Saint-Félix and laid siege to a *castrum* of theirs known as Les Cassés."[85] The insurrection spread from her husband's vas-

sals to her own men, who, we are told, "treacherously and secretly" provided arms and supplies to the other side and set her camp on fire, so that
she was compelled, "aggrieved," to abandon the siege.[86] In her frustration
at the political turmoil in the county of Toulouse, Joan turned, not to
her husband Raymond, but to her brother Richard, who had twice rescued her from peril in the Mediterranean, who had taken her to the Holy
Land on the Third Crusade with him, and in whose company she had been
found as recently as the previous Easter. William of Puylaurens continues,
"Shaken with grief at this injury, she rushed to see her brother King Richard and to expose to him the injury,"[87] but only to learn that he had died
on April 6. Before he expired, Richard had magnanimously pardoned the
soldier whose arrow had caused his death, but, the Annalist of Winchester
relates, "Mercadier sent him secretly from the king to Joan, . . . the king's
sister, who had his fingernails, toenails, and eyes torn out, and afterwards
had him skinned and drawn apart by horses."[88] Whatever mercy Richard
may have wished to exhibit to his killer, Mercadier believed that Joan possessed the right to exact the appropriate vengeance, which she carried out.
Like William of Puylaurens, who portrays Joan as "a spirited and provident
woman" who refuses to allow her husband's authority to be defied, this
annalist depicts her as "a woman transcending the weakness of the female
sex with the constancy of a manly spirit,"[89] who, again, refuses to allow
her brother to go unavenged. There is no evidence of a particular inclination toward God by this point in Joan's life, but there is much evidence
of an inclination toward justice, as we can see in her punishing of those
who would rebel against her husband or raise their crossbow against her
brother. It was after her engagement with the secular world was thwarted,
with her men rising up against her and her brother dying, that she turned
to Fontevraud and to her mother.

When Joan set out for Eleanor, the queen was making the circuit of her
lands in an effort to shore up support for John's reign, but she welcomed
her distraught daughter. Joan may have reached Eleanor in Niort, and she
accompanied her on her travels at least as far as La Rochelle, in May of
1199,[90] and perhaps Puyravault shortly afterward,[91] where she served as a
witness of her charters. In June and July, Eleanor continued on her tour
to Jean-d'Angély and Bordeaux, but Joan withdrew to Fontevraud, where
the necrology describes her as "remaining for a short time with us, where
she was brought up."[92] We find Joan back at Eleanor's side by August 1, in
Rouen, where one of the queen's charters is again witnessed by "our dearest daughter Queen Joan."[93] She remained in the Norman capital with her
mother, the newly crowned John, and the major ecclesiastics of the court,

including Hubert Walter, Archbishop of Canterbury, and Luke, Abbot of Turpenay. By the end of this month, it was clear that she was ailing and was not expected to survive. On August 26, John approved a charter "by the advice of his dearest lady and mother Eleanor, Queen of the English,"[94] as well as the ecclesiastics, in which he finally reimbursed Joan for the money she had lent Richard during the Third Crusade, though he did so at this point only in anticipation of her immanent death. In her last will and testament, Joan left funds to many churches and religious orders,[95] but she made the most extensive bequests to Fontevraud, including funds for the abbey church "for the anniversary of the King of Sicily and herself." From the evidence of a letter she wrote at this time, Eleanor traveled to Gascony with the original testament of "her dearest daughter Queen Joan" so that Raymond VI of Toulouse would see the document and be moved to comply with his late wife's bequests, "as he loves God and her, to the honor of God and to the advantage of the queen's soul."[96] Attaching herself to her mother during these last months of her life, Joan sought to set her affairs in order, financially but also spiritually.

As Joan was dying in Rouen, we are told, she determined to become a nun of Fontevraud because she expected that by doing so, she would be able better to resist the devil in her last hours. Andreas of Fontevraud quotes Hilary of Poitiers, who claimed that "The said enemies . . . are present at the death of everyone, no matter how holy. . . . Because the Enemy, by nature, can do no harm at all to the good after their deaths, he does not cease to persecute them as long as they are in this world, especially at the end, in order to frighten and trouble them."[97] According to the necrology of Fontevraud, it was in the expectation that the devil would come to tempt her on her deathbed and lead her into damnation that Joan sought the protection of the veil of Fontevraud. She begged Hubert Walter, "O Lord Father, have pity on me, and fulfill my desire, so that I may go to fight the Adversary with the arms of religion, so that my body may be strengthened, and so that my soul may be represented more freely to its Creator. I know and I believe that, with my heart joined to the Order of Fontevraud, if my body were also joined, I would be able to escape eternal punishment." Like a warrior faced with an opponent in battle, she believes she will be better prepared to fight the devil "with the arms" of this holy order. Joan is a married woman, still bound to Raymond VI of Toulouse, and she is again pregnant and, indeed, far along in her pregnancy. While the archbishop protested that a married lady could not become a nun without her husband's permission, according to the author of the necrology, he was ultimately persuaded to grant Joan's wish. We are told that "With his own hand, he consecrated her with the veil in the presence of her mother [*praesente matre sua*], the Abbot of Turpenay, and many other nuns of God and the Order of Fontevraud." The devil does come to Joan, but she is now able to brandish the veil she has just received before him and declare, "I am a sister and nun of Fontevraud. Strengthened by such devotion, I do not fear." Having thus deterred the devil, Joan is rewarded for her resolve by the Virgin Mary, whom, "rejoicing," she claims to have seen at this time.[98] The nun's veil, always the marker of a girl or woman's entrance into Fontevraud, has become a talisman for the dying woman, protecting her from the devil and providing her with access to the Virgin.

Dying as a nun of Fontevraud, Joan looks forward to becoming a member of this community, even if only in its burial site. As we have seen, if she wishes to be joined to the order "in her body," it is because she already feels herself to be joined to its community "in her heart." According to Honorat Nicquet, she expresses her wish "that I be buried in the holy monastery of Fontevraud, in order to be joined in body after my death to such a holy company of many nuns, to whom, during my life, I was joined by the ties of a very affectionate friendship."[99] She had been a member of this community of nuns during her life, having been raised here until she was eleven years old, when she was sent off to Sicily to be married, and she wishes to remain in their community after her death, until the time of the Resurrection, as she feels it will help her attain salvation. In her will, Joan made special gifts to particular individuals at the abbey, including "Lady Agatha and Lady Alix, nuns of Fontevraud" and two chaplains of Fontevraud "who shall celebrate divine service forever for her soul and those of her ancestors."[100] She died on September 4.[101] Her child was removed from her by Caesarian section, perhaps while she was still alive, perhaps afterward,[102] and he lived long enough to be baptized[103] and possibly named Richard.[104] Alix, Prioress of Fontevraud, having been sent for in the place of the abbess, arrived after Joan's death and retroactively approved Joan's admission to the order. While the newborn son was buried in the Cathedral of Our Lady in Rouen, Joan's body was transported to Fontevraud, in accordance with her wishes, to be buried in its choir, "with the ceremony that a person of this quality deserved."[105] As Joan is dying, she seeks to join this community on account of the love she feels for its nuns and the love they feel for her, as that love is what assures her of their continued prayers and, hence, of her salvation.

Because the story of Joan's deathbed experience first appears in seventeenth-century sources, one might suspect it is an early modern interpolation were it not for the fact that it mirrors so closely the death-bed experience of a nun of Fontevraud of Joan's time. The nun is identified only as a certain "Angelucia," and the remarkable account of her passing was written, or at least dictated, by a nun who was present at her death,[106] perhaps Margaret, the daughter of Theobald "the Great," II Count of Champagne, IV Count of Blois and Chartres, and the sister-in-law of Eleanor's daughters Marie and Alix.[107] The text was preserved in a mortuary scroll sent to affiliated religious houses, including the Cistercian Monastery of the Blessed Mary of the Mercy of God in Châtellerault, where it was later discovered, in order to inform their residents of recent deaths in the community and solicit their prayers for the departed. Like Joan, Angelucia struggled with the devil as she was dying in the monastery's infirmary and was rewarded for doing so with a visit from the Virgin Mary. As dawn comes, she informs the other nuns, "Here My Lady is present, my queen, with a great entourage and a great procession rejoicing and exulting." She leads the nuns in singing the Marian hymns *"Ave maris stella,"* *"Salve Regina Misericordia,"* and *"Virgines castae,"* with herself singing the loudest, clapping and beating out the time with her fingers. Like Joan, Angelucia sees herself as a member of a community, all of whom strive to assist each other in their spiritual struggles. As she is dying, she lies in her bed, surrounded by changing shifts of nuns who question her about what she is perceiving at this transitional moment between the earthly and the heavenly realms. When the Virgin Mary arrives to Angelucia, we are told, "They interrogated her as to what she said," and they begged, "Tell us, bride of God, what appears to you."[108] The nuns cannot hear her singing without being stirred by her piety, and they cannot look at her radiant face without weeping a font of tears. It is said, "We looked at her, and we were refreshed by a joy and sweetness like heavenly bread." As Angelucia is exulting in the presence of the heavenly Bridegroom, the other nuns are exulting in the presence of Angelucia, whose extraordinary piety inspires their own devotion. Stirred by the love of her "beloved sisters,"[109] Angelucia advises them to strive to love their Bridegroom and to serve him well, as she has done, and she promises them that, if they do so, they will partake in the spiritual ecstasy she is undergoing. She loves the other nuns and they love her, but this love is no secular friendship of women for each other; it is the sacred attachment of souls attempting to aid and be aided by each other in their journey to Paradise. Both Joan and this virgin nun will succeed in overcoming the devil as a member of the order of Fontevraud, and their sisters in that order will assist them in gaining salvation.

Like Joan, Eleanor is said to have taken the habit of Fontevraud shortly before dying, but not because she feared struggling with the devil. By the time the queen arrived at Fontevraud, there was a long tradition of royal and aristocratic women retreating to this abbey or its priories to repent of their sins, including Bertrade of Montfort, the wife of Fulk IV, Count of Anjou, who was later the mistress and then "wife" of Philip I, King of France,[110] and Juliana, the illegitimate daughter of Henry I of England, who had rebelled against her father and even attempted to kill him with a crossbow.[111] Even Queen Guinevere, the wife of King Arthur, is said to have ended her life as a nun at the Fontevrist priory of Amesbury, where she atoned for her adultery with Lancelot.[112] Given Eleanor's disordered youth, it might have been expected that she, too, would repent of her sins as she turned toward Fontevraud so that she could die in a state of grace. And it is true that the Cistercian chronicler Alberic of Trois-Fontaines refers in his *Chronica* (1232–41) to "the queen, that is, Eleanor, who amended her life so that she finished it in a good state."[113] In the seventeenth, eighteenth, and nineteenth centuries, Eleanor would be remembered as having atoned for her many misdeeds. Balthazar Pavillon claims that she followed in the footsteps of William X, who had done penance by traveling to Saint James of Compostella and, in doing so, had taught his daughter "the science of dying well."[114] Abbé "Edouard" (a pseudonym for Abbé Armand Biron) claimed that Eleanor underwent a change of heart with her entry into religion: "She took the nuns' habit and adopted with it their spirit and austere practices. She redeemed the distractions of her youth with tears and abundant alms."[115] Another author remarks that "All the extremities of human beings met in this woman."[116] Yet we have no firm evidence of Eleanor's change of heart in the medieval or even the modern sources. We have no accounts of a dramatic deathbed conversion, as we do for the Young King and Joan. According to the necrology, the epitaph on the monument raised to Eleanor's memory offered bland praise of her "honesty . . . of life, grace . . . of manners, . . . and incomparable honor of probity,"[117] in which she exceeded all other queens, but it made no reference to her holiness, let alone to her penitential practices. Because Eleanor had been described as beautiful, spirited, and amorous in her younger years and because she affiliated herself with a monastery in her old age, these authors extrapolate that she rejected her former, sinful life and embraced this later, virtuous one, but there is no reason to make such an assumption.

If Eleanor took the habit of Fontevraud shortly before dying—and we have only the abbey's tradition to assure us that she did—it seems to have been less out of devotion to God than out of affection for the nuns. In a charter from around 1200, she makes a donation of ten Poitevin pounds in usufruct "to our beloved protégée [*alumpne*] Alix, Prioress of Fontevraud" (338). The necrology generalizes about the fondness Eleanor showed to the nuns of this abbey at the end of her life, so that it is, not just this one prioress, but many nuns who become the object of her interest: "Whatever nuns of our order, wherever they were found, even the lowliest, she supported with such honor and favored with such love that she adopted them as her own daughters." It is the affection that Eleanor felt for the nuns that led her to adopt the veil herself, we are informed. According to the necrology, "In the end, she was affected by a bond of such sincere love for us that, as if rejecting other religious orders, she preferred to take the veil of our order and be buried in our church."[118] While Eleanor had originally intended merely to live at the abbey in the years before her death in a secular state, Baltazar Pavillon writes, "The charms she found in the life of these holy girls brought her in the end to take their habit and to associate herself with them shortly before dying, following the example of Queen Joan her daughter."[119] These documents are all from the seventeenth century, but their interpretation of Eleanor's motivation in entering religious life is not without interest. As Eleanor loves the nuns like a daughter, she wishes to become a nun among them. And as she had loved her daughter Joan, who became one of these nuns before she died, she wishes to act as Joan had acted, taking the veil before her death.

In joining the order of Fontevraud, Eleanor would have joined, not only the nuns, for whom she was said to have had such fondness, but her five daughters, each of whom was associated with the order, either directly or through her own daughters. Marie de Champagne retired to the Fontevrist priory of Château de Fontaines-les-Nonnes near Meaux, where she died in 1198.[120] Marie's sister Alix of Blois died in the secular world in 1197 or 1198, but her youngest daughter, also named Alix, was a nun at Fontevraud when Eleanor was living there. In a charter from the time of her daughter Alix's death, Eleanor makes a donation "to our beloved granddaughter Alix, daughter of Alix, of happy memory, once Countess of Blois, our dearest daughter," and she asks that the funds be used "to celebrate the anniversaries of our said granddaughter and her mother in that church" (340). Expressing affection for her daughter and granddaughter, Eleanor subsidizes Masses that will not only preserve the memories of these women but will link them to herself. Matilda of Saxony had died in 1189, but the "M[atilda], Countess of Le Perche" mentioned in charters as attending Eleanor at this time was this Matilda's daughter, who had joined her grandmother's entourage.[121] Young Eleanor, married and living in Castile, did not affiliate herself with a Fontevrist community per se, but in 1187 she founded the Cistercian Abbey of Santa María la Real de Las Huelgas, another powerful monastery of nuns and final resting place of a royal family, which is often thought to have been modeled on Fontevraud.[122] Joan, as we have seen, died as a nun of Fontevraud, with her mother by her side. Linked through this abbey during their lives, these women were linked through its nuns' prayers after their deaths, as were their menfolk. In addition to "Our Lady Eleanor, Queen of England, our most famous mother,"[123] much of Eleanor's family is listed in Fontevraud's necrology, including her grandparents William IX and Philippa; her aunt Audiarda; her father William X; her uncle Ralph of Faye; her husband Henry; her sons the Young King, Richard, and John; her daughters Eleanor and Joan; her grandsons Henry III, King of England, and Raymond VII, Count of Toulouse; and her great-grandson Edward I, King of England. Thanks to the donations Eleanor and these relatives had made to Fontevraud, they expected to benefit from the gratitude of the nuns of this abbey and from the prayers of these holy women, who, it was hoped, would aid in their progress toward Heaven.

In the last months of Eleanor's life, her family's land holdings on the Continent were vanishing. In December of 1203, John had abandoned Normandy. In March of 1204, Castle Gaillard, the great fortress Richard had built to protect the Seine Valley from French incursions, fell to Philip, and the Norman barons deserted John for the French king. Before long, Rouen, having been left exposed by the loss of this castle, also succumbed. On March 31 or April 1, 1204, at the age of at least eighty-two, Eleanor died, perhaps at Fontevraud,[124] but perhaps in Poitiers[125] or elsewhere.[126] Most chroniclers mention simply the year[127] or perhaps the date and the year[128] at which she passed away, without the place. John mourned the passing of his mother in the customary ways, by releasing prisoners "for the love of God and for the salvation of our dearest mother's soul,"[129] by making gifts to Fontevraud,[130] and by arranging for Masses to be said on the anniversary of her death. Yet the consequences of Eleanor's demise were, for John, political as well as personal. Soon after Eleanor expired, her onetime vassals in Poitou and Aquitaine recognized Philip as their lord.[131] Polydore Vergil would connect Eleanor's death to the dissolution of the Angevin realm, the news of which would have come to the abbey: "At this time, Eleanor, the mother of John, a most prudent woman [*mulier longe prudentissima*], died, more of sadness of spirit than consumed by disease [*magis moerore animi quam morbo consumpta*]."[132] As Eleanor gave up her spirit out of grief at losing these lands, John, it was said, lost these lands out of grief of losing his mother. According to the *Annales Sancti Albini Andegavenis*, "With her death, the king, most vehemently saddened, feared greatly for himself and was disquieted enough to withdraw from Normandy."[133] By August of that year, John would still be King of England, but with no land holdings on the Continent except Aquitaine.

THE TOMB SCULPTURE

She lies there still, in the abbey church of Fontevraud. She is reclining on a draped bed of state with her head propped up by a cushion as well as by the curve of the bed, so that she can read the book she is holding open on her chest. Underneath her crown, she is wearing a white wimple with a chin-strap and a short veil. A blue mantle is drawn over her shoulders and then gathered up again over the middle third of her body. Beneath the mantle, a white, pleated gown, girt at the waist with a belt, flows down over her body to her feet. We do not know if Eleanor ever looked like this statue—the woman depicted here is ageless and expressionless—but the clothes she is wearing are the fashions of the early thirteenth century. Henry lies on his own bed of state next to her, crowned like his wife and holding a scepter in the place of a book, and Richard reclines at Henry's feet.[134] The sculptures are life-sized and carved out of the local tuffeau limestone. Their current colors date from the sixteenth or seventeenth century, but they would have been painted when they were first fashioned. These statues are the first *gisants*, that is, the first tomb sculptures that represent the departed, not as standing figures who happen to be laid down horizontally, but as recumbent figures who are actually reclining, with their garments flowing over their bodies as they would naturally do in this position.[135] In their size and their realistic details, they seem like actual human beings, resting in anticipation of the end of time and the Resurrection, when they will rise again in these beautiful forms. Surviving as she does in this effigy, Eleanor in particular feels curiously alive, as if she is holding up her book to read, while her companions lie still, and she therefore feels curiously present, as if she continues to haunt the church and the abbey where she spent so much time in her last years.

It is generally agreed that Eleanor arranged for the sculptures of Henry, Richard, and herself to be carved and placed in the abbey church.[136] In March of 1189, when Henry died at Chinon, Roger of Howden writes that his body was brought "to the Abbey of Fontevraud, and there [Richard] buried him in the nuns' choir."[137] While the precise location of the "nuns' choir" at this time is not entirely clear, it seems that, by the late twelfth century, the nuns would have been seated in the nave of the church, with a barrier protecting them from the sight of the brothers in the choir.[138] The dead were thus buried in the nave, presumably in the easternmost bays, just below the transept. The effigies of both Henry and Richard are believed to have been commissioned by Eleanor shortly after Richard's death, at a time when she was making substantial donations in the memory of her beloved son, and to have been carved by the same artist. They were placed over these kings' tombs, so that anyone wishing to visit the tombs would have seen them.[139] It would not be until the early thirteenth century that women would come to be held responsible for praying for their deceased family members to ascend from Purgatory to Paradise,[140] but Eleanor's daughters had already constructed memorials for their husbands, including Marie de Champagne's effigy for her husband, Henry I the Liberal, Count of Champagne, at the collegiate church of Saint Stephen in Troyes, and Matilda of Saxony's effigy for her husband, Henry the Lion, Duke of Saxony, in Brunswick Cathedral. It would not be until the fourteenth century that individuals were recorded as having commissioned their own tombs, but it has been speculated that Eleanor may have anticipated this trend.[141] When it came her time to die, the necrology reports, "Eleanor . . . ordered that she finally be buried there."[142] Her *gisant* is thought to have been carved by a different artist from the one who fashioned her husband's and son's statues, and one of superior ability,[143] sometime before 1210, within six years of her death.[144] Eleanor and her daughters did not leave us written accounts of their lives, but they did leave us these memorials of themselves and their families.

The story of Joan's internment is more complicated than that of her parents and her brother. Eleanor was present when her youngest daughter died in Rouen, when she was transported back to the abbey, and when she was buried, as Roger of Howden puts it, "among the veiled women [*inter velatas*]."[145] Roger's phraseology has led some scholars to believe that Joan was originally interred, not near her father and brother, but in the cemetery of the nuns, among whom she now belonged. Yet Henry, as we have seen, was also described as having been buried "among the veiled women" in the sense that he was buried in the abbey complex, and other sources explicitly locate Joan's tomb among her family members, not her sister religious. William of Puylaurens is describing the arrangement of the tombs retrospectively, after Eleanor had died as well, when he writes of Joan that "She was buried at the feet of her mother Eleanor, Queen of England, next to her brother Richard, who is buried at the feet of their father, King Henry, in the church at Fontevraud."[146] The author of the necrology likewise attests that Joan's body "was placed next to her brother."[147] While Joan's tomb may have been marked only by an inscribed slab, a tradition holds that a *gisant* was made for her as well.[148] There would have been a symmetry in having Joan lie at her mother's feet, just as Richard was lying at his father's feet, and at having her rest until the Resurrection next to the brother for whom she cared so deeply. After Joan's son Raymond VII, Count of Toulouse, died in 1249, at his request he was buried near his mother at Fontevraud, underneath a stone *gisant*.[149] In 1638, when Abbess Jeanne-Baptiste de Bourbon was supervising renovations in the church, she had Joan's and Raymond's *gisants* replaced by marble praying statues (*priants*), which represented Joan kneeling at the head of her father's sepulcher, with her hands clasped and her head bent down, and Raymond kneeling and facing his mother, perhaps striking his breast in penance for his onetime dalliance with the heretical Cathar faith.[150] The statues of mother and son both disappeared during the revolutionary tumult of 1793, though fragments of Raymond's statue were rediscovered in the twentieth century.[151]

In the abbey church, in the company of her husband, her son, and, at one point, her daughter, Eleanor is represented, not as a nun, but as a queen. When the Angevin kings died, it seems that their bodies were dressed in the same clothing and accoutrements they had worn on the day of their coronation. According to Roger of Howden, as we have seen, when Henry was borne to be buried at Fontevraud, "he was clothed with regal splendor,"[152] with the crown, gloves, ring, scepter, and sword he would have worn during his coronation. Something similar seems to have happened when Richard was carried back to this abbey. And as the appearance of these dead kings on their funeral bier recalled that of the living kings at the site of their coronation, the appearance of these sculpted kings on their stone beds of state recalls that of the dead kings on their funeral bier. Indeed, in the last quarter of the twelfth century, the development of funeral ceremonies for deceased rulers seems to have led to the commissioning of funeral sculptures like these *gisants*,[153] which replicated the public exposure of these rulers' recumbent bodies as an object of mourning. Nothing is known of Eleanor's funeral or the funeral of any other queen of her time, but when her formidable granddaughter Blanche of Castile, Queen of France, passed away in 1252, her dead body was treated like those of these kings.[154] According to the *Grandes chroniques de France*, "When she was dead, the noble men of the country carried her on a gold pulpit throughout Paris, all clothed like a queen, the gold crown on her head."[155] No equally grand ceremony could have accompanied Eleanor's burial, given her son's tenuous control over the territory in which Fontevraud was located at this time, but it stands to reason that she too would have been "all clothed like a queen, the gold crown on her head," as she was when crowned Queen of England and as she is depicted in her *gisant*. Far from having turned away from her earlier secular life, the Eleanor of this statue is affirming her identity as a crowned queen, positioned next to her husband, the crowned king, as she would have been during their corona-tion,[156] and adjacent to her son, another crowned king and, at one point, her daughter, another crowned queen. By lying in an abbey church, she associates herself, not with the nuns, but with her royal family members.

Though a queen, Eleanor the *gisant* is focused, not on the outer life of government, but on the inner life of meditation. While Henry and Richard lie with their eyes fully closed, as if slumbering in death as they await the Resurrection, Eleanor reclines with her eyes half open, as if hovering some-where in between life and death. Scholars speak of the "idealization"[157] of Eleanor's features in this *gisant*, usually with disappointment, as if they would prefer to see her as she "really" was, yet in the Middle Ages, no one ever contrasted the "ideal" and the "real" in this manner. Insofar as medi-eval people did oppose what can be perceived with the intellect and what can be perceived with the senses, they deemed the fixed, perfected appear-ance of a glorified human being, as she will exist for eternity, to be more "real" than her mutable, flawed appearance as it is in our temporal world. What we apprehend as "realism," they saw, as one scholar puts it, as "the values of the surface, . . . *vanitas* and impermanence, and hence mortal-ity."[158] The early twelfth-century theologian Honorius of Autun wrote in his popular handbook the *Elucidarium* that the bodies of the resurrected would be "immortal, incorruptible, and transparent, like bright glass," "full of all beauty," with their members "healthy and whole,"[159] and that their age would be that of Jesus Christ when he was resurrected.[160] Represented in this glorified body, Eleanor is anticipating the world to come, not remem-bering the world in which she had lived for so many years.

Focused as she is on the inner life of meditation, Eleanor holds a book open on her chest.[161] There were already tomb sculptures of the dead car-rying closed books, often against their side,[162] but this is the earliest depic-tion of anyone, male or female, holding an open book.[163] Some commen-tators have wished to see the book as a collection of troubadour poetry or a romance, in accordance with their vision of Eleanor as a patroness of vernacular literature,[164] but ladies generally listened to such works of en-tertainment being read aloud at this time.[165] Instead, the book is presum-ably a psalter, which both laywomen and nuns were accustomed to read and which we see the nuns of Fontevraud reading by the side of the dying Angelucia or the dead Henry. Yet, though Eleanor is holding the book, she cannot be reading it; her gaze is fixed above its pages. Her line of vision symbolizes the spiritual meditation to which nuns' lives were given over, a meditation prompted by and supported by a text but ultimately transcending it. The model reader at someplace like Fontevraud would be, not a scholar of Latin theology or a peruser of vernacular songs, but the Virgin Mary, who was commonly represented as reading in her chamber, in a way that evokes visually the intensity of her inner communion with God. The fact that Eleanor holds a book, and not a scepter, as Fredegond, the wife of the Merovingian King Chilperic I, does in her effigy at Saint-Denis, or even as she herself does in her seals,[166] has seemed to observers to reflect her prioritization of piety over power, contemplation over action,[167] and by extension, "retreat, political retrenchment, and burial, in a community of devout women," over the secular world of her husband and son.[168] Though Eleanor lies next to members of her royal family, she acts as the nuns of this abbey would have acted every day, including in the very church where they would have beheld this statue.

The nuns deserve the final word in this chapter. In the early twelfth century, Petronilla of Chemillé indicated that she took no pleasure in running the abbey. She is reported to have said, "The embellishment of reading and prayers often having been neglected, we turn to the management of temporal goods for the advantage of our successors, which indeed we do so that, when we are sleeping in our tombs, we will be worthy to be helped by their prayers before God."[169] This abbess would have preferred to remain a contemplative nun, abandoning herself to the delights of meditation, but she was obliged to assume an active role in this community for the benefit of those who would come after her. The reward she seeks is, not the admiration of future generations of historians, but the prayers of future generations of nuns, whose devotions on her behalf will help her attain Heaven. In a similar manner, the author of the account of Angelucia's death makes no mention of the names of the holy nun's parents, the place from which she hailed, or even the year of her passing,[170] which would have enabled us to identify her, but records only the month and day of her heroic end, as it was on the anniversary of that day that future members of this community would remember her. In 1911, the nuns of Saint Mary of Fontevraud of Boulaur, who had revived the Fontevrist priory in the 1840s,[171] composed the first and only history of Fontevraud written by nuns of this order. They remark that their task was not an easy one, "as innumerable nuns ... seem to have taken to task to accomplish literally this advice of the pious author of the *Imitation of Jesus Christ*: 'Love to be unknown and to be counted as nothing.'"[172] It was on account of their spiritual vocation, these authors suggest, that their predecessors at Fontevraud sought anonymity. Instead of projecting themselves into the temporal future, as individuals worthy of honor and commemoration in this world, they sought to live entirely in the temporal present, as souls humble and free of self-consciousness, in order to prepare themselves for the eternal future. The life of a nun, as they saw it, was "an angelic life,"[173] outside time and, hence, outside history. Yet just as the twelfth-century nuns of Fontevraud believed themselves to have aided Richard on crusade through their spiritual efforts on his behalf, their modern-day descendants remind us that "Through prayer, man participates in the government of the world."[174] With this abbey's respect for both contemplation and action—for both retreat from the world and involvement in it—it is no surprise that it welcomed Eleanor in her final years.

THE LIONESS
IN WINTER

Poetry, Theater, Cinema

Three hundred years after Eleanor had been buried in the Abbey of Fontevraud, an aspect of her story that had been almost entirely neglected by medieval chroniclers took on new interest. In the sixteenth century, it was recalled, the English royal household had been peopled, not only by Eleanor and Henry's family members, retainers, and servants, but by a certain number of unattached young women, including foster-daughters like Margaret and Alys of France, kept "in custody" (*in custodia*) until they were of age to be married; prisoners like Eleanor, the Fair Maid of Brittany, kept confined to prevent them from claiming their ancestral lands; hostages like the mysterious Daughter of the King of Cyprus, retained as a form of leverage over their untrustworthy fathers; and concubines like Rosamund Clifford or the prostitutes who were kept on the court payroll.[1] Given the simultaneously protective and carceral connotations of being held "in custody" in medieval Latin, as in modern English, these young female members of the court could occupy all these roles at once. Medieval chroniclers made clear that these maidens were not infrequently Henry's mistresses, but early modern poets and playwrights were the first to try to imagine Eleanor's response to this situation. Did the queen see these young women as unwilling pawns in arrangements made by the men around them, or did she regard them as willing partners in love affairs with her husband? Did she experience sympathy toward these girls, whose education she had often supervised, or jealousy toward sexual competitors at a time when her own physical charms were fading? In an environment where the personal and the political were so inextricably intertwined, what did it mean for anyone in this household, whether Eleanor, Henry, or these young women, to love or be loved? The image of Eleanor as a bitter old woman seeking vengeance on her rivals that has dominated the vast majority of the postmedieval representations of the queen has its origins in these early modern works.

In the medieval chronicles, when Henry's mistresses were mentioned, it was not Eleanor who was condemned for her behavior toward them but her husband. As William of Newburgh sees it, Henry possessed many virtues appropriate to a king, but "He was susceptible . . . to certain vices which especially disgraced a Christian prince. He [was] prone to lust. . . . Having lived with the queen a sufficient time to have offspring, when she ceased to give birth, following his desire, he had illegitimate children."[2] From what William attests, Henry used Eleanor to serve his dynastic purposes and then discarded her in favor of other women. Yet the king was not able to pursue women with impunity, the chronicler Ralph Niger reports. If he imprisoned Eleanor in 1173, this chronicler claims, it was, not just to prevent her from conspiring with his sons, but to prevent her from interfering with his pursuit of other sexual partners: "He enclosed the queen in a house prison so that he might have leisure to occupy himself more freely with debauchery."[3] From what Ralph suggests, Eleanor had so little power that she was locked up by her husband, but were she at liberty, she would have possessed so much power that she could have potentially impeded his amorous adventures. While the queen is imagined to be hostile toward the king's infidelities, she is imagined as seeking to act on that hostility by inhibiting his pursuit of women—perhaps by her mere presence at court—not by taking vengeance on the women he pursued.

If the judgment on Eleanor's interactions with these young women changed over the course of the centuries, it is largely because the values brought to bear on their situation shifted. The medieval chroniclers were concerned with public morality. What example did Eleanor, Henry, and Rosamund set for others through their immoral behavior? What effect did their actions have on others in this kingdom? In contrast, the Renaissance poets were concerned with private morality. What led this queen, this king, and this damsel to act as they did? What degree of responsibility did they therefore bear for their actions? Turning away from both the medieval and the early modern precedents, James Goldman, in his 1966 play *The Lion in Winter*, and Anthony Harvey, in his 1968 film version of the drama,[4] with Katharine Hepburn's Academy Award–winning turn as Eleanor, do not focus on morality at all, but, rather, on politics as it plays out within this family circle. In both the theatrical and cinematic versions of this work, Eleanor has been temporarily released from imprisonment for Henry's 1183 Christmas court at Chinon, where she and her husband are joined by Richard, Geoffrey, and John, and by Alys of France (here called Alais), Louis's daughter by his second wife, Constance of Castile.[5] The sons are all jockeying to be designated heir to the throne, with Alais and her significant dowry to be given to whoever among them succeeds. Whether Henry's mistress is Rosamund or Alais, she and Eleanor represent two models of feminine comportment, the one sweet, gentle, and accommodating to the men around her, the other fierce and rebellious against their plans. With moral considerations having been pushed aside by political ones, Eleanor is evaluated, no longer in terms of how virtuously she acted toward those around her, but in terms of how skillfully she retained power, and on that score she is praised.

FAIR ROSAMUND

For many centuries after the Middle Ages, Eleanor's treatment of "Fair Rosamund" was seen as her darkest hour. While in the medieval texts Rosamund is referred to simply by her Christian name, she can reasonably be identified as Rosamund Clifford, the daughter of the Anglo-Norman marcher lord Walter de Clifford from Herefordshire, on the Welsh border. At the end of the twelfth century, Gerald of Wales recounts how Henry took Rosamund as his concubine following his sons' rebellion against him, that is, in 1174 or 1175.[6] The young woman died around 1176 and was buried at the Benedictine nunnery of Godstow,[7] in between Woodstock and Oxford, where members of the Clifford family may have already been interred. Rosamund's father later made gifts to the abbey "for the souls of my wife Margaret Clifford and our daughter Rosamund,"[8] and her brother-in-law did the same, referring to the two women "whose bodies rest there."[9] It was around the time of Rosamund's burial that Henry made Godstow into a royal abbey under his protection[10] and showered it with bequests.[11] After these scattered historical references to Rosamund in twelfth-century sources, the more legendary accounts of this maiden started to develop in the fourteenth and fifteenth centuries,[12] and they flourished in the sixteenth and seventeenth centuries, especially in the form of ballads and other poems. Though tales of Rosamund continued to inspire countless poems,[13] plays,[14] operas,[15] and paintings[16] well into the modern era, it was during the Elizabethan period that Eleanor first emerged as Rosamund's murderer, stirred to kill the maiden by motives both political and personal. While Henry is seen as destroying the maiden by debauching her, Eleanor is seen as destroying her by punishing her for this debauchery,

In the earliest medieval accounts of Rosamund, Henry is represented as loving this maiden during her lifetime. Gerald of Wales refers to "the maiden Rosamund, whom the king had loved so excessively with his adulterous embraces."[17] While Gerald emphasizes the sexual nature of Henry's attraction to Rosamund, he also stresses the amorous nature of this bond. This is not courtly love, which was considered impossible between a powerful man and a low-ranked woman like Rosamund, given the pressure that such a man could bring to bear on such a woman for her sexual favors, but rather the affection of a ruler for a subject's daughter.[18] So much did Henry value this young woman, we are told, that he concealed her in the royal residence at Woodstock, with its a vast enclosed park and menagerie, in order to keep her safe. The Benedictine chronicler Ranulph Higden was perhaps inspired by the sight of this walled park and its exotic beasts when he relates, in the first part of the fourteenth century, that "The king had an enclosure of marvelous construction built at Woodstock for the most-watched maiden, winding in a Daedalus-like way, lest perhaps she be discovered easily by the queen, but she died soon thereafter."[19] Ranulph suggests that, like Daedalus, who built a labyrinth in Crete, with intricate passageways designed to prevent any intruder from tracking down the Minotaur in its midst,[20] Henry built an enclosure whose halls within halls were designed to prevent Eleanor from tracking down his concubine.[21] So unruly was this queen, he implies, that Henry could not simply order her to stay away from his mistress, nor could he simply punish her if she defied his command; he could only use artifice to try to stop her. In these earliest accounts, there is no indication that Eleanor found Rosamund in the labyrinth, let alone harmed her, yet Ranulph's juxtaposition of the queen's potential menace and the maiden's early death is suggestive. Once again, Eleanor is characterized, not by what she did, but by what she could have or would have done had she not been prevented from doing so.

Even after Rosamund had died, we are told, Henry continued to cherish her. According to Roger of Howden, Hugh, Bishop of Lincoln, was once paying visits to the religious houses in his diocese when he stopped by Godstow Abbey. There, he noticed a tomb positioned before the altar, covered by a silken cloth and surrounded by candles. Roger relates, "He asked those standing around whose tomb it was which was held in such reverence. They told him that it was the tomb of Rosamund, whom Henry, King of England, so loved that, for love of her, he had enriched with many great revenues this house, which had earlier been poor and begging. He had adorned it with noble buildings, and he had conferred a great revenue on this church for the unfailing light which is to be found around this tomb."[22] So bereft was Henry at the death of his "beloved [*amica*],"[23] as Rosamund is termed, we are told, that he did all that one could in the Middle Ages when a cherished woman passed away: he had her buried honorably, in an abbey of religious virgins, in the chapel mentioned here or perhaps in the chapterhouse;[24] he had her memory preserved with everlasting vigilance by those virgins, who kept the candles surrounding her tomb alit; and he supported this abbey with generous donations. By having virgins honor the tomb of a concubine, Henry had them honor a sentimental love out of respect for his power and gratitude for his bequests, however contrary that love might seem to their own professed chastity,

Yet in these same accounts, Henry is criticized for his love of Rosamund. Gerald of Wales writes of the king, "When his wife, Queen Eleanor, had been imprisoned for some time, . . . he who had previously been a secret adulterer afterwards became a manifest one, publicly and impudently abusing . . . Rosamund. . . . And because 'that world is ordered by the example of the king,' he offended not only by his deed but much more by his example."[25] Though Henry kept Rosamund hidden away in Woodstock, he let it be known that he was keeping her as his paramour. In doing so, Gerald asserts, he sinned, not just by committing adultery, but by flagrantly committing adultery and, hence, by giving royal sanction to this crime. In depicting Henry as "abusing [*abutendo*]" Rosamund, Gerald suggests that the king used this maiden wrongly or improperly in committing adultery with her, but he could also be suggesting that he subjected her to ill-treatment or even violated her sexually. Whatever the degree of her consent to Henry's abuse, it is clear that Rosamund was stained by the king's treatment of her. When Hugh of Lincoln learned that her body was in the church of Godstow, he told those who were with him, "Take her out of here, for she was a harlot, and the love that existed between the king and her was illicit and adulterous. Bury her with the other dead outside the church so that the Christian religion is not debased and so that other women, frightened, beware of illicit and adulterous concubinage from her example."[26] Whatever love there was between Henry and his mistress — and Hugh acknowledges that there was some love — it was contrary to divine and human law, and it should be recognized as such. As Gerald worried that Henry's open adultery was giving permission to his subjects to keep concubines, Hugh worries that the nuns' veneration of the concubine's tomb was giving permission to these subjects' wives and daughters to engage in such sinful behavior. To honor a harlot is to honor harlotry, and Rosamund was, in her essence, a wayward woman.

The epitaph on Rosamund's tomb epitomizes the foulness these me-

dieval chroniclers attribute to this maiden. Playing on her name, Gerald
of Wales writes that she was "not indeed called 'rose of the world' [*Rosa-
mundi*], as the name is wrongly and frivolously interpreted, but more truly
'rose of the unclean' [*immundi rosa*]."[27] Ranulph Higden recalls Gerald's
words when he relates that her epitaph read: "Here lies in the tomb the
Rose of the World [*Rosa mundi*], not a clean rose [*rosa munda*]. She does
not emit a good odor, but stinks who used to emit a good odor [*Non re-
dolet sed olet quod redolere solet*]."[28] Whereas Gerald contrasts Rosamund's
physical beauty and her moral foulness, the author of these verses contrasts
the sweet smell she had exuded as a living maiden and the repugnant odor
she now gives off as a decomposing corpse. In the late fifteenth century, we
are told that when Henry returned from foreign travels and found Rosamund buried, he had her tomb pried open "for the great love that he had
for her," only to find a toad lying between her breasts, an adder encircling
her waist, and a foul odor emanating from her body.[29] Like a death's head,
Rosamund has become a memento mori, an image of the end that awaits
us all, and more particularly, an image of the punishment that awaits sinners after death. In contrast to a saint's body, whose incorruptible flesh and
sweet smell reflect that person's blessedness, this sinner's demonic companions and rank odor convey her damned state. If one interprets Rosamund's
name correctly, Gerald indicates, one apprehends her true, foul nature as
a harlot, a nature that was concealed by her corporeal beauty during her
lifetime but is now made manifest in her flesh after her demise.

By the time we get to the Renaissance literary accounts of Rosamund,
which shift from the maiden's outer appearance to her inner thoughts, we
see her, not just as a harlot, but as a young woman who was to some degree compelled to become Henry's paramour. In Samuel Daniel's "Complaint of Rosamund" (1592), the maiden feels no attraction to this lord.
She explains, "He is my King and may constrain me, / Whether I yield
or not I live defamed: / The world will think authority did gain me, / I
shall be judged his love, and so be shamed."[30] It is not that Henry is forcing her to become his concubine, but that he *may* force her to do so; if
she is thus compelled, she realizes, she will be no less dishonored than
if she had agreed to this arrangement. For that reason, she succumbs to
Henry's advances, recognizing, ". . . if I yield, tis honorable shame, / If not,
I live disgraced, yet thought the same."[31] The first night Rosamund and
Henry spent together, she recalls, she experienced, not "the sweet-stolen
sports, of joyful meeting lovers," but ". . . the hand of lust most undesired
/ . . . / Which yields no mutual pleasure when 'tis hired."[32] She might have
known sexual delight if she had been joined with a lover of her own age to

whom she was attracted, but she took no such enjoyment in this "loathed bed"[33] with its older bedmate. Henry quickly satisfies himself with the young woman, given his aged libido, and he falls asleep next to her, but she remains awake alone, already repenting of what has occurred. In other poems, Rosamund pleads with Eleanor for her life, kneeling before her, weeping, and wringing her hands. She insists, "So farforth as it lay in me I did . . . withstand, / But what may not so great a King by means or force command?"[34] She portrays herself, not as raped per se—she is not physically pinned down and assaulted—but as consenting under constraint. For that reason, she begs Eleanor for compassion for her sufferings: "Take pity on my youthful years, / . . . / And for the fault which I have done, / Though I was forced thereto."[35]

Yet in the Renaissance poems, Rosamund also blames herself for having become Henry's concubine. In Samuel Daniel's "Complaint of Rosamund," she at first resists his overtures, but an older woman who is sent to break her will warns her, with the carpe diem topos popular at this time, that her beauty will soon fade and she will repent of not having taken sufficient advantage of men's admiration when she had the chance. This duenna teaches her that a woman suffers shame, not for what she does, but for what she is known to do, so that a discreet paramour may therefore preserve her honor. And even if she should suffer shame, she advises, her action will not be disgraceful because her lover will be a king: "The Majesty that doth descend so low, is not defiled, but pure remains therein, / And being sacred, sanctifies the sin."[36] On the night before her deflowering, Henry gives Rosamund a casket decorated with the images of Amymone being seized by Neptune, "From whom she striv'd and struggled to be gone,"[37] and Io, beloved of Jove, ". . . kept with jealous eyes, / always in danger of her hateful spies."[38] Though these images presage the abuse to which Henry, the new Neptune and the new Jove, is about to submit Rosamund and the surveillance with which Eleanor, the new Juno, would now pursue her, the maiden is not deterred. She relates, "I saw the sin wherein my foot was ent'ring, / I saw how that dishonor did attend it, / I saw the shame whereon my flesh was vent'ring, / Yet had I not the power for to defend it."[39] With these repeated recollections of "I saw . . . , / I saw . . . , / I saw . . . ," she recognizes that she beheld her fate in the images from Greek mythology, but this foreknowledge did not save her from perdition, "For that must hap decreed by heavenly powers, / Who work our fall, yet make the fault still ours."[40] As she had accepted to sleep with Henry under coercion, she later accepted to die under coercion, so that her half-willed punishment mirrors her half-willed misdeed. When she lifts the poisoned cup

Eleanor has given her to her lips, she observes, "That mouth that newly gave consent to sin, / Must now receive destruction in thereat."[41] When she dies, her body collapses on the bed where it had lain in wantonness. Neither entirely innocent nor entirely guilty, Rosamund goes wrong, she recognizes, not because of her will, but because of her weakness, or what she terms her "frailty."[42] For that reason, she demands of Eleanor, not just compassion for her sufferings, but forgiveness for her sins: "I dare not hope you should so far relent, / Great queen, as to forgive the punishment / That to my foul offence is justly due."[43]

In the Renaissance poems, Eleanor briefly feels sympathy for Rosamund. Learning that Henry has left England for France, she tracks down his concubine, perhaps by finding the ball of thread (the "clew") that would enable Henry to find his way to the center of the labyrinth. We are told, "Like Procne, seeking Philomela, she sought and found / The bower that lodged her husband's love."[44] According to Ovid's *Metamorphoses*, Procne, having discovered that her husband, Tereus, King of Thrace, had brutally raped her sister Philomela, avenged the wronged party. With this brief allusion, Eleanor is compared to a queen who, when learning of her husband's attraction to another woman, responded, not with jealousy for a rival in love, but with sympathy for a victim of violence. At other times, it is not so much pity for the vulnerable girl as admiration for her beauty that gives Eleanor pause. We are informed that "When the queen did view [Rosamund], / ... / The beauty and splendor of the person and the place / Amazed her." She declares, "No marvel, ... / That often the court did miss the King. / ... / Now, trust me, were she not a whore, or any whore but his, / She would be pardoned."[45] So extraordinary is the beauty she beholds in the maiden that she would be ready to forgive her if only that beauty had not attracted her husband. Elsewhere, it is said that when Eleanor saw Rosamund, "Even she herself did seem to entertain / Some ruth,"[46] that is, some pity or compassion. When death had undone Rosamund, it is said, "Her chief foe did plainly confess that she was a glorious creature."[47] Even if Eleanor is not, in the end, moved by the constrained circumstances under which Rosamund became her husband's concubine, she hesitates to extinguish such a lovely thing.

Despite her initial sympathy for Rosamund, in the Renaissance poems, Eleanor hardens her heart and brings about the maiden's death.[48] "Strumpet," the queen cries out as she rushes at her, "I need not speak at all; my sight may be / Enough expression of my wrongs."[49] She is described as "furious,"[50] "wrathful,"[51] and even "enrag'd with madness."[52] If Eleanor kills Rosamund, these authors indicate, it is because she sees the maiden as attempting to usurp her position as queen, for which, "envious,"[53] she seeks revenge. In William Warner's *Albions England* (1586), she demands, "Did I come from France as Queen Dowager . . . to pay so dear / For bringing him so great wealth as to be cuckqueened here?"[54] Because she brought so much property into the marriage, she feels that she should be treated with more respect. Like a man cuckolded by his wife, she is a woman "cuckqueened" by her husband. She raves, "But in faith I must not pardon this. / A queen corivalled with a queen? Nay, kept at rack and manger? / A husband to his honest bed through her become a stranger?" She cannot bear the thought that she, the queen, faces a rival in this upstart; that she, the wife, is losing her husband to this outsider to their marriage; and that she, the legitimate ruler and spouse, is being yoked together with the illegitimate concubine, like animals foddered together at a trough. She rails at Rosamund sarcastically, ". . . best he take thee to the Court, Be thou his Queen, do call / Me to attendance, if his Lust may stand for law in all." She imagines that Henry will treat Rosamund as he used to treat her, his proper consort, and that his sexual desire will thus determine these women's relative rank instead of their legal status. Determined to thwart their plans, she announces, "But lo, I live, and live I will, at least to mar that game."[55] Whatever violence she may visit on Rosamund, she makes clear, she commits to prevent this usurper from claiming her own rightful role.

There were Renaissance authors who claimed that Eleanor responded to Henry's love affair with Rosamund, not by murdering her husband's mistress, but by inspiring her sons to rebel against their father. Raphael Holinshed asserts that when the Young King was quarreling with Henry, "The Queen Mother Eleanor did what she could to prick him forward in his disobedient attempts. For she, being enraged with her husband because he kept sundry concubines"—he goes on to name Rosamund in particular—"and therefore delighted the less in her company, cared not what mischief she procured against him."[56] Holinshed blames Henry, in part, for this insurrection. Instead of limiting his attentions to the mother of his children, the king undermined the bodily integrity of the family, and he deserved to suffer the rebellion of this family as punishment for his sin. He writes, "Note here how God stirs up the wife of his own bosom and the sons descending from his own loins to be thorns in his eyes and goads in his sides for profaning so divine and holy an ordinance." Yet this chronicler also blames Eleanor, in part, for these wars. However much she was "dishonor[ed]" by her husband's infidelity, he writes, she should not have stirred up discord between a father and his sons, but, rather, should "have lulled the contention asleep and done what she possibly could to quench the fervent fire of strife with the water of pacification." As he sees Henry as divinely punished for his incontinence through the rebellion of his wife and his sons, he sees Eleanor as divinely punished for her "discontented or rather malicious mind" through her husband's confinement of her. After having subdued his sons in the war, Henry consigned to prison "so smoking a firebrand (as Queen Eleanor had proved herself to be)."[57] Poets of these years imagine Eleanor to have spent her time in prison weeping, repenting of the dissension she had aroused between her husband and her sons and acknowledging the justice of her punishment.[58] Most of all, they see her as regretting having offended Henry to the point where he no longer wishes to have anything to do with her. While a wife should be "kind,"[59] that is, filled with a natural affection for her husband and their kin, and "patient" if her husband should go astray, Eleanor is said to recognize that, ". . . most unkind, / I brought myself in such disdain: / That now the king cannot abide / I should be lodged by his side."[60] Whatever insurrection she raised against her husband was perpetrated, not just out of political resentment, but out of personal jealousy, and she is the one who, spurned by her spouse, most suffers its consequences.

In *The Lion in Winter*, Eleanor and her family are gathering for Christmas several years after Rosamund's death, at a point when the queen can make light of what she sees as Henry's infatuation with this maiden. As she tells the story to Alais, "He found Miss Clifford in the mists of Wales and brought her home for closer observation. Liking what he saw, he scrutinized her many years. He loved her deeply and she him. And yet, . . . when Henry had to choose between his lady and my lands—" (I, 2, pp. 16–17). While Eleanor acknowledges that Henry loved Rosamund and she loved him, she suggests ironically with her unfinished sentence that his passion was so profound that, when the question arose as to whether he would forsake Eleanor and her lands in order to marry this girl, there was no question at all. The queen affects blithe indifference toward her husband's sexual escapades: "Believe me, Henry's bed is Henry's province: he can people it with sheep for all I care. Which, on occasion, he has done" (I, 2, pp. 16–17). Again she acknowledges that he slept with another woman, but again she qualifies that recognition by asserting, mockingly, that he is indiscriminate in whom he sleeps with to the point of bestiality. While Henry was unfaithful to her, Eleanor recalls, she was also unfaithful to him. Even now, she taunts him with the rumors of her dalliances with Thomas Becket and his own father, Geoffrey Plantagenet: "I've never touched you without thinking, 'Geoffrey, Geoffrey' . . . I've put more horns on you than Louis ever wore" (II, 1, p. 83). Whatever pain he has caused her through his love affairs, she has caused him an equal pain in return. A king like Henry is a king, Eleanor indicates. He may fall in love with a woman, but his heart lies with his kingdom. He may sleep with any woman he likes, but the availability of so many women for his bed makes his liaison with any one of them without significance. And a queen like Eleanor is, in the end, a queen. Henry's political power may have been matched by his sexual prowess, but she has gone toe to toe with him in this regard. In a moral context where neither Henry's nor Eleanor's infidelities are held against them, adultery serves as a means by which to insult a spouse and, by doing so, assert dominance in the marriage.

Yet even as Eleanor makes light of Henry's love affair with Rosamund in *The Lion in Winter*, it becomes clear that she was hurt by what happened. Part of the anger she felt toward Henry at that time of this dalliance was political. She expresses indignation that he replaced her with Rosamund in her position as queen: "He put her in my place, you see, and that was very hard. . . . She headed Henry's table; that's my chair" (II, 1, p. 70). As Henry had attempted to unseat her by taking Rosamund as his companion, she attempted to unseat him by stirring up an insurrection. When he complains, "You led too many civil wars against me," she counters, "And I damn near won the last one" (I, 2, p. 18). Yet part of the anger Eleanor felt toward Henry was also personal. She reminiscences that, years ago, "We were fond. There was no Thomas Becket then, or Rosamund. No rivals" (I, 3, p. 29). When Henry charges her with having thrown him out of her bed for Richard, who became the primary object of her affection, she retorts, "Not until you threw me out for Rosamund" (II, 1, p. 78). Even now, in her chamber in Chinon, she sits at a table, tries on jewels, and admires herself. She hesitates to pick up the mirror, but when she does so, she exclaims, "My, what a lovely girl. How could her king have left her?" (I, 5, p. 53). The fact that Henry turned toward another woman makes her uncertain about her beauty, even as she tries to reassure herself of her continued attractiveness. While Eleanor cannot admit to having been hurt by Henry's love affair with Rosamund, she was clearly offended at having been displaced, both as his queen and as his beloved.

In the end, literary, theatrical, and cinematic commentators conclude that Eleanor and Henry were two of a kind. In the Renaissance poetry, Rosamund sees herself as the victim of both Henry and Eleanor. As she compares Henry to Jove, the god who seduces or rapes helpless young women, she compares Eleanor to Juno, Jove's goddess wife, who pursues his objects of desire, or to Argus, Juno's hundred-eyed servant, who keeps so close a watch on one such maiden.[61] Eleanor does not so much kill Rosamund as demand that the maiden kill herself, offering her a bowl of poison, perhaps with the option of a dagger should she prefer an alternate means of death.[62] Like her husband, she gives the maiden a choice that is no choice at all, so that once again it is Rosamund who acts to her own perdition. After the maiden swallows the poison, she laments of herself, "Oh poor weak conquest both for him and her."[63] As Henry conquers her by seducing her, Eleanor conquers her by bringing about her death. In both cases, the rulers assert their power over her, crushing someone much weaker than themselves. With the generosity of spirit that marks her end, Rosamund prays as she dies, "Forgive, O Lord, . . . / Him that dishonored, her that murdered me."[64] It was the king and queen who destroyed her, the one inspired by lust, the other inspired by wrath, the one using his power to get what he wants, the other using her power to eliminate a rival. As royals, both are able to act with impunity in their crimes. In *The Lion in Winter*, Eleanor and Henry look back regretfully on their many years of marriage. Eleanor laments, "Oh, Henry, we have mangled everything we've touched." Henry concedes her point, admitting, "and all for Rosamund." Yet Eleanor corrects him, observing that his explanation is too simple: "Life, if it's like anything at all, is like an avalanche. To blame the little ball of snow that starts it all, to say it is the cause, is just as true as it is meaningless" (II, 1, p. 78). Henry acted by taking Rosamund as his concubine, and Eleanor responded by inciting her sons to rise up against him. But Rosamund, they agree, was the mere snowball who set these great figures' catastrophic deeds into motion, without ever intending to cause this avalanche.

ALYS OF FRANCE

We have no evidence that Eleanor ever encountered Rosamund Clifford, despite all the literary, theatrical, and operatic works that brought these two women together, but we know that she had extensive dealings with Margaret and Alys of France, Louis's two daughters by his second wife, Constance of Castile. In November of 1160, when Margaret was two and Alys just a few weeks old, Henry and Louis met for negotiations, in the course of which it was arranged that "The King of France should give his two daughters, . . . one of whom was called Margaret and the other Alys, in marriage to the two sons of King Henry, namely, Henry and Richard, who were as yet but little children."[65] It was agreed that Margaret would receive as her dowry the Vexin, the buffer region between Normandy and the Ile-de-France, with its important castles of Gisors, Neaufles, and

Châteauneuf-sur-Epte, and that the Knights Templar would hold these fortresses until that marriage took place. At the time of this betrothal, the loss of the Vexin to the English seemed a distant prospect, but Louis had underestimated what Henry was capable of once he had the girl in his custody. Instead of waiting for Margaret and the Young King to come of age, he had them married immediately with the help of a papal dispensation, "although they were as yet but little children, crying in the cradle."[66] In the years that followed, we catch a glimpse of the six-year-old Margaret living in Eleanor's household at Salisbury. John of Salisbury refers to the child "whom I had lately seen healthy when I took leave of the Lady Queen."[67] We see her again as a fifteen-year-old "staying with the queen at Caen."[68] The Young King was being crowned at Westminster Abbey, but the Young Queen had been left behind, "as if repudiated, to the disgrace and contempt of her father,"[69] though she would be crowned not long thereafter. We see her on a ship with Eleanor, being transported back to England during the Young King's revolt against his father, for all intents and purposes Henry's prisoner like her mother-in-law.[70] Yet whatever humiliations Margaret suffered among the Angevins, her younger sister's fate was far worse.

Kept in custody at the royal court for over two decades, Alys was at risk of never being married at all. In 1169, when the princess was eight years old, she was formally betrothed to Richard and placed in her prospective in-laws' guard, perhaps in Eleanor's household alongside Margaret.[71] But in the spring of 1173, when Alys was twelve, the queen was arrested and imprisoned by Henry, and Alys seems to have been shifted into the king's care. As the years went by, Henry repeatedly swore that he would have Richard marry her, but he haggled with Louis and then Philip about her dowry. On behalf of Pope Alexander III, Cardinal Peter of Saint Chrysogonus threatened to place England's continental possessions under interdict if he did not have Richard marry Alys, "whom the King of England had kept in his custody for a long time, beyond the period that had been agreed upon between them."[72] Stories circulated as to the real reason why Henry had not proceeded with the match. Gerald of Wales relates, "It was said and rumored among the people that, after the death of the girl Rosamund, whom the King had loved so excessively with his adulterous embraces, he most shamelessly and unfaithfully dishonored this virgin, who was the daughter of his lord and had been entrusted to him in good faith."[73] By 1175 or 1176, when Alys was fourteen or fifteen, Henry took her as his mistress, fathering on her, it was said, a son[74] or a daughter,[75] who died shortly after birth. While Gerald indicates that Henry entered into the liaison with Rosamund out of love for this maiden, he suggests that the king took advantage of Alys out of contempt for her father. He observes, "The sister of King Philip and daughter of Louis had been committed to the custody of the King of the English by her most pious father in good faith, to be joined in marriage to his son Richard, Count of Poitou,"[76] yet, far from keeping this maiden intact for this honorable purpose, he corrupted her. While Gerald identified Rosamund by her Christian name alone, he identifies Alys by her relation to Henry's French overlords, whom the king was offending by taking advantage of their kinswoman. By this time, Henry had already debauched other noble maidens under his care. John of Salisbury writes of Odo II, Viscount of Porhoët and husband of a kinswoman to the king, that in 1168, "Odo . . . deplored the fact that [Henry] had impregnated his virgin daughter, whom he had given to him as a hostage of peace," thus acting "as a traitor, an adulterer, and an incestuous man."[77] To place one's children in another man's custody, whether he is one's vassal or one's lord, is to entrust him with one's offspring, and for that guardian to exploit the situation by seducing the girls is for him to abuse the confidence he has been given. As a lord, Henry was said to be "a corruptor of chastity, . . . exercising his lures first with the spouses, then with the daughters of his vassals."[78] The problem is not the harm that Henry may have done to Odo's daughter or these other maidens, but the breaking of the social bonds with their fathers and brothers that he perpetrated through his intercourse with them. Whether Alys and these other young women were forcibly raped, whether they freely consented to their liaisons with Henry, or whether they were partly coerced and they partly consented, they were dishonored, and they were the means by which their male relatives were dishonored as well.

During Henry's reign, there was little Eleanor did or probably could have done to help Alys. When the maiden became Henry's mistress, the queen was her husband's prisoner and, from what we are told, the object of his wrath and suspicion, as were her rebellious sons. According to Gerald of Wales, in October of 1175, "[Henry] proposed, it was said, after that great and inexorable hatred that had arisen between him and his sons and their mother the queen, to be divorced from Queen Eleanor and be joined to the other one in marriage, for he always strove to devise illicit schemes. . . . By means of the heirs born from her, and with both his power and that of the French, he might all the more effectively disinherit the older sons he had had by Eleanor who had attacked him."[79] Disgusted with the wife who had stirred their sons to rise up against him as well as with the sons themselves, Henry longed to have a new wife and new children. He invited the papal legate Cardinal Hugh Pierleone to Winchester, where he flattered him and plied him with gifts in an attempt to persuade him to support the annulment of his marriage, and he wrote letters to Philip, who was by now King of France, angling for his support as he elevated his sister to the English throne. Yet Philip was still friends with Richard at that point, and he immediately forwarded these missives to his companion, who was said to be so angered by his father's intention to disinherit him that he regarded him with suspicion ever after. It would have been to Alys's honor to marry Henry and to bear him the next King of England, but it would have been to Eleanor and her sons' shame to tolerate their own replacement, and, for whatever reason, the king's plot never came to fruition. When the Young King died in 1183 and Margaret was left a widow, her dowry of the Vexin was transferred to Alys in expectation of her marriage to Richard. Philip demanded that the dowerlands Margaret had received at the time of her marriage be transferred to his sister as well, but Henry sent his messengers to England, "ordering that Queen Eleanor, his wife, who had been retained for a long time in the king's custody, be freed and that she go through her dowerlands, wishing that she preserve them against the request of the King of France."[80] Whatever the queen may have felt toward Alys at this time, when the question was who was to rule England, who was to have her son inherit the throne, and who was to possess these dowerlands, their interests were not aligned.

If Eleanor passively suffered Alys's mistreatment during Henry's reign, she actively contributed to her misfortune by thwarting her marriage to one of her sons in the years that followed. After his father's death in 1189, Richard repeatedly renewed his promise to marry Alys, even reassuring Philip of his intentions shortly before their departure on the Third Crusade. It was only when the two kings were in Sicily in 1191 and news arrived that Eleanor was bringing Berengaria of Navarre for him to wed that Richard definitively turned against this earlier engagement. As William of Tyre's continuator tells the story, Eleanor decided to prevent the marriage between Richard and Alys because "She hated the heirs of King Louis of France, her former husband, and she had no desire for her heirs to come together with the heirs of the said king,"[81] but there is little to confirm his interpretation of the situation. Far from hating Louis, Eleanor allied herself with him during the Young King's revolt against Henry, to the point that Louis was said to have warned Henry that he would never make peace with him "except with the assent of your wife and your sons."[82] Far from hating Louis's heirs, she was generally seen as aiming to strengthen the bond between the Angevins and the Capetians. When William the Breton chastises Richard at one point for waging war against Philip, he reminds him that "Your mother taught you never to enter into conflict with your lord, but reverently to render him honor."[83] Whatever reasons Eleanor had for bringing Berengaria, and not Alys, to Sicily for her son to wed, Richard was said to have informed Philip at this time "that he would on no account whatsoever take his sister as his wife because the King of England, his own father, had known her and had had a son by her," and he was ready to produce numerous witnesses to testify to this fact.[84] If Richard would not marry Alys and make her queen, Philip determined, he would conspire to have John do so, but Eleanor again prevented this match from going forward. (Alys would finally wed William IV Talvas, Count of Ponthieu, in 1195, at the advanced age of thirty-five, and would have two daughters with him.) Again, it would have been to Alys's honor to marry Richard or John, but, as Eleanor saw it, it would not have been to her family's or her kingdom's advantage for her to do so, and the marriage did not happen.

In *The Lion in Winter*, the only major work to explore Alys's situation in depth, Henry seems to prefer Alais (that is, Alys) to Eleanor. He professes love to this mistress, claiming that, of all the people he has known, "Nowhere in God's Western world have I found anyone to love but you" (I, 1, p. 4). Alais is young—in history and in the play, twenty-three to Henry's fifty, and in the film, twenty-seven to his thirty-six—and beautiful, but there are other reasons why he is so attached to her. When he wonders if she will turn against him at some point, she asks, "If I decided to be trouble, Henry, how much trouble could I be?" to which he concedes, "Not much" (I, 1, p. 4). Eleanor and his sons have all led rebellions against him, rousing their own vassals and allies to oppose his rule, and he has reason to fear that they may do so again. But Alais, alone among members of his household, presents no such threat, if only because she cannot present such a threat. Far from worrying that she will wield power over him, Henry is confident that he wields power over her. As he has taken her for himself, he can give her to whichever son he chooses. He reminds her, "If I say you and I are done, we're done. If I say, marry John, it's John. I'll have you by me, and I'll use you as I like" (I, 1, p. 4). Brutal as these words may be, he speaks them affectionately, with his hands on her shoulders and his head bent toward hers. The thought of his ability to do with his mistress whatever he likes fills him with tenderness for her. As Henry professes love for Alais, he claims hatred for Eleanor. When Alais worries that he still loves his old queen, he scoffs, "The new Medusa? My good wife? . . . Don't be jealous of the gorgon. . . . I haven't kept the great bitch in the keep for ten years out of passionate attachment" (I, 1, p. 4). Eleanor is a monster whom he holds in such horror, he insists, that he has held her imprisoned for all these years. He would rather have a sweet, pliant woman in his life than an angry, potentially dangerous one.

Yet despite his preference for Alais, Henry is continually lured back to Eleanor. After he declares his love to the princess, he explains to Eleanor dismissively, "I talk like that to keep her spirits up" (I, 4, p. 38). Eleanor is old—sixty-one in the history, the play, and the film—but she commands the screen. When she arrives at Chinon on her barge, she does so seated on a throne, looking straight ahead in regal ease as the men row. As she is approaching the castle, Henry races along the ramparts with Alais scurrying along behind him so that that he can be at the dock when she lands. He shouts out to his wife as she comes closer, "How was your crossing? Did the Channel part for you?" as if she were Moses. She calls back, "It went flat when I told it to. I didn't think to ask for more," laughingly acknowledging her divinely sent powers. Eleanor smiles continually, not with the smile of a subordinate eager to curry favor with a master, but with the smile of a master confident of her control over a situation, even as she refers to that smile as "the way I register despair." While all the other members of court, including Alais, wear muted browns, greens, and blues, Eleanor parades about in a brilliant red-orange dress or a silver dressing gown, like a peacock among the swallows. Throughout, Henry recognizes that Eleanor is a great figure in a way that meek Alais will never be. When he speculates as to what future historians will write about him, he imagines them saying that he was the ablest soldier at an able time and the ruler of a state as great as Charlemagne's, but also that "He married, out of love, a woman out of legend. Not in Alexandria, or Rome, or Camelot has there been such a queen" (I, 6, p. 66). Eleanor, as Henry sees her, may not be a woman anxious to please him, like Alais, but she is a woman who will go down in history books alongside Cleopatra and Guinevere. Her greatness as a queen mirrors his own greatness as a king, in a way that enhances his prestige. She does defy him. When Henry discloses his plan to have their marriage annulled and to marry Alais in order to beget more tractable sons, Eleanor threatens, "You go to Rome, we'll rise against you . . . Richard, Geoffrey, John, and Eleanor of Aquitaine" (II, 1, p. 81). She drags out the full title by which she will be known in history, reminding him whom he is daring to take on. When Henry has his sons thrown in the dungeon to prevent them from rising up against him in his absence, she gains access to their cell and supplies them with knives, with which they consider killing their father. Yet however much she defies him, Henry cannot help but admire his wife for having the spirit to cause him so much trouble, in contrast to the young woman now by his side. After he abandons his plan to wed Alais, the young woman offers to warm some wine for him, and he retorts, "I've shot your world, you silly bitch, and there you stand, all honey and molasses. Sweet? You make my teeth ache" (II, 3. p. 100).

Like Henry, Eleanor loves "gentle Alais" (I, 2, p. 12), as she calls her. When the queen first sees the maiden, she interrupts her formal curtsy and embraces her warmly: "No, no; greet me like you used to. Fragile I am not: affection is a pressure I can bear" (I, 2, p. 12). At one point, when Richard, Geoffrey, and John are all clamoring for the crown, Eleanor confesses to Henry that she does not much like their children, but she then turns to Alais, adding, "Only you—the child I raised but didn't bear" (I, 2, p. 16). She recalls brushing and braiding her hair and kissing away her tears when she was a child, and she takes pride in the learning she sees her ward has retained from their lessons. When Richard refers to Alais as "the family whore," she objects: "I brought her up and she is dear to me and gentle" (I, 2, p. 11). While Eleanor recalls Alais's years under her tutelage with affection, Alais has mixed feelings toward her foster-mother. Now that she is grown, she sees how the queen manipulates people to her own ends. She asks, "Were you always like this? Years ago, when I was young and worshiped you, is this what you were like?" to which Eleanor replies, "Most likely" (II, 1, p. 71). In retrospect, Alais realizes, "You never cared for me." However great a figure Eleanor may be and however much fondness she may claim to feel for her, Alais concludes, the queen is, at her core, heartless. Because Alais grasps that Eleanor will stop at nothing to get Richard and herself into power after Henry's death, she realizes that if Henry should marry her and give her a son, she and her child would find themselves in mortal danger. When Eleanor inquires if Alais really believes she could bring herself to hurt her, she replies, "Eleanor, with both hands tied behind you" (I, 2, p. 16). Yet despite all Alais's wariness of her, Eleanor consistently expresses love for this young woman. She recognizes that, though Alais has Henry, her position, as a mere mistress, is insecure, and the hostility that she expresses to the queen derives from that insecurity. "Why aren't you happy?" Eleanor asks the "poor child" (II, 1, p. 70). Alais tells Eleanor that for Christmas, "I should like to see you suffer" (II, 1, p. 71), yet she bursts into tears after uttering these words and throws herself into her arms, sobbing, "*Maman, oh, Maman. . . . J'ai peur, Maman*," while Eleanor caresses her and comforts her, murmuring, "*Ma petite*." Both native French speakers, they lapse into their common maternal tongue. Though Eleanor recognizes the weakness of Alais's character as well as her position, she never expresses contempt for her as Henry does, only sympathy.

If there is dissension between Eleanor and Henry and the young adults in *The Lion in Winter*, it is because the royal couple do not distinguish love from honor in the way the younger generation wishes they would. Though Eleanor's historical sons never exhibited anything but devotion to her, these theatrical or cinematic sons all complain that she did not love them when they were children, as a modern, middle-class mother might be expected to love her progeny.[85] Geoffrey protests. "Never once can I remember anything from you or Father warmer than indifference" (I, 5. p. 50). Even now, he feels, "There's no affection for me here" (I, 2, p. 16). John reproaches his mother for having had him brought up by midwives, and he spurns her belated attempt to mother him now out of resentment of this fact: "Let you put your arms around me just the way you never did?" (I, 3, pp. 25–26). Even Richard, though acknowledged to be Eleanor's favorite, expresses only bitterness toward her. The queen herself admits to her sons, "I never nursed you, warmed you, washed you, fed you" (II, 3, p. 98). Just as Eleanor is said not to truly love her sons, she is said not to truly love her husband. Alais informs her, "You love Henry but you love his kingdom, too. You look at him and you see cities, acreage, coastline, taxes. All I see is Henry. Leave him to me, can't you?" (II, 1, p. 71). Because Alais loves Henry for himself in a way that Eleanor has never done—that is, as a man, not just as a ruler—she feels she has a right to him in a way that Eleanor does not. Yet for Eleanor and Henry, they *are* the lands they possess. In a passage that recalls the medieval descriptions of Henry's considerations when marrying Eleanor, the king remarks, "It's been my luck to fall in love with landed women. When I married Eleanor, I thought: 'You lucky man. The richest woman in the world. She owns the Aquitaine, the greatest province on the Continent—and beautiful as well'" (I, 1, p. 6). Just as Eleanor *is* "Eleanor of Aquitaine" for Henry, Henry *is* Henry of England for Eleanor. Neither Eleanor nor Henry can distinguish people from the lands they possess, whether they are speaking of their spouses, their children, or even themselves. When Henry is plotting how to get Aquitaine for John, Alais complains to him, "I talk people and you answer back in provinces," to which he replies, "They get mixed up" (I, 4, p. 37). While the young adults in this work can imagine Eleanor and Henry as private individuals, defined by the domestic sphere and their relations with each other, this queen and king conceive of themselves as entirely public figures, defined by their political roles.

As Eleanor and Henry do not distinguish love from honor, they do not distinguish honor from love. Because Henry spends so much of this work attempting to have John designated as heir to the throne of England, the throne becomes marked as the object of his desire. When he asks Eleanor if she truly cares who will be king, she answers, "I care because you care so much" (I, 2, p. 19). She wants to decide who will rule because he wants to decide who will rule. Similarly, when Henry plots to have Eleanor sign Aquitaine over to him so he can give it to John, the province becomes meaningful because Eleanor resists giving it to him. As he puts it at one point, "What's the Aquitaine to Eleanor? It's not a province. It's a way to torture me" (I, 4, p. 37). So long as she retains title to this land, she possesses leverage over him, and she will use that leverage against him. At one point, in despair at her situation, Eleanor finally agrees to sign Aquitaine over to him, but Henry refuses to accept this long-sought offer. "Dear God, the pleasure I still get from goading you" (II, 1, p. 75), he exclaims. His aim was never to obtain her lands, but only to outmaneuver her, and if he can obtain the lands without outmaneuvering her, he does not want them. Both spouses want the lands that the other possesses, but both want those lands because the one who possesses them values them so much. Both despair at the struggles between them, which have poisoned their lives and the lives of their children, but both relish the conflict in which they are engaged. In the beginning of the work, Eleanor proposes to Henry that they not transmit their lands to any of their children but, rather, live forever, "tusk to tusk through all eternity" (I, 2, p. 12), as Henry puts it. Like two boars charging at each other, they relish their combat. In his last words to Eleanor, as her barge is bearing her off, Henry shouts, "You know, I hope we never die. . . . You think there's any chance of it?" (II, 3, p. 103). As Henry laughs, throwing his head back and spreading his arms wide, Eleanor stands up in the barge, smiling and waving goodbye. Despite all the fighting over the future and which son will inherit the throne, they both would prefer to remain in the present, sparring with each other.

Once again, Eleanor and Henry are two of a kind. When Henry informs Eleanor that he wants a new wife who will bear him new sons, she is broken-hearted, but she is also furious with him. Confronted with her rage, he asks, "Eleanor, what do you want?" She answers with perhaps Katharine Hepburn's greatest speech in the movie: "Just what you want: a king for a son. You can make more. I can't. You think I want to disappear? One son is all I've got and you can blot him out and call me cruel. For these ten years you've lived with everything I've lost and loved another woman through it all. And I'm cruel? I could peel you like a pear and God himself would call it justice" (II, 1, p. 80). If Henry does not understand her, she makes clear, it is because he does not appreciate that she is just like him. Both of them are rulers. But for ten years he has kept her locked up, without a kingdom to rule or a partner at her side, while he has enjoyed his reign and his mistress. Both of them want a son to succeed them. But she cannot make new sons, whereas he can, and this new heir stands to disinherit her progeny. Earlier during this visit, Eleanor had claimed to be satisfied with her castle prison and her maids-in-waiting. Now, she fantasizes flaying Henry as casually as she might peel a piece of fruit, as if that violence would be nothing compared to the pain he has caused her in the past ten years, of which he seems blithely unaware. She expresses not self-pity but outrage, and an outrage all the more impressive for having been concealed thus far during her visit. By proclaiming that God himself would approve that vengeance, she makes clear that she is, not pleading with Henry for mercy, but damning him for his injustice. Throughout this speech, she looks her husband straight in the eye, with her gaze firm despite the tears on her cheeks and her intonation and diction exquisitely controlled. Weak though she may be as his prisoner, she speaks from a position of strength as his equal and partner.

According to history, literature, and film, what mattered in these Angevin and Capetian circles was, not love, but honor. Henry was said to have loved Rosamund. He hid her away in Woodstock to consort with her as he pleased, and when she died, he had her tomb venerated at Godstow. But this love, such as it was, brought the maiden only "honorable shame," as Samuel Daniel quotes Rosamund saying. Henry seduced her, debauched her, and degraded her, so that her body, reeking after her death, reflected the state of her damned soul. We do not know whether Henry loved Alys, but he prevented her from marrying Richard for many years, despite their betrothal, and he deflowered her, so that after his death she would not be a desirable bride. Eleanor may not seem to have loved her sons from a modern perspective, but she sought their honor. She supported the Young King's rebellion against his father, though she would suffer many years of imprisonment as a result. She administered Richard's kingdom in his absence, protecting it from his younger brother's attempted usurpation; she raised the ransom that would bring about his release from captivity; and she advised him how to act to ensure this liberation. However difficult to handle John had been during Richard's early reign, when it came his turn to rule, she traveled throughout her ancestral lands, ensuring that her vassals would recognize him as their lord and attacking their cities if they failed to do so. What mattered was not bestowing hugs and endearments, but enabling someone to rule in accordance with his right to do so, and these sons appreciated the political talent Eleanor deployed to that end.

Insofar as the film of *The Lion in Winter* succeeds, it is because Katharine Hepburn convinces us that Eleanor was herself an actress. At one point, as she proceeds through a crowded dining hall arm in arm with Henry, she is smiling and nodding to their cheering barons but under her breath she is also threatening her husband that she will make him lose the Vexin if he does not let Richard marry Alais. She claims to love Henry at one moment and undercuts these words the next. In her affectionate moods, she may be voicing the fondness she truly feels for him, she may be pretending to feel fondness to get him to do what she wishes, or she may be pretending to pretend to feel fondness because any admission of genuine feeling for this man would leave her too vulnerable. It is possible that Eleanor herself does not know what she feels or that she feels one thing at one moment and something else at another. "If there were some God," Eleanor muses, "then I'd exist in his imagination, like Antigone in Sophocles'. I'd have no contradictions, no confusions, . . . and then, . . . then I'd make some sense" (II, 1, p. 74). She is not a character, that is, a single, unified, coherent personality, who either loves or does not love, but, rather, a series of discrete poses with a center as unknown to herself as to anyone else. The affected and mannered style of Hepburn's acting becomes the style of Eleanor's political manipulations. As one critic observes, "Hepburn's Eleanor is that unusual thing, indeed, an actress fully aware of the pretenses of her acting, as though for her—at these critical moments in her life—performance, appearance, and reality are all the same"[86]

Yet insofar as *The Lion in Winter* works as a film, it is also because Katharine Hepburn convinces us Eleanor was Katharine Hepburn. Like the queen, the woman who played her was a famous beauty from an aristocratic family. Like the queen, she was intelligent, well-educated, and imperious. Like the queen, she was known for her love affairs in her youth and she remained compelling to men in her advanced years. Like the queen, she functioned in a world where women were commonly controlled by powerful men but where she had succeeded in holding her own. The persona of the medieval queen becomes subsumed into that of the mercurial Hollywood star.[87] And indeed, it may be that Eleanor was Katharine Hepburn *avant la lettre*. However attractive both women have been to feminists, both fit uneasily into modern notions of feminism. Whatever disadvantages they suffered as women in the male-dominated worlds of twelfth-century France and England or twentieth-century Hollywood were overwhelmingly offset by the advantages of their class, their wealth, their beauty, their confidence, and their strength of character. Both enjoyed a privilege almost unique to royalty and celebrities: for them, the public sphere was the arena in which the private self could be fully actualized. As Katharine Hepburn said of herself, "I'm a personality as well as an actress. Show me an actress who isn't a personality, and you'll show me a woman who isn't a star."[88] It is often said that, despite her record-setting four Best Actress Oscars, she never actually acted: whether as Tracy Lord, Linda Seton, Tess Harding, or Eleanor of Aquitaine, she played herself, that is, a wealthy, entitled, and intelligent woman, temporarily cast down through the power of circumstances but ready to rise up again by the end of the film. As tempting as it may be to set Eleanor within the category of medieval queens, and as illuminating as it is in many ways to do so, it is her similarly irreducible individuality that, for almost a thousand years, has made her compelling for so many readers and audiences.

CONCLUSION

In the final analysis, when we are dealing with the world in which Eleanor lived, we are dealing with a world where the personal was political and the political was personal. Marriages were an affair of state, uniting, not just Eleanor and Louis or Henry, but Aquitaine and France or England. The children of such marriages were, not just sons and daughters, but the future rulers of England, Sicily, and Castile, as well as of Aquitaine, Anjou, Brittany, Champagne, Normandy, and Saxony. With the personal and the political as entwined as they were, moral character was, not just a private matter, but a public area of concern. If a king was cowardly like Louis, energetic like Henry, courageous like Richard, or indolent like John, his traits would determine whether his subjects would invade other countries or be invaded, remain at peace or erupt into civil war, and see their homelands expand or disintegrate. The ruler's sexual behavior was far from irrelevant to these subjects' day-to-day lives. A king like Henry, who debauched his vassals' wives and daughters, could stoke hatred in his subjects' hearts, which might lead them to ally themselves with his sons in one of their periodic uprisings. A king like John, who stole the young Isabella of Angoulême from her betrothed, Hugh IX "le Brun," seigneur of Lusignan, could spark an insurrection among that lord's family members and their allies. While it may seem to us misogynistic to condemn Eleanor for her wantonness,[1] her contemporaries criticized Henry,[2] Richard,[3] and John[4] for the same fault and praised Louis[5] for his continence. What we now consider personal matters were not just personal at a time when they had such political consequences.

When the people of Eleanor's time condemned her, they typically viewed her as willful. At a time when loyalty and fidelity were the paramount feudal virtues, they saw the queen as betraying her "husband" and "lord" (*seigneur*) at Antioch. At a time when the royal class was supposed to be distinguished, not just by wealth and power, but by prudence, wisdom, and reason, they saw her as abandoning herself to folly. She had spurned "regal dignity" in having a love affair and, in doing so, had acted, "not like a queen, but like a whore." One could object that we do not know what happened in Antioch, that Eleanor may well have committed no crime at all, and that she may even have been abducted and raped. But whatever did or did not occur, the incident ruined her reputation, so that she became known throughout western Europe as a woman of loose morals. Not many years after Eleanor traveled through Germany en route to the Holy Land, an anonymous poet of that country would fantasize about her in sexual terms: "If all the world were mine from the sea up to the Rhine, I would willingly forsake it all in order to have the Queen of England lie in my arms."[6] Back in France, Eleanor was seen as having rid herself of one husband in order to acquire another who was more appealing to her eyes and more congenial to her character. She had mettlesome sons with this second husband, and when they were grown, she was said to have urged them to rebel against their father, thus tearing asunder the familial body of which they were all a part and of which he was the head. By following her desires rather than her duty, Eleanor did not reinforce the political, social, and moral order of her society, as someone of her position was expected to do, but, on the contrary, weakened it.

Yet even as Eleanor's contemporaries saw her as willful, they also saw her as free. She was envisioned as an eagle, "rapacious and regal," spreading her wings over two kingdoms. When released from her first marriage and the authority of her first husband, she was imagined as "an eagle having broken free of her pact,"[7] flying back to her own lands, which she possessed by hereditary right. She would acquire a second husband, but for the time being, she was said to have enjoyed the devotion of the vassals who served her, the poet who sang her praises in his *cansos*, and other ladies who joined her in deliberations about amorous questions. For years, Eleanor suffered imprisonment by her second husband. When her most beloved son finally replaced him on the throne, she sent messengers throughout the kingdom ordering that other people who had been unjustly imprisoned be released, "inasmuch as she had learned by experience in her own person that confinement is repellant to men and that it is a most delightful refreshment of the spirits to emerge from it." Her son would win praise as a great warrior and crusader king, but when he too was taken captive, she would overturn heaven and earth to secure to his deliverance. After she succeeded in ransoming him, he was said to be "free and released . . . into the arms of his mother Eleanor," as all those around them shed tears of joy. Though the queen had earlier refused to allow herself to be "shut up . . . in a nun's habit," at the end of her life she lived in proximity to a cloister though not confined by it. When Eleanor was regarded from the perspective of the political, social, and moral order she was defying, she was criticized as willful, but when she was considered from the point of view of those who were being oppressed by this order, she was celebrated.

By the end of her life, Eleanor was regarded, not just as a powerful queen, but, when all was said and done, as an admirable and remarkable woman. Despite the vilification she had suffered in her younger days, she now received praise. An obscure Londoner writing in the year of her death states, "The queen was called Eleanor, a generous queen indeed, and a spirited and well-landed lady."[8] Matthew Paris refers to her as "the noble Queen Eleanor, an admirable lady of beauty and astuteness."[9] These authors emphasize Eleanor's beauty and great lands, as was common in descriptions of queens, but they also stress her liberality, her intelligence, and her energy. In 1192, Richard of Devizes describes her as "Queen Eleanor, an incomparable woman, beautiful and chaste, powerful and gentle, humble and well-spoken, qualities which are most rarely found in a woman."[10] He sees the queen as putting herself forward into the public realm with her commanding appearance, her dominant rank, and her eloquence, but as tempering this self-assertion with reserve and tact. Her authority derived, not from her place within the administrative state—she never held an official position in the government—but from her capacity to work with others to achieve what needed to be done. From what we are told, she mediated, she negotiated, and she conciliated, even using tears. She did not break men, but she persuaded them to bend, willingly, to her will. She did not set herself above the secular and ecclesiastical lords with whom she was interacting, and she did not display what was seen in the Empress Matilda, who had attempted to rule England on her own, as "womanly arrogance, aspiring to uncustomary things higher than her sex."[11] Even as she assumed men's clothes and conducted wars, she functioned, not as a man, but as a woman, yet in a way that was thought to make her unlike other women.[12] These chroniclers of Eleanor's last years are interested, not just in the fact that the queen had power, but in how she behaved as someone in power— and at this point in her history, they believe she behaved well. It is by attuning ourselves to the cultural categories that were available to Eleanor's contemporaries and to Eleanor herself as they made sense of her life—even if these categories are not to our liking—that we can appreciate the feminisms of the Middle Ages, which are so different from our own.

ACKNOWLEDGMENTS

I am grateful to Richard Aldous and Francine Prose for their valuable responses to sections of this manuscript; to Michael Staunton for many stimulating conversations about the Angevin rulers and their times; to Owen Duff, Menahem Haike, and Kaleth Torrens-Martin for their assistance at various stages of my research; to Omar Encarnación and Lydia Davis for their thoughts on the writing process; to David Ungvary for his insights into several unexpected turns of phrase; to the Press's anonymous readers for their much-appreciated recommendations; to Nicole Balant for her meticulous editing of the manuscript; and, as always, to Randy Petilos, for his wise guidance of the project from start to finish.

NOTES

ABBREVIATIONS

CCCM   *Corpus Christianorum Continuatio Medievalis*

CCM   *Cahiers de civilisation médiévale*

HGL   *Histoire générale de Languedoc.* Ed. Claude De Vic and Joseph Vaissete. 16 vols. Toulouse: Editions Privat, 1872–1892.

MGH   *Monumenta Germaniae Historica.* Ed. Georg Heinrich Pertz et al. Stuttgart; Hanover: [Various publishers], 1826–present.

PL   *Patrologiae Cursus Completus, series Latina.* Ed. Jacques-Paul Migne. 221 vols. Paris: Garnier Brothers, 1844–64.

RHF   *Recueil des historiens des Gaules et de la France.* Ed. Martin Bouquet et al. 22 vols. Paris: Les Libraires associés, 1738–1865. New edition. Ed. Léopold Delisle. 24 vols. Paris: Palmé, 1869–1904.

RS   Rolls Series. *Rerum Britannicarum Medii Aevi Scriptores / Chronicles and Memorials of Great Britain and Ireland during the Middle Ages.* 253 vols. London: Longman, 1858–1911.

INTRODUCTION

1. Roger of Howden, *Chronica Magistri Rogeri de Houedene*, ed. William Stubbs, 4 vols., RS, vol. 51 (London: Longman, 1868–71), vol. 3, p. 204. All translations are my own.

2. Gervase of Canterbury, *Chronica*, in *The Historical Works of Gervase of Canterbury*, ed. William Stubbs, 2 vols., RS, vol. 73 (London: Longman, 1879–80), vol. 1, pp. 1–594, at p. 515.

3. Ambroise, *The History of the Holy War: Ambroise's "Estoire de la guerre sainte,"* ed. Marianne Ailes and Malcolm Barber (Woodbridge, UK: Boydell Press, 2003), vv. 1155–57.

4. William of Newburgh, *Historia rerum Anglicarum*, in *Chronicles of the Reigns of Stephen, Henry II, and Richard I*, ed. Richard Howlett, 4 vols., RS, vol. 82 (London: Longman, 1884–85), vol. 2, V, 5, p. 424.

5. *Fragmentum genealogicum ducum Normanniae et Angliae regum*, RHF, vol. 18, p. 241. William X, Duke of Aquitaine, IX Count of Poitou, died on April 9, 1137, which was a Good Friday. The dating of William's death to 1136 in this text may result either from error or from

a reckoning of the new year from Easter. And William left behind two daughters, not one. Alfred Richard, in *Histoire des comtes de Poitou, 778–1204*, 2 vols. (Paris: Alphone Picard & Fils, 1903), vol. 1, p. 488, contended, based on unclear evidence, that Eleanor was born in 1122, but Andrew W. Lewis has argued persuasively, in "The Birth and Childhood of King John: Some Revisions," in *Eleanor of Aquitaine: Lord and Lady*, ed. Bonnie Wheeler and John Carmi Parsons (Basingstoke: Palgrave, 2002), pp. 159–75, at pp. 161 and 170–71n12, that her birth year was more likely 1124. I will use the 1124 date in calculating Eleanor's age throughout.

6. While it is often believed that Eleanor and Henry had five sons (William, who died young; Henry the Young King; Richard; Geoffrey; and John), in addition to three daughters (Matilda, Eleanor, and Joan), Ralph of Diceto, in *Ymagines historiarum*, in *Radulfi de Diceto Decani Lundoniensis opera historica / The Historical Works of Master Ralph of Diceto, Dean of London*, ed. William Stubbs, 2 vols., RS, vol. 68 (London: Longman, 1876), vol. 1, pp. 291–440, and vol. 2, pp. 3–176, at p. 17, refers to Henry as having had "six sons from legitimate matrimony." Lewis, in "The Birth and Childhood of King John," p. 161, argues that the additional unnamed son could have been born between Geoffrey and young Eleanor or between young Eleanor and Joan.

7. See *Encomium Emma Reginae*, ed. Alistair Campbell (Cambridge: Cambridge University Press, 1998); Turgot of Durham, *Vita sanctae Margaretae Scotorum reginae*, ed. James Raine, in *Symeonis dunelmensis opera et collectanea*, ed. J. Hodgson Hinde (Durham, UK: Andrews and Co., 1868), vol. 1, pp. 234–54; and Caesarius of Heisterbach, *Das Leben der Heiligen Elisabeth*, ed. Ewald Könsgen (Marburg: Elwert, 2007). See also Nicholas Vincent, "The Strange Case of the Missing Plantagenet Biographies of the Kings of England, 1154–1272," in *Writing Medieval Biography, 750–1250: Essays in Honour of Frank Barlow*, ed. David Bates, Julia Crick, and Sarah Hamilton (Woodbridge, UK: Boydell & Brewer, 2006), pp. 237–58.

8. *Chroniques de Saint-Martial de Limoges*, ed. Henri Duplès-Agier (Paris: Renouard, 1874), p. 69.

9. John of Salisbury, *Historia pontificalis / Memoirs of the Papal Court*, ed. Marjorie Chibnall (London: Thomas Nelson, 1956; rpt., Oxford: Clarendon Press, 1986), Prologue, p. 4.

10. See Lois L. Huneycutt, "Intercession and the High-Medieval Queen: The Esther Topos," in *Power of the Weak: Studies on Medieval Women*, ed. Jennifer Carpenter and Sally-Beth MacLean (Urbana: University of Illinois Press, 1990), pp. 126–46; and John Carmi Parsons, "The Queen's Intercession in Thirteenth-Century England," in *Power of the Weak*, pp. 147–77.

11. See Theresa Earnenfight, *Queenship in Medieval Europe* (New York: Palgrave Macmillan, 2012), esp. pp. 4–12, on the difficulty of documenting queens' lives.

12. Gervase of Canterbury, *Chronica*, p. 149.

13. William of Newburgh, *The History of English Affairs*, ed. P. G. Walsh and M. J. Kennedy, 2 vols. (Oxford: Aris & Phillips, 1988; rpt., 2007), vol. 1, I, 31, p. 128.

14. Ralph of Diceto, *Ymagines historiarum*, vol. 1, p. 355.

15. Gerald of Wales, *Expugnatio Hibernica: The Conquest of Ireland*, ed. A. Brian Scott and F. X. Martin (Dublin: Royal Irish Academy, 1978), p. 128.

16. Gervase of Canterbury, *Chronica*, p. 149.

17. *The Chronicle of Richard of Devizes of the Time of King Richard the First*, ed. John T. Appleby (London: Thomas Nelson, 1963), pp. 24–26. Adding to the mystery, in one of the two manuscripts of his chronicle, Richard writes these words in the form of an inverted triangle surrounded by a thick, wavy line.

18. Gervase of Canterbury, *Chronica*, p. 87.

19. William of Tyre, *Chronicon*, ed. R. B. C. Huygens, 2 vols., CCCM, vol. 63 (Turnhout: Brepols, 1986), Prologue, vol. 1, p. 98.

20. William of Malmesbury, *Gesta regum Anglorum: The History of the English Kings*, ed. R. A. B. Mynors, R. M. Thomson, and M. Winterbottom, 2 vols. (Oxford: Clarendon Press, 1998–99), vol. 1, Prologue to Book 2, p. 150.

21. William of Malmesbury, *Gesta regum Anglorum*, vol. 1, Letter 2, from the Monks of Malmesbury to Empress Matilda, pp. 6–9.

22. William of Tyre, *Chronicon*, XVI, 27, vol. 2, pp. 754–75.

23. *The Correspondence of Thomas Becket, Archbishop of Canterbury (1162–1170)*, ed. Anne Duggan, 2 vols. (Oxford: Clarendon Press, 2000), vol. 1, Letter 51, of John of Poitiers, Bishop of Le Mans, to Archbishop Thomas of Canterbury, p. 216.

24. Michael Staunton, in *The Historians of Angevin England* (Oxford: Oxford University Press, 2017), explores the way in which Eleanor's contemporaries made sense of this queen through reference to a long series of classical and biblical prototypes, including Bathsheba, for her marriage to a king who took her from her rightful husband (p. 181); Livia, for her persecution of Henry's illegitimate son Geoffrey (p. 106); and Helen (p. 312), Amata (p. 196), and Cleopatra (p. 312), for stirring men to war and dissension.

25. As the French word *prudence* would not enter widespread circulation until the midthirteenth century, the Latin word *prudentia* was often translated as "wisdom" (*sagesse*) before that time.

26. Gerald of Wales, *Instruction for a Ruler / De principis instructione*, ed. Robert Bartlett (Oxford: Clarendon Press, 2018), I, 11, p. 138.

27. Turgot of Durham, *Vita sanctae Margaretae Scotorum reginae*, p. 238.

28. Peter of Blois, *Epistolae*, *PL*, vol. 207, cols. 1–559, at Letter 154, cols. 448–49.

29. Gervase of Canterbury, *Chronica*, pp. 242–43.

30. *Epistolae Cantuarienses: The Letters of the Prior and Convent of Christ Church, Canterbury, from A.D. 1187 to A.D. 1199*, ed. William Stubbs, in *Chronicles and Memorials of the Reign of Richard I*, 2 vols., RS, vol. 38 (London: Longman, 1865), vol. 2, Letter 399, from Richard the Lionheart to Eleanor of Aquitaine, p. 362.

31. Marion Meade, *Eleanor of Aquitaine: A Biography* (New York: Hawthorn Books, 1977), p. ix.

32. Jane Martindale, "Eleanor of Aquitaine," in *Richard Coeur de Lion in History and Myth*, King's College Medieval Studies VII, ed. Janet Nelson (London: King's College London, 1992), pp. 17–50, at p. 44.

33. Martindale, "Eleanor of Aquitaine," p. 40.

34. Natasha Hodgson, *Women, Crusading, and the Holy Land in Historical Narrative* (Woodbridge, UK: Boydell Press, 2007), p. 133.

35. See Steven Runciman, *A History of the Crusades*, 3 vols. (Cambridge: Cambridge University Press, 1951–54), vol. 2, p. 279; and Régine Pernoud, *Aliénor d'Aquitaine* (Paris: Albin Michel, 1965), pp. 74–75.

36. See Jean Flori, *Aliénor d'Aquitaine: La reine insoumise* (Paris: Payot, 2004), p. 15.

37. Ralph V. Turner, in *Eleanor of Aquitaine: Queen of France, Queen of England* (New Haven: Yale University Press, 2009), p. 91.

38. If scholars have assumed that Eleanor sought to acquire and retain power, it is because they have assumed that queens in general were motivated by such an ambition. The editors of the Queenship and Power series at Palgrave Macmillan, which includes sixty volumes at the time of this writing, state, "This series . . . aims to broaden our understanding of the strategies that

queens . . . pursued in order to wield political power within the structures of male-dominant societies" (https://www.palgrave.com/gp/series/14523).

39. The anonymous Nun of Barking offers a prayer for Henry and Eleanor, in *La vie d'Edouard le confesseur, poème Anglo-normand du xiie siècle*, ed. Östen Södergård (Uppsala: Almqvist & Wiksells, 1948), vv. 5001–6.

40. *Hildegardis Bingensis Epistolarium*, ed. Lieven Van Acker and Monika Klaes-Hachmoller, 3 vols., CCCM, vol. 91b (Turnhout: Brepols, 1991–2001), vol. 3, 78, ep. 318 (1154–70), p. 78.

CHAPTER ONE

1. Hugh of Saint Victor, *De sacramentis*, *PL*, vol. 176, col. 488.

2. Jean-Baptiste Molin and Protais Mutembe, *Le rituel du mariage en France du XIIe au XVIe siècle* (Paris: Beauchesne, 1973), p. 286.

3. See John Gillingham, "Love, Marriage, and Politics in the Twelfth Century," *Forum for Modern Language Studies* 25 (1989): 292–303, esp. p. 295.

4. See Richard of Poitiers, *Ex chronico Richardi Pictaviensis*, *RHF*, vol. 12, pp. 411–21, at p. 413; and Orderic Vitalis, *Historia ecclesiastica*, in *The Ecclesiastical History of Orderic Vitalis*, ed. Marjorie Chibnall, 6 vols. (Oxford: Clarendon Press, 1969–80), vol. 6, XIII, 30, pp. 480–82.

5. Orderic Vitalis, in *Historia ecclesiastica*, vol. 6, XIII, 32, states that Louis VI died on August 4, a date that is supported by the obituary of Argenteuil (490). But all other sources agree that he died on August 1. See Achille Luchaire, *Louis VI le Gros* (Paris: Alphonse Picard, 1890), nos. 590, 595.

6. See Jane Martindale, "Succession and Politics in the Romance-Speaking World, c. 1000–1140," in *England and Her Neighbors, 1066–1453: Essays in Honour of Pierre Chaplais*, ed. M. Jones and M. Vale (London: Bloomsbury, 1989), pp. 19–41; and Lois L. Huneycutt, "Female Succession and the Language of Power in the Writings of Twelfth-Century Churchmen," in *Medieval Queenship*, ed. John Carmi Parsons (Stroud, UK: Sutton Publishing, 1994), pp. 189–201.

7. *Chronicle of the Abbey of Morigny: A Translation of the "Chronicle" of the Abbey of Morigny, France, c. 1100–1150*, ed. Richard Cusimano (Lewiston, ME: Edwin Mellen Press, 2003), III, 2, pp. 124–25.

8. Suger of Saint-Denis, *Vita Ludovici VI Regis Philippi filii qui Grossus dictus*, *RHF*, vol. 12, pp. 10–63, at p. 62.

9. In an apparently inauthentic will, supposedly written before his departure and signed by William and "Eleanor his daughter," in the presence of over a dozen witnesses, William refers to Eleanor as she "to whom I leave Aquitaine and Poitou." See *Ex fragmentis chronicorum comitum Pictaviae, ducum Aquitaniae, auctore, ut videtur, monacho S. Maxentii*, *RHF*, vol. 12, pp. 408–11, at pp. 409–10. This document suggests that the duke was at least remembered to have designated Eleanor as his heir.

10. *Chronicle of the Abbey of Morigny*, III, 2, pp. 124–25.

11. Robert of Torigni, *Appendice ad Sigebertum*, *RHF*, vol. 13, pp. 283–326, at p. 330.

12. See *Chronique de Saint-Maixent (751–1140)*, ed. Jean Verdon, Les classiques de l'histoire de France au Moyen Age (Paris: Les Belles Lettres, 1979), pp. 194–96.

13. Yves of Chartres, *Addenda ad Ivonis epistolas*, *PL*, vol. 162, cols. 287–505, at Letter 243, to Galen, Bishop of Paris, col. 251.

14. *Corpus iuris canonici*, ed. Emil Friedberg and Aemilius Ludwig Richter, 2 vols. (Leipzig: Ex

officina Bernhardi Tauchnitz, 1879–81; rpr. Graz: Akademische Druck- u. Verlagsanstalt, 1959), vol. 1, *Decretum Magistri Gratiani*, [Part II], C. 27, q. 2, d. a. c. 1, at col. 1062.

15. Hugh of Saint-Victor, *De sacramentis*, II, 11, 4, col. 482.

16. John of Salisbury, *The Letters of John of Salisbury*, vol. 1, *The Early Letters (1153–1161)*, ed. W. J. Millor and H. E. Butler; rev. ed., C. N. L. Brooke (London: Thomas Nelson, 1955–79), Letter 131, from Archbishop Theobald to Pope Alexander III (c. October–November 1160), p. 235.

17. Peter Lombard, *Sententiae*, in *Magistri Petri Lombardi sententie in IV libris distinctae*, [no editors], 2 vols., Spicilegium Bonaventurianum 4–5, 3rd ed. (Grottaferrata [Romae]: Editiones Collegii S. Bonaventurae ad Claras Aquas, 1981), IV, dist. 28, vol. 2, ch. 2, p. 433.

18. Peter Lombard, *Sententiae*, IV, dist. 28, vol. 2, ch. 2, p. 433.

19. Ephesians 5:25.

20. Justinian, *Digest*, XXIII, titl. 1, l. 7, 11, and 12, quoted in Yves of Chartres, *Decretum*, *PL*, vol. 161, cols. 47–1037, at VIII, 11, ch. 20, col. 588.

21. *Corpus iuris canonici*, vol. 1, *Decretum Magistri Gratiani*, [Part II], C. 27, q. 2, d. a. c. 1, at col. 1062.

22. *Le roman d'Eneas: Edition critique d'après le manuscrit BN fr. 60*, ed. Aimé Petit, Lettres Gothiques (Paris: Le Livre de Poche, 1997), vv. 8341, 8488, et passim.

23. *Le roman d'Eneas*, vv. 8775–78.

24. *Le roman d'Eneas*, v. 4203.

25. *Le roman de Thèbes: Edition du manuscrit S (Londres, Brit. Lib., Add. 34114)*, ed. Francine Mora-Lebrun, Lettres Gothiques (Paris: Le Livre de Poche, 1995), v. 4240.

26. *Le roman de Thèbes*, vv. 4244–53.

27. See Orderic Vitalis, *Historia ecclesiastica*, vol. 6, XIII, 26, p. 466, and 30, pp. 480–82.

28. *Ex fragmentis chronicorum comitum Pictaviae*, p. 409.

29. Richard of Poitiers, *Ex chronico*, p. 413.

30. Richard of Poitiers, *Ex chronico*, p. 413.

31. Cercamon, "Lo plaing comenz iradamen," in *The Poetry of Cercamon and Jaufre Rudel*, ed. George Wolf and Roy Rosenstein (New York: Garland Publishing, 1983), I, pp. 32–35, at vv. 13–18. The troubadour Marcabru similarly urges, "Antioch, here, Guyenne and Poitou, weep for worthiness and valor. May God conduct the count to his washing-place and put his soul in peace," in "Pax in nomine Domini," *Marcabru: A Critical Edition*, ed. Simon Gaunt, Ruth Harvey, and Linda Paterson (Woodbridge, UK: D. S. Brewer, 2000), XXXV, pp. 434–53, at vv. 67–70.

32. William X was conflated with William of Malavalle, a knight from Aquitaine who died a recluse in Castiglione della Pescaia in Tuscany in 1157. See Jean Bouchet, *Les annales d'Aquitaine: Faicts et gestes en sommaire des roys de France et d'Angleterre, et païs de Naples & de Milan* (Poitiers: Marnef & Bouchet, 1545; rev., 1557), fol. 75; and François de Belle-Forest, *Grandes annales et histoire générale de France*, 2 vols (Paris: Gabriel Buon, 1579), vol. 1, p. 510.

33. Suger of Saint-Denis, *Vita Ludovici VI Regis*, p. 62.

34. Orderic Vitalis, *Historia ecclesiastica*, vol. 6, XIII, 32, p. 490.

35. Orderic Vitalis, *Historia ecclesiastica*, vol. 6, XIII, 32, pp. 490–91.

36. Suger of Saint-Denis, *Vita Ludovici VI Regis*, p. 61.

37. *Chronicle of the Abbey of Morigny*, III, 2, pp. 126–27.

38. Suger of Saint-Denis, *Vita Ludovici VI Regis*, p. 62.

39. Orderic Vitalis, *Historia ecclesiastica*, vol. 6, XIII, 32, p. 490.

40. Suger of Saint-Denis, *Vita Ludovici VI Regis*, p. 62.

41. *Chronicle of the Abbey of Morigny*, III, 2, pp. 128–29.

42. Michael Evans, in "The Missing Queen? Eleanor of Aquitaine in the Early Reign of Louis VII," in *Louis VII and His World*, ed. Michael L. Bardot and Laurence W. Marvin (Leiden: Brill, 2018), pp. 105–13, stresses the lack of evidence that Eleanor played a powerful role as Queen of France and the speculations historians have relied on to argue otherwise.

43. See Marie Hivergneaux, "Aliénor d'Aquitaine: Le pouvoir d'une femme à la lumière de ses chartes (1152–1204)," in *La cour Plantagenêt (1154–1204): Actes du colloque tenu à Thouars du 30 avril au 2 mai 1999*, ed. Martin Aurell (Poitiers: Université de Poitiers, 2000), pp. 63–87; and "Autour d'Aliénor d'Aquitaine: Entourage et pouvoir au prisme des chartes (1137–1189)," in *Plantagenêts et Capétiens: Confrontations et héritages*, ed. Martin Aurell and Noël-Yves Tonnerre (Turnhout: Brepols, 2006), pp. 61–73. Louis signed twenty-nine charters concerning Aquitaine between 1137 and 1152. Eleanor appears in sixteen of them, simply giving her consent in twelve. When Eleanor was married to Henry, she was mentioned in only eleven charters. It was only when she became a widow that things changed. Forty of her eighty acts were prepared between 1189 and 1204.

44. Geoffrey of Auxerre, *S. Bernardi vita prima, liber tertius-quintus, PL*, vol. 185, cols. 303–68, at IV, 3, 18, col. 332. See also Geoffrey's *Fragmenta ex vita tertia Sancti Bernardi, PL*, vol. 185, cols. 523–30, at VIII, col. 527.

45. Geoffrey of Auxerre, *S. Bernardi vita prima*, IV, ch. 3, 18, col. 332.

46. The marriage between Petronilla and Ralph of Vermandois would not be a happy one. The couple had three children but none had heirs, and their one son succumbed to leprosy. They would divorce in 1151, and Ralph would marry another woman, after which Petronilla returned to Eleanor's entourage.

47. Geoffrey of Auxerre, *S. Bernardi vita prima*, IV, 3, 18, col. 332.

48. Geoffrey of Auxerre, *Fragmenta ex vita tertia*, VIII, col. 527.

49. Geoffrey of Auxerre, *S. Bernardi vita prima*, IV, ch. 3, 18, col. 332.

50. Geoffrey of Auxerre, *Fragmenta ex vita tertia*, VIII, col. 527.

51. Constance Britain Bouchard argues in "Eleanor's Divorce from Louis VII: The Uses of Consanguinity," in *Eleanor of Aquitaine: Lord and Lady*, ed. Bonnie Wheeler and John Carmi Parsons (Basingstoke, UK: Palgrave, 2002), pp. 223–35, at p. 232, that Eleanor and Louis's divorce marked a "key transition" in attitudes toward consanguinity: whereas earlier clerics had argued against consanguineous marriages and nobles had defended them, now, in the twelfth century, nobles argued against these unions when they saw them as no longer in their interest and clerics defended them.

52. Ralph of Diceto, in *Ymagines historiarum*, vol. 1, p. 366, reports that William X rose up against his father to avenge this insult to his mother, but whatever animosity he felt toward him must have been appeased by 1121, when he married Aénor of Châtellerault.

53. See Robert of Torigni, *Appendice ad Sigebertum*, X, 31, p. 758; and Wace, *Roman de Brut: A History of the British*, ed. Judith Weiss (Exeter: University of Exeter Press, 1999), vv. 22–23.

54. John of Salisbury, *Historia pontificalis*, XXIX, p. 61.

55. John of Salisbury, *Historia pontificalis*, XLI, p. 82.

56. Mark 10:7–9.

57. Bernard of Clairvaux, *Epistolae, in Sancti Bernardi Opera*, ed. Jean LeClercq, C. H. Talbot, and Henri Rochais, 8 vols. in 9 (Rome: Editiones Cistercienses, 1957–77), vol. 7, Letter 224, to Stephen, Bishop of Palestrina (1144), pp. 91–93, at p. 93. Though Bernard was not present at the Council of Beaugency, he is said to have advised that Eleanor and Louis's marriage be dissolved, perhaps through Godefroy de la Roche Vanneau, Archbishop of Langres, who was

his cousin and a onetime prior of Clairvaux. See *Anonymous Blandiniensis, appendicula ad Sigebertum*, *RHF*, vol. 14, pp. 16–21, at p. 21. Other sources confirming the consent of Eugenius, Bernard of Clairvaux, and Godefroy of Langres to the annulment include Richard of Poitiers, *Ex chronico*, p. 416; and Bernard Gui, *Ex libro Bernardi Guidonis de origine regum Francorum*, *RHF*, vol. 12, pp. 230–33, at p. 231.

58. Stephen of Rouen, *Draco Normannicus*, in *Chronicles of the Reigns of Stephen, Henry II, and Richard I*, ed. Richard Howlett, 2 vols., RS, vol. 82 (London: Longman, 1885), vol. 2, pp. 585–781, at II, vv. 107–11. See also John of Salisbury, *Historia pontificalis*, XXIII, p. 53.

59. *Historia gloriosi Regis Ludovici VII, filii Ludovici Grossi*, *RHF*, vol. 12, pp. 124–33, at p. 127.

60. *Chronicon Turonese magnum*, ed. André Salmon, in *Recueil de chroniques de Touraine* (Tours: Imprimerie Ladevéze, 1854), pp. 64–161, at p. 136.

61. See Alberic of Trois-Fontaines, *Ex chronico Albrici Trium-Fontium monachi*, *RHF*, vol. 13, pp. 683–713, at p. 703; Ralph of Coggeshall, in *Chronicon Anglicanum*, ed. Joseph Stevenson, RS, vol. 66 (London: Longman, 1875), pp. 1–208, at p. 13; *Continuatio Aquicinctina*, *PL*, vol. 160, cols. 294–348, at cols. 294–95; *Fragmentum genealogicum ducum Normanniae et Angliae regum*, pp. 241–42; and *Annales Monasterii de Waverleia* (AD 1–1291), ed. Henry Richards Luard, in *Annales monastici*, 5 vols., RS, vol. 36 (London: Longman, 1865), vol. 2, pp. 129–411, at p. 234.

62. *De origine comitum Andegavensium*, *RHF*, vol. 12, pp. 534–39, at p. 537.

63. John of Salisbury, *Historia pontificalis*, XXIX, p. 61.

64. See John of Salisbury, *The Letters of John of Salisbury*, vol. 1, *The Early Letters (1153–1161)*, Letter 131, Archbishop Theobald to Pope Alexander III (c. October–November 1160), p. 235.

65. See, for example, Turner, *Eleanor of Aquitaine*, pp. 105–6.

66. *Récits d'un ménestrel de Reims*, ed. Natalis de Wailly (Paris: Renouard, 1876), II, 11, p. 6.

67. *Récits d'un ménestrel de Reims*, II, 11, p. 6.

68. Matthew Paris, *Chronica majora*, ed. Henry Richards Luard, 7 vols., RS, vol. 57 (London: Longman, 1872–83), p. 186.

69. All references in this section will be to Philippe Mouskés, *Chronique rimée*, ed. Frédéric-Auguste-Ferdinand-Thomas Reiffenberg, 2 vols. (Brussels: M. Hayez, 1836–38), vol. 2.

70. [*Histoire des rois d'Angleterre*], Cambridge University Library, Manuscripts, Ii.6.24, fol. 95r–100v, at fol. 98r. For critical editions, see Paul Meyer, "Notice sur le manuscrit II, 6, 24 de la Bibliothèque de l'Université de Cambridge," *Notices et extraits des manuscrits de la Bibliothèque nationale et autres bibliothèques* 32, pt. 2 (1888): 37–38; and Daniel Power, "The Stripping of a Queen: Eleanor in Thirteenth-Century Norman Tradition," in *The World of Eleanor of Aquitaine: Literature and Society in Southern France between the Eleventh and Thirteenth Centuries*, ed. Marcus Bull and Catherine Léglu (Woodbridge, UK: Boydell Press, 2005), pp. 115–35, at p. 134.

71. [*Chronique de Normandie*], Paris, Bibliothèque de l'Arsenal, Manuscrits, 3516, fol. 304v–315r, at fol. 314r. For a critical edition, see Power, "The Stripping of a Queen," pp. 135–36. Meyer, in "Notice sur le manuscrit," pp. 63–64, suggests that the Cambridge and Arsenal texts were attempting to make Eleanor and the barons converse in a kind of Occitan.

72. Walter Map, *De nugis curialium / Courtiers' Trifles*, ed. M. R. James, rev. C. N. L. Brooke and R. A. B. Mynors (Oxford: Clarendon Press, 1983), Dist. ii, c. 13, p. 160.

73. Gerald of Wales, *Expugnatio Hibernica*, I, Preface, p. 6.

74. Geoffrey of Auxerre, in his *Super apocalypsim*, ed. Ferruccio Gastaldelli (Rome: Edizioni di Storia a Letteratura, 1970), at pp. 183–84, cites a priest in Sicily, who came to light when the

Duke of Burgundy's sister was engaged to Roger the Magnificent, King of Sicily, and "whose good reputation is attested by neighbors and officials," as the source of his report.

75. Gervase of Tilbury, in *Otia imperialia / Recreations for an Emperor*, ed. S. E. Banks and J. W. Binns (Oxford: Clarendon Press, 2002), III, 57, p. 664, claims to have heard about such demonic ladies "from men of completely proven and sincere religion."

76. Jean d'Arras, in *Mélusine: Roman du XIVe siècle, publié pour la première fois d'après le manuscrit de la Bibliothèque de l'Arsenal avec les variantes des manuscrits de la Bibliothèque nationale*, ed. Louis Stouff (Dijon: Imprimerie Bernigaud et Privat, 1932), pp. 1–3, bases his knowledge of marvels on Gervase of Tilbery's *Otia imperialia*, which he would have known from the fourteenth-century translation of Jehan de Vignay, which was available in John of Berry's library.

77. Gervase of Tilbury, *Otia imperialia*, I, 15, p. 86.

78. Gerald of Wales speaks of the Countess of Anjou in *Instruction for a Ruler*, III, 27, p. 688.

79. The ten different manuscripts of this fourteenth-century romance, *Richard Coer de Lyon*, differ markedly. Karl Brunner used the longest manuscript—Cambridge, Gonville and Caius MS 175—as the basis of his *Der mittelenglische Versroman über Richard Löwenherz* (Vienna: W. Braumüller, 1913), which he supplemented with material from sixteenth-century editions. I am relying on *Richard Coer de Lyon*, ed. Peter Larkin, Middle English Texts Series (Kalamazoo, MI: Medieval Institute Publications, 2015).

80. Gerald of Wales, *Instruction for a Ruler*, III, 27, pp. 688, 690.

81. Caesarius of Heisterbach, *Dialogus miraculorum*, ed. Joseph Strange, 2 vols. (Cologne: J. M. Heberle, 1851), vol. 1, dist. 3, 12, p. 324.

82. Lambert of Waterlos, *Ex Lamberti Waterlosii chronico Cameracensi Autbertino*, *RHF*, vol. 13, pp. 497–532, at p. 507.

83. John of Salisbury, *Historia pontificalis*, XXIII, p. 53.

84. John of Salisbury, *Historia pontificalis*, XXIX, p. 61.

85. Aelred of Rievaulx, *De spirituali amicitia*, ed. Anselm Hoste, in *Opera omnia*, ed. Anselm Hoste, C. H. Talbot, Gaetano Raciti, Domenico Pezzini, and Francesco Marzella, 7 vols., CCCM, vols. 1–3A (Turnhout: Brepols, 1971–), vol. 1, pp. 287–330, at III, 2, p. 317.

86. Aelred of Rievaulx, *De spirituali amicitia*, I, 41, p. 296.

87. Aelred of Rievaulx, *De spirituali amicitia*, II, 59, p. 313.

88. Aelred of Rievaulx, *De spirituali amicitia*, II, 59, p. 313.

89. Walter Map, *De nugis curialium*, dist. IV, c. 9, p. 348.

90. Geoffrey of Auxerre, *Super apocalypsim*, Sermo 15, p. 186.

91. Gerald of Wales, *Instruction for a Ruler*, III, 27, p. 68; and Mouskés, *Chronique rimée*, vv. 18800–18801.

92. Map, *De nugis curialium*, dist. IV, c. 9, p. 348; Gervase of Tilbury, *Otia imperialia*, III, 57, p. 664; *Richard Coer de Lyon*, vv. 229–30.

93. Gervase of Tilbury, *Otia imperialia*, I, 15, p. 90.

94. See Map, *De nugis curialium*, dist. ii, c. 13, p. 160; Jean d'Arras, *Mélusine*, p. 253; and Geoffrey of Auxerre, *Super apocalypsim*, ed. Gastaldelli, sermo 15, pp. 184–85.

95. 2 Corinthians 11:14.

96. [*Histoire des rois d'Angleterre*], Cambridge University Library, Ii.6.24, fol. 98r.

97. Lambert of Waterlos, *Chronico Cameracensi Autbertino*, *RHF*, vol. 13, p. 507.

98. Gervase of Tilbury, *Otia imperialia*, I, 15, p. 90.

99. Jean d'Arras, *Mélusine*, p. 4.

100. See Laurence Harf-Lancner, *Les fées au Moyen Âge: Morgane et Mélusine: La naissance aux fées* (Geneva: Champion, 1984), p. 57. The Castle of Lusignan was erected in the tenth

century by Hugh II of Lusignan. It was razed in the sixteenth century, during the Wars of Religion.

101. John of Salisbury, *Historia pontificalis*, XXIII, p. 53.

102. Hugh of Saint-Victor, *De sacramentis*, II, 11, 11, col. 499.

103. Gervase of Canterbury, *Chronica*, p. 149.

104. William of Newburgh, *The History of English Affairs*, vol. 1, I, 31, p. 128.

105. William of Newburgh, *The History of English Affairs*, vol. 1, I, 31, p. 128.

106. Stephen of Paris, *Fragmentum historicum de Ludovico VII, Francorum Rege, excerptum ex Stephani Pariensis Commentario Ms. in Regulam S. Benedicti*, RHF, vol. 12, pp. 89–91, at p. 89. On Stephen of Paris, see Caroline Walker Bynum, "Stephen of Paris and His Commentary on the Benedictine Rule," *Revue bénédictine* 81 (1971): 67–91.

107. *Historia gloriosi Regis Ludovici VII, filii Ludovici Grossi*, p. 127.

108. *Ex fragmentis chronicorum comitum Pictaviae, ducum Aquitaniae, auctore, ut videtur, monacho S. Maxentii*, p. 410.

109. Gervase of Canterbury, *Chronica*, p. 149.

110. William of Newburgh, *The History of English Affairs*, vol. 1, I, 31, p. 128.

111. Stephen of Rouen, *Draco Normannicus*, II, v. 113.

112. Wace, *Roman de Brut*, vv. 24–26.

113. [*Histoire des rois d'Angleterre*], Cambridge University Library, Ii.6.24, fol. 98r.

114. Power, "The Stripping of a Queen," p. 127.

115. [*Histoire des rois d'Angleterre*], Cambridge University Library, Ii.6.24, fol. 98r.

116. *Continuatio Aquicinctina*, col. 294.

117. William of Newburgh, *The History of English Affairs*, vol. 1, I, 31, p. 130.

118. *Récits d'un ménestrel de Reims*, II, 11, pp. 6–7.

119. Later medieval chroniclers echo the Minstrel of Reims's criticism of Louis. See the *Chronique abrégée*, Paris Bibliothèque nationale de France, Manuscrits, fr. 9222, fols. 16v–17t; Jean d'Outremeuse, *Ly myreur des histors: Chronique de Jean de Preis dit l'Outremeuse*, ed. Adolphe Borgnet, 6 vols. (Paris: Librairie Renouard, 1864–80), vol. 4, pp. 400–401; and Pierre Cochon, *Chronique normande*, ed. Charles de Robillard de Beaurepaire (Rouen: A. Le Brunment, 1870), pp. 2–3.

120. William of Saint-Denis suggests, in *Sugerii vita*, ed. Françoise Gasparri, in *Oeuvres*, 2 vols. Classiques de l'Histoire de France au Moyen Age 37e and 41e (Paris: Les Belles Lettres, 1996–2001), vol. 2, pp. 292–373, at p. 306, that if Suger had still been alive at this point, he would have prevented the great duchy of Aquitaine from being cut off from France. See also Hugh of Poitiers, *Ex historia Vizeliacensis Monasterii*, RHF, vol. 12, pp. 317–44, at p. 341.

121. *Récits d'un ménestrel de Reims*, II, 11, p. 6.

122. "Queen Eleanor's Confession," in *The Traditional Tunes of the Child Ballads with Their Texts, According to the Extant Records of Great Britain and America*, ed. Francis James Child, rev. Bertrand Harris Bronson, 4 vols. (Princeton: Princeton University Press, 1959–72), vol. 3, no. 156, pp. 105–6.

123. Robert Courson, in his *Summa*, XXXI, 15–16, still only found on the Bibliothèque nationale de France, Manuscrits, lat. 14524, takes issue with Eleanor's marriage to Henry, which was tolerated by the Church despite the consanguinity of the spouses and despite the absence of necessity, utility, or just cause.

124. Louis was Eleanor's third cousin once removed and Henry was her fourth cousin. See C. N. L. Brooke, "The Marriage of Henry II and Eleanor of Aquitaine," *Historian: The Magazine for Members of the Historical Association* 20 (1988): 3–8, at p. 5.

125. William of Newburgh, *The History of English Affairs*, vol. 1, I, 31, pp. 128–30.

126. See *Corpus iuris canonici*, vol. 1, *Decretum Magistri Gratiani*, [Part II], C. 36, q. 1, d. p. c. 2, at col. 1289; and Peter Lombard, *Sententiae*, IV, dist. 41, ch. 5–9, vol. 2, p. 500.

127. The Arab-Andalusian historian Al-Bakri tells this story. His account has been lost, but the relevant passage was transcribed by Muḥammad ibn ʿAbd Allāh Ḥimyarī in *Kitab ar rawd al-mitar fi habar al-haktar*, ed. and trans. in Evariste Levi-Provençal, *La Péninsule Ibérique au Moyen Age* (Leiden: E. J. Brill, 1938), pp. 54–55.

128. Gerald of Wales, *Instruction for a Ruler*, III, 27, p. 684.

129. Geoffrey du Breuil of Vigeois, *Chronicon Lemovicense: Ex chronico Gaufredi Coenobitae, Monasterii S. Martialis Lemovicensis ac Prioris Vosiensis Coenobii*, RHF, vol. 12, pp. 421–51, at p. 435.

130. Gervase of Tilbury, *Otia imperialia*, II, 21, p. 482.

131. Gerald of Wales, *Instruction for a Ruler*, III, 27, pp. 686–88.

132. Judges 19:25.

133. Walter Map likewise reproaches Henry for marrying Eleanor, in *De nugis curialium*, dist. V, c. 6, pp. 474–76, "though she was secretly rumored to have shared Louis's bed with his father Geoffrey."

134. See Matthew Strickland, *Henry the Young King* (New Haven: Yale University Press, 2016), pp. 72–73; and Michael Staunton, *The Historians of Angevin England*, p. 32. Henry became seneschal of France in 1158, and both the Young King and his brother Geoffrey occupied this position. See the treatise *De majoratu et senescalcia Franciae*, probably by the Angevin retainer Hugh de Clers, in *Chroniques des comtes d'Anjou et des seigneurs d'Amboise*, ed. Louis Halphen and René Poupardin (Paris: A. Picard, 1913), pp. 239–46.

135. *Chronicon Turonese magnum*, p. 136.

136. See Pierre Souty, "Aliénor d'Aquitaine et l'embuscade de Port-de-Piles (1152)," *Bulletin Trimestriel de la Société Archéologique de Touraine* 37 (1973): 194–95.

137. Hélinand of Froidmont, *Chronicon*, PL, vol. 212, cols. 971–1082, at cols. 1057–58.

138. William of Tyre, *Chronicon*, XVII, 8, p. 770; *Chronicon Turonese magnum*, pp. 136–37; and *Annales prioratus de Wigornia*, ed. Henry Richards Luard, in *Annales monastici*, ed. Henry Richards Luard, 5 vols., RS, vol. 36 (London: Longman, 1869), vol. 4, pp. 355–562, at p. 380.

139. Thomas Wykes, *Chronicon*, in *Annales monastici*, ed. Henry Richards Luard, 5 vols., RS, vol. 36 (London: Longman, 1869), vol. 4, pp. 6–352, at p. 28; and Bernard Gui, *Ex libro . . . de origine regum Francorum*, p. 231.

140. Matthew Paris, *Chronica majora*, p. 186; Lambert of Waterlos, *Chronico Cameracensi Autbertino*; Gervase of Tilbury, *Otia imperialia*, II, 21, p. 484; and *Annales Monasterii de Waverleia*, p. 234.

141. Lambert of Waterlos, *Chronico Cameracensi Autbertino*, p. 507.

142. *Historia gloriosi Regis Ludovici VII*, p. 127; and Ralph of Coggeshall, *Chronicon Anglicanum*, p. 13.

143. William of Tyre, *Chronicon*, XVII, 8, p. 770.

144. *The Chronicle of Robert of Torigni, Abbot of the Monastery of St. Michel-in-Peril-of-the-Sea*. In *Chronicles of the Reigns of Stephen, Henry II, and Richard I*, ed. Richard Howlett, 4 vols., RS, vol. 82 (London: Longman, 1884–89), vol. 4, pp. 3–315, at p. 165.

145. Gervase of Canterbury, *Chronica*, p. 149.

146. Henry of Huntingdon, *Historia Anglorum*, X, 31, p. 758.

147. Richard of Poitiers, *Ex chronico*, p. 417.

148. Thomas Wykes, *Chronicon*, p. 28.

149. Aelred of Rievaulx, *De spirituali amicitia*, I, 45, p. 296.

150. Gerald of Wales, *Instruction for a Ruler*, III, 27, p. 688. The term "domino suo" could be translated as "her lord" or "her husband," but also as "his lord." When Gerald lists Henry's crimes, in *Instruction for a Ruler*, II, 39, at p, 539, he mentions, not only his killing of Becket, but (citing Pope Lucius III's reprimand of this king) "the height of injury, [his] taking [of Louis's] wife Eleanor unjustly and having heirs from such a union."

151. Gerald of Wales, *Instruction for a Ruler*, III, 27, p. 688.

152. Gerald of Wales, *Instruction for a Ruler*, II, 1, p. 444.

153. Gerald of Wales, *Instruction for a Ruler*, I, 20, p. 382, and III, 1, p. 566.

154. Walter Map, *De nugis curialium*, dist. V, c. 6, p. 476.

155. William of Newburgh, *The History of English Affairs*, vol. 1, I, 31, p. 128.

156. William of Newburgh, *Historia rerum Anglicarum*, vol. 1, III, 26, p. 281.

157. William of Newburgh, *The History of English Affairs*, vol. 1, 31, p. 128.

158. Thomas Wykes, *Chronicon*, p. 28.

159. Gervase of Canterbury, *Chronica*, p. 149.

160. *Fragmentum historicum vitam Ludovici VII summatim complectens*, RHF, vol. 12, pp. 285–87, at p. 286.

161. *Récits d'un ménestrel de Reims*, II, 12, p. 7.

162. *Continuatio Aquicinctina*, col. 194–95.

163. William of Newburgh, *The History of English Affairs*, vol. 1, I, 31, p. 128.

164. Gervase of Canterbury, *Chronica*, p. 149.

165. Walter Map, *De nugis curialium*, dist. V, c. 6, p. 474.

166. William of Newburgh, *The History of English Affairs*, vol. 1, I, 31, p. 128.

167. Thomas Wykes, *Chronicon*, p. 28.

168. Walter Map, *De nugis curialium*, dist. V, c. 6, p. 474.

169. Adam of Eynsham, *Magna Vita Sancti Hugonis: The Life of St. Hugh of Lincoln*, ed. Decima L. Douie and Dom Hugh Farmer, 2 vols. (London: Thomas Nelson and Sons, 1961–62), vol. 2, V, 16, p. 184.

170. William of Newburgh, *Historia rerum Anglicarum*, vol. 1, III, 26, p. 281.

171. *The Letters and Charters of Gilbert Foliot, Abbot of Gloucester (1139–48), Bishop of Hereford (1148–63) and London (1163–87)*, ed. Z. N. Brooke, Adrian Morey, and C. N. L. Brooke (Cambridge: Cambridge University Press, 1967), Letter 26, to Brian FitzCount (1143–44), p. 63.

CHAPTER TWO

1. *Historia gloriosi Regis Ludovici VII*, p. 126.

2. Odo of Deuil, *De profectione Ludovici VII in orientem: The Journey of Louis VII to the East*, ed. Virginia Gingerick Berry (New York: W. W. Norton, 1948), vol. 1, pp. 16–18.

3. The Byzantine official Niketas Choniatēs, in his *Historia*, ed. Jan-Louis van Dieten, 2 vols. (Berlin: Novi Eboraci: De Gruyter, 1975), vol. 2, p. 60, describes a band of women warriors among the crusaders in Constantinople who rode their horses astride like men and bore lances and other weapons. He records, "One stood out from the rest as another Penthesilea. From the embroidered gold which ran around the hem and fringes of her garment, she was called 'Goldfoot.'" Given that Eleanor is the only noteworthy woman to have participated in the Second Crusade, it has often been assumed that Choniatēs was describing her in this passage, but there is little to support this view. The chronicler makes no allusion to the French

army or to Louis, let alone to Eleanor herself, and his description of women dressed as Amazons participating on the crusade is confirmed by no other account of the crusade. In the seventeenth century, Isaac de Larrey, Eleanor's first biographer, in *L'héritière de Guyenne, ou histoire d'Eleonor, femme de Louis VII roy de France et en-suite de Henri II roy d'Angleterre* (Rotterdam: Chez Reinier Leers, 1691), p. 40, inaugurated the legend that the queen and her ladies dressed up as Amazons when embarking on the crusade, though he does not seem to have been familiar with Choniatēs's chronicle or any other source text. Matthew Bennett, in "Virile Latins, Effeminate Greeks, and Strong Women: Gender Definitions on Crusade," in *Gendering the Crusades*, ed. Susan Edgington and Sarah Lambert (Cardiff: University of Wales Press, 2001; rpt., New York: Columbia University Press, 2002), pp. 16–30, at p. 24; and Michael Evans, in "Penthesilea on the Second Crusade: Is Eleanor of Aquitaine the Amazon Queen of Niketas Choniates?" *Crusades* 8 (2009): 23–30; have both argued against the identification of Choniatēs's woman warrior as Eleanor.

4. This figure is from Turner, *Eleanor of Aquitaine*, pp. 86, 88.

5. See Flori, *Aliénor d'Aquitaine*, pp. 69–70; Hodgson, *Women, Crusading, and the Holy Land in Historical Narrative*, p. 133; Pernoud, *Aliénor d'Aquitaine*, pp. 74–75; and Runciman, *A History of the Crusades*, vol. 2, p. 279.

6. See Peggy McCracken, "Scandalizing Desire: Eleanor of Aquitaine and the Chroniclers," in *Eleanor of Aquitaine*, ed. Bonnie Wheeler and John Carmi Parsons (Basingstoke: Palgrave, 2002), pp. 247–63, at p. 254.

7. All references in this section will be to William of Tyre, whether his *Chronicon*, vol. 2, or *Guillaume de Tyr et ses continuateurs: Texte français du XIIIe siècle*, ed. Paulin Paris (Paris: Firmin Didot, 1879), as indicated.

8. There is even some evidence that information about Eleanor may have been excised from his account. See Odo of Deuil, *De profectione Ludovici VII in orientem*, p. xxiii n. 67.

9. Philip Handyside, in *The Old French William of Tyre* (Leiden: Brill, 2015), pp. 6–7, counts fifty-one such manuscripts. Peter W. Edbury and John G. Rowe, in *William of Tyre: Historian of the Latin East* (Cambridge: Cambridge University Press, 1988), p. 4, count at least fifty-nine.

10. References here are to William of Tyre, *Chronicon*.

11. John of Salisbury, *Historia pontificalis*, XXIII, p. 52.

12. Gerhoh von Reichersberg, *De investigatione Antichristi*, ed. Jodo Stülz, *Archiv für Kunde österreichischer Geschichts-Quellen* 20 (1859): 127–88, at 64, p. 160.

13. William of Nangis, *Ex Guillelmi Nangii chronico, RHF*, vol. 20, pp. 543–763, at p. 734.

14. John of Salisbury, *Historia pontificalis*, XXIII, pp. 52–53.

15. In recognition of the heroism Raymond displayed at this time, the story of his death was recounted, not only in William of Tyre's and William of Newburgh's chronicles (*The History of English Affairs*, vol. 1, I, 20–21, pp. 94–97); but also in the *Chanson des chétifs* (early 1200s), in *The Old French Crusade Cycle*, ed. Jan A. Nelson and Emanuel J. Mickel, Jr., vol. 5, ed. G. M. Myers (Tuscaloosa: University of Alabama Press, 1981), vv. 1778–79, a part of the Old French Crusade Cycle, which Raymond had sponsored. This poem addresses the Crusade of 1101, in which Eleanor's grandfather, William IX, had participated. Linda M. Paterson proposes, in "Occitan Literature and the Holy Land," in *The World of Eleanor of Aquitaine*, pp. 85–89, that Raymond had this work composed for Eleanor and Louis's visit to Antioch.

16. William of Newburgh, *The History of English Affairs*, vol. 1, I, 31, p. 128.

17. Henry of Huntingdon, *Historia Anglorum: The History of the English People*, ed. Diana Greenway (Oxford: Clarendon Press, 1996), X, 27, p. 752. Cf. Psalms 57:8 and 2:6 (53:5).

18. Henry of Huntingdon, in *Historia Anglorum*, X, 27, p. 752, writes that both monarchs fled "ignominiously" with a few followers, first to Antioch and later to Jerusalem. If Louis later attacked Damascus, he states, it was only "in order to do something to repair his damaged reputation."

19. Odo of Deuil, *De profectione Ludovici VII in orientem*, I, p. 10.

20. The *Chronicle of the Abbey of Morigny*, III, 7, pp. 160–61, extols the piety Louis exemplified in calling for the crusade but deplores the guilelessness he exhibited in conducting it.

21. John of Salisbury, *Historia pontificalis*, XXIII, p. 52.

22. John of Salisbury, *Historia pontificalis*, XXIII, p. 53.

23. On the eunuch as the "perfect servant," see Kathryn M, Ringrose, *The Perfect Servant: Eunuchs and the Social Construction of Gender in Byzantium* (Chicago: University of Chicago Press, 2003), esp. pp. 194–211.

24. The twelfth-century Byzantine author Theophylact of Ochrid describes the malice, jealousy, and viciousness attributed to eunuchs at his time. See *Théophylacte d'Achrida: Discours, traité, poésies*, ed. Paul Gautier, Corpus Fontium Historiae Byzantinae, 2 vols. (Thessalonica: Association de Recherches Byzantines, 1980–1986), vol. 1, pp. 288–331.

25. Peter Abelard writes, in his *Historia calamitatum*, in *The Letter Collection of Peter Abelard and Heloise*, ed. David Luscombe (Oxford: Oxford University Press, 2013), p. 46, that his castration made him "a monstrous spectacle to all." See the chapters on Abelard's castration in *Becoming Male in the Middle Ages*, ed. Jeffrey Jerome Cohen and Bonnie Wheeler (New York: Routledge, 2015).

26. S. F. Tougher writes, in "Images of Effeminate Men: The Case of Byzantine Eunuchs," in *Masculinity in Medieval Europe*, ed. Dawn M. Hadley (London: Longman, 1999), pp. 89–100, at p. 100, "Notably, emperors who made heavy use of eunuchs in their regimes were themselves likely to be characterized as weak and feeble."

27. Gerhoh von Reichersberg, *De investigatione Antichristi*, 64, p. 160.

28. John of Salisbury, *Historia pontificalis*, XXIII, p. 53.

29. In William of Tyre's chronicle, "dignity" (*dignitas*) refers to the quality of someone's comportment that makes an individual seem worthy of a certain high office, even to strangers. On kings and emperors who exhibit dignity or fail to do so, see *Chronicon*, vol. 2, XVI, 1, p. 715; XVIII, 25, p. 848; and XIX, 3, p. 867. There is no one rendering of the word in the French translation.

30. Hélinand of Froidmont, *Chronicon*, cols. 1057–58.

31. Alberic of Trois-Fontaines writes in *Ex chronico*, p. 703, "King Louis relinquished her on account of the incontinence of this woman, who did not act like a queen, but exhibited herself like a common woman [*communem*]."

32. Bernard Gui reports in *Ex libro . . . de origine regum Francorum*, p. 231, "Hélinand wrote in his *Chronicle* that he did this on account of the incontinence of this woman, who acted not like a queen, but like a whore [*meretrix*]."

33. See Ruth Mazo Karras, "Prostitution and the Question of Sexual Identity in Medieval Europe," *Journal of Women's History* 11, no. 2 (Summer 1999): 159–77, at p. 162; as well as *Common Women: Prostitution and Sexuality in Medieval England* (Oxford: Oxford University Press, 1996).

34. See Marie de France, *Lanval*; *Le roman des sept sages de Rome*; *La châtelaine de Vergi*; and *Le roman de silence*.

35. John of Salisbury, *Historia pontificalis*, XXIII, p. 53.

36. Suger, *Epistolae Sugeri*, in *Oeuvres*, ed. Françoise Gasparri, 2 vols., Classiques de l'histoire de

France au Moyen Age 37e and 41e (Paris: Les Belles Lettres, 1996–2001), vol. 2, pp. 2–98, Letter to Louis (before April 3, 1149), pp. 32–39, at p. 39.

37. William of Newburgh, *The History of English Affairs*, vol. 1, I, 31, p. 128.

38. *Fragmentum historicum vitam Ludovici VII summatim complectens*, p. 286.

39. *Ex libro III historiae regum Francorum ab origine gentis ab MCCXIV*, *RHF*, vol. 12, pp. 217–21, at p. 220.

40. *Extrait d'un abrégé de l'histoire de France*, *RHF*, vol. 12, pp. 222–27, at p. 225.

41. *Fragmentum historicum vitam Ludovici VII summatim complectens*, p. 286.

42. *Extrait d'un abrégé de l'histoire de France*, p. 225.

43. Matthew Paris, *Historia Anglorum*, vol. 1, p. 288. He writes in *Chronica majora*, ed. Henry Richards Luard, 7 vols., RS, vol. 57 (London: Longman, 1872–83), vol. 2, p. 186, "She was defamed of adultery, even with an infidel."

44. *Fragmentum historicum vitam Ludovici VII summatim complectens*, p. 286.

45. *Chronique de Flandres*, BN, Ms. fr. 1799, fol. 16ᵛ, cited in Gaston Paris, "La légende de Saladin," *Journal des savants* (May–August 1893): 354–65; rpt. in *La légende de Saladin* (Paris: Imprimerie nationale, 1893), p. 36.

46. *Istore et croniques de Flandres, d'après les textes de divers manuscrits*, ed. Kervyn de Lettenhove, 2 vols. (Brussels: F. Hayez, 1879), vol. 1, p. 44.

47. All references in this section will be to the Minstrel of Reims, *Récits d'un ménestrel de Reims*.

48. Jean d'Outremeuse, *Ly myreur des histors*, vol. 4, p. 396.

49. William of Newburgh, *The History of English Affairs*, vol. 1, I, 31, p. 128.

50. Gervase of Canterbury, *Chronica*, p. 149.

51. Gervase of Canterbury, *Chronica*, p. 149.

52. *Chronique abrégée*, Paris, Bibliothèque nationale de France, Manuscrits, fr. 9222, fols. 16v–17r, cited in McCracken, "Scandalizing Desire: Eleanor of Aquitaine and the Chroniclers," p. 261n13.

53. Pierre Cochon, *Chronique normande*, pp. 2–3.

54. *Istore et croniques de Flandres*, vol. 1, pp. 44–55.

55. Jean d'Outremeuse, *Ly myreur des histors*, vol. 4, p. 396.

56. See, for example, the famous *vida* of Jaufre Rudel, where the troubadour—also a knight on the Second Crusade—falls in love with the Countess of Tripoli without ever having seen her.

57. *Extrait d'un abrégé de l'histoire des rois de France*, Ms. de la Bibliothèque de l'Abbaye de S. Victor de Paris, *RHF*, vol. 12, pp. 228–30, at p. 229.

58. Theodor Heinermann, in "Zeit und Sinn der Karlreise," *Zeitschrift für romanische Philologie* 56 (1936): 497–562, connects Charlemagne and the unnamed queen of this poem to Louis and Eleanor, as does Rita Lejeune, in "Rôle littéraire d'Aliénor d'Aquitaine et de sa famille," *Cultura neolatina* 14 (1954): 5–57, at p. 15.

59. *The Pilgrimage of Charlemagne / Le Pèlerinage de Charlemagne*, ed. Glyn S. Burgess and Anne Elizabeth Cobby (New York: Garland Publishing, 1988), vv. 12, 814–16; and Chrétien de Troyes, *Erec et Enide*, ed. Mario Roques (Paris: Honoré Champion, 1990), v. 2589.

60. *Pilgrimage of Charlemagne*, vv. 53–56.

61. Chrétien de Troyes, *Erec et Enide*, vv. 2996–97.

62. See *The Annals of Quintus Ennius*, ed. Otto Skutsch (Oxford: Clarendon Press, 1984), VII, 222–26, p. 461; Plautus, *Aulularia* 62; Plautus, *Menaechmi* 1073; Terence, *Andria* 642043; and Cato, *Oratio contra Servium Galbam*, frag. 172.13.

63. Chrétien de Troyes, *Erec et Enide*, vv. 2588–604.

64. Chrétien de Troyes, *Erec et Enide*, vv. 3102–3.

65. Paris, Bibliothèque nationale de France, Manuscrits, fr. 5003, fol. 180ᵛ, cited in Gaston Paris, "La légende de Saladin," pp. 36–37.

66. *Fragmentum historicum vitam Ludovici VII summatim complectens*, p. 286.

67. *Layettes du trésor des Chartes*, ed. Alexandre Teulet, Joseph de Laborde, Elie Berger, and Henri François Delaborde, 5 vols. (Paris: Henri Plon, 1863–1909), vol. 1, no. 508, p. 209. See Jean Hubert, "L'origine de la parenté entre la famille de Chauvigny et les Plantagenêts," *Revue du Berry et du Centre*, 1927, pp. 38–40.

68. Jehan de la Gogue, *Saladin*, in *Esquisses biographiques du département de l'Indre; ou, Aperçu historique sur la principauté de Déols, Baronnie, comté et marquisat et enfin duché de Chateauroux (ancien Bas-Berri)*, ed. Amadour Grillon des Chapelles, 2nd ed., 3 vols. (Paris: Benjamin Duprat, 1864–65), vol. 3, pp. 314–83; reprinted in *Saladin: Suite et fin du deuxième cycle de la croisade*, ed. Larry S. Crist (Geneva: Librairie Droz, 1972), pp. 219–69. All references in this section will be to *Saladin*, ed. Crist.

69. See *La fille du comte de Ponthieu, conte en prose: Versions du XIIIe et du XVe siècle*, ed. Clovis Brunel, SATF (Paris: Honoré Champion, 1923), p. 44. This story, originally composed around 1223, was retold by Ernoul in his *Histoire d'outremer et du roi Saladin* (1200s), in *La chronique d'Ernoul et de Bernard le Trésorier*, ed. M. L. de Mas-Latrie (Paris: Jules Renouard, 1871); and by the anonymous author of the Second Crusade Cycle (1465–68). Matthew Paris writes of Saladin in his *Historia Anglorum*, vol. 1, p. 430, "He was born from a noble, Christian, English woman, a slave, who had been seized from her husband."

70. This anonymous version of *Saladin* was composed for Charles de Charolais, the future Charles the Bold, Duke of Burgundy. It survives in two manuscripts: Paris, Bibliothèque de l'Arsenal, Manuscrits, f.fr., 5208, fols. 122ᵛ–192ᵛ; and Paris, Bibliothèque nationale de France, Manuscrits, f.fr., 12572, fols. 165ʳ–262ʳ. The edition in *Saladin: Suite et fin du deuxième cycle de la croisade*, ed. Crist, pp. 21–170, follows the second manuscript.

71. The version of *Saladin* by Jehan de La Gogue, dated to 1482 at the latest, is available only in the copy of a copy of an incomplete manuscript from the late fifteenth or early sixteenth century with numerous lacunas and indecipherable words.

72. McCracken argues, in "Scandalizing Desire: Eleanor of Aquitaine and the Chroniclers," p. 258, that, by this point in history, "chroniclers' accounts of Eleanor of Aquitaine's adulterous desire for Saladin [are] less a story about Eleanor herself than a story about queenship in which Eleanor has become exemplary."

73. Minstrel of Reims, *Récits d'un ménestrel de Reims*, II, 7, p. 4.

74. *De origine comitum Andegavensium*, pp. 537–38.

75. *De origine comitum Andegavensium*, p. 537.

76. See *La continuation de Guillaume de Tyr (1184–1192)*, ed. Margaret R. Morgan (Paris: Librairie orientaliste P. Geuthner, 1982), 142, p. 151. For a discussion of this proposed alliance, see Adnan A. Husain and Margaret Aziza Pappano, "The One Kingdom Solution? Diplomacy, Marriage, and Sovereignty in the Third Crusade," in *Cosmopolitanism and the Middle Ages*, ed. John M. Ganim and Shayne Aaron Legassie (New York: Palgrave Macmillan, 2013), pp. 121–40.

77. See Bahā' al-Dīn Ibn Shaddād, *The Rare and Excellent History of Saladin or al-Nawadir al-Sultaniyya wa'l-Mahasin al-Yusufiyya*, ed. and trans. D. S. Richards (New York: Ashgate, 2002), p. 187.

78. Bahā' al-Dīn Ibn Shaddād, *The Rare and Excellent History of Saladin*, p. 188.

79. 'Imâd ad-dîn Al-Isfahâni, *Conquête de la Syrie et de la Palestine par Saladin (al-Fath al-qussî fî l-fath al-qudsî)*, trans. Henri Massé (Paris: Librairie orientaliste P. Geuthner, 1972), p. 351. Yet

another Arabic source recounts that "Rumina," a woman warrior and sister to Richard, was taken captive in battle, converted, and married Saphadin. This romance is published in a German translation in *Arabische Quellenbeiträge zur Geschichte der Kreuzzüge*, ed. and trans. E. P. Goergens and Reinhold Röhricht (Berlin: Weidmannsche Buchhandlung, 1879), pp. 283–91.

CHAPTER THREE

1. Wace, *The Roman de Rou*, vv. 17–24. Wace makes no mention of Eleanor in his *Brut* (c. 1150–55), but the English poet Layamon, in *Layamon's Arthur: The Arthurian Section of Layamon's "Brut" (lines 9229–14297)*, ed. W. R. J. Barron and S. C. Weinberg (Liverpool: Liverpool University Press, 1989), claims that, after having written his book, Wace "presented it to the noble Eleanor, who was the great King Henry's queen" (vv. 22–23).

2. Benoît de Sainte-Maure, in *Le roman de Troie*, vol. 2, v. 13468, refers to the "rich lady of a rich king." On this passage, see Peter Damian-Grint, "Benoît de Sainte-Maure et l'idéologie des Plantagenêts," in *Plantagenêts et Capétiens: Confrontations et héritages*, ed. Martin Aurell and Noël-Yves Tonnerre (Turnhout: Brepols, 2006), pp. 413–27; and Tamara F. O'Callaghan, "Tempering Scandal: Eleanor of Aquitaine and Benoît de Sainte-Maure's *Roman de Troie*," in *Eleanor of Aquitaine*, ed. Wheeler and Parsons, pp. 301–17, esp. p. 312.

3. Philippe de Thaon's *Bestiare*, ed. Emmanuel Walberg (Paris: Lund, 1900), having originally been dedicated to Aélis de Louvain, the wife of Henry I, King of England, was rededicated around 1152 to Eleanor (vii).

4. Cercamon, "Car vei fenir a tot dia," in *The Poetry of Cercamon and Jaufre Rudel*, II, pp. 36–39, at vv. 50–54.

5. Cercamon, "Lo plaing comenz iradamen," vv. 31–36.

6. See Marcabru, "Emperaire, per mi mezeis," in *Marcabru*, XXII, pp. 308–18, at vv. 55–57.

7. Cercamon, "Ab lo pascor m'es bel qu'eu chan," in *The Poetry of Cercamon and Jaufre Rudel*, VII, pp. 54–59, at v. 39.

8. Cercamon, "Ab lo pascor m'es bel qu'eu chan," v. 42. See also Marcabru, "Cortesamen vuoill comensar," in *Marcabru*, XV, pp. 200–207, at vv. 27–30.

9. Gaston Paris, "Etudes sur les romans de la Table Ronde: *Lancelot du Lac*," *Romania* 12 (1883): 459–534, at p. 523.

10. Alfred Jeanroy, "La poésie provençale au Moyen Age. III. La chanson," *Revue des deux mondes* 13 (1903), I: 661–92, at p. 667. More recently, Margaret Aziza Pappano has argued, in "La *regina bisperta*: Aliénor d'Aquitaine et ses relations littéraires au XII siècle," in *Aliénor d'Aquitaine* [*exposition, Abbaye de Fontevraud, 2004*], ed. Martin Aurell (Nantes: 303, 2004), pp. 150–55, at p. 154, that Eleanor played the role of a cultural mediator thanks to her double identity as a southerner living in northern lands. See also Pappano, "Marie de France, Aliénor d'Aquitaine, and the Alien Queen," in *Eleanor of Aquitaine: Lord and Lady*, ed. Wheeler and Parsons, pp. 337–67.

11. Jeanroy, *La poésie lyrique des troubadours*, vol. 1, pp. 151–52.

12. Rita Lejeune, "La femme dans les littératures françaises et occitanes du XIe au XIIIe siècles," *CCM* 20 (1977): 201–17, at p. 211. See also Rita Lejeune, "Rôle littéraire d'Aliénor d'Aquitaine et de sa famille," *Cultura neolatina* 14 (1954): 5–57; and Rita Lejeune, "Rôle littéraire de la famille d'Aliénor d'Aquitaine," *CCM* 1, no. 3 (1958): 319–37.

13. See Karen Broadhurst, "Henry II of England and Eleanor of Aquitaine: Patrons of Literature in French?" *Viator* 27 (1996): 53–84.

14. See Diana B. Tyson, "Patronage of French Vernacular History Writers in the Twelfth and Thirteenth Centuries," *Romania* 100 (1979): 180–222. Ruth E. Harvey claims, in "Eleanor of Aquitaine and the Troubadours," in *The World of Eleanor of Aquitaine*, ed. Bull and Léglu, pp. 101–14, at p. 106, that Tyson's criteria for establishing patronage of a work are excessively stringent, given how few works from the twelfth century could fulfill them. Tyson herself admits that only four works from this time period satisfy these demands.

15. See Jean Markale, *Aliénor d'Aquitaine: La vie, la légende, l'influence d'Aliénor, comtesse de Poitou, duchesse d'Aquitaine, reine de France, puis d'Angleterre, dame des troubadours et des bardes bretons* (Paris: Payot, 1979); and Pernoud, *Aliénor d'Aquitaine*, chapter 14, "La reine des troubadours," p. 160.

16. Chrétien de Troyes, *Le chevalier de la charrette, ou Le roman de Lancelot*, ed. Charles Méla, in *Romans* (Paris: Livre de Poche, 1994), pp. 795–704, at vv. 1–3.

17. See Flori, *Aliénor d'Aquitaine*, p. 125.

18. No source from the Low Countries reports this story. Ruth E. Harvey, in "Cross-Channel Gossip in the Twelfth Century," in *England and the Continent in the Middle Ages: Studies in Memory of Andrew Martindale*, ed. John Mitchell (Stamford, UK: Paul Watkins Press, 2000), pp. 48–59, doubts its veracity.

19. Roger of Howden, *Chronica Magistri Rogeri de Houedene*, vol. 2, pp. 82–83.

20. See Ralph of Diceto, *Ymagines historiarum*, vol. 1, p. 402.

21. Paris, "Etudes sur les romans de la Table Ronde," p. 534.

22. Jeanroy, "La poésie provençale au Moyen Age," p. 668.

23. Reto Bezzola, *Les origines et la formation de la littérature courtoise en Occident (500–1200)*, 3 vols. in 5 (Paris: E. Champion, 1944–63), part 3, vol. 1, at pp. 247–91; vol. 2, pp. 313–14.

24. Denis de Rougemont, *L'amour et l'Occident* (Paris: Plon, 1956), p. 111.

25. Moshé Lazar, *Amour courtois et "fin amors" dans la littérature du XIIe siècle* (Paris: Klincksieck, 1964), p. 14. See also Lazar, "Cupid, the Lady, and the Poet: Modes of Love at Eleanor of Aquitaine's Court," in *Eleanor of Aquitaine: Patron and Politician*, ed. William W. Kibler (Austin: University of Texas Press, 1977), pp. 35–60; and Mary Dominica Legge, "La littérature anglo-normande au temps d'Aliénor d'Aquitaine," *CCM* 29 (1986): 113–18.

26. Lejeune, "Rôle littéraire d'Aliénor d'Aquitaine et de sa famille," pp. 18–20.

27. See D. W. Robertson, *A Preface to Chaucer: Studies in Medieval Perspective* (Princeton: Princeton University Press, 1962); and D. W. Robertson, "The Concept of Courtly Love as an Impediment to the Understanding of Medieval Texts," in *The Meaning of Courtly Love: Papers of the First Annual Conference of the Center for Medieval and Early Renaissance Studies, State University of New York at Binghamton (March 17–18, 1967)*, ed. Francis X. Newman (Albany: State University of New York Press, 1968), pp. 1–18.

28. John F. Benton, "Clio and Venus: A Historical View of Medieval Love," in *The Meaning of Courtly Love*, ed. Newman, pp. 19–42, at pp. 19–20.

29. Benton, "Clio and Venus," p. 20.

30. Joseph J. Duggan, "Ambiguity in Twelfth-Century French and Provençal Literature: A Problem or a Value?" in *Jean Misrahi Memorial Volume: Studies in Medieval Literature*, ed. Hans R. Runte, Henri Niedziekski, and William K. Hendrickson (Columbia, SC: French Literature Publications, 1977), pp. 136–49, at p. 145.

31. William D. Paden, Jr., "*Utrum copularentur*: Of *Cors*," *L'esprit créateur* 19, no. 4 (Winter 1979): 70–83, at p. 70.

32. Duggan, "Ambiguity in Twelfth-Century French and Provençal Literature," p. 145.

33. Geoffrey du Breuil of Vigeois, *Chronicon Lemovicense*, p. 438.

34. Geoffrey du Breuil of Vigeois, *Chronicon Lemovicense*, p. 445.

35. I will be citing Bernart de Ventadorn, *The Songs of Bernart de Ventadorn*, ed. Stephen G. Nichols, Jr., John A. Galm, and A. Bartlett Giamatti (Chapel Hill: University of North Carolina Press, 1965). See also *Bernard de Ventadour, troubadour du XIIe siècle: Chansons d'amour*, ed. Moshé Lazar (Paris: Klincksieck, 1966; rpt., Moustier Ventadour: Carrefour Ventadour, 2001).

36. Bernart de Ventadorn, "Lo temps vai e ven e vire," *The Songs of Bernart de Ventadorn*, vv. 22–23.

37. Ebles III, Viscount of Ventadorn, was married to Margarida, the daughter of Raymond I, Viscount of Turenne, with whom he had one daughter, but the marriage was dissolved by 1151, when Margarida married William VI, Count of Taillefer. By 1156, the viscount had wed Azalaïs, the daughter of William VI, seigneur of Montpellier, who would bear his only son, Ebles IV. As Bernart's *vida* refers to Ebles IV as the son of the viscountess whom Bernart loved, it seems to be Azalaïs who is being indicated.

38. Bernart de Ventadorn and Uc de Saint-Circ both seem to have had the impression that Eleanor inherited the duchy of Normandy from her mother, instead of acquiring it through her marriage to Henry, who had inherited it through his maternal line. See *Biographies des troubadours: Textes provençaux des XIIIe et XIVe siècles*, ed. Jean Boutière and A.-H. Schutz (Toulouse: E. Privat; Columbus: Ohio State University Press, 1950), p. 81. References in this section will be to this book.

39. Bernart de Ventadorn, "Pel doutz chan que·l rossinhols fai," in *The Songs of Bernart de Ventadorn*, p. 139, vv. 43–45. The *tornada* is missing from Manuscripts Q and N. Ruth E. Harvey remarks, in "Eleanor of Aquitaine and the Troubadours," p. 107, "'Queen of the Normans' has the air of a topical compliment inspired by recent developments, which may will fit with the queen's séjour in Normandy in the autumn of 1154, and it is possible to imagine that Bernart's praise of Henry's (newly acquired?) extensive dominions dates from the same-period."

40. When the *vidas* speak of the places of the troubadours' birth, the social status of their families, and the nature of their professions, this information is typically accurate and, indeed, often confirmed by external sources. See Jeanroy's discussion of *vidas* in *La poésie lyrique des troubadours*, vol. 1, p. 131. Stanislaw Stronski defends the accuracy of many facts in the *vidas* in *La poésie et la réalité aux temps des troubadours: The Taylorian Lecture* (Oxford: Clarendon Press, 1943), esp. pp. 22–23.

41. For discussion of the manuscripts, see *Biographies des troubadours*, pp. 26–28. All page references that follow will refer to the reference.

42. To put this argument in theoretical terms, Bernart de Ventadorn's *vida* functioned as what Gérard Genette defines as a "paratext," in *Seuils* (Paris: Editions du Seuil, 1987), p. 2, that is, as the seemingly extraneous, seemingly supplementary material framing a text, often supplied by someone other than the author himself, which shapes how the audience is expected to receive and interpret what they are hearing.

43. See the *vidas* of Peirol and Raimon de Miraval, in *Biographies des troubadours*, p. 250 and p. 286.

44. Nicola Zingarelli has argued in "Ricerche sulla vita e le rime de Bernart de Ventadorn," *Studi medievali* I (1905): 309–93, 594–611, that the *vidas*' account of Bernart's lowly origins could have been drawn, not from the author's knowledge of Bernart's life, but from Peire d'Alvernha's satire, "Canterai d'aqestz trobadors" (1155–73), in *Liriche*, ed. Alberto del Monte (Turin: Loescher, 1955), pp. 118–34, which itself may have been drawn from a reading of

Bernart's "Be m'an perdut lai enves Ventadorn." Walter T. Pattison, in "The Troubadours of Peire d'Alvernhe's Satire in Spain," *Modern Philology* 31, no. 1 (August 1933): 19–34, proposes that Peire's song would have been sung when the party that was accompanying Eleanor and Henry's daughter, young Eleanor, to Castile to marry Alfonso VIII, stayed at the Castle of Puivert in what is now the Aude district.

45. For other examples of troubadours who, though of humble birth, achieve success through their talents, see the *vidas* of Arnaut de Mareuil, Giraut de Bornelh, and Perdigon, in *Biographies des troubadours*, pp. 18–19, pp. 190–99, and p. 253.

46. Enric II and Guillem de Mur, "Guilhem, d'un plag novel," *The Troubadour "Tensos" and "Partimens": A Critical Edition*, ed. Ruth Harvey and Linda Paterson, 3 vols. (Rochester, NY: D. S. Brewer, 2010), vol. 1, pp. 310–13, at vv. 24–25.

47. Lantelm and Raimon, "Raimond, una dona pros e valenz," in *Troubadour "Tensos" and "Partimens,"* vol. 3, pp. 914–19, vv. 14–15.

48. *Biographies des troubadours*, p. 333.

49. *Biographies des troubadours*, p. 101.

50. Bernart de Ventadorn, "Per melhs cobrir lo mal pes e·l cossire," in *The Songs of Bernart de Ventadorn*, pp. 142–44, at v. 13.

51. Bernart de Ventadorn, "Ges de chantar no·m pren talans," in *The Songs of Bernart de Ventadorn*, pp. 97–99, at v. 50. Peter Dronke argues, in "Peter of Blois and Poetry at the Court of Henry II," *Mediaeval Studies* 38 (1976): 185–235, at p. 188, that Henry II is mentioned in five of Bernart's poems, but Margaret Aziza Pappano, in "Territorial Desire: Bernart de Ventadorn's Plantagenet Poems and Marie de France's *Chievrefueil*," *Culture politique des Plantagenêts (1154–1224), Actes du Colloque tenu à Poitiers du 2 au 5 mai 2002*, ed. Martin Aurell (Poitiers: CESCM, 2003), pp. 61–74, at 65n14, is more conservative.

52. Bernart de Ventadorn, "Ges de no·m pren talans," in *The Songs of Bernart de Ventadorn*, vv. 53–56.

53. Bernart de Ventadorn, "Ges de chantar no·m pren talans," in *The Songs of Bernart de Ventadorn*, vv. 17–21. See also "En cossirer et en esmai," in the same volume, pp. 86–88, vv. 4–8. Raimbaut de Vaqueiras similarly claims, in "Era·m requier sa costum'e us," in *The Poems of the Troubadour Raimbaut de Vaqueiras*, ed. Joseph Linskill (The Hague: Mouton, 1964), pp. 146–47, at vv. 36–38, that even if he were the King of England or France, he would still fulfill his lady's commands.

54. Bernart de Ventadorn, "Tuih cil que·m preyon qu'eu chan," in *The Songs of Bernart de Ventadorn*, pp. 173–75, vv. 40–42.

55. Bernart de Ventadorn, "Lancan vei per mei la landa," in *The Songs of Bernart de Ventadorn*, pp. 114–16, vv. 36–45.

56. Margaret Aziza Pappano points out in "Territorial Desire," p. 62, that, while the *vidas* relate that Henry took Eleanor away from Bernart, scholars have read "Lancan vei per mei la landa" as reporting that he kept Bernart with him in England, while Eleanor was living in Poitiers. She notes, "The locational terms in 'Lancan vei' are extremely ambiguous, rendering both readings possible."

57. Bernart de Ventadorn, "Pois preyatz me, senhor," in *The Songs of Bernart de Ventadorn*, vv. 13–18.

58. Bernart de Ventadorn, "Tan ai mo cor ple de joya," in *The Songs of Bernart de Ventadorn*, vv. 73–76.

59. Bernart de Ventadorn, "Ges de chantar no·m pren talans," in *The Songs of Bernart de Ventadorn*, vv. 25–32.

60. Bernart de Ventadorn, "Can vei la lauzeta mover," in *The Songs of Bernart de Ventadorn*, pp. 97–99, at pp. 97–98, vv. 17–18.

61. Bernart de Ventadorn, "Can vei la flor, l'erba vert e la folha," in *The Songs of Bernart de Ventadorn*, pp. 163–65, at p. 163, v. 15.

62. Jean-Baptiste de La Curne de Sainte-Palaye and C. F. X. Millot, *Histoire littéraire des troubadours: Contenant leurs vies, les extraits de leurs pièces, & plusieurs particularités sur les moeurs, les usages, & l'histoire du douzième & du treizième siècles*, 3 vols. (Paris: Chez Durand, 1774; rpt., Geneva: Slatkine, 1967), vol. 1, pp. 30–35, at p. 30. See also Jean-Pierre Papon, *Histoire générale de Provence*, 4 vols. (Paris: Chez Moutard, 1777–86), vol. 2, pp. 437–40.

63. La Curne de Sainte-Palaye, *Histoire littéraire des troubadours*, p. 33. See also Papon, *Histoire générale de Provence*, vol. 2, pp. 437–40.

64. Friedrich Diez, *Leben und Werke der Troubadours: Ein Beitrag zur nähern Kenntniss des Mittelalters* (Leipzig: J. A. Barth, 1829; rpt., 1882), p. 25.

65. Claude Fauriel, *Histoire de la poésie provençale* (Paris: J. Labitte, 1846; rpt., Paris: Classiques Garnier, 2011), p. 30.

66. See Carl Appel, *Bernart von Ventadorn: Seine Lieder mit Einleitung und Glossar* (Halle a. S.: Max Niemeyer, 1915).

67. Joseph Anglade, *Les troubadours: Leurs vies, leurs oeuvres, leurs influence* (Paris: Librairie Armand Colin, 1908), p. 111.

68. Gaston Paris, "Jaufré Rudel," *Revue historique* 53 (1893): 225–60, at p. 256.

69. Stronski, *La poésie et la réalité aux temps des troubadours*, p. 23.

70. Zingarelli, in "Ricerche sulla vita e le rime de Bernart de Ventadorn," performed a minute analysis of the passages from Bernart's songs that seemed to justify the plot of the *vidas* and demonstrated how the ambiguity of their language complicated any effort to do so.

71. Bernart de Ventadorn, *Chansons d'amour*, p. 14.

72. See Stanislaw Stronski, *Le troubadour Folquet de Marseille* (Krakow: Académie des Sciences, 1910), pp. 27–43, esp. p. 30n1.

73. Jeanroy, *La poésie lyrique des troubadours*, vol. 2, p. 140.

74. Stronski, *La poésie et la réalité aux temps des troubadours*, p. 25.

75. Bernart de Ventadorn, "Ara no vei luzir solelh," in Bernart de Ventadorn, *The Songs of Bernart de Ventadorn*, pp. 59–61, vv. 57–60.

76. See Bernart de Ventadorn, "Amics Bernartz de Ventadorn," in *The Songs of Bernart de Ventadorn*, pp. 45–47; "Bernart de Ventadorn, del chan," pp. 78–79; and "Chantars no pot gaire valer," pp. 80–82, vv. 53–54.

77. Bernart de Ventadorn, "A, tantas bonas chansos," in *The Songs of Bernart de Ventadorn*, vv. 47–48.

78. Bernart de Ventadorn, "Lancan vei la folha," in *The Songs of Bernart de Ventadorn*, pp. 110–12, vv. 49–60.

79. *Biographies des troubadours*, 42.

80. *Biographies des troubadours*, p. 42.

81. *Biographies des troubadours*, p. 43.

82. Giraut de Bornelh and Alamanda (d'Esctanc?), "S'ie·us qier conseill, bella amia Alamanda," in *Troubadour "Tensos" and "Partimens,"* vol. 2, pp. 708–13, vv. 1–6.

83. For many years, Andreas Capellanus was understood to have been Marie de Champagne's personal chaplain and to have produced this work at her court. Theodore Evergates, in *Marie of France: Countess of Champagne, 1145–1198* (Philadelphia: University of Pennsylvania Press, 2019), pp. 59–60, argues persuasively that this was the case. The name of a chaplain called "Andreas" appears in nine charters from her court between 1182 and 1186.

84. Alfred Karnein has demonstrated, in "Auf der Suche nach einem Autor: Andreas, Verfasser von *De amore*," *Germanisch-Romanische Monatsschrift*, n.f. 28 (1978): 1–20, that surviving charters from Paris in the final decade of the twelfth century signed by a certain "Andreas Cambellanus" testify to the presence of a chaplain by this name at the royal court.

85. See, for example, the late twelfth-century *Altercatio Phyllidis et Florae*, included in part in the *Carmina Burana*, where the maidens Phyllis and Flora disagree as to the relative merits of their lovers—one a knight and the other a cleric—and travel to the God of Love so that he may resolve their dispute. The *Concilium Romarici Monti* addresses the same theme. For the influence of such works on Andreas, see Don A. Monson, *Andreas Capellanus: Scholasticism, and the Courtly Tradition* (Washington, DC: Catholic University of America, 2005), pp. 111–12.

86. P. G. Walsh, in *Andreas Capellanus on Love*, ed. P. G. Walsh (London: Gerald Duckworth, 1982), p. 260n37, identifies "the Countess of Flanders" as Elizabeth of Vermandois, who was Countess of Flanders between 1168 and her death in 1183. Elizabeth was succeeded by Philip's second wife, Theresa of Portugal, who was countess between 1183 and 1191. When Philip died childless in 1191, his sister, Margaret of Alsace, claimed the county. Elizabeth, Theresa, and Margaret could thus all be considered Countesses of Flanders, in addition to Sibyl of Anjou, Philip and Margaret's mother.

87. Robertson, *A Preface to Chaucer*, pp. 420n57, 444; and John F. Benton, in "The Court of Champagne as a Literary Center," *Speculum* 36 (1961): 551–91, at p. 581, have argued that Andreas was making fun of Eleanor by having her pass judgment on cases that echo her scandalous amorous history, but their arguments do not bear out. If Andreas were mocking Eleanor for having contracted two consanguineous marriages despite her alleged horror of incest, he would also be mocking over half the rulers of France and England during her lifetime, who committed the same crime. If he were criticizing her seniority in age to Henry when he has her express a preference for younger men in bed, he would be criticizing her second marriage on grounds for which it was never reproached in the Middle Ages, despite the many complaints that were raised about it. Throughout this treatise, Andreas is speaking of extramarital liaisons, not marriages, which he places, emphatically, in a separate category.

88. Drouart la Vache, *Li livres d'amours*, ed. Robert Bossuat (Paris: Honoré Champion, 1926), vv. 5667, 6143, and 6225 (as "the Queen of Germany"); vv. 5749 and 6233 (as "the Queen"). Drouart eliminates the question about the consanguineous lovers. He alludes twice to "the Queen of England" (v. 2527, v. 1486), but there is no indication that he identifies her as Eleanor.

89. See Monson, *Andreas Capellanus*, p. 62.

90. See June Hall Martin McCash, "Marie de Champagne and Eleanor of Aquitaine: A Relationship Reexamined," *Speculum* 54 (1979): 698–711.

91. Similar *tensons* and *jeux-partis* have come down to us in French, though only dated to the early thirteenth century. Of the 182 such poems, six have women judges. See *Recueil général des jeux-partis français*, ed. Arthur Långfors, with Alfred Jeanroy and Louis Brandin, 2 vols. (Paris: Edouard Champion, 1926), vol. 1, pp. 153–55, 157–59, 279–81; vol. 2, pp. 29–32, 213–15, 251–53.

92. See *Troubadour "Tensos" and "Partimens*," vol. 1, pp. xix–xx; and *Recueil général des jeux-partis français*, vol. 1, p. vii.

93. Guillem de la Tor and Sordel, "Uns amics et un'amia," in *Troubadour "Tensos" and "Partimens*," vol. 2, pp. 648–51, vv. 65–66.

94. Guillem Raimon de Gironela and Ponzet, "Del joi d'amor agradiu," in *Troubadour "Tensos" and "Partimens*," vol. 2, pp. 614–17, vv. 53–56.

95. A Lord and Albert, "N'Albert, en sui en error," in *Troubadour "Tensos" and "Partimens,"* vol. 1, pp. 380–83, v. 2.

96. Guillem Peire de Cazals and Bernart de la Barta, "Bernart de la Bart'ancse·m platz," in *Troubadour "Tensos" and "Partimens,"* vol. 2, pp. 604–9, v. 4.

97. For civil law, see *The Digest of Justinian*, ed. Theodor Mommsen and Paul Krueger, 5 vols. (Philadelphia: University of Pennyslvania Press, 1985), 5.1.12, at vol. 1, p. 166, and 50, 17, 2, at vol. 4, p. 957. For canon law, see Gratian, *Corpus iuris canonici*, vol. 1, *Decretum Magistri Gratiani*, [Part II], C. 33 q. 5 c. 17, at col. 1255, and C. 3, q. 7, c. 1, at col. 524.

98. See the discussion in Rüdiger Schnell, *Andreas Capellanus: Zur Rezeption des römischen und kanonischen Rechts in 'De Amore'* (Munich: Wilhelm Fink Verlag, 1982), pp. 83–85.

99. *Calendar of Documents Preserved in France Illustrative of the History of Great Britain and Ireland*, vol. 1, *AD 918–1206*, ed. J. Horace Round (London: Eyre and Spottiswoode, 1899), vol. 1, no. 1087, pp. 385–86. The charter is preserved in the Gaignières copy from the seventeenth century in Paris, Bibliothèque nationale de France, Manuscrits, lat. 5480, vol. 1, pp. 73–74.

100. B. R. Kemp, *Reading Abbey Cartularies: British Library Manuscripts, Egerton 3031, Harley 1708, and Cotton Vespasian E XXV*, 2 vols. (London: Offices of the Royal Historical Society, University College, London, 1986–87), no. 466; and H. G. Richardson, "The Letters and Charters of Eleanor of Aquitaine," *English Historical Review* 291 (1959): 195n3.

101. *Calendar of Documents Preserved in France*, vol. 1, no. 1092, p. 338.

102. *Epistolae Cantuarienses*, Vol. 2, Letter 393, from the Prior and Convent to Eleanor of Aquitaine (January 1192), p. 358.

103. See Pierre Tisset, "Placentin et son enseignement à Montpellier, droit romain et coutume dans l'ancien pays de Septimanie," *Recueil des mémoires et travaux anciens pays de droit écrit* 2 (1951): 67–95, at p. 72; and André Gouron, "Les étapes de la pénétration du droit romain au XIIe siècle dans l'ancien Septimanie," *Annales du Midi* 69 (1957): 103–120, at p. 103.

104. Louis VII, *Regis Ludovici VII et variorum ad eum volumen epistolarum, RHF*, vol. 16, at Letter 281, to Ermengarda of Narbonne (1164), p. 91.

105. See *Corpus iuris canonici*, vol. 1, *Decretum Magistri Gratiani*, [Part II], C. 2, q. 6, c. 33, at col. 478.

106. Yvonne Bongert, *Recherches sur les cours laïques du Xe au XIIIe siècle* (Paris: A. & J. Picard, 1949), pp. 107, 168.

107. *Corpus iuris canonici*, vol. 2, Decretalium D. Gregorii Papae IX, lib. 1, tit. 43, ch. 4, at col. 231.

108. Jehan de Nostredame's *Les vies des plus celebres et anciens poets provensavx qui ont floury du temps des Comtes de Prouence* (Lyon: Alexandre Marsilii, 1575); rpt. as *Les vies des plus célèbres et anciens poètes provençaux*, ed. Camille Chabaneau (Paris: Honoré Champion, 1913), p. 11.

109. Pierre de Caseneuve, *L'origine des Jeux-Fleureaux de Toulouse* (Toulouse: R. Bosc, 1659), pp. 34–46.

110. Giovanni Mario Crescimbeni, *Istoria della volgar poesia* (Venice: L. Basegio, 1730–31); Pierre Jean-Baptiste Legrand d'Aussy, *Fabliaux ou contes des douzième et treizième siècle, traduits ou extraits d'après les manuscrits* (Paris: Onfroy, 1779); and Barthélemy-Gabriel Rolland de Chambaudoin d'Erceville (M. le Président Rolland), *Recherches sur les prérogatives des dames chez les Gaulois, sur les cours d'amour . . .* (Paris: Chez Nyon l'aîné, 1787).

111. Johann Christoph Aretin, *Aussprüche der Minnegerichte: Aus alten Handschriften hrsg. und mit einer historischen Abhandlung über die Minnegerichte des Mittelalters begleitet* (Munich: Scherer, 1803); and Jean-Charles Léonard Simonde de Sismondi, *De la littérature du midi de l'Europe* (Paris: Treuttel et Würtz, 1813).

112. Jacques Lafitte-Houssat, *Troubadours et cours d'amour*, 4th ed. (Paris: Presses universitaires de France, 1950), p. 80.

113. François-Juste-Marie Raynouard, *Des troubadours et des cours d'amour* (Paris: Firmin Didot, 1817). There had been editions of Andreas's *De amore* in the fifteenth and seventeenth centuries, but they had not received attention.

114. In Stendhal's *Le rouge et le noir* (1830), the hero Julien Sorel, apparently following Andreas's advice, pretends to be in love with another woman in order to arouse the interest of the haughty Mathilde de la Mole.

115. Raynouard, *Des troubadours et des cours d'amour*, p. lxxviii.

116. The tradition developed that Eleanor was herself a trobairitz and that she presided over the Consistory of the Gay Science (*Consistori del Gay Saber*), a poetic academy founded in Toulouse in 1323 (well over a century after her death) to revive the art of the troubadours. At this academy's festivals (sometimes called "Courts of Love"), she sat in judgment with a conclave of her ladies, passed judgment on the troubadours' performances before her, and rewarded the best of them with a violet. See Agnes Strickland, *Lives of the Queens of England, from the Norman Conquest; with Anecdotes of Their Courts, Now First Published from Official Records and Other Authentic Documents, Private as well as Public*, 12 vols. (London: H. Coburn, 1840–48; 4th ed., 1854), vol. 1, p. 243. Alfred Lord Tennyson, in *Becket*, in *The Works of Alfred Lord Tennyson*, 6 vols. (London: Macmillan, 1884), vol. 8, pp. 1–218, at p. 26, depicts Eleanor claiming, "I am a Troubadour, you know, and won the violet at Toulouse" and referring to "My Courts of Love." In all this, Eleanor was apparently being conflated with the semilegendary Clémence Isaure, who was said to have revived the Consistori del Gay Saber in the form of the Jeux-Floreaux of Toulouse in the fifteenth century. See also Paris, "Etudes sur les romans de la Table Ronde," p. 529; and E. Trojel, *Middelalderens Elskovshoffer, literaturhistorisk-kritisk undersøgelse / Les cours d'amour du Moyen Age: Etude critique d'histoire littéraire* (Copenhagen: C. A. Reitzel, 1888).

117. Amy Kelly, "Eleanor of Aquitaine and Her Courts of Love," *Speculum* 12, no. 1 (1937): 3–19, at p. 15.

118. Rita Lejeune, "Rôle littéraire d'Aliénor d'Aquitaine et de sa famille," p. 42.

119. Jean-Pierre Papon, *Voyage littéraire de Provence, . . . et cinq lettres sur les trouvères et les troubadours* (Paris: Barrois l'Aîné, 1780), p. 178.

120. Friedrich Diez, *Beiträge zur Kenntniss der romantischen Poesie: Uber die Minnehöfe* (Berlin: G. Reimer, 1825). p. 73.

121. Diez, *Beiträge zur Kenntniss der romantischen Poesie*, p. 91.

122. Paris, "Etudes sur les romans de la Table Ronde," p. 529.

123. Jacques Lafitte-Houssat, *Troubadours et cours d'amour*, p. 80.

124. Paul Rémy, "Les 'Cours d'amour': Légende et réalité," *Revue de l'Université de Bruxelles* 7 (1954–55): 179–97, at p. 196.

125. Paul Meyer, *Le salut d'amour dans les littératures provençale et française: Mémoire, suivi de huit saluts inédits* (Paris: Franck, 1867), p. 128.

126. All references in this section are to *The History of William Marshal*, ed. A. J. Holden, 3 vols. (London: Anglo-Norman Text Society, 2002), including here, to vv. 19072–73.

127. David Crouch, *William Marshal: Court, Career, and Chivalry in the Angevin Empire (1142–1219)* (London: Longmans, 1990); rev. ed., *William Marshal: Knighthood, War and Chivalry, 1147–1219* (London: Longmans, 2002); 3rd ed., *William Marshal* (Abington, UK: Routledge, 2016), p. 181.

128. See Antonia Grandsen, *Historical Writing in England, c. 550 to c. 1307*, 2 vols. (Ithaca: Cornell University Press, 1974), p. 348.

129. Evelyn Mullally, "The Reciprocal Loyalty of Eleanor of Aquitaine and William the Marshal," in *Eleanor of Aquitaine*, ed. Wheeler and Parsons, pp. 237–45, at p. 243.

130. Robert of Torigni writes in his *Chronicle*, at p. 236, that Earl Patrick was buried at the Church of Saint Hilary in Poitiers. Eleanor established an endowment for an annual Mass to be said in his name at this church.

131. Georges Duby, *Guillaume le Maréchal, ou, Le meilleur chevalier du monde* (Paris: Fayard, 1984), pp. 97–98.

132. No other source mentions this rumor of the affair. Roger of Howden writes that, in 1183, the Young King sent Margaret to King Philip, but this may be, not because he wanted to separate from her, but because he was preparing to wage war against Richard. Philip received her honorably and provided for her every need (*Chronica*, ed. Stubbs, vol. 1, p. 296).

133. *Lancelot: Roman en prose du treizième siècle*, ed. Alexandre Micha, 9 vols. (Genève: Droz, 1978–82), vol. 4, pp. 398–99.

134. Béroul, *The Romance of Tristran*, ed. Norris J. Lacy (New York: Garland Publishing, 1989), vv. 773–74.

135. Béroul, *Romance of Tristran*, v. 1061.

136. Béroul, *Romance of Tristran*, v. 2566.

137. *La mort le Roi Artu*, ed. Jean Frappier (Genève: Droz, 1936), 118, pp. 154–55.

138. *Le roman de Tristan en prose*, ed. Renée Curtis, 3 vols. (Cambridge: D. S. Brewer, 1963–85), vol. 2, 561, p. 157.

139. See David Crouch, *William Marshal*, p. 2.

140. The ballad itself would not be published until the seventeenth century, in the broadside "Queen Eleanor's Confession" (London: Printed for C. Bates, at the Sun & Bible, 1685?).

141. *The Traditional Tunes of the Child Ballads*, ed. Child, p. 106.

142. Elizabeth Carney, in "Fact and Fiction in 'Queen Eleanor's Confession,'" *Folklore* 95, no. 2 (1984): 167–70, argues that the charge of Eleanor's adultery with the Marshal recalls the charge of Margaret of France's adultery with this knight.

CHAPTER FOUR

1. *The Chronicle of Richard of Devizes*, p. 3. Cf. Statius, *Thebaid: A Song of Thebes*, ed. Jane Wilson Joyce (Ithaca: Cornell University Press, 2006), vv. 16–17.

2. William Hazlitt, "Coriolanus" (December 15, 1816), in *A View of the English Stage* (1818), in *The Collected Works of William Hazlitt: Lectures on the English Comic Writers. A View of the English Stage. Dramatic Essays from "The London Magazine,"* ed. A. R. Waller and Arnold Glover (London: J. M. Dent, 1903), pp. 173–379, at p. 349.

3. Hazlitt, "Coriolanus," p. 349.

4. *History of William Marshal*, vol. 2, vv. 11877–79.

5. See Roger of Howden, *Chronica*, vol. 2, p. 46.

6. Geoffrey du Breuil of Vigeois, *Chronicon Lemovicense*, p. 443.

7. Ralph of Diceto, *Ymagines historiarum*, vol. 1, p. 350.

8. Roger of Howden, *Gesta Regis Henrici secundi*, vol. 1, p. 42.

9. William of Newburgh, *The History of English Affairs*, vol. 2, II, 27, p. 118. Strickland argues, in *Henry the Young King*, pp. 134–35, that Eleanor sent Richard and Geoffrey to join the Young King at the Capetian court, given that danger that the Young King would have faced if he himself went back for them.

10. Ralph of Diceto, *Ymagines historiarum*, vol. 1, p. 355.

11. Matthew Paris, *Chronica majora*, vol. 2, p. 286.

12. Gervase of Canterbury writes, in *Chronica*, p. 242, "It was said that all things had been arranged from her machinations and counsel."

13. William of Newburgh, *The History of English Affairs*, vol. 2, 27, p. 118, and 38, p. 154; Gervase of Canterbury, *Chronica*, p. 242.

14. Roger of Howden, *Gesta Regis Henrici secundi*, vol. 1, p. 42.

15. In *Ex actis Pontificatus Alexandri Papae III* (1173), *RHF*, vol. 13, pp. 665–72, at p. 671, we read that the Young King rose up against his father, "and, together with his mother and his brothers, tried heedlessly to expel him from all the kingdom."

16. All references in this chapter will be to Peter of Blois's letters. The vast majority of those letters can be found in Peter of Blois, *Epistolae, PL*, vol. 207, cols. 1–559. The three letters Peter wrote to Pope Celestine III in Eleanor's voice in 1193 can be found in *Variorum ad Coelestinam III epistolae, PL*, vol. 206, cols. 1261–80, at cols. 1262–72 (where they are incorrectly dated to 1192). They include Letter 2, cols. 1262–65; Letter 3, cols. 1265–68; and Letter 4, cols. 1268–72.

17. Genesis 2:24; Ephesians 5:23.

18. *The Chronicle of Melrose*, p. 40.

19. Roger of Howden, *Chronica*, vol. 2, p. 48.

20. Walter Map, *De nugis curialium*, dist. 4, c. 1, p. 280.

21. William of Newburgh, *The History of English Affairs*, vol. 2, II, 27, p. 116.

22. Dante Alighieri, *The Divine Comedy*, ed. Charles S. Singleton, *Inferno* (Princeton: Princeton University Press, 1990), XXVIII, vv. 134–41.

23. Richard FitzNeal, *Dialogus de Scaccario / The Course of the Exchequer*, ed. Charles Johnson, F. E. L. Carter, and D. E. Greenway (Oxford: Clarendon Press, 1983), p. 76.

24. Gervase of Canterbury, *Gesta regum*, p. 80. Gervase refers to Eleanor fleeing, "her women's clothes having been changed," in *Chronica*, p. 242.

25. Geoffrey du Breuil of Vigeois, *Chronicon Lemovicense*, p. 319.

26. Gervase of Canterbury, *Chronica*, p. 256.

27. Gervase of Canterbury, *Gesta regum*, p. 80.

28. Gerald of Wales, *Instruction for a Ruler*, III, 28, p. 696. Cf. III, 9, p. 609.

29. William of Newburgh, *Historia rerum Anglicarum*, vol. 2, V, 7, pp. 233–34.

30. See Roger of Howden, *Chronica*, vol. 2, p. 279.

31. See William of Newburgh, *Historia rerum Anglicarum*, vol. 1, III, 7, p. 234.

32. *The Chronicle of Robert of Torigni*, p. 306.

33. See William of Newburgh, *Historia rerum Anglicarum*, vol. 1, III, 7, p. 235.

34. *History of William Marshal*, vv. 7152–53. See a *razo* for Bertran de Born's "Pois lo gens terminis floris," *Biographies des troubadours*, 53, for a similar story.

35. Thomas Agnellus, *Sermo de morte et sepultura Henrici Regis Angliae Junioris*, ed. Joseph Stevenson, RS, vol. 66 (London: Longman, 1875), pp. 263–73, at p. 273.

36. Geoffrey of Monmouth, *The History of the Kings of Britain: An Edition and Translation of "De gestis Britonum"* [*Historia regum Britanniae*], ed. Michael D. Reeve (Woodbridge, UK: Boydell Press, 2007), VII, p. 148.

37. Ralph of Diceto, *Ymagines historiarum*, vol. 2, p. 67. Ralph Niger, in *Radulfi Nigri chronica / The Chronicles of Ralph Niger*, ed. Robert Anstruther (London: Printed for the Members of the Caxton Society, 1851), p. 98, identifies the covenant that Eleanor broke as the betrothal of Richard and Alys of France (98).

38. In 1174, Guernes de Pont Sainte-Maxence commented, in *La vie de saint Thomas de Canterbury*, ed. Jacques T. E. Thomas (Louvain: Peeters, 2002), XII, vv. 6133–36, "More than three

times and three she has already nested; the third nesting of England made her heart happy. About this one and the others, if it pleases God, she will rejoice."

39. Richard of Poitiers, *Ex chronico*, p. 420.

40. According to Gerald of Wales, Henry also imagined himself as an eagle, though one perse-cuted by his young. At Winchester, this chronicler reports, the king had a painting made of himself as an eagle with four eaglets poised on top of him, "keenly watching the moment to peck out the eyes of its parent" (*Instruction for a Ruler*, III, 26, p. 678). It had been proph-esied of Henry that "The womb of his wife shall rise up against him" (Roger of Howden, *Chronica*, vol. 2, p. 356; Roger of Howden, *Gesta Regis Henrici secundi*, vol. 2, p. 55; and Gerald of Wales, *Instruction for a Ruler*, III, 9, p. 608), and the eaglets born of Eleanor's womb behaved as had been foreseen.

41. Ralph of Diceto, *Ymagines historiarum*, vol. 2, p. 67. According to Markale, in his *Aliénor d'Aquitaine*, p. 224, a certain Jean d'Etampes met with Eleanor at the Council of Sens in 1140 and identified her as the eagle with its wings stretched over France and England. But Markale cites no source for his anecdote. Flori repeats Markale's tale in *Aliénor d'Aquitaine*, p. 161.

42. Matthew Paris, *Chronica majora*, vol. 1, p. 206.

43. Ralph of Diceto, *Ymagines historiarum*, vol. 1, p. 350.

44. Richard of Poitiers, *Ex chronico*, p. 420.

45. Thomas Agnellus, *Sermo de morte et sepultura Henrici Regis Angliae Junioris*, p. 273.

46. Even Gerald of Wales, in his *Instruction for a Ruler*, II, 4, at p. 458, refers to Eleanor having been imprisoned "perhaps as a punishment for the ending of her first marriage and her con-sent to the second." He suggests that her confinement was due, not to Henry's punishment of a rebel against his authority, but to God's punishment of an adulteress.

47. Only Roger of Howden, in *Gesta Regis Henrici secundi*, would track Eleanor's movements during her captivity: see vol. 1, pp. 305, 313, 333, 334, 337, 345. Geoffrey du Breuil of Vigeois. *Chronicon Lemovicense*, p. 442, states that she was primarily held in Salisbury. The *An-nales Monasterii de Waverleia*, p. 241, record for 1179 that "King Henry and Queen Eleanor were reconciled," but there is no confirmation of this report, and Eleanor remained impris-oned. See also the Pipe Rolls' evidence of Eleanor's residences during these years, especially as quoted in R. W. Eyton, *The Court, Household, and Itinerary of Henry II, Instancing Also the Chief Agents and Adversaries of the King in His Government, Diplomacy, and Strategy* (London: Taylor and Co., 1878).

48. Ralph of Diceto, *Ymagines historiarum*, vol. 2, p. 67.

49. Ralph of Diceto, *Ymagines historiarum*, p. 68.

50. Roger of Howden, *Gesta Regis Henrici secundi*, vol. 1, p. 335.

51. Roger of Howden, *Gesta Regis Henrici secundi*, vol. 2, p. 304.

52. Roger of Howden, *Gesta Regis Henrici secundi*, vol. 1, p. 336.

53. Geoffrey du Breuil of Vigeois, *Chronicon Lemovicense*, p. 442.

54. *History of William Marshal*, vv. 9507–10.

55. Roger of Howden, *Chronica*, p. 4. See Jane Martindale, in "Eleanor of Aquitaine and a 'Queenly Court'?" in *Eleanor of Aquitaine*, ed. Wheeler and Parsons, pp. 423–39, at p. 429, on the unusual phrase "reginalem curiam."

56. Roger of Howden, *Chronica*, vol. 3, p. 5.

57. Gervase of Canterbury, *Chronica*, p. 457.

58. Ralph of Diceto, *Ymagines historiarum*, vol. 2, p. 67.

59. Matthew Paris, *Chronica majora*, p. 346.

60. Roger of Howden, *Chronica*, vol. 3, p. 4.

61. Roger of Howden, *Chronica*, p. 4.

62. *La continuation de Guillaume de Tyr*, 102, p. 103.

63. Roger of Howden, *Chronica*, vol. 3, pp. 195–96.

64. Gervase of Canterbury, *Chronica*, p. 515.

65. Roger of Howden, *Gesta Regis Henrici secundi*, vol. 2, pp. 236–37.

66. John Gillingham, in *Richard I* (New Haven: Yale University Press, 1999), pp. 139–40; in "Richard I and Berengaria of Navarre," *Bulletin of the Institute of Historical Research* 53 (1980): 157–73; and in *Richard Coeur de Lion: Kingship, Chivalry and War in the Twelfth Century* (Hambledon Press, London, 1994; rpt., 2003), pp. 119–39; argues that Richard had made overtures to the King of Navarre about Berengaria as early as 1186 and that he did so because he sought to ally himself with the royal house of Navarre, whose assistance he desired to defend the southern frontier of his lands.

67. Richard de Templo, *Itinerarium peregrinorum et Gesta Regis Ricardi*, ed. William Stubbs, RS, vol. 38 (London: Longman, 1864), II, 26, p. 175.

68. Ambroise, *The History of the Holy War*, vol. 1, vv. 1151–52.

69. *La continuation de Guillaume de Tyr*, 110, p. 113.

70. William of Tyre's continuator mistakes Berengaria for Sancho VI's sister, and he believes Eleanor to have missed Richard in Sicily and to have entrusted Berengaria to her daughter Joan in his stead.

71. Roger of Howden, *Gesta Regis Henrici secundi*, vol. 2, p. 161.

72. William of Newburgh, *Historia rerum Anglicarum*, IV, 19, p. 346.

73. William of Newburgh, *Historia rerum Anglicarum*, IV, 19, p. 346.

74. *The Chronicle of Richard of Devizes*, p. 25.

75. *The Chronicle of Richard of Devizes*, p. 28.

76. Richard de Templo, *Itinerarium peregrinorum et Gesta Regis Ricardi*, II, 26, p. 175.

77. Richard de Templo, *Itinerarium peregrinorum et Gesta Regis Ricardi*, II, 26, p. 176.

78. Ambroise, *The History of the Holy War*, vol. 1, vv. 1155–61.

79. *History of William Marshal*, vv. 9872–76.

80. Roger of Howden, *Gesta Regis Henrici secundi*, vol. 2, pp. 236–37.

81. Roger of Howden, *Gesta Regis Henrici secundi*, vol. 2, p. 237.

82. *The Chronicle of Richard of Devizes*, pp. 59–61.

83. Roger of Howden, *Chronica*, vol. 3, p. 207.

84. Peter of Blois writes, in a letter to William Longchamp from sometime between 1191 and 1193, *PL*, vol. 207, Letter 87, col. 276, "I turned myself to the Lady Queen." Between 1192 and 1194, he attested two of Eleanor's charters.

85. See Beatrice Lees, "Notes and Documents: The Letters of Queen Eleanor of Aquitaine to Pope Celestine III," *English Historical Review* 21 (1906): 78–93. In addition to the letters attributed to Eleanor, Peter of Blois wrote letters to Celestine in the name of Walter of Coutances and his suffragens (Letter 64) and to Conrad, Archbishop of Mainz, whom he knew from his studies (Letter 143), making many of the same points. He also wrote two poems on this theme (*Petri Blesensis Carmina*, ed. Carstin Wollin, CCCM, vol. 128 [Turnhout: Brepols, 1998], 2.3, "In nova fert animus," pp. 249–56; and 2.7, "Insurgant in Germaniam," pp. 367–70).

86. For many centuries, it was assumed that Eleanor dictated these letters to Peter of Blois, who was serving as her secretary, and that they therefore reflect her true feelings. John Bale wrote in the sixteenth century, in his *Scriptorum illustrium majoris Britanniae . . . catalogus* (Ipswich and Wesel: John Overton, 1548), fol. 253, "Queen Eleanor, the mother of King John of

the English, a learned woman, wrote letters to Pope Celestine III." More recently, Lena Wahgren, in *The Letter Collections of Peter of Blois* (Göteborg: Acta Universitatis Gothoburgensis, 1993), pp. 13–14, though not arguing that the letters were commissioned by Eleanor or sent to the pope, does maintain that we cannot establish otherwise. John D. Cotts, in in *The Clerical Dilemma: Peter of Blois and Literate Culture in the Twelfth Century* (Washington, DC: Catholic University of America Press, 2009), pp. 77, 79, 141, 150, 152, 157; and Egbert Türk, *Pierre de Blois: Ambitions et remords sous les Plantagenêts* (Turnhout: Brepols, 2006), p. 360; regard the letters as authentic.

87. *Histoire de Guillaume le Maréchal*, vv. 9821–22.

88. Roger of Howden, *Chronica*, vol. 3, p. 210.

89. Roger of Howden, *Chronica*, vol. 3, p. 212.

90. See *The Chronicle of Jocelin of Brakelond Concerning the Acts of Samson, Abbot of the Monastery of St. Edmund*, ed. H. E. Butler (New York: Oxford University Press, 1949), pp. 46–47.

91. William Dugdale, *Monasticon Anglicanum, or, The History of the Ancient Abbies, and Other Monasteries, Hospitals, Cathedral and Collegiate Churches in England and Wales*, ed. J. Caley et al., 6 vols. (London: Bohn, 1846), vol. 3, p. 154.

92. In the Gospel of Luke 18:3, a widow whose son has been murdered persists in demanding that a judge hear the case until he consents, if only to make her cease pestering him. In the same gospel 7:12, a woman outside the city of Naim is weeping for her dead son, "the only son of his mother, and she was a widow," until Jesus Christ takes pity on her and revives the young man. Readers not infrequently combined the two stories, so that they remembered the importunate widow's appeal as the reason that Christ raises her dead son. For example, when Walter of Coutances writes to Hugh, Bishop of Durham, in February of 1193, requesting that he have prayers said for Richard during his captivity, he points out, according to Roger of Howden's *Chronica*, vol. 3, p. 197, "The importunate woman in the Gospel was deemed deserving to be heard, and, as it is there said, Christ raised her son, because for him many tears were shed."

93. See Cassius Dio, *Historia Romana*, LXVIII, and Bahāʾ al-Dīn Ibn Shaddād, *The Rare and Excellent History of Saladin or al-Nawadir al-Sultaniyya waʾl-Mahasin al-Yusufiyya*, ed. and trans. D. S. Richards (New York: Ashgate, 2002), p. 148.

94. *Epistolae Cantuarienses*, Letter 399, from Richard the Lionheart to Eleanor of Aquitaine (March 30, 1193), pp. 362–63, at p. 362.

95. Roger of Howden claims, however, in his *Chronica*, vol. 3, p. 208, that Pope Celestine threatened to place the empire under interdict unless the emperor quickly freed Richard and to place France under interdict unless Philip ceased persecuting this king.

96. Otto of Saint-Blasien, in *Chronica*, ed. Hofmeister, p. 58, relates that many people regarded it as sacrilege to take a crusader captive. Even Rigord, in *Gesta Philippi Regis*, in *Oeuvres de Rigord et de Guillaume le Breton: Historiens de Philippe-Auguste*, ed. H. François Delaborde, 2 vols. (Paris: Renouard, 1882), vol. 1, pp. 1–167, at p. 121, writes that the arrest "was against all the custom of Christian states, which guaranteed free passage to all Christians."

97. *Annalium Salisburgensium additamentum*, ed. W. Wattenach, *MGH*, *Scriptores*, vol. 13, pp. 236–41, at p. 240.

98. Roger of Howden, *Chronica*, vol. 3, p. 229.

99. Roger of Howden, *Chronica*, vol. 3, p. 231.

100. Roger of Howden, *Chronica*, vol. 3, p. 201.

101. Roger of Howden, *Chronica*, vol. 3, pp. 233–34.

102. *The History of William Marshal*, vv. 10108–12.

103. *The Chronicle of Richard of Devizes*, p. 58.

104. *The Chronicle of Richard of Devizes*, p. 60. This was not the only time when Eleanor took pity on suffering commoners. According to the *Miraculorum gloriosi martyris Thomae, Cantuariensis Archiepiscopi*, in *Materials for the History of Thomas Becket, Archbishop of Canterbury*, ed. James Craigie Robertson, 7 vols., RS, vol. 67 (London: Longman, 1875), vol. 1, pp. 173–546, at II, 32, p. 213, Eleanor once found a street child, "destitute of the maternal bosom," and arranged for him to be raised at Abingdon Abbey.

105. *The Chronicle of Richard of Devizes*, p. 60.

106. Roger of Hoveden, *Chronica*, vol. 3, p. 240.

107. Roger of Hoveden, *Chronica*, vol. 3, p. 248.

108. William of Newburgh, *Historia rerum Anglicarum*, vol. 2, V, 5, p. 424.

109. *The Chronicle of Richard of Devizes*, p. 14. Richard had been advised that John would conspire against him as soon as he left for the Holy Land. See William of Newburgh, *Historia rerum Anglicarum*, vol. 1, IV, 3, pp. 301–2.

110. Roger of Howden, *Gesta Regis Henrici secundi*, vol. 1, p. 106.

111. *The Chronicle of Richard of Devizes*, p. 14. Raphael Holinshed, in *Chronicles of England, Scotland, and Ireland*, ed. Ellis, 6 vols. (London: J. Johnson, 1807–8), vol. 2, p. 210, would later suggest that Eleanor persuaded Richard to revoke that decree "lest it seem to the world that her sons stood in fear of one another."

112. William of Newburgh, *Historia rerum Anglicarum*, vol. 2, V, 5, p. 424.

113. *History of William Marshal*, vv. 11761–67.

114. Ralph of Coggeshall, *Chronicon Anglicanum*, p. 96.

115. *Layettes du trésor des Chartes*, no. 489, Letter of Eleanor of Aquitaine to the Public (April 21, 1199), p. 200.

116. See Roger of Howden, *Chronica*, p. 289; and Adam of Eynsham, *Magna Vita Sancti Hugonis*, vol. 1, V, 6, p. 255. Left to her own resources, Berengaria settled in Beaufort-en-Vallée, in the Maine, and in 1229 founded the Cistercian Abbey of L'Épau near her dower city of Le Mans. On this neglected queen, see Ann Trindade, *Berengaria: In Search of Richard the Lionheart's Queen* (Dublin: Four Courts Press, 1999).

117. Roger of Howden, *Chronica*, vol. 4, p. 88.

118. Roger of Wendover, *Liber qui dicitur Flores historiarum*, ed. Henry G. Hewlett, 3 vols., RS, vol. 84 (London: Longman, 1886–89), vol. 1, p. 286.

119. See Hivergneaux, "Aliénor d'Aquitaine," pp. 63–87. Eleanor issued more charters immediately after Richard's death that at any other time in her widowhood.

120. See, for example, *Histoire de la ville de La Rochelle et du Pays d'Aulnis composée d'après les auteurs et les titres originaux, et enrichie de divers plans*, ed. Louis-Etienne Arcère et al., 2 vols. (La Rochelle: Chez René-Jacob Desbordes, 1756–57), vol. 2, p. 647; or "Chartes de Fontevrault concernant l'Aunis et La Rochelle [second article]," ed. Paul Marchegay, *Bibliothèque de l'Ecole des Chartes* 19 (1858): 321–347, at p. 333.

121. Rigord, *Gesta Philippi Augusti*, in *Oeuvres de Rigord et de Guillaume le Breton*, ed. H. François Delaborde, 2 vols. (Paris: Renouard, 1882–85), vol. 1, pp. 168–320, at 129, p. 146.

122. Guy of Thouars, Aimery's younger brother, had married Constance of Brittany in the fall of 1199 and, as stepfather to young Arthur, was naturally an important champion of his claim to the English throne.

123. *Foedera, conventiones, litterae, et cujuscunque generis acta publica inter reges Angliae, et alios quosvis imperatores, reges, pontifices, principes, vel communitates*, ed. Thomas Rymer and Robert Sanderson, 20 vols. (London: n.p., 1704–35); rev. ed. George Holmes, 17 vols. (The Hague: Apud Joannem Nealme, 1735–47), Letter of Eleanor of Aquitaine to John (1200), vol. 1, p. 39.

124. Letter of Eleanor of Aquitaine to John (1200), vol. 1, p. 36.

125. Gervase of Canterbury, *Gesta regum*, pp. 92–93.

126. Ralph of Coggeshall, *Chronicon Anglicanum*, p. 137.

127. Matthew Paris, *Chronica majora*, vol. 2, p. 478.

128. Ralph of Coggeshall, *Chronicon Anglicanum*, p. 137.

129. *Continuatio Chronici Willelmi de Novoburgo ad annum 1298*, in *Chronicles of the Reigns of Stephen, Henry II, and Richard I*, ed. Richard Howlett, 4 vols., RS, vol. 82 (London: Longman, 1884–85), vol. 2, pp. 503–83, at p. 507.

130. Matthew Paris, *Chronica majora*, vol. 2, p. 478.

131. *Biographies des troubadours*, 72.

132. *Histoire des Ducs de Normandie et des Rois d'Angleterre*, ed. Francisque Michel (Paris: Jules Renouard, 1840), p. 95.

133. William the Breton, *Philippide*, in *Oeuvres de Rigord et de Guillaume le Breton*, vol. 2, pp. 1–385, at VI, vv. 394–95.

134. For other accounts of John's relief of this siege, see *Chronicon Turonese magnum*, pp. 146–47; *Ex Annalibus Waverleiensis Monasterii*, p. 192; Ralph of Coggeshall, *Chronicon Anglicanum*, p. 137; and *History of William Marshal*, vol. 2, vv. 12059–68.

135. Ralph of Coggeshall, *Chronicon Anglicanum*, p. 137.

136. *Histoire des Ducs de Normandie et des Rois d'Angleterre*, p. 93.

137. William the Breton, *Philippide*, VI, vv. 371–75.

138. William the Breton, *Philippide*, VI, v. 377.

139. Polydore Vergil, *Anglica Historia*, ed. Dana J. Sutton (Birmingham, UK: Library of Humanistic Texts at the Philological Museum of University of Birmingham's Shakespeare Institute, 2005), XV, 1.

140. Holinshed, *Chronicles of England, Scotland, and Ireland*, vol. 2, p. 274.

141. Vergil, *Anglica Historia*, XV, 1.

142. Holinshed, *Chronicles of England, Scotland, and Ireland*, vol. 2, p. 274.

143. Vergil, *Anglica Historia*, XV, 1.

144. Holinshed, *Chronicles of England, Scotland, and Ireland*, vol. 2, p. 274.

145. William Shakespeare, *The Life and Death of King John*, ed. Claire McEachern (New York: Penguin Books, 2000), II, 1, 63.

146. In *Julius Caesar*, Shakespeare has Mark Antony lament Julius Caesar's murder by imagining, "And Caesar's spirit, ranging for revenge, / With Atë by his side come hot from Hell, / Shall in these confines with a monarch's voice / Cry 'Havoc!' and let slip the dogs of war" (III, 1, 285–88).

147. Shakespeare, *The Life and Death of King John*, II, 1, 468.

148. Shakespeare, *The Life and Death of King John*, II, 1, 491–92.

149. George Peele, *The Troublesome Reign of John, King of England*, ed. Charles R. Forker (Manchester: Manchester University Press, 2016), I, 4, 126–27.

150. Shakespeare, *King John*, I, 1, 40. According to William Lowes Rushton, *Shakespeare's Legal Maxims* (Liverpool: Henry Young & Sons, 1859), p. 12, Shakespeare may have had in mind the maxim, "Where the right is equal, the claim of the party in possession shall prevail."

151. Dorothea Kehler, "'So Jest with Heaven': Deity in *King John*," in *King John: New Perspectives*, ed. Deborah T. Curren-Aquino (Newark: University of Delaware Press, 1989), pp. 99–113, at p. 101.

152. Marsha Robinson, "The Historiographic Methodology of King John," in *King John: New Perspectives*, pp. 29–40, at p. 31.

153. Phyllis Rackin, "Patriarchal History and Female Subversion in King John," in *King John: New Perspectives*, pp. 76–90, at p. 81.

154. Peele, *The Troublesome Reign of John*, I, 4, 163.

155. Peele, *The Troublesome Reign of John*, I, 4, 99.

156. Peele, *The Troublesome Reign of John*, II, 2, 18–20.

157. Shakespeare, *King John*, IV, 2, 182.

158. John Watkins, "Losing France and Becoming England: Shakespeare's *King John* and the Emergence of State-Based Diplomacy," in *Shakespeare and the Middle Ages*, ed. Curtis Perry and John Watkins (Oxford: Oxford University Press, 2009), pp. 78–102, at p. 88.

159. Juliet Dusineberre, "*King John* and Embarrassing Women," *Shakespeare Survey* 42 (1989): 37–52, at p. 41.

160. Peele, *The Troublesome Reign of John*, I, 4, 184–85.

161. Peele, *The Troublesome Reign of John*, I, 9, 11–12.

162. On April 16, 1203, around the time of Arthur's disappearance, John wrote to Eleanor and to several other parties from the Castle of Falaise in Normandy, where the boy had been kept imprisoned, and advised them to heed certain unspecified information his messenger would pass along orally. He added cryptically, as cited in *Rotuli litterarum patentium in turri Londinensi asservati*, ed. Thomas Duffus Hardy (London: Commission on the Public Records of the Kington, 1835), p. 28f, "The grace of God is even more with us than he can tell you [*gratia Dei meli[us] stat nobis q[uam] ille vobis d[ice]re possit*]." John's words have traditionally been taken as a veiled reference to Arthur's murder. See Turner, *Eleanor of Aquitaine*, p. 293, who builds on Richard, *Histoire des comtes de Poitou*, vol. 2, pp. 424–25; and Maurice Powicke, *Loss of Normandy, 1198–1204* (Manchester: Manchester University Press, 1913), p. 325.

163. Shakespeare, *King John*, III, 3, 19.

164. Shakespeare, *King John*, III, 3, 18.

165. See Peter Alexander, ed., *The BBC Shakespeare: King John*, dir. David Giles (London: British Broadcasting Corp., 1986), p. 27.

166. See *King John*, dir. Pat Patton, Oregon Shakespeare Festival (Ashland, Summer, 1985), as reviewed by Charles Frey, "King John at Ashland," *Journal of Dramatic Theory and Criticism* 1, no. 2 (Spring 1987): 167–74.

167. Vergil, *Anglica Historia*, XV, 1.

168. See Edmond-René Labande, *Pour une image véridique d'Aliénor d'Aquitaine* (La Crèche: Société des Antiquaires de l'Ouest et des Musées de Poitiers, 1952); rpt., in *Bulletin de la Société des Antiquairies de l'Ouest*, ed. Martin Aurell (Poitiers: Geste Éditions / Société des Antiquaires de l'Ouest, 2005), p. 105; Turner, *Eleanor of Aquitaine*, pp. 251, 280; and Turner, "Eleanor of Aquitaine in the Governments of Her Sons Richard and John," in *Eleanor of Aquitaine: Lord and Lady*, pp. 77–95, at p. 87.

169. Peele, *The Troublesome Reign of John*, I, 2, 100–102.

170. Shakespeare, *King John*, II, 1, 193–94.

171. Gerald of Wales, *Instruction for a Ruler*, III, 27, p. 684.

172. Shakespeare, *King John*, II, 1, 177–82.

173. Peele, *The Troublesome Reign of John*, I, 9, 7–10.

CHAPTER FIVE

1. Voltaire, *La pucelle* (1752), in *Les oeuvres complètes de Voltaire*, ed. Jeroom Vercruysse, 200 vols. (Oxford: Oxford University Press, 1968–present), vol. 7 (1970), vv. 241–42.

2. See Baldric of Bourgueil, *Historia magistri Roberti*, in *Les deux vies de Robert d'Arbrissel, fondateur de Fontevraud: Légendes, écrits et témoignages: Editions des sources avec introductions et traductions française*, ed. Jacques Dalarun, Geneviève Giordanengo, Armelle Le Huërou, and Jean Longère (Turnhout: Brepols, 2006), pp. 130–87; and Andreas of Fontevraud, *Supplementum historiae vitae Roberti*, in *Les deux vies de Robert d'Arbrissel*, pp. 190–300. All references in this section will be to Andreas of Fontevraud's *Supplementum historiae vitae Roberti*, in this edition. Both *vitae* come down to us in French translations from the sixteenth century as well as Latin editions from the seventeenth century.

3. Yves Magistri, *Baston de deffense et mirouer des professeurs de la vie régulière de l'Abbaye et de l'Ordre de Fontevrault* (Angers: par Anthoine Hernault libraire, 1586).

4. Laurent Pelletier (attributed), *Légende de Robert d'Arbrissel avec un catalogue des abbesses de Fontevrault* (Angers: n.p., 1586).

5. Honorat Nicquet, *Histoire de l'Ordre de Font-Evraud* (Paris: Chez Michel Soly, 1642).

6. Baltazar Pavillon, *La vie du bienheureux Robert d'Arbrissel, patriarche des solitaires de la France et instituteur de l'Ordre de Font-Evraud* (Saumur: François Ernov, 1666).

7. Jean Lardier edited seventy-two volumes of documents, most of which were dispersed at the time of the French Revolution. The *Inventaire des titres*, also named the *Thrésor de l'Ordre de Fontevraud* (1646–58) has survived in seven manuscript volumes, preserved in the Archives Départementales de Maine-et-Loire. In 1699, the antiquarian François-Roger de Gaignières collected a number of extracts and copies of this cartulary in his *Chartularium monasterii Fontis-Ebraldi, in dioecesi Pictaviensi*, which is preserved in Paris, Bibliothèque nationale de France, Manuscrits, lat. 5480.

8. *Clypeus nascentis Fontebraldensis Ordinis contra priscos et novos ejus calumniatores*, ed. Jean de La Mainferme, 3 vols. (Paris: Apud Georgium et Ludovicum Josse, 1682–92).

9. Nicquet, *Histoire de l'Ordre de Font-Evraud*, III, 5, p. 417.

10. See Geoffrey of Vendôme, *Epistola ad Robertum*, in *Les deux vies de Robert d'Arbrissel*, pp. 568–77.

11. "The Miracle of Rouen," in *Les deux vies de Robert d'Arbrissel*, pp. 301–23, at p. 322.

12. Baldric of Bourgueil, *Historia magistri Roberti*, pp. 168–69.

13. See William of Malmesbury, *Gesta regum Anglorum*, vol. 1, 493, pp. 782–84.

14. See Marbod of Rennes, *Epistola ad Robertum*, in *Les deux vies de Robert d'Arbrissel*, 30, p. 554.

15. See Jacques Dalarun, "Robert d'Arbrissel et les femmes," *Annales* 39, no. 6 (1984): 1140–60; and Fiona Griffiths, "The Cross and the *Cura monialium*: Robert of Arbrissel, John the Evangelist, and the Pastoral Care of Women in the Age of Reform," *Speculum* 83 (2008): 303–30.

16. Gerald of Wales, *Instruction for a Ruler*, III, 28, p. 692.

17. Roger of Howden, *Chronica*, vol. 2, p. 367.

18. *History of William Marshal*, vv. 9410–21; and Gerald of Wales, *Instruction for a Ruler*, 28, p. 694. But see Roger of Howden, *Gesta Regis Henrici secundi*, vol. 2, p. 71.

19. In his 1182 will, Henry bequeathed 5,000 silver marks to the Templars, 5,000 to the Hospitalers, 3,000 to the Order of Grandmont, 2,000 to Cîteaux, and 2,000 to the Charterhouse, but he also gave 2,000 marks to the largely female Fontevraud, leaving the Cluniacs, the Premonstratensians, and the Saint-Sulpiciens with significantly less. See Gerald of Wales, *Instruction for a Ruler*, II, 17, p. 504; and Jean-Marc Bienvenu, "Henri II Plantagenêt et Fontevraud," *CCM* 37, nos. 145–46 (January–June 1994): 25–32, at p. 26.

20. Charles T. Woods, in "La mort et les funérailles d'Henri II," trans. Marie-Hélène Bradley, *CCM* 37, nos. 145–46 (January–June 1994), Actes du Colloque de Fontevraud (September 23–

October 1, 1990): 119–23, at p. 121, believes that Henry was buried at Fontevraud because the abbey was nearby and his body would have decomposed quickly in the summer heat if it had been carried a longer distance. Yet Alain Erlande-Brandenburg, in *Les rois à Fontevrault: Henri II, Richard Coeur de Lion, Aliénor, Isabelle d'Angoulême: Mort, sépulture et sculpture (1189–1204)* (Fontevraud: Centre Culturel de l'Ouest, 1979), argues that people at this time customarily sought to fulfill the wishes of the dying person regarding the place of their burial and that numerous examples exist of bodies being transported for long distances in order to conform to their wishes.

21. William of Newburgh, *Historia rerum Anglicarum*, vol. 1, III, 25, p. 278.

22. *History of William Marshal*, vv. 9294–9303.

23. Gerald of Wales, *Instruction for a Ruler*, III, 28, p. 694.

24. Roger of Howden, *Chronica*, vol. 2, p. 367; Gerald of Wales, *Instruction for a Ruler*, III, 28, p. 692.

25. Gervase of Canterbury, *Chronica*, p. 449.

26. *Grand cartulaire de Fontevraud: Pancarta et cartularium Abbatissae et Ordinis Fontis Ebraudi*, ed. Jean-Marc Bienvenu, with Robert Favreau and Georges Pon, 2 vols. (Poitiers: Société des Antiquaires de l'ouest, 2000–2005), vol. 1, 360, p. 360; vol. 1, 947, p. 898; vol. 2, 711, pp. 668–69 et passim.

27. Roger of Howden, *Chronica*, vol. 2, p. 356.

28. Gerald of Wales, *Instruction for a Ruler*, III, 28, p. 696; cf. III, 9, p. 609. Amy Kelly, in *Eleanor of Aquitaine and the Four Kings*, p. 190, states that Henry offered the abbacy to Eleanor. While her suggestion has been repeated by many scholars, she offers no proof of this point.

29. *Ex Annalibus Waverleiensis Monasterii*, p. 189.

30. William of Newburgh, *Historia rerum Anglicarum*, vol. 1, III, 25, p. 279.

31. *History of William Marshal*, vol. 1, vv. 9228–44.

32. See William of Newburgh, *Historia rerum Anglicarum*, vol. 1, III, 25, pp. 278–79; and *Ex Annalibus Waverleiensis Monasterii*, p. 189.

33. William of Newburgh, *Historia rerum Anglicarum*, vol. 1, III, 25, p. 279.

34. Pavillon, *La vie du bienheureux Robert d'Arbrissel*, p. 583.

35. Roger of Howden, *Chronica*, vol. 4, p. 84.

36. Roger of Wendover, *Liber qui dicitur Flores historiarum*, vol. 1, p. 283.

37. See Lionel Landon, in *The Itinerary of King Richard I, With Studies on Certain Matters of Interest Connected with His Reign*, Publications of the Pipe Roll Society (London: J. W. Ruddock, 1935), p. 145.

38. Adam of Eynsham, *Magna Vita Sancti Hugonis*, vol. 2, V, 10, p. 137.

39. *Histoire des Ducs de Normandie et des Rois d'Angleterre*, p. 90.

40. See *Calendar of Documents Preserved in France*, vol. 1, no. 1086, p. 385.

41. Nicquet, *Histoire de l'Ordre de Font-Evraud*, III, 7, p. 255.

42. Religieuses de Sainte-Marie de Fontevrault, *Histoire de l'Ordre de Fontevrault (1100–1908)*, 2 vols. (Auch: Imprimerie Léonce Cocharaux, 1911), vol. 2, p. 79.

43. Nicquet, *Histoire de l'Ordre de Font-Evraud*, III, 7, p. 256.

44. Adam of Eynsham, *Magna Vita Sancti Hugonis*, vol. 2, V, 11, p. 138. For the rule preventing visitors from entering the Abbey of Fontevraud except in the presence of the abbess, see "The Revised Statutes," in *Les deux vies de Robert d'Arbrissel*, pp. 406–27, at p. 412.

45. Adam of Eynsham, *Magna Vita Sancti Hugonis*, pp. 138–39.

46. Stories circulated about the danger cloistered nuns faced from predatory male visitors, including the danger a nun of Fontevraud once faced from Richard. See Odo of Cheriton, *Les*

fabulistes latins, ed. Léopold Hervieux, 5 vols. (Paris: Firmin-Didot, 1893–1899, 1896), vol. 4, no. 120, p. 311; and Stephen of Bourbon, *Anecdotes historiques, légendes et apologues tirés du recueil inédit d'Etienne de Bourbon, Dominican du XIIIe siècle*, ed. A. Lecoy de la Marche (Paris: Renouard, 1877), no. 248. pp. 211–12; no. 500, p. 431.

47. Adam of Eynsham, *Magna Vita Sancti Hugonis*, vol. 2, V, 11, p. 139. Cf. Matthew 15:1–13.

48. See Werner Robl, *Heloisas Herkunft: Hersindis Mater* (Munich: Olzog, 2001).

49. Heloise, *The Letter Collection of Peter Abelard and Heloise*, ed. David Luscombe (Oxford: Oxford University Press, 2013), Letter 6, from Heloise to Peter Abelard, p. 222.

50. "The Revised Statutes," in *Les deux vies de Robert d'Arbrissel*, p. 412.

51. Adam of Eynsham, *Magna Vita Sancti Hugonis*, p. 139.

52. Cited in Pavillon, *La vie du bienheureux Robert d'Arbrissel*, p. 535, no. 90.

53. See Roger of Howden, *Chronica*, vol. 4, p. 82; Ralph of Coggeshall, *Chronicon Anglicanum*, p. 94; and Roger of Wendover, *Liber qui dicitur Flores historiarum*, vol. 1, p. 282.

54. Adam of Eynsham, *Magna Vita Sancti Hugonis*, vol. 2, V, 10, p. 133.

55. All references after this point will be to "Chartes de Fontevraud concernant l'Aunis et La Rochelle [second article]."

56. Adam of Eynsham, *Magna Vita Sancti Hugonis*, vol. 2, V, 10, p. 135.

57. Adam of Eynsham, *Magna Vita Sancti Hugonis*, vol. 2, V, 16, p. 184.

58. RaGena C. DeAragon observes in "Wife, Widow, and Mother: Some Comparisons between Eleanor of Aragon and Noblewomen of the Anglo-Norman and Angevin World," in *Eleanor of Aquitaine: Lord and Lady*, pp. 97–113, at p. 106, that only 10 percent of dowager countesses joined a religious community or retired to a monastery.

59. Katherine Clark Walter, *The Profession of Widowhood: Widows, Pastoral Care, and Medieval Models of Holiness* (Washington, DC: Catholic University of America, 2018), p. 181.

60. Walter, *The Profession of Widowhood*, pp. 195–96.

61. Rodrigo Jiménez de Rada, *De rebus Hispaniae sive historia Gothica*, ed. Juan Fernández Valverde, CCCM, vol. 71 (Turnhout: Brepols, 1987), V, ch. 24, p. 173.

62. *Biographies des troubadours*, p. 61. This line is from a *razo* for Bertran de Born's *sirventes* "Qan vei pels vergiers despleiar."

63. *Clypeus nascentis Fontebraldensis Ordinis*, vol. 1, p. 147.

64. See a charter from 1114 recorded in *HGL*, vol. 8, p. 846; and the *Grand cartulaire de Fontevraud*, vol. 1, 43, p. 36.

65. William of Malmesbury, *Gesta regum Anglorum*, vol. 1, 439, p. 784. See also Hildebert of Lavardin, *Carmina minora*, ed. A. Brian Scott (Leipzig: Teubner, 1969), p. 39; and Orderic Vitalis, *Historia ecclesiastica*, vol. 6, XII, 21, p. 268.

66. Baldric of Bourgueil, *Historia magistri Roberti*, 22, pp. 178–79. Cf. 1 Timothy 2:4.

67. Roscelin, Letter to Peter Abelard, in *Les deux vies de Robert d'Arbrissel*, pp. 628–30, at p. 630.

68. Unedited document from the *Cartularium breve Fontisebraldense*, Archives Départementales de Maine-et-Loire, Angers, 101 H, 225 *bis*, quoted in Szabolcs de Vajay, "Ramire II le Moine, roi d'Aragon, et Agnès de Poitou dans l'histoire et dans la légende," in *Mélanges offerts à René Crozet à l'occasion de son soixante-dixième anniversaire, par ses amis, ses collègues, ses élèves*, 2 vols. (Poitiers: Société d'études médiévales, 1966): 727–50, at vol. 2, p. 743n117. In the obits of Fontevraud in *La vie du bienheureux Robert d'Arbrissel*, Pavillon lists "Audiarda, sacred to God, the daughter of the Duke of Aquitaine" (579).

69. It has often been assumed that Philippa died in 1117 or 1118, but there is evidence that she may have been alive in 1119, when a Countess of Poitou is said to have confronted her husband, William IX, at the Council of Reims, or even in the 1120s or the 1130s, when other figures

named in some of her charters were active. See François Villard. "Guillaume IX d'Aquitaine et le concile de Reims de 1119," *CCM* 16 (1973): 295–302, at p. 296.

70. Eugène Hucher, "Notice sur deux chartes de Louis VII et d'Aliénor d'Aquitaine, en faveur de l'Abbaye de Fontevraud," *Revue des sociétés savantes de la France et de l'étranger*, 5th series, vol. 3 (January 1872): 49–54, at p. 53.

71. Orderic Vitalis, *Historia ecclesiastica*, XII, 33, p. 330.

72. Eleanor may also have met Henry's cousin, Matilda of Flanders (the daughter of his aunt Sibyl of Anjou), who had entered this abbey at the age of fourteen and would become abbess in 1189; his former hostage and mistress, Alix of Porhoët, the daughter of Odo II, Viscount of Porhoët; and his cousin Bertha, Duchess of Brittany, who would become abbess in 1209.

73. Hucher, "Notice sur deux chartes de Louis VII et d'Aliénor d'Aquitaine," p. 52.

74. Hucher, "Notice sur deux chartes de Louis VII et d'Aliénor d'Aquitaine," p. 53.

75. *Recueil des documents relatifs à l'Abbaye de Montierneuf de Poitiers, 1076–1319*, ed. François Villard (Poitiers: Société des archives historiques du Poitou, 1973), April 11, 1126, p. 115.

76. Fontevraud was not the only religious institution whose piety Eleanor appraised and whose needs she subsidized. See her similar remarks about the Benedictine Abbey of Sauve-Majeure, on the road to Compostella, in a charter from Bordeaux dated July 1, 1199 (*Foedera, conventiones*, ed. Rymer, vol. 5, pp. 1, 80), and the pleasure she was said to have taken at the blessing Gilbert of Sempringham gave Richard and John in *The Book of St. Gilbert*, ed. Raymonde Foreville and Gillian Keir (Oxford: Clarendon Press, 1987), 29, p. 92.

77. Roger of Hoveden, *Chronica*, vol. 4, p. 114.

78. Letter of Eleanor to John (1200), in *Foedera, conventiones*, vol. 1, p. 39.

79. Bertran de Born, "Qan vei pels vergiers despleiar," *The Poems of the Troubadour Bertran de Born*, ed. William D. Paden, Jr., T. Senkovitch, and P. H. Stäblein (Berkeley: University of California Press, 1986), pp. 274–81, vv. 41–48.

80. Gérard Gourian, in "Les Débuts du héraut d'armes en littérature et les premières chansons de guerre de Bertran de Born (1181–83)," *Summa* 4 (Autumn 2014): 45–61, at p. 46, characterizes this tale as "an anecdote, to say the least doubtful," which Bertran would have learned from the Catalan troubadour Guillem de Berguedà. Alfonso II had recently aided Richard in overtaking Bertran's castle of Hautefort and giving it to Bertran's brother Constantine, so Bertran had reason to malign him.

81. The editors of *The Poems of the Troubadour Bertran de Born*, at p. 289nn41–48, identify the Abbess of Fontevraud at this point as Matilda of Flanders, but Matilda was only elected to this position in 1189. A certain "Gilles" or "Gillette" was abbess at this time, but little is known about her.

82. *Biographies des troubadours*, p. 61.

83. *Calendar of Documents Preserved in France*, vol. 1, no. 1091, p. 387.

84. De Vic and Vaissete, *HGL*, vol. 6, XX, 62, p. 190, deny that Joan had any children with Raymond aside from the future Raymond VI. But an obituary from the Abbey of Vaissy in Auvergne refers to a certain Joan of Toulouse as Joan's daughter.

85. William of Puylaurens, *Chronique (1145–1275) / Chronica Magistri Guillelmi de Podio Laurentis*, ed. Jean Duvernoy (Toulouse: Le Pérégrinateur, 1976), 5, p. 44.

86. William of Puylaurens, *Chronique*, 5, p. 44.

87. William of Puylaurens, *Chronique*, 5, p. 46.

88. *Annales Monasterii de Wintonia*, ed. Henry Richards Luard, in *Annales monastici*, 5 vols., RS, vol. 36 (London: Longman, 1865), vol. 2, pp. 3–125, at p. 71. Roger of Howden, in

Chronica, vol. 4, pp. 83–84, relates that Richard ordered this man to be given one hundred shillings and released, but that Mercadier, without the king's knowledge, had him flayed and then hanged.

89. *Annales Monasterii de Wintonia*, ed. Luard, p. 64.

90. *Histoire de la ville de La Rochelle et du Pays d'Aulnis*, ed. M. Arcère, 2 vols. (La Rochelle: René-Jacob Desbordes, 1752), vol. 2, pp. 660–61. "Our dearest daughter Queen Joan," cited in *Autographes de personnages ayant marqué dans l'histoire de Bordeaux et de la Guyenne*, Société des Archives Historiques de la Gironde (Bordeaux: Imprimerie G. Gounouilhou, 1895), vol. 30, p. 7, serves as a witness for a charter at Niort in 1199.

91. *Cartulaire Saintongeais de la Trinité de Vendôme*, ed. Charles Métais (Paris: Picard, 1893), 72, p. 118.

92. *Clypeus nascentis Fontebraldensis Ordinis*, vol. 2, p. 160.

93. *Calendar of Documents Preserved in France*, vol. 1, p. 387n4.

94. *Calendar of Documents Preserved in France*, vol. 1, no. 1103, p. 392.

95. Colette Bowie, in *The Daughters of Henry II and Eleanor of Aquitaine* (Turnhout: Brepols, 2014); and in "Shifting Patterns in Angevin Marriage Policies: The Political Motivations for Joanna Plantagenet's Marriages to William II of Sicily and Raymond VI of Toulouse," in *Les stratégies matrimoniales (IXe–XIIIe siècle)*, ed. Martin Aurell (Turnhout: Brepols, 2013), pp. 155–167; stresses Joan's relative poverty at this point in her life. See also Bowie's "To Have and Have Not: The Dower of Joanna Plantagenet, Queen of Sicily (1177–1189)," in *Queenship in the Mediterranean: Negotiating the Role of the Queen in the Medieval and Early Modern Eras*, ed. Elena Woodacre (New York: Palgrave Macmillan, 2013), pp. 27–50.

96. *Calendar of Documents Preserved in France*, vol. 1, no. 1105, p. 393.

97. Andreas of Fontevraud, *Supplementum historiae vitae Roberti*, 43, pp. 270–71. The editor suspects that Andreas is confusing Hilary of Poitiers with Sulpicius Severus, whose *Epistula ad Bassulum*, 16, p. 342, echoes this passage.

98. *Clypeus nascentis Fontebraldensis Ordinis*, vol. 2, p. 161.

99. Nicquet, *Histoire de l'Ordre de Font-Evraud*, III, 7, p. 257.

100. *Calendar of Documents Preserved in France*, vol. 1, no. 1105, p. 393.

101. Nicquet, *Histoire de l'Ordre de Font-Evraud*, III, 7, p. 258.

102. Pavillon, in *La vie du bienheureux Robert d'Arbrissel*, pp. 509–10, claims that Joan requested this operation so the child could be baptized before it died and thus assured of salvation. Bowie and Vaissete say that he was born posthumously.

103. *Clypeus nascentis Fontebraldensis Ordinis*, vol. 2, p. 161; Nicquet, *Histoire de l'Ordre de Font-Evraud*, III, 7, p. 258.

104. Bouchet, *Annales d'Aquitaine*, III, 5, p. 89.

105. Pavillon, *La vie du bienheureux Robert d'Arbrissel*, p. 509.

106. In *De felici obitu Angeluciae virginis sanctimonialis Fontebraldensis*, in *Thesaurus novus anecdotarum*, ed. Edmond Martène and Ursin Durand, 5 vols. (Lutetiae Parisiorum: Sumptibus Fl. Delaulne, 1717), vol. 3, cols. 1703–10, at cols. 1703–4, the editors identify the author as "either . . . a monk from among those who were subject to the nuns or one of the sisters." The Benedictine Monks of the Congregation of Saint-Maur and the Académie des Inscriptions et Belles-Lettres, in *Histoire littéraire de la France* (Paris: Firmin Didot, 1814), vol. 13, pp. 599–600, at p. 600, speak of the author as a nun of Fontevraud who had been an eyewitness to these events.

107. In *Histoire de l'Ordre de Font-Evraud*, IV, 35, p. 529, Nicquet cites "Margaret, the daughter of Thibaut, Count of Chartres and Champagne" as a distinguished individual buried in the ab-

bey church. This Margaret seems to have been the daughter of Thibaut "the Great," II Count of Champagne, IV Count of Blois and Chartres. See Jean-Marc Bienvenu, "Une visionnaire fontévriste du XIIe siècle: Angelucia," in *Les religieuses dans le cloître et dans le monde des origines à nos jours*, ed. Bouter, pp. 139–48, at p. 139.

108. *De felici obitu Angeluciae virginis sanctimonialis Fontebraldensis*, col. 1708.

109. *De felici obitu Angeluciae virginis sanctimonialis Fontebraldensis*, col. 1707.

110. Andreas of Fontevraud, *Supplementum historiae vitae Roberti*, 74, p. 297.

111. Orderic Vitalis, *Historia ecclesiastica*, vol. 6, XII, 22, p. 278. See also *Calendar of Documents Preserved in France*, vol. 1, no. 1054, p. 373.

112. Thomas Malory, *The Works of Sir Thomas Malory*, ed. Eugene Vinaver and P. J. C. Field, 3rd ed. (Oxford: Clarendon Press, 1990), vol. 3, p. 1249.

113. Alberic des Trois-Fontaines, *Chronica*, p. 876.

114. Pavillon, *La vie du bienheureux Robert d'Arbrissel*, vol. 2, p. 87.

115. Edouard (pseudonym of Abbé A. Biron), *Fontevrault et ses monuments, ou Histoire de cette royale abbaye depuis sa foundation jusqu'à sa suppression (1100–1793)*, 2 vols. (Paris: Aubry Librairie, 1873–74), vol. 2, p. 117.

116. Religieuses de Sainte-Marie de Fontevrault, *Histoire de l'Ordre de Fontevrault*, vol. 2, p. 86.

117. *Clypeus nascentis Fontebraldensis Ordinis*, vol. 2, p. 158.

118. *Clypeus nascentis Fontebraldensis Ordinis*, vol. 2, pp. 158–59.

119. Pavillon, *La vie du bienheureux Robert d'Arbrissel*, p. 512.

120. See *Obituaires de la province de Sens*, ed. Auguste Longnon et al., 4 vols. in 5 (Paris: Imprimerie nationale: Librairie C. Klincksieck, 1902–23), vol. 4, p. 190.

121. *Layettes du trésor des Chartes*, 200, no. 489 (Fontevraud, 1199).

122. See Elizabeth M. Hallam, in "Royal Burial and the Cult of Kingship in France and England, 1060–1330," *Journal of Medieval History* 8, no. 4 (1982): 359–80, at p. 371; and José Manuel Cerda, "Leonor Plantagenet and the Cult of Thomas Becket in Castile," in *The Cult of St. Thomas Becket in the Plantagenet World, c. 1170–c. 1220*, ed. Paul Webster and Marie-Pierre Gelin (Woodbridge, UK: Boydell & Brewer, 2016), pp. 144–45, at p. 143.

123. Pavillon, *La vie du bienheureux Robert d'Arbrissel*, p. 578.

124. The author of *Chronicle of Saint-Martial de Limoges*, ed. Henri Duplès-Agier (Paris: Renouard, 1874), p. 69, relates, "Eleanor, Queen of the English, died. She was buried at Fontevraud," but he does not observe that she died at the abbey.

125. The chronicler of Saint-Aubin d'Angers writes, in *Annales Sancti Albini Andegavensis*, in *Recueil d'annales Angevines et Vendômoises*, ed. Louis Halphen (Paris: Alphonse Picard, 1903), pp. 1–49, "Item Eleanor, formerly Queen of England and mother of the King, withdrew in death in Poitou," *Chroniques des églises d'Anjou*, ed. Paul Marchegay and Emile Mabille (Paris: Renouard, 1869), p. 52.

126. Matthew Paris, *Historia Anglorum*, vol. 2, p. 102, claims that Eleanor died in the Cistercian Abbey of Beaulieu, in Hampshire.

127. Ralph of Coggeshall, *Chronicon Anglicanum*, p. 144; *Continuatio Chronici Willelmi de Novoburgo ad annum 1298*, p. 507; *Annales de Margan*, ed. Henry Richards Luard, in *Annales monastici*, 5 vols., RS, vol. 36 (London: Longman, 1864), vol. 1, pp. 1–40, at pp. 26–27.

128. *Annales Monasterii de Waverleia*, p. 256.

129. *Rotuli litterarum patentium in turri Londinensi asservati*, ed. Thomas Duffus Hardy (London: G. Eyre and A. Spottiswoode, 1835), pp. 54a–b.

130. See Paul Webster, *King John and Religion* (Woodbridge, UK: Boydell Press, 2015), pp. 32, 93–94.

131. Gascony alone, under the command of the Archbishop of Bordeaux, remained independent of the French crown.

132. Polydore Vergil, *Anglica Historia*, XV, 8.

133. *Annales Sancti Albini Andegavenis*, p. 21.

134. On the identification of these kings, see Alain Erlande-Brandenburg, "Le gisant d'Aliénor d'Aquitaine," in *Aliénor d'Aquitaine [exposition, Abbaye de Fontevraud, 2004]*, ed. Martin Aurell (Nantes: 303, 2004), pp. 175–79.

135. Erwin Panofsky, *Tomb Sculpture: Four Lectures on Its Changing Aspects from Ancient Egypt to Bernini*, ed. H. W. Jansen (New York: Harry N. Abrams, 1964), p. 57. The *gisants* are also among the first full, three-dimensional depictions of living or recently deceased rulers from this time. See Kathleen Nolan, "The Queen's Choice: Eleanor of Aquitaine and the Tombs at Fontevraud," in *Eleanor of Aquitaine*, ed. Wheeler and Parsons, pp. 377–405, at p. 382.

136. Alain Erlande-Brandenburg identifies Eleanor as the primary instigator of the construction of the "Cemetery of Kings" in a series of books and articles, including "Le 'cimitière des rois' à Fontevrault," *Congrès archéologique de France* 122 (Paris: Société française d'archéologie, 1964): 482–92; *Les rois à Fontevrault: Henri II, Richard Coeur de Lion, Aliénor, Isabelle d'Angoulême: Mort, sépulture et sculpture (1189–1204)* (Fontevraud: Centre Culturel de l'Ouest, 1979); *La figuration des morts dans la chrétienté médiévale jusqu'à la fin du premier quart du XIVe siècle (Colloque, 26–28 mai 1988, Abbaye royale de Fontevraud)*, ed. Roger Grégoire (Fontevraud: Centre culturel de Fontevraud, 1989), pp. 3–12, at p. 4; and "Les cimitières royaux en France à l'époque gothique," *Hortus Artium Medievalium* 10 (2004): 43–54, at p. 47. Michael Clanchy, in "Images of Ladies with Prayer Books: What Do They Signify?" *The Church and the Book* 38 (2004): 106–22, at p. 116, agrees, as does Kathleen Nolan, in *Queens in Stone and Silver: The Creation of a Visual Imagery of Queenship in Capetian France* (New York: Palgrave Macmillan, 2009), p. 112.

137. Roger of Howden, *Chronica*, vol. 2, p. 367.

138. Loraine N. Simmons, "The Abbey Church at Fontevraud in the Later Twelfth Century: Anxiety, Authority, and Architecture in the Female Spiritual Life," *Gesta* 31 (1992): 99–107.

139. See Erlande-Brandenburg, "Les cimitières royaux en France"; and Simmons, "The Abbey Church at Fontevraud," p. 105. Nicquet, relying on the records of Father Lardier and a map of the abbey church from 1760, states that the *gisants* were originally located in the northern arm of the transept, near the western column.

140. See Walter, *The Profession of Widowhood*, p. 188; and Nolan, "The Queen's Choice," p. 378.

141. See Erlande-Brandenburg, *Les rois à Fontevrault*. Adelaide of Maurienne, Louis's mother, planned her tomb at the Benedictine monastery for women of Saint Peter in Montmartre, most likely when Eleanor was still her daughter-in-law.

142. *Clypeus nascentis Fontebraldensis Ordinis*, vol. 2, p. 158.

143. See Erlande-Brandenburg, "Le 'cimitière des rois' à Fontevrault," p. 492; *Les rois à Fontevrault*, p. 20; and "La sépulture funéraire vers les années 1200: Les gisants de Fontevrault," in *The Year 1200: A Symposium* (New York: Metropolitan Museum of Art, 1975), pp. 561–77, at p. 566; as well as Nolan, in *Queens in Stone and Silver*, p. 111.

144. Erlande-Brandenburg, "Le 'cimitière des rois' à Fontevrault," p. 492.

145. Roger of Howden, *Chronica*, vol. 4, p. 96.

146. William of Puylaurens, *Chronique*, 5, pp. 46.

147. *Clypeus nascentis Fontebraldensis Ordinis*, vol. 2, p. 161.

148. Francis Sandford states, in *A Genealogical History of the Kings of England and Monarchs of Great Britain* (London: Tho. Newcomb, 1677), p. 71, that Joan was buried "under a marble, upon which her effigies was carved."

149. Raymond VII's will is reproduced in De Vic and Vaissete, *HGL*, vol. 8, col. 1255.

150. Nicquet, *Histoire de l'Ordre de Font-Evraud*, III, 7, p. 256.

151. In 1910, Lucien Magne found four coffins at Fontevraud, one of which was determined to be Raymond VII's, as he recounted in "Rapport sur les tombeaux trouvés dans le transept de l'église abbatiale de Fontevrault, le 14 juin 1919," *Congrès archéologique, Angers et Saumur* (1910), vol. 2, pp. 154-57.

152. Roger of Howden, *Gesta Regis Henrici secundi*, vol. 2, p. 71.

153. Hallam, "Royal Burial and the Cult of Kingship in France and England," p. 361.

154. See Alain Erlande-Brandenburg, *Le roi est mort: Etude sur les funérailles, les sépultures et les tombeaux des rois de France jusqu'à la fin du XIIIe siècle* (Paris: Arts et Métiers Graphiques, 1975), p. 24.

155. *Grandes chroniques de France*, ed. Paulin Paris, 6 vols. (Paris: Techener Librairie, 1836-38), vol. 1, 64, col. 1019.

156. Panofsky, *Tomb Sculpture*, p. 57.

157. See André Vauchez, "Le devenir du corps après la mort chez les théologiens du XIIe siècle," p. 274; and Paul Binski, *Medieval Death: Ritual and Representation* (Ithaca: Cornell University Press, 1996), pp. 93-94.

158. See Binski, *Medieval Death*, p. 103.

159. Honorius of Autun, *Elucidarium*, *PL*, vol. 172, III, 11, col. 1166.

160. Honorius of Autun, *Elucidarium*, *PL*, vol. 172, III, 16, col. 1169.

161. The early engravings of the Fontevraud effigies—by Roger de Gaignières in the seventeenth century and Bernard de Montfaucon in the eighteenth—show Eleanor holding the book at the same angle we see today. In Charles A. Stothard's 1816 drawing of the effigy, in *The Monumental Effigies of Great Britain* (London, C. A. Stothard, 1817-32), plates 4 and 5, Eleanor's hands and the book have disappeared. Michael Clanchy, in "Images of Ladies with Prayer Books," pp. 117-18, interprets the book we see now, with its realistic binding and leafed folios, as a nineteenth-century restoration of the original sculpture rather than a wholesale replacement. See also Nolan, *Queens in Stone and Silver*, p. 112.

162. See Clanchy, "Images of Ladies with Prayer Books," pp. 115-16.

163. See Nolan, *Queens in Stone and Silver*, p. 112.

164. Lejeune, "Rôle littéraire d'Aliénor d'Aquitaine et de sa famille," p. 49; Binski, in *Medieval Death*, p. 101.

165. See Susan Bell, "Medieval Women Book Owners: Arbiters of Lay Piety and Ambassadors of Culture," *Signs* 7 (1982): 742-68; rpt. *Women and Power in the Middle Ages* (Athens, GA: University of Georgia Press, 1988), pp. 149-87; David N. Bell, *What Nuns Read: Books and Libraries in Medieval English Nunneries* (Kalamazoo, MI: Cistercian Publications, 1995); and David N. Bell, "What Nuns Read: The State of the Question," in *The Culture of Medieval English Monasticism*, ed. James G. Clark (Woodbridge, UK: Boydell & Brewer, 2007), pp. 113-33.

166. On Eleanor's seals, see Nolan, *Queens in Stone and Silver*, pp. 78-86.

167. Nolan, *Queens in Stone and Silver*, p. 213.

168. Nolan, "The Queen's Choice," p. 394.

169. *Grand cartulaire de Fontevraud*, Paris, Bibliothèque nationale de France, Manuscrits, nouv. acq. lat. 2414, fol. 71v.

170. The mortuary roll states that Angelucia died on Sunday, October 9, but it makes no mention of the year (which could have been 1166, 1177, 1183, or 1188, as those were years when October 9 fell on a Sunday). As Jocelyn Wogan-Browne writes, in "Dead to the World? Death and the Maiden Revisited in Medieval Women's Convent Culture," in *Guidance for Women in*

Twelfth-Century Convents, trans. Vera Morton (Cambridge: D. S. Brewer, 2003), pp. 157–80, at pp. 169–70, the cyclical anniversaries of the deaths of those attached to Fontevraud, like the anniversaries of the death and Resurrection of Jesus Christ, are "more important than the linear chronology of historical time, and provide . . . the framework within which the latter is experienced."

171. In 1956, the community of Chemillé was absorbed into that of the Benedictine sisters of Saint Bathilda of Vanves. But the Cistercian Abbey of Saint Mary of Boulaur is thriving as of today, with twenty-five nuns.

172. Religieuses de Sainte-Marie de Fontevrault, *Histoire de l'Ordre de Fontevrault*, vol. 1, pp. vi–vii.

173. Religieuses de Sainte-Marie de Fontevrault, *Histoire de l'Ordre de Fontevrault*, vol. 2, p. 66.

174. Religieuses de Sainte-Marie de Fontevrault, *Histoire de l'Ordre de Fontevrault*, vol. 2, p. 80.

CHAPTER SIX

1. On the complex status of women kept in custody, see Gwen Seabourne, *Imprisoning Medieval Women: The Non-Judicial Confinement and Abduction of Women in England, c. 1170–1509* (Farnham, UK: Ashgate Publishing, 2011).

2. William of Newburgh, *Historia rerum Anglicarum*, vol. 1, III, 26, p. 280.

3. Ralph Niger, *Chronica*, pp. 167–68.

4. James Goldman, *The Lion in Winter: A Play* (New York: Random House, 1966). All references in this chapter will be to this play. If a citation from *The Lion in Winter* does not accompany a quotation, it is because the line appears in the 1968 film but not in the play.

5. According to Anselme de Sainte-Marie, in *Histoire généalogique et chronologique de la maison royale de France*, 9 vols., 3rd ed. (Paris: Compagnie des Librairies, 1726–33), vol. 1 p. 77, which many historians have followed, Alys was born in 1170 and was therefore the daughter of Adela of Champagne, Louis's third wife. But Alys was in fact born in 1160, which means that she must have been Constance of Castile's child.

6. The jurors of Corfham, one of Walter's manors, attested in 1274, in *Rotuli Hundredorum Temp. Hen. III et Ed. I*, 2 vols. (n.p.: n.p., 1812–18), vol. 2, pp. 93–94, that this land had once been part of the royal domain but that "King Henry . . . gave [it] to [Walter] de Clifford for love of his daughter Rosamund." This record suggests that the liaison between the king and this maiden had become common knowledge.

7. Robert of Gloucester, writing in the mid- to late thirteenth century, in *The Metrical Chronicle of Robert of Gloucester*, ed. William Aldis Wright, 2 vols., RS, vol. 86 (London: Longman, 1887), vol. 2, at vv. 9856–59, confirms that Rosamund was buried in Godstow.

8. *The Latin Cartulary of Godstow Abbey*, ed. Emilie Amt (Oxford: Oxford University Press, 2014), no. 213, p. 114; no. 214, p. 115; no. 684, p. 317. This Latin cartulary was compiled in 1403–4 and translated into *The English Register of Godestow Nunnery, near Oxford, Written about 1450*, ed. Andrew Clark (London: Kegan Paul, Trench, Trübner & Co., 1911).

9. *The Latin Cartulary of Godstow Abbey*, no. 681, p. 315.

10. See *The Latin Cartulary of Godstow Abbey*, no. 8, p. 10.

11. For a listing of Henry's gifts to Godstow, see *The Latin Cartulary of Godstow Abbey*, p. xxviii n. 69 and no. 68, p. 45.

12. See Henry Knighton's *Chronicon* (before 1396); John Brompton's *Chronicon* (c. 1436); and *Dives et pauper* (1493).

13. See Charles Brifaut's *Rosamonde, poème en trois chants suivie de poésies diverses* (1813) and Thomas Miller's *Fair Rosamond, or the Days of King Henry II* (1839).

14. See Thomas Hull's *Henry the second: or, the fall of Rosamond. A Tragedy* (1774); Emile de Bonnechose's *Rosemonde, tragédie en cinq actes et en vers* (1826); and Charles Algernon Swinburne's *Rosamond*.

15. See Thomas Clayton's *Rosamond*, which was based on Thomas May's *The Death of Rosamond* (early 1600s); Thomas Arne's *Rosamond* (1733), which was based on Joseph Addison's *Rosamond* (1707); Gaetano Donizetti's *Rosmonda d'Inghilterra* (1834); and John Barnett's *Fair Rosamond* (1837). For a full overview of literary depictions of Rosamund, see Virgil B. Heltzel, *Fair Rosamund: A Study of the Development of a Literary Theme* (Evanston, IL: Northwestern University Press, 1947).

16. See Marie-Philippe Coupin de la Couperie's *Queen Eleanor and Rosamund* (1826), Arthur Hughes's *Fair Rosamund* (1854), Frederick Sandys's *Queen Eleanor* (1858), Edward Burne-Jones's *Beautiful Rosamund and Queen Eleanor* (1862), Evelyn De Morgan's *Queen Eleanor and the Fair Rosamund* (1901–2), John William Waterhouse's *Fair Rosamund* (1917), and Frank Cadogan Cowper's *Fair Rosamund and Queen Eleanor* (1920).

17. Gerald of Wales, *Instruction for a Ruler*, III, 2, p. 574.

18. See Giraut de Bornelh and King Alfonso II of Aragon, "Be·m plairia, Seingner En Reis," in *Troubadour "Tensos" and "Partimens,"* vol. 2, pp. 700–703.

19. Ranulph Higden, *Polychronicon*, ed. Churchill Babington, RS, vol. 7–8, 9 vols. (London: Longmans, 1865), vol. 8, VII, 22, pp. 51–54; trans. John of Trevisa as Ranulph Higden, *Polychronicon*, VII, 22, pp. 55–55.

20. For discussion of labyrinths at this time, see Penelope Reed Doob, *The Idea of the Labyrinth from Classical Antiquity through the Middle Ages* (Ithaca: Cornell University Press, 1990), pp. 106–7.

21. In Renaissance accounts, the place where Rosamund is hidden became a "bower," which was originally understood to be a rustic abode or an inner chamber in a mansion and eventually envisioned as a shady recess covered with foliage. Raphael Holinshed, in *Holinshed's Chronicles*, ed. Ellis, vol. 2, p. 200, refers to it as a "knot garden" or "maze," like those that were being constructed out of hedges at this time.

22. Roger of Howden, *Gesta Regis Henrici secundi*, vol. 2, pp. 231–32.

23. Roger of Howden, *Chronica*, vol. 3, p. 168.

24. Higden, *Polychronicon*, vol. 8, VII, 22, p. 54.

25. Gerald of Wales, *Instruction for a Ruler*, II, 4, pp. 458–60. Cf. Claudian, *Panegyricus dictus Honorio Augusto quartum consuli*, 299–300.

26. Roger of Howden, *Gesta Regis Henrici secundi*, vol. 2, pp. 231–32.

27. Gerald of Wales, *Instruction for a Ruler*, II, 4, p. 458.

28. Higden, *Polychronicon*, vol. 8, VII, 22, p. 54; Higden, *Polychronicon*, trans. John of Trevisa, vol. 8, VII, h. 22, p. 55.

29. *Dives et pauper*, the Sixth Commandment, ch. 14, quoted in *Life and Times of Anthony Wood, Antiquary of Oxford, 1632–1695, Described by Himself, Collected from his Diaries and Other Papers*, ed. Andrew Clark, 5 vols. (Oxford: Clarendon Press, 1891–1900), vol. 1, p. 341n2.

30. Samuel Daniel, "The Complaint of Rosamund," in *Poems and a Defence of Ryme*, ed. Arthur Colby Sprague (Cambridge, MA: Harvard University Press, 1930), pp. 39–63, vv. 337–40.

31. Daniel, "The Complaint of Rosamund," vv. 342–43.

32. Daniel, "The Complaint of Rosamund," vv. 434–38.

33. Daniel, "The Complaint of Rosamund," v. 441.

34. William Warner, *Albions England* (London: By Thomas Orwin, 1592), VIII, 41, p. 201.

35. Thomas Deloney, "A Mournfull Dittie, on the Death of *Rosamond*, King Henry the Second's Concubine" (also entitled "The Faire Lady Rosamund") in *The Works of Thomas Deloney*, ed. Francis Oscar Mann (Oxford: Clarendon Press, 1912), pp. 297–302, at vv. 161–68.

36. Daniel, "The Complaint of Rosamund," vv. 292–94.

37. Daniel, "The Complaint of Rosamund," vv. 381–82.

38. Daniel, "The Complaint of Rosamund," vv. 405–6.

39. Daniel, "The Complaint of Rosamund," vv. 421–24.

40. Daniel, "The Complaint of Rosamund," vv. 412–13.

41. Daniel, "The Complaint of Rosamund," vv. 598–99.

42. Daniel, "The Complaint of Rosamund," vv. 61, 214, 733.

43. Thomas May, "The Death of Rosamond," in *Specimens of the British Poets*, ed. Thomas Campbell (Philadelphia: Henry Carey Baird, 1854), pp. 252–53, at pp. 252–53.

44. Warner, *Albions England*, VIII, 41, p. 200.

45. Warner, *Albions England*, VIII, 41, p. 201.

46. May, "The Death of Rosamond," p. 252.

47. Deloney, "A Mournfull Dittie, on the Death of *Rosamond*," vv. 187–88. I have translated the word "wight" as "creature."

48. In the mid-fourteenth century, the *Croniques de London depuis l'an 44 Hen. III jusqu'à l'an 17 Edw. III*, ed. George James Aungier (London: Camden Society, 1844), p. 3, alleges for the first time that Eleanor killed Rosamund (in a remarkably gruesome way), but it is conflating her with the unpopular Eleanor of Provence, the wife of Henry III.

49. May, "The Death of Rosamond," p. 252.

50. Daniel, "The Complaint of Rosamund," vv. 589–95; Warner, *Albions England*, VIII, 41, p. 200; Deloney, "A Mournfull Dittie, on the Death of *Rosamond*," v. 173; May, "The Death of Rosamond," p. 252.

51. Daniel, "The Complaint of Rosamund," vv. 596–602.

52. Daniel, "The Complaint of Rosamund," vv. 582–88.

53. Deloney, "A Mournfull Dittie, on the Death of *Rosamond*," v. 135.

54. Warner, *Albions England*, VIII, 41, p. 200.

55. Warner, *Albions England*, VIII, 41, p. 201.

56. Holinshed, *Chronicles*, vol. 2, p. 149.

57. Holinshed, *Chronicles*, vol. 2, p. 159.

58. Deloney, "The Imprisonment of Queen Elenor, wife to King Henrie the Second," in *The Works of Thomas Deloney*, ed. Mann, pp. 397–99, vv. 1–6.

59. Michael Drayton, "Henry to Rosamund," in *The Works of the English Poets from Chaucer to Cowper*, ed. Samuel Johnson, 21 vols. (London: H. Hughs and John Nichols, 1810), vol. 4, pp. 58–60.

60. Deloney, "The Imprisonment of Queen Elenor," vv. 21–24.

61. Daniel, "The Complaint of Rosamund," vv. 544–81.

62. May, "The Death of Rosamond," p. 252.

63. Daniel, "The Complaint of Rosamund," in *The Complete Works in Verse and Prose of Samuel Daniel*, ed. Alexander B. Grosart, 4 vols. (London: Hazell, Watson, & Viney, 1885), vol. 1, pp. 81–113, at v. 637. This edition reproduces a different version of the poem than Sprague's.

64. May, "The Death of Rosamond," p. 253.

65. Roger of Howden, *Chronica*, vol. 1, p. 218.

66. Roger of Howden, *Chronica*, vol. 1, p. 218.

67. *The Correspondence of Thomas Becket*, vol. 1, Letter 24 (1165), from John of Salisbury to Thomas Becket, p. 70. Another manuscript has "Saresberie" instead of "sanam."

68. *The Correspondence of Thomas Becket*, vol. 2, Letter 297 (after June 14, 1170), from a loyal friend to Thomas Becket, p. 1252.

69. *The Correspondence of Thomas Becket*, vol. 2, Letter 296 (before June 14, 1170), from a friend to Thomas Becket, p. 1246.

70. Robert of Torigni, *Appendice ad Sigebertum*, p. 318.

71. Gervase of Canterbury, *Chronica*, p. 208.

72. Roger of Howden, *Chronica*, vol. 2, p. 143.

73. Gerald of Wales, *Instruction for a Ruler*, III, 2, p. 574.

74. Roger of Howden, *Chronica*, vol. 3, p. 99.

75. Thomas de Burton, in *Chronica Monasterii de Melsa*, ed. Edward Augustus Bond, RS, vol. 43, 2 vols. (London: Longman, 1866), vol. 1, 26, p. 256, a fifteenth-century Cistercian chronicler, claims that the child was a daughter, who died young.

76. Gerald of Wales, *Instruction for a Ruler*, III, 2, p. 574.

77. John of Salisbury, *The Letters of John of Salisbury*, vol. 2, *The Later Letters (1163–1180)*, ed. W. J. Millor and C. N. L. Brooke (London: Thomas Nelson, 1955–79), Letter 279, to Master Lombardus (July 1168), p. 602. Odo of Porhoët's daughter Alix became a nun of Fontevraud and eventually abbess between 1209 and 1218.

78. Ralph Niger, *Chronica*, p. 168.

79. Gerald of Wales, *Instruction for a Ruler*, III, 2, p. 574.

80. Roger of Howden, *Gesta Regis Henrici secundi*, vol. 1, p. 305.

81. *La continuation de Guillaume de Tyr*, 110, p. 111.

82. Peter of Blois, *Epistolae*, Letter 153, to Henry II (1173), col. 447.

83. William the Breton, *Philippide*, vv. 448–49.

84. Roger of Howden, *Chronica*, vol. 3, p. 99.

85. Modern scholars influenced by psychological theories of the twentieth century, like Elizabeth A. R. Brown, in "Eleanor of Aquitaine: Parent, Queen, and Duchess," in *Eleanor of Aquitaine: Patron and Politician*, pp. 9–23, and "Eleanor of Aquitaine Reconsidered: The Woman and Her Seasons," in *Eleanor of Aquitaine: Lord and Lady*, pp. 1–54, have criticized Eleanor as a neglectful mother. But other scholars have pointed out that, if anything, Eleanor was a more attentive mother than other women of her class. See Ralph V. Turner, "Eleanor of Aquitaine and Her Children: An Inquiry into Medieval Family Attachment," *Journal of Medieval History* 14 (1988): 21–35.

86. Homer B. Petty, "Katharine Hepburn in *The Lion in Winter*," in *Close-Up: Great Cinematic Performances*, ed. Murray Pomerance and Kyle Stevens, 2 vols. (Edinburgh: Edinburgh University Press, 2018), vol. 1, pp. 56–66, at pp. 57–58.

87. See Michael R. Evans's discussion of Katharine Hepburn as Eleanor in *Inventing Eleanor: The Medieval and Post-Medieval Image of Eleanor of Aquitaine* (London: Bloomsbury, 2014), pp. 111–17.

88. "Obituary: Katharine Hepburn," *BBC News*, June 30, 2003.

CONCLUSION

1. See Jane Martindale, "Eleanor of Aquitaine," p. 22.

2. See Ralph Niger, *Chronica*, p. 168; William of Newburgh, *Historia rerum Anglicarum*, vol.

1, III, 26, p. 280; Gerald of Wales, *Instruction for a Ruler*, III, 2, p. 574; and John of Salisbury, *The Letters of John of Salisbury*, vol. 2, Letter 279 (July 1168), to Master Lombardus, p. 602.

3. See Roger of Howden, *Gesta Regis Henrici secundi*, vol. 1, p. 292; and Adam of Eynsham, *Magna Vita Sancti Hugonis*, vol. 1, V, 6, p. 255.

4. See a *razo* for Bertran de Born *fils*'s "Cant vei lo temps renovelar," in *Biographies des troubadours*, pp. 71–72; and *History of William Marshal*, vol. 3, vv. 11984–12006. See also Ralph V. Turner, *King John: England's Evil King* (Stroud, UK: History Press, 2009), p. 166.

5. See Gerald of Wales, *Instruction for a Ruler*, p. 377.

6. *Carmina Burana*, ed. David A. Traill, Dumbarton Oaks Medieval Library, 2 vols. (Cambridge, MA: Harvard University Press, 2018), vol. 2, 145a, p. 142. Traill retains the original "king [*künic*]" in the *Carmina Burana* manuscript (Munich clm 4660 and 4660a), instead of the "queen [*künigen*]" to which this verse is usually corrected.

7. Stephen of Rouen, *Draco Normannicus*, vv. 116–17.

8. Felix Liebermann, "A Contemporary Manuscript of the *Leges Anglorum Londoniis collectae*," *English Historical Review* 112 (October 1913): 732–45, at p. 742.

9. Matthew Paris, *Historia Anglorum*, vol. 2, p. 102.

10. *The Chronicle of Richard of Devizes*, p. 25.

11. William of Malmesbury, *Gesta regum Anglorum*, III, 256, p. 474. William is speaking of Richildis, Countess of Hainault, the widow of Baldwin VI, Count of Flanders.

12. James Goldman writes of Eleanor in his stage notes to *The Lion in Winter*, I, 2, pp. 10–11, "She is the most unusual thing: a genuinely feminine woman thoroughly capable of holding her own in a man's world."

SELECTED
BIBLIOGRAPHY

PRIMARY SOURCES

Adam of Eynsham. *Magna Vita Sancti Hugonis: The Life of St. Hugh of Lincoln*. Ed. Decima L. Douie and David Hugh Farmer. 2 vols. Oxford: Nelson, 1961–62.

Ambroise. *The History of the Holy War: Ambroise's "Estoire de la guerre sainte."* Ed. Marianne Ailes and Malcolm Barber. 2 vols. Woodbridge, UK: Boydell Press, 2003.

Andreas Capellanus on Love. Ed. P. G. Walsh. London: Gerald Duckworth, 1982.

Annales monastici. Ed. Henry Richards Luard. 5 vols. RS, vol. 36. London: Longman, 1864–69.

Benedict of Peterborough (*see also* Roger of Howden).

Benedict of Peterborough. *Miracula Sancti Thomae Cantuariensis*. In *Materials for the History of Thomas Becket, Archbishop of Canterbury*. Ed. James Craigie Robertson. 7 vols. RS, vol. 67, issue 2. London: Longman, 1875–88, vol. 2, pp. 21–282.

Bernart de Ventadorn. *Bernard de Ventadour, troubadour du XIIe siècle: Chansons d'amour*. Ed. Moshé Lazar. Paris: Klincksieck, 1966. Rpt., Moustier Ventadour: Carrefour Ventadour, 2001.

———. *The Songs of Bernart de Ventadorn*. Ed. Stephen G. Nichols, Jr., John A. Galm, A. Bartlett Giamatti, Roger J. Porter, Seth J. Wolitz, and Claudette M. Charbonneau. Chapel Hill: University of North Carolina Press, 1965.

Bertran de Born. *The Poems of the Troubadour Bertran de Born*. Ed. William D. Paden, Jr., T. Senkovitch, and P. H. Stäblein. Berkeley: University of California Press, 1986.

Biographies des troubadours: Textes provençaux des XIIIe et XIVe siècles. Ed. Jean Boutière and A.-H. Schutz. Toulouse: E. Privat; Columbus: Ohio State University Press, 1950.

Caesarius of Heisterbach. *Dialogus miraculorum*. Ed. Joseph Strange. 2 vols. Cologne: H. Lempertz, 1851.

Calendar of Documents Preserved in France Illustrative of the History of Great Britain and Ireland. Vol. 1. *AD 918–1206*. Ed. J. Horace Round. London: Eyre and Spottiswoode, 1899.

Carmina Burana. Ed. David A. Traill. 2 vols. Dumbarton Oaks Medieval Library. Cambridge, MA: Harvard University Press, 2018.

Cercamon. *The Poetry of Cercamon and Jaufre Rudel*. Ed. George Wolf and Roy Rosenstein. New York: Garland Publishing, 1983.

"Chartes de Fontevraud concernant l'Aunis et La Rochelle [first article]." Ed. Paul Marchegay. *Bibliothèque de l'Ecole des Chartes* 19 (1858): 132–70.

"Chartes de Fontevraud concernant l'Aunis et La Rochelle [second article]." Ed. Paul Marchegay. *Bibliothèque de l'Ecole des Chartes* 19 (1858): 321–347.

Chronicle of the Abbey of Morigny: A Translation of the "Chronicle" of the Abbey of Morigny, France, c. 1100–1150. Ed. Richard Cusimano. Lewiston, ME: Edwin Mellen Press, 2003.

Chronicon Turonese magnum. Ed. André Salmon. In *Recueil de chroniques de Touraine*. Tours: Imprimerie Ladevéze, 1854, pp. 64–161.

[*Chronique de Normandie*]. Paris, Bibliothèque de l'Arsenal, Manuscrits, 3516, fol. 304v–315r.

Chronique de Saint-Maixent (751–1140). Ed. Jean Verdon. Les classiques de l'histoire de France au Moyen Age. Paris: Les Belles Lettres, 1979.

Chroniques d'Anjou. Ed. Paul Marchegay and André Salmon. Société de l'Histoire de France. Paris: Renouard, 1856.

Chroniques de Saint-Martial de Limoges. Ed. Henri Duplès-Agier. Paris: Renouard, 1874.

Chroniques des comtes d'Anjou et des seigneurs d'Amboise. Ed. Louis Halphen and René Poupardin. Paris: A. Picard, 1913.

Epistolae Cantuarienses: The Letters of the Prior and Convent of Christ Church, Canterbury, from A.D. 1187 to A.D. 1199. Ed. William Stubbs. In *Chronicles and Memorials of the Reign of Richard I*. 2 vols. RS, vol. 38. London: Longman, 1865, vol. 2, pp. 1–540.

Foedera, conventiones, litterae, et cujuscunque generis acta publica inter reges Angliae, et alios quosvis imperatores, reges, pontifices, principes, vel communitates. Ed. Thomas Rymer and Robert Sanderson. 20 vols. London: n.p., 1704–35. Rev. ed., George Holmes, 17 vols. The Hague: Apud Joannem Nealme, 1735–47.

Fragmentum historicum vitam Ludovici VII summatim complectens. RHF, ed. Delisle, vol. 12, pp. 285–87.

Geoffrey du Breuil of Vigeois. *Chronicon Lemovicense: Ex chronico Gaufredi Coenobitae, Monasterii S. Martialis Lemovicensis ac Prioris Vosiensis Coenobii. RHF*, ed. Delisle, vol. 12, pp. 421–50 (for the years 1060–1182); vol. 18, cols. 211–23 (for the years 1183–84).

Geoffrey of Auxerre. *Fragmenta ex vita tertia Sancti Bernardi. PL*, vol. 185, cols. 523–30.

———. *S. Bernardi vita prima, liber tertius-quintus. PL*, vol. 185, cols. 303–68.

Geoffrey of Clairvaux. *See* Geoffrey of Auxerre.

Geoffrey of Vinsauf. *See* Richard de Templo.

Gerald of Wales. *Giraldi Cambrensis opera*. Ed. J. S. Brewer, James F. Dimock, and George F. Warner. 8 vols. RS, vol. 21. London: Longman, 1861–91.

———. *Instruction for a Ruler / De principis instructione*. Ed. Robert Bartlett. Oxford: Clarendon Press, 2018.

Gerhoh of Reichersberg. *De investigatione Antichristi*. Ed. Jodo Stülz. *Archiv für Kunde österreichischer Geschichts-Quellen* 20 (1859): 127–88.

Gervase of Canterbury. *Chronica*. In *The Historical Works of Gervase of Canterbury*. Ed. William Stubbs. 2 vols. RS, vol. 73. London: Longman, 1879–80, vol. 1, pp. 1–594.

———. *Gesta regum*. In *The Historical Works of Gervase of Canterbury*. Ed. William Stubbs. 2 vols. RS, vol. 73. London: Longman, 1879–80, vol. 2, pp. 3–324.

Grand cartulaire de Fontevraud: Pancarta et cartularium Abbatissae et Ordinis Fontis Ebraudi. Ed. Jean-Marc Bienvenu, with Robert Favreau and Georges Pon. 2 vols. Poitiers: Société des Antiquaires de l'ouest, 2000–2005.

Hélinand of Froidmont. *Chronicon. PL*, vol. 212, cols. 971–1082.

Henry II. *The Letters and Charters of Henry II: King of England, 1154–1189*. Ed. Nicholas Vincent. 7 vols. Oxford: Oxford University Press, 2020.

[*Histoire des rois d'Angleterre*]. Cambridge University Library, Manuscripts, Ii.6.24, fol. 95r–100v.

History of William Marshal. Ed. A. J. Holden. 3 vols. London: Anglo-Norman Text Society, 2002.

Itinerarium peregrinorum et Gesta Regis Ricardi. See Richard de Templo.

Jehan de la Gogue. *Saladin.* In *Esquisses biographiques du département de l'Indre; ou, Aperçu historique sur la principauté de Déols, Baronnie, comté et marquisat et enfin duché de Chateauroux (ancien Bas-Berri).* Ed. Amadour Grillon des Chapelles. 2nd ed., 3 vols. Paris: Benjamin Duprat, 1864–65, vol. 3, pp. 314–83. Reprinted in *Saladin: Suite et fin du deuxième cycle de la croisade.* Ed. Larry S. Crist. Geneva: Librairie Droz, 1972, pp. 219–69.

John of Salisbury. *Historia pontificalis / Memoirs of the Papal Court.* Ed. Marjorie Chibnall. London: Thomas Nelson, 1956. Rpt., Oxford: Clarendon Press, 1986.

———. *The Letters of John of Salisbury.* Vol. 1. *The Early Letters (1153–1161).* Ed. W. J. Millor and H. E. Butler; rev. ed., C. N. L. Brooke. Vol. 2, *The Later Letters (1163–1180).* Ed. W. J. Millor and C. N. L. Brooke. London: Thomas Nelson, 1955–79.

Lambert of Waterlos. *Ex Lamberti Waterlosii chronico Cameracensi Autbertino. RHF,* vol. 13, pp. 497–532.

Layettes du trésor des Chartes. Ed. Alexandre Teulet, Joseph de Laborde, Elie Berger, and Henri François Delaborde. 5 vols. Paris: Henri Plon, 1863–1909.

The Letters and Charters of Henry II: King of England, 1154–1189. Ed. Nicholas Vincent. 7 vols. Oxford: Oxford University Press, 2020–23.

Marcabru: A Critical Edition. Ed. Simon Gaunt, Ruth Harvey, and Linda Paterson. Cambridge: D. S. Brewer, 2000.

Matthew Paris. *Chronica majora.* Ed. Henry Richards Luard. 7 vols. RS, vol. 57. London: Longman, 1872–83.

———. *Historia Anglorum, sive, ut vulgo dicitur, historia minor.* Ed. Frederic Madden. 3 vols. RS, vol. 44. London: Longman, 1866–69.

Minstrel of Reims. *Récits d'un ménestrel de Reims.* Ed. Natalis de Wailly. Paris: Renouard, 1876.

Odo of Deuil. *De profectione Ludovici VII in orientem: The Journey of Louis VII to the East.* Ed. Virginia Gingerick Berry. New York: Columbia University Press, 1948.

Peter of Blois. *Epistolae. PL,* vol. 207, cols. 1–559.

———. [Letters from Eleanor of Aquitaine to Pope Celestine III]. In *Variorum ad Coelestinam III epistolae. PL,* vol. 206, cols. 1261–80, at cols. 1262–72.

Philippe Mouskés. *Chronique rimée.* Ed. Frédéric-Auguste-Ferdinand-Thomas Reiffenberg. 2 vols. Brussels: M. Hayez, 1836–38.

Pierre Cochon. *Chronique normande.* Ed. Charles de Robillard de Beaurepaire. Rouen: A. Le Brunment, 1870.

"Queen Eleanor's Confession." In *The Traditional Tunes of the Child Ballads with Their Texts, According to the Extant Records of Great Britain and America.* Ed. Francis James Child. Rev. Bertrand Harris Bronson, 4 vols. Princeton: Princeton University Press, 1959–72, vol. 3, no. 156, pp. 105–6.

Ralph Niger. *Radulfi Nigri chronica / The Chronicles of Ralph Niger.* Ed. Robert Anstruther. London: Printed for the Members of the Caxton Society, 1851.

Ralph of Coggeshall. *Chronicon Anglicanum.* Ed. Joseph Stevenson. RS, vol. 66. London: Longman, 1875, pp. 1–208.

Ralph of Diceto. *Ymagines historiarum.* In *Radulfi de Diceto Decani Lundoniensis opera historica / The Historical Works of Master Ralph of Diceto, Dean of London.* Ed. William Stubbs. 2 vols. RS, vol. 68. London: Longman, 1876, vol. 1, pp. 291–440; vol. 2, pp. 3–176.

Ranulph Higden. *Polychronicon Ranulphi Higden, with Trevisa's Translation.* Vols. 1 and 2, ed. Churchill Babington. Vols. 3 and 4, ed. Joseph Rawson Lumby. RS, vol. 41. London: Longman, 1865–1872.

Recueil d'annales Angevines et Vendômoises. Ed. Louis Halphen. Paris: Alphonse Picard, 1903.

Richard Coer de Lyon. Ed. Peter Larkin. Middle English Texts Series. Kalamazoo, MI: Medieval
  Institute Publications, 2015.

Richard de Templo. *Das "Itinerarium peregrinorum": Eine Zeitgenössische englische Chronik zum
  dritten Kreuzzug in Ursprünglicher Gestalt.* Ed. Hans E. Mayer. Stuttgart: Anton Hiersemann,
  1962.

———. *Itinerarium peregrinorum et Gesta Regis Ricardi.* Ed. William Stubbs. RS, vol. 38. London:
  Longman, 1864 [formerly attributed to Geoffrey of Vinsauf].

Richard FitzNeal. *"Dialogus de Scaccario" / "The Course of the Exchequer" and "Constitutio domus
  regis" / "The Establishment of the Royal Household."* Ed. Charles Johnson, with F. E. L. Carter
  and D. E. Greenway. Oxford: Clarendon Press, 1983.

Richard of Devizes. *The Chronicle of Richard of Devizes of the Time of King Richard the First.* Ed.
  John T. Appleby. London: Thomas Nelson, 1963.

Richard of Poitiers. *Ex chronico Richardi Pictaviensis. RHF,* vol. 12, pp. 411–21.

Rigord. *Gesta Philippi Regis.* In *Oeuvres de Rigord et de Guillaume le Breton: Historiens de Philippe-
  Auguste.* Ed. H. François Delaborde. 2 vols. Paris: Renouard, 1882, vol. 1, pp. 1–167.

Robert of Torigni. *Appendice ad Sigebertum. RHF,* vol. 13, pp. 283–326.

———. *The Chronicle of Robert of Torigni, Abbot of the Monastery of St. Michel-in-Peril-of-the-Sea.*
  In *Chronicles of the Reigns of Stephen, Henry II, and Richard I.* Ed. Richard Howlett. 4 vols. RS,
  vol. 82. London: Longman, 1884–89, vol. 4, pp. 3–315.

Robertus de Monte. *See* Robert of Torigni.

Roger of Howden. *Chronica Magistri Rogeri de Houedene.* Ed. William Stubbs. 4 vols. RS, vol. 51.
  London: Longman, 1868–71.

———. *Gesta Regis Henrici secundi Benedicti Abbatis: The Chronicle of the Reigns of Henry II and
  Richard I, AD 1169–1192.* Ed. William Stubbs. 2 vols. RS, vol. 49. London: Longman, 1867
  [formerly attributed to Benedict of Peterborough].

Roger of Wendover. *Liber qui dicitur Flores historiarum ab anno domini MCLIV annoque Henrici
  Anglorum Regis Secundi primo.* Ed. Henry G. Hewlett. 3 vols. RS, vol. 84. London: Longman,
  1886–89.

Rotuli chartarum in turri Londinensi asservati. Ed. Thomas Duffus Hardy. London: G. Eyre and
  A. Spottiswoode, 1837.

Rotuli litterarum patentium in turri Londinensi asservati. Ed. Thomas Duffus Hardy. London:
  G. Eyre and A. Spottiswoode, 1835.

Saladin. In *Saladin: Suite et fin du deuxième cycle de la croisade.* Ed. Larry S. Crist. Geneva: Librairie Droz, 1972, pp. 21–170.

Stephen of Paris. *Fragmentum historicum de Ludovico VII, Francorum Rege, excerptum ex Stephani
  Pariensis Commentario Ms. in Regulam S. Benedicti. RHF,* vol. 12, pp. 89–91.

Stephen of Rouen. *Draco Normannicus.* In *Chronicles of the Reigns of Stephen, Henry II, and Richard I.* Ed. Richard Howlett. 2 vols. RS, vol. 82. London: Longman, 1885, vol. 2, pp. 585–781.

Suger of Saint-Denis. *Oeuvres,* ed. Françoise Gasparri. 2 vols., Classiques de l'histoire de France au
  Moyen Age 37e and 41e. Paris: Les Belles Lettres, 1996–2001.

———. *Vita Ludovici VI Regis Philippi filii qui Grossus dictus. RHF,* vol. 12, pp. 10–63.

Thomas Agnellus. *Sermo de morte et sepultura Henrici Regis Angliae Junioris.* Ed. Joseph Stevenson.
  RS, vol. 66. London: Longman, 1875, pp. 263–73.

Thomas Becket. *The Correspondence of Thomas Becket, Archbishop of Canterbury (1162–1170).* Ed.
  Anne Duggan. 2 vols. Oxford: Clarendon Press, 2000.

Wace. *Roman de Brut: A History of the British.* Ed. Judith Weiss. Exeter: University of Exeter Press,
  1999.

————. *The Roman de Rou.* Ed. Anthony J. Holden. St. Helier, UK: Société Jersiaise, 2002.

Walter Map. *De nugis curialium / Courtiers' Trifles.* Ed. M. R. James. Rev. C. N. L. Brooke and R. A. B. Mynors. Oxford: Clarendon Press, 1983.

William of Nangis. *Ex Guillelmi Nangii chronico. RHF,* vol. 20, pp. 543–763.

William of Newburgh. *Historia rerum Anglicarum.* In *Chronicles of the Reigns of Stephen, Henry II, and Richard I.* Ed. Richard Howlett. 4 vols. RS, vol. 82. London: Longman, 1884–85, vols. 1 (Books I–IV) and 2 (Book V), pp. 410–500.

————. *The History of English Affairs.* Ed. P. G. Walsh and M. J. Kennedy. 2 vols. Oxford: Aris & Phillips, 1988. Rpt., 2007 (Books I and II).

William of Newburgh, Continuator of. *Continuatio Chronici Willelmi de Novoburgo ad annum 1298.* In *Chronicles of the Reigns of Stephen, Henry II, and Richard I.* Ed. Richard Howlett. 4 vols. RS, vol. 82. London: Longman, 1884–85, vol. 2, pp. 503–83.

William of Tyre. *Chronicon.* Ed. R. B. C. Huygens. 2 vols. CCCM, vol. 63. Turnhout: Brepols, 1986.

————. *Guillaume de Tyr et ses continuateurs: Texte français du XIIIe siècle.* Ed. Paulin Paris. Paris: Firmin Didot, 1879.

William of Tyre, Continuator of. *La continuation de Guillaume de Tyr (1184–1192).* Ed. Margaret R. Morgan. Paris: Librairie orientaliste P. Geuthner, 1982.

William the Breton. *Gesta Philippi Augusti.* Ed. H. François Delaborde. In *Oeuvres de Rigord et de Guillaume le Breton.* 2 vols. Paris: Renouard, 1882–85, vol. 1, pp. 168–320.

————. *Philippide.* Ed. H. François Delaborde. In *Oeuvres de Rigord et de Guillaume le Breton.* 2 vols. Paris: Renouard, 1882–85, vol. 2, pp. 1–385.

SECONDARY SOURCES

Aurell, Martin. "Aliénor d'Aquitaine (1124–1204) et ses historiens: La destruction d'un mythe?" In *Guerre, pouvoir et noblesse au Moyen Age: Mélanges en honneur de Philippe Contamine.* Ed. Jacques Paviot and Jacques Verger. Paris: Presses de l'Université de Paris-Sorbonne, 2000, pp. 43–49.

————. "Aliénor d'Aquitaine en son temps." In *Aliénor d'Aquitaine* [*exposition, Abbaye de Fontevraud, 2004*], ed. Martin Aurell. Nantes: 303, 2004, pp. 6–17.

————, ed. *Aliénor d'Aquitaine* [*exposition, Abbaye de Fontevraud, 2004*]. Nantes: 303, 2004.

————. "Aux origines de la légende noire d'Aliénor d'Aquitaine." In *Royautés imaginaires (XIIe-XVIe siècles): Actes du colloque organisé par le Centre de Recherche d'Histoire Sociale et Culturelle (CHSCO) de l'Université de Paris X-Nanterre (26 au 27 septembre 2003).* Ed. Anne-Hélène Alliot, Gilles Lecuppre, and Lydwine Scordia. Turnhout: Brepols, 2005, pp. 89–102.

Barber, Richard. "Eleanor of Aquitaine and the Media." In *The World of Eleanor of Aquitaine: Literature and Society in Southern France between the Eleventh and Thirteenth Centuries.* Ed. Marcus Bell and Catherine Léglu. Woodbridge, UK: Boydell Press, 2005, pp. 13–28.

Benton, John F. "The Court of Champagne as a Literary Center." *Speculum* 36 (1961): 551–91.

Bezzola, Reto. *Les origines et la formation de la littérature courtoise en Occident (500–1200).* 3 vols. in 5. Paris: Champion, 1954–63.

Bienvenu, Jean-Marie. "Aliénor d'Aquitaine et Fontevraud." *CCM* 29 (1986): 15–27.

————. "Henri II Plantagenêt et Fontevraud." *CCM* 37 (1994): 25–32. Rpt. in *Henri II Plantagenêt et son temps: Actes du Colloque de Fontevraud (29 septembre–1er octobre 1990).* Poitiers: Université de Poitiers, Centre d'Etudes Supérieures de Civilisation Médiévale, pp. 35–32.

Bouchard, Constance Britain. "Eleanor's Divorce from Louis VII: The Uses of Consanguinity." In *Eleanor of Aquitaine: Lord and Lady*. Ed. Bonnie Wheeler and John Carmi Parsons. Basingstoke, UK: Palgrave, 2002, pp. 223–35.

Bourgain, Pascale. "Aliénor d'Aquitaine et Marie de Champagne mises en cause par André le Chapelain." *CCM* 113–14 (1986): 29–36.

Broadhurst, Karen. "Henry II of England and Eleanor of Aquitaine: Patrons of Literature in French?" *Viator* 27 (1996): 53–84.

Brooke, C. N. L. "The Marriage of Henry II and Eleanor of Aquitaine." *Historian: The Magazine for Members of the Historical Association* 20 (1988): 3–8.

Brown, Elizabeth A. R. "Eleanor of Aquitaine: Parent, Queen, and Duchess." In *Eleanor of Aquitaine: Patron and Politician*. Ed. William W. Kibler. Austin: University of Texas Press, 1977, pp. 9–23.

———. "Eleanor of Aquitaine Reconsidered: The Woman and Her Seasons." In *Eleanor of Aquitaine: Lord and Lady*. Ed. Bonnie Wheeler and John Carmi Parsons. Basingstoke, UK: Palgrave, 2002, pp. 1–54.

Brundage, James A. "The Canon Law of Divorce in the Mid-Twelfth Century: Louis VII and Eleanor of Aquitaine." In *Eleanor of Aquitaine: Lord and Lady*. Ed. Bonnie Wheeler and John Carmi Parsons. Basingstoke, UK: Palgrave, 2002, pp. 212–21.

Bull, Marcus, and Catherine Léglu, eds. *The World of Eleanor of Aquitaine: Literature and Society in Southern France between the Eleventh and Thirteenth Centuries*. Woodbridge, UK: Boydell Press, 2005.

Carney, Elizabeth. "Fact and Fiction in 'Queen Eleanor's Confession.'" *Folklore* 95, no. 2 (1984): 167–70.

Castor, Helen. *She-Wolves: The Women Who Ruled England before Elizabeth*. New York: Harper-Perennial, 2011.

Chambers, Frank McMinn. "Some Legends Concerning Eleanor of Aquitaine." *Speculum* 16, no. 4 (1941): 459–68.

Chapman, R. L. "Note on the Demon Queen Eleanor." *Modern Language Association Notes* 70, no. 6 (June 1955): 193–396.

Cheney, C. R. "A Monastic Letter of Fraternity to Eleanor of Aquitaine." *English Historical Review* 51, no. 203 (July 1936): 488–93.

Clypeus nascentis Fontebraldensis Ordinis contra priscos et novos ejus calumniatores. Ed. Jean de La Mainferme. 2 vols. Paris: Georgius and Ludovicus Josse, 1684–88.

Cockerill, Sara. *Eleanor of Aquitaine: Queen of France and England, Mother of Empires*. Stroud, UK: Amberly Publishing, 2019.

DeAragon, RaGena C. "Wife, Widow, and Mother: Some Comparisons between Eleanor of Aragon and Noblewomen of the Anglo-Norman and Angevin World." In *Eleanor of Aquitaine: Lord and Lady*. Ed. Bonnie Wheeler and John Carmi Parsons. Basingstoke, UK: Palgrave, 2002, pp. 97–113.

Duby, Georges. *Dames du XIIe siècle: Héloise, Aliénor, Iseut et quelques autres*. Paris: Gallimard, 1995.

Duggan, Anne J. "On Finding the Voice of Eleanor of Aquitaine." In *Voix des femmes au Moyen Age: Actes du Colloque du Centre d'Etudes Médiévales Anglaises de Paris—Sorbonne (26–27 mars 2010)*. Ed. Leo Martin Carruthers. Paris: Société des anglicistes de l'enseignement supérieur, 2011, pp. 129–58.

Erlande-Brandenburg, Alain. "Le gisant d'Aliénor d'Aquitaine." In *Aliénor d'Aquitaine* [exposition, Abbaye de Fontevraud, 2004]. Ed. Martin Aurell. Nantes: 303, 2004, pp. 174–79.

Evans, Michael R. *Inventing Eleanor: The Medieval and Post-Medieval Image of Eleanor of Aquitaine*. London: Bloomsbury, 2014.

———. "The Missing Queen? Eleanor of Aquitaine in the Early Reign of Louis VII." In *Louis VII and His World*. Ed. Michael L. Bardot and Laurence W. Marvin. Leiden: Brill, 2018, pp. 105–13.

———. "Penthesilea on the Second Crusade: Is Eleanor of Aquitaine the Amazon Queen of Niketas Choniates?" *Crusades* 8 (2009): 23–30.

———. "A Remarkable Woman? Popular Historians and the Image of Eleanor of Aquitaine." In *Studies in Medievalism XVIII: Defining Medievalism(s)*. Ed. Karl Fugelso. Woodbridge, UK: Boydell & Brewer, 2010, pp. 244–64.

Favreau, Robert. "Aliénor d'Aquitaine et Fontevraud." In *Aliénor d'Aquitaine* [*exposition, Abbaye de Fontevraud, 2004*]. Ed. Martin Aurell. Nantes: 303, 2004, pp. 40–45.

Flori, Jean. *Aliénor d'Aquitaine: La reine insoumise*. Paris: Payot, 2004.

———. "Aliénor l'insoumise: Le rôle de la personnalité d'Aliénor dans l'histoire de son temps." In *Aliénor d'Aquitaine* [*exposition, Abbaye de Fontevraud, 2004*]. Ed. Martin Aurell. Nantes: 303, 2004, pp. 52–57.

Gillingham, John. "Telle Mère, tel fils: Aliénor et Richard." In *Aliénor d'Aquitaine* [*exposition, Abbaye de Fontevraud, 2004*]. Ed. Martin Aurell. Nantes: 303, 2004, pp. 26–33.

Harvey, Ruth E. "Eleanor of Aquitaine and the Troubadours." In *The World of Eleanor of Aquitaine: Literature and Society in Southern France between the Eleventh and Thirteenth Centuries*. Ed. Marcus Bull and Catherine Léglu. Woodbridge, UK: Boydell Press, 2005, pp. 101–14.

Hivergneaux, Marie. "Aliénor d'Aquitaine: Le pouvoir d'une femme à la lumière de ses chartes (1152–1204)." In *La cour Plantagenêt (1154–1204): Actes du colloque tenu à Thouars du 30 avril au 2 mai 1999*. Ed. Martin Aurell. Poitiers: Université de Poitiers, 2000, pp. 63–87.

———. "Autour d'Aliénor d'Aquitaine: Entourage et pouvoir au prisme des chartes (1137–1189)." In *Plantagenêts et Capétiens: Confrontations et héritages*. Ed. Martin Aurell and Noël-Yves Tonnerre. Turnhout: Brepols, 2006, pp. 61–73.

———. "Queen Eleanor and Aquitaine, 1137–1189." In *Eleanor of Aquitaine: Lord and Lady*. Ed. Bonnie Wheeler and John Carmi Parsons. Basingstoke, UK: Palgrave, 2002, pp. 55–76.

Huneycutt, Lois L. "*Alianora Regina Anglorum*: Eleanor of Aquitaine and her Anglo-Norman Predecessors as Queens of England." In *Eleanor of Aquitaine: Lord and Lady*. Ed. Bonnie Wheeler and John Carmi Parsons. Basingstoke, UK: Palgrave, 2002, pp. 115–32.

Kelly, Amy. "Eleanor of Aquitaine and Her Courts of Love." *Speculum* 12, no. 1 (1937): 3–19.

———. *Eleanor of Aquitaine and the Four Kings*. Cambridge, MA: Harvard University Press, 1950.

Kibler, William W., ed. *Eleanor of Aquitaine: Patron and Politician*. Austin: University of Texas Press, 1977.

Labande, Edmond-René. "Les filles d'Aliénor d'Aquitaine: Étude comparative." *CCM* 113–14 (1986): 101–12.

———. *Pour une image véridique d'Aliénor d'Aquitaine*. La Crèche: Société des Antiquaires de l'Ouest et des Musées de Poitiers, 1952. Rpt. *Bulletin de la Société des Antiquairies de l'Ouest*. Ed. Martin Aurell. Poitiers: Geste Éditions / Société des Antiquaires de l'Ouest, 2005.

Larrey, Isaac de. *L'héritière de Guyenne, ou histoire d'Eleonor, femme de Louis VII roy de France et en-suite de Henri II roy d'Angleterre*. Rotterdam: Chez Reinier Leers, 1691.

Lazar, Moshé. "Cupid, the Lady, and the Poet: Modes of Love at Eleanor of Aquitaine's Court." In *Eleanor of Aquitaine: Patron and Politician*. Ed. William W. Kibler. Austin: University of Texas Press, 1977, pp. 35–60.

Lees, Beatrice A. "The Letters of Queen Eleanor of Aquitaine to Pope Celestine III." *English Historical Review* 21 (1906): 78–93.

Lejeune, Rita. "La femme dans les littératures françaises et occitaines du XIe au XIIIe siècles." *CCM* 20 (1977): 201–17.

———. "Rôle littéraire d'Aliénor d'Aquitaine et de sa famille." *Cultura neolatina* 14 (1954): 5–57.

———. "Rôle littéraire de la famille d'Aliénor d'Aquitaine." *CCM* 1, no. 3 (1958): 319–37.

Martindale, Jane. "Eleanor of Aquitaine." In *Richard Coeur de Lion in History and Myth, King's College Medieval Studies VII*, ed. Janet Nelson. London: King's College London, 1992, pp. 17–50.

———. "Eleanor of Aquitaine and a 'Queenly Court'?" In *Eleanor of Aquitaine: Lord and Lady*. Ed. Bonnie Wheeler and John Carmi Parsons. Basingstoke, UK: Palgrave, 2002, pp. 423–39.

———. "Eleanor of Aquitaine: The Last Years." In *King John: New Interpretations*. Ed. S. D. Church. Woodbridge, UK: Boydell Press, 1999, pp. 137–64.

McCash, June Hall Martin. "Marie de Champagne and Eleanor of Aquitaine: A Relationship Reexamined." *Speculum* 54 (1979): 698–711.

McCracken, Peggy. *The Romance of Adultery: Queenship and Sexual Transgression in Old French Literature*. Philadelphia: University of Pennsylvania Press, 1998.

———. "Scandalizing Desire: Eleanor of Aquitaine and the Chroniclers." In *Eleanor of Aquitaine: Lord and Lady*. Ed. Bonnie Wheeler and John Carmi Parsons. Basingstoke, UK: Palgrave, 2002, pp. 247–63.

Meade, Marion. *Eleanor of Aquitaine: A Biography*. New York: Hawthorn Books, 1977.

Mullally, Evelyn. "The Reciprocal Loyalty of Eleanor of Aquitaine and William the Marshal." In *Eleanor of Aquitaine: Lord and Lady*. Ed. Bonnie Wheeler and John Carmi Parsons. Basingstoke, UK: Palgrave, 2002, pp. 237–45.

Nolan, Kathleen D. "The Queen's Choice: Eleanor of Aquitaine and the Tombs at Fontevraud." In *Eleanor of Aquitaine: Lord and Lady*. Ed. Bonnie Wheeler and John Carmi Parsons. Basingstoke, UK: Palgrave, 2002, pp. 377–405.

Nuñez Rodriguez, Manuel. "Leonor de Aquitania en Fontevraud: La iconografía funeraria como expresión de poder." In *Muerte, religiosidad y cultura popular: Siglos XIII–XVIII*. Ed. E. Serrano Martín. Saragossa, 1994, pp. 451–70.

O'Callahan, Tamara. "Tempering Scandal: Eleanor of Aquitaine and Benoît de Sainte-Maure's *Roman de Troie*." In *Eleanor of Aquitaine: Lord and Lady*. Ed. Bonnie Wheeler and John Carmi Parsons. Basingstoke, UK: Palgrave, 2002, pp. 301–17.

Owen, Douglas D. R. *Eleanor of Aquitaine: Queen and Legend*. Oxford: Blackwell, 1993.

Pappano, Margaret Aziza. "La *regina bisperta*: Aliénor d'Aquitaine et ses relations littéraires au XII siècle." In *Aliénor d'Aquitaine [exposition, Abbaye de Fontevraud, 2004]*. Ed. Martin Aurell. Nantes: 303, 2004, pp. 150–55.

———. "Marie de France, Aliénor d'Aquitaine, and the Alien Queen." In *Eleanor of Aquitaine: Lord and Lady*. Ed. Bonnie Wheeler and John Carmi Parsons. Basingstoke, UK: Palgrave, 2002, pp. 337–67.

Paris, Gaston. "La légende de Saladin." *Journal des savants* (May–August 1893): 354–65. Rpt., *La légende de Saladin*. Paris: Imprimerie nationale, 1893.

Parsons, John Carmi. "Mothers, Daughters, Marriage, Power: Some Plantagenet Evidence, 1150–1500." In *Medieval Queenship*. Ed. John Carmi Parsons. New York: St. Martin's Press, 1993, pp. 63–78.

Pavillon, Baltazar. *La vie du bienheureux Robert d'Arbrissel*. Samur: François Ernov, 1666.

Pernoud, Régine. *Aliénor d'Aquitaine*. Paris: Albin Michel, 1965.

Power, Daniel. "The Stripping of a Queen: Eleanor in Thirteenth-Century Norman Tradition."
  In *The World of Eleanor of Aquitaine: Literature and Society in Southern France between the
  Eleventh and Thirteenth Centuries*. Ed. Marcus Bull and Catherine Léglu. Woodbridge, UK:
  Boydell Press, 2005, pp. 115–35.

Richard, Alfred. *Histoire des comtes de Poitou, 778–1204*. 2 vols. Paris: Alphone Picard & Fils, 1903.

Richardson, H. G. "The Letters and Charters of Eleanor of Aquitaine." *English Historical Review*
  74 (1959): 193–213.

Sanford, Francis. *A Genealogical History of the Kings and Queens of England, and Monarchs of Great
  Britain, etc., from the Conquest, anno 1066, to the year 1707*. London: Printed by M. Jenour, for
  John Nicholson and Robert Knaplock, 1707.

Staunton, Michael. *The Historians of Angevin England*. Oxford: Oxford University Press, 2017.

Strickland, Agnes [and Elizabeth Strickland]. *Lives of the Queens of England, from the Norman
  Conquest; with Anecdotes of Their Courts, Now First Published from Official Records and Other
  Authentic Documents, Private as well as Public*, 12 vols. London: H. Coburn, 1840–48; 4th ed.,
  1854.

Swabey, Fiona. *Eleanor of Aquitaine, Courtly Love, and the Troubadours*. Westport, CT: Green-
  wood Press, 2004.

Tolhurst, Fiona. "What Ever Happened to Eleanor? Reflections of Eleanor of Aquitaine in Wace's
  Roman de Brut and Lawman's *Brut*." In *Eleanor of Aquitaine: Lord and Lady*. Ed. Bonnie
  Wheeler and John Carmi Parsons. Basingstoke, UK: Palgrave, 2002, pp. 319–36.

Turner, Ralph V. "Eleanor of Aquitaine and Her Children: An Inquiry into Medieval Family
  Attachment." *Journal of Medieval History* 14 (1988): 21–35.

———. "Eleanor of Aquitaine in the Governments of Her Sons Richard and John." In *Eleanor of
  Aquitaine: Lord and Lady*. Ed. Bonnie Wheeler and John Carmi Parsons. Basingstoke, UK:
  Palgrave, 2002, pp. 77–95.

———. *Eleanor of Aquitaine: Queen of France, Queen of England*. New Haven: Yale University
  Press, 2009.

Verger, Jacques. "Aliénor et la Renaissance intellectuelle du XIIe siècle." In *Aliénor d'Aquitaine
  [exposition, Abbaye de Fontevraud, 2004]*. Ed. Martin Aurell. Nantes: 303, 2004, pp. 136–41.

Vincent, Nicholas. "Aliénor, Reine d'Angleterre." In *Aliénor d'Aquitaine [exposition, Abbaye de
  Fontevraud, 2004]*. Ed. Martin Aurell. Nantes: 303, 2004, pp. 58–63.

———. "Patronage, Politics, and Piety in the Charters of Eleanor of Aquitaine." In *Plantagenêts et
  Capétiens: Confrontations et héritages*. Ed. Martin Aurell and Noël-Yves Tonnerre. Turnhout:
  Brepols, 2006, pp. 17–60.

Vollrath, Hanna. "Aliénor d'Aquitaine et ses enfants: une relation affective?" In *Plantagenêts et
  Capétiens: Confrontations et héritages*. Ed. Martin Aurell and Noël-Yves Tonnerre. Turnhout:
  Brepols, 2006, pp. 113–23.

Vones-Liebenstein, Ursula. *Eleonore von Aquitanien: Herrscherin zwischen zwei Reichen*.
  Göttingen-Zurich: Muster-Schmidt, 2000.

Weir, Alison. *Eleanor of Aquitaine: By the Wrath of God, Queen of England*. London: Vintage,
  2000. Published in the United States as *Eleanor of Aquitaine: A Life*. New York: Ballantine
  Books, 2000.

Wheeler, Bonnie and John Carmi Parsons, eds. *Eleanor of Aquitaine: Lord and Lady*. Basingstoke,
  UK: Palgrave, 2002.

Wood, Charles T. "Fontevraud, Dynasticism, and Eleanor of Aquitaine." In *Eleanor of Aquitaine:
  Lord and Lady*. Ed. Bonnie Wheeler and John Carmi Parsons. Basingstoke, UK: Palgrave,
  2002, pp. 407–22.

INDEX